Inventing Baseball

The 100 Greatest Games of the 19th Century

edited by
Bill Felber

Introduction by John Thorn

Phoenix, AZ

Inventing Baseball:
The 100 Greatest Games of the 19th Century

Edited by Bill Felber
Photo Editor: Mark Fimoff
Associate Editors: Bob Bailey, Jerry Casway, Len Levin, Peter Mancuso, John Thorn, Robert L. Tiemann and Craig Waff, with special thanks to Skip McAfee

Copyright © 2013
Society for American Baseball Research, Inc.

All rights reserved. Reproduction in whole or part without permission is prohibited.

Photograph permissions are indicated in the photo credit list at the back of the book. Uncredited photos are considered to be in the public domain.

ISBN: 978-1-933599-42-7 (paperback)
ISBN: 978-1-933599-43-4 (ebook)

Design and production: Bryan Davidson and Jon Franke

The Society for American Baseball Research, Inc.
4455 E. Camelback Road, Ste. D-140
Phoenix, AZ 85018
Phone: (800) 969-7227 or (602) 343-455

Web: www.sabr.org
Facebook: Society for American Baseball Research
Twitter: @SABR

Names and nicknames in past centuries were represented in many variations, all of which were considered "correct" at the time. For the sake of consistency we have standardized names of clubs, organizations, and players as they are found in Peter Filichia's reference book *Professional Baseball Franchises* (Facts on File, 1993). Even player statistics and numbers are mutable through time as new research has been uncovered. We have used *Total Baseball, 8th Edition*, as our common reference.

Table of Contents

Dedication

Preface xi

Introduction: Toward the Game We Know xiii
   by John Thorn

The One Hundred Greatest

July 4, 1833: In The Beginning—Olympics. vs. Camden 1
   by Richard Hershberger

Spring 1840: The Legendary Doubleday Game 3
   by Mark Pestana

October, 1845: The First Recorded Games—Brooklyn vs. New York 6
   by John Thorn

June 3, 1851: Match Play—Knicks vs. Gothams 8
   by John Zinn

July to September, 1858: The Rivalry Begins—Brooklyn vs. New York 10
   by John Zinn

Sept. 9, 1858: The New York Rules in New England—Portland Eons vs. Tri Mountains 13
   by Casey Tibbitts

June 30, 1859: Caught On The Fly—Excelsiors of South Brooklyn vs. the Knickerbockers of New York 16
   by Craig Waff

July 1, 1859: Baseball Goes To College—Amherst vs. Williams 19
   by Jim Overmyer

Oct. 11, 1859: The Massachusetts Champions—Excelsiors of Upton vs. Unions of Medway 22
   by Joanne Hulbert

July 2–11, 1860: The Grand Excursion—The Excelsiors of South Brooklyn vs. six upstate New York teams 24
   by Craig Waff

Aug. 23, 1860: No Gentlemen's Game—Excelsiors vs. Atlantics at the Putnam Grounds, Brooklyn 28
   by Craig Waff

July 24, 1860: The First Enclosed Ballpark—Olympics of Philadelphia vs. St. George 32
   by Jerrold Casway

September 22-24 1860: The Grand Excursion, Part II—Excelsiors of Brooklyn vs. Excelsiors of Baltimore and vs. a picked nine in Philadelphia 34
   by Craig Waff

July 4, 1862: The POW Game—Captive Union soldiers play a baseball game at Salisbury, NC 36
   by Patricia Millen.

Sept. 18, 1862: The "Silver Ball" Game—Eckfords vs. Atlantics at the Union Grounds in Williamsburg, Brooklyn 39
   by Craig Waff

Table of Contents

Oct. 14, 1862: The Martyrdom of Jim Creighton—Excelsiors of Brooklyn vs. Unions 43
  by Rich Bogovich

Sept. 28, 1865: The First Fixed Game—Eckfords vs. Mutuals 46
  by Phil Dixon

July 16, 1866: Lipman Pike's Home Run Record—Athletic vs. Danville 49
  by Jerrold Casway

October, 1866: Moneyball—Atlantics vs. Athletics 51
  by Eric Miklich

July 25, 1867: The Most Important Game in Baseball History?—Rockford vs. Washington 55
  by John Thorn

Oct. 3, 1867: Put On Yer Coats, Put on Yer Coats, Das All!—
Excelsiors of Philadelphia vs. Uniques of Brooklyn 58
  by Irv Goldfarb

October 7, 1867: Candy Cummings Debuts The Curve—Excelsiors vs. Harvard 60
  by Mark Pestana

June 15, 1869: A Cunning Play Saves The Streak—Cincinnati Red Stockings at Mutuals 63
  by Greg Rhodes

Aug. 26, 1869: Unbeaten, But Tied—Cincinnati vs. Unions 65
  by Greg Rhodes

Sept. 3, 1869: Inter-racial Baseball—The Pythians vs. The Olympics 68
  by Jerrold Casway.

June 14, 1870: The Atlantic Storm—Cincinnati Red Stockings vs. Atlantics 71
  by Greg Rhodes.

July 23, 1870: The First "Chicago" Game—New York at Chicago 74
  by Rich Bogovich and Mark Pestana

Nov. 1, 1870: The Birth of the NA—Mutuals vs. Chicago 77
  by Bob Tiemann

May 4, 1871: Association Ball—Forest City of Cleveland at Kekionga of Fort Wayne 79
  by John Thorn

Oct. 30, 1871: The First Pennant Race—Chicago at Athletic of Philadelphia 81
  by Bob Tiemann

July & August, 1874: New Game in The Old Country—Boston and Philadelphia exhibitions in England 84
  by John Bauer

May 29, 1875: The First No-Hitter—Princeton vs. Yale 87
  by Rich Bogovich

June 3, 1875: The Unbeatable Red Caps—Boston at St. Louis 90
  by Bill Nowlin

June 19, 1875: The "Model" Game—Hartford at Chicago 93
  by David Arcidiacano

July 28, 1875: The First Professional No-Hitter—Chicago at Philadelphia 95
  by Casey Tibbitts

Table of Contents

April 22, 1876: A New Age Begins—Boston at Philadelphia 97
   by John Zinn

July 15, 1876: Wearin' of the "Grin"—Hartford at St. Louis 100
   by Parker Bena

May 1, 1877: The Double Shutout—Syracuse at St. Louis 103
   by W. Lloyd Johnson

August 20, 1877: Gray Outcomes—Louisville at Hartford 106
   by Bob Bailey

May 8, 1878: Three In One?—Boston at Providence 108
   by Kathy Torres

Oct. 14, 1878: Farewell To Old-style Ball—Buffalo vs. Syracuse 110
   by W. Lloyd Johnson

June 2, 1879: Lee Richmond's No-Hit Debut—Chicago at Worcester 113
   by John Husman

June 21, 1879: The Cameo of Bill White—Cleveland at Providence 116
   by John Husman

June 12, 1880: Baseball Perfection—Cleveland at Worcester 119
   by John Husman

June 17, 1880: Perfection Revisited—Buffalo at Providence 122
   by John Husman

Sept. 2, 1880: Night Baseball—Jordan Marsh vs. R.H. White at Nantasket Beach, Mass 125
   by Craig Waff

June 25, 1881: George Gore's Theft Spree—Providence at Chicago 127
   by Jerry Grillo

June 26, 1881: Mullane vs. Reccius For Eighteen Innings—Louisville vs. Akron 130
   by Dick McBane

Sept. 10, 1881: Roger Connor's Grand Slam—Worcester at Troy 133
   by John Husman

May 2, 1882: The Beer and Whiskey League: Day One 135
   by John W. Bauer

July 18, 1882: Mullane Goes Both Ways—Louisville at Baltimore 138
   by Jerry Grillo

Aug. 17, 1882: Radbourn The Slugger—Detroit at Providence 141
   by Edward Achorn

Sept. 13, 1882: The Innovative Mind of King Kelly—Providence at Chicago 144
   by Bob Tiemann

October 6, 1882: The First Meeting of Champions—Chicago vs. Cincinnati 147
   by Greg Rhodes

Aug. 10, 1883: Cap Anson vs. Fleet Walker—Chicago at Toledo 149
   by John Husman

Table of Contents

Sept. 10–13, 1883: Grasshopper Snatches the Pennant—Chicago at Boston 152
    by Mark Pestana

Sept. 13, 1883: One Hand, No Hits—Cleveland at Philadelphia 155
    by Jon Barnes

September 21–23, 1883: Nipped At The Wire—Philadelphia at St. Louis 158
    by James Rygelski

May 1, 1884: Fleet Walker's Major League Debut—Toledo at Louisville 161
    by John Husman

June 7, 1884: Sweeney Strikes Out Nineteen—Providence at Boston 164
    by Edward Achorn

July 7, 1884: One-Arm Daily Strikes Out 19 (or 20)—Chicago at Boston, Union Association 167
    by Mark Pestana

July 28, 1884: Hoss Radbourn: 59 or 60?—Providence at Philadelphia 170
    by Ed Achorn

October 25, 1884: The First "World Series"—Providence vs. New York 172
    by Peter Mancuso

September 29 to Oct. 3, 1885: Capping A Pennant Chase—New York at Chicago 175
    by Bob Tiemann

July 21, 1886: "A Glorious Victory"—Cuban Giants vs. Cincinnati 178
    by Paul Browne

Aug. 15, 1886: Guy Hecker, Hitting Pitcher—Baltimore at Louisville 180
    by Bob Bailey

Oct. 3, 1886: Matt Kilroy, Strikeout King—Baltimore at Louisville 182
    by Jimmy Keenan

Oct. 23, 1886: Curt Welch's Winning Slide—Chicago vs. St. Louis 184
    by Bob Tiemann

May 2, 1887: The First African American Battery—Newark at Buffalo 187
    by Peter Mancuso

July 14, 1887: The Color Line is Drawn—Chicago at Newark 189
    by Peter Mancuso

Oct. 21, 1887: Sam's Triple Trouble—Detroit vs. St. Louis 192
    by Mike Harrington

Aug. 14, 1888: Tim Keefe Finally Loses—Chicago at New York 195
    by Peter Mancuso

Sept. 4, 1888: The Little Steam Engine That Could—Pittsburgh at Indianapolis 198
    by Mark Pestana

Feb. 9, 1889: A Wondrous Ballpark—White Stockings vs. All-Americas at Giza, Egypt 201
    by Bill Felber

June 22, 1889: Sad-sack Colonels—St. Louis at Louisville 204
    by Bob Bailey

Table of Contents

Sept. 7, 1889: The Candlelight Game—St. Louis at Brooklyn 208
    by Bob Tiemann

Oct. 2, 1889: A King's Downfall—Boston at Cleveland 211
    by Jean-Pierre Caillault

Oct. 5, 1889: The Giants Win the Pennant on the Last Day—New York at Cleveland 214
    by Donald Jensen

Oct. 18, 1889: Genesis of a Rivalry—Brooklyn at New York 217
    by Cliff Blau

October 29, 1889: Giants Win Back-To-Back World Series—New York at Brooklyn 219
    by Peter Mancuso

April 19, 1890: Debut of the Players League 222
    by John W. Bauer

May 12, 1890: The Kid, The Bolt and Silent Mike—Boston at New York 225
    by Peter Mancuso

June 21, 1890: No Hits—But No Win—Brooklyn at Chicago Pirates 228
    by John Zinn

Oct. 6, 1890: The First Worst To First—Baltimore at Louisville 231
    by Jimmy Keenan

Sept. 28-30, 1891: The Clouded Finish—New York at Boston 234
    by Lyle Spatz

June 10, 1892: Seven Hits in Seven Tries—St. Louis at Baltimore 237
    by Jimmy Keenan

Oct. 15, 1892: Bumpus Jones: No-Hit Phenom—Pittsburgh at Cincinnati 239
    by Jerry Grillo

October 1892: The Split-Season Playoff—Boston vs. Cleveland 241
    by Terry Gottschall

Aug. 16, 1893: Bill Hawke's No-Hitter—Baltimore at Washington 244
    by Jimmy Keenan

May 15, 1894: "It Was a Hot Game, Sure Enough"—Baltimore at Boston 246
    by Terry Gotschall

May 30, 1894: Four For Bobby Lowe—Cincinnati at Boston 248
    by Charles Faber

July 13, 1896: Ed Delahanty's Four Home-Run Game—Philadephia at Chicago 251
    by Jerrold Casway

May 16, 1897: Arrested on a Day Of Rest—Washington at Cleveland 254
    by Bill Felber

June 19, 1897: Hit 'Em Where They Ain't—Baltimore at Pittsburg 257
    by Bill Felber

June 29, 1897: The Colts' Record Romp—Louisville at Chicago 259
    by Bill Felber

Circa Sept. 19, 1897: Cap Anson's 3,000th Hit?—Louisville at Chicago 262
    by Bill Felber

Sept. 27, 1897: Good vs. Evil—Boston at Baltimore 265
    by Bill Felber

July 25, 1898: The Ducky Holmes Game—Baltimore at New York 268
    by William Lamb

Sept. 16, 1899: The Misfits—Cleveland at Cincinnati 270
    by Frank Vaccaro

April 19, 1900: A "Basket Of Fresh Goose Eggs": The American League's
No-Hit Debut—Buffalo vs. Detroit 272
    by Jeff Samoray

Photo Credits 275

Contributor Biographies 279

Index

Name Index 282

Team/Club Index 287

Subject Index 289

This book is dedicated to the memory of Craig D. Waff, scientist and researcher, whose precision, commitment, passion and knowledge made it better.

Preface

I'll offer a friendly challenge to even those most versed in 19th-century baseball to fail to find something in this book that they did not already know.

For me, the previously unknown factoid was that until the mid-1890s the pitcher worked off flat ground rather than off a mound. I was vaguely aware that there had been such a time, but I was not as cognizant as I ought to have been that it extended more than two decades into "big league" ball.

You may find your "I did not know that" moment in our departed colleague Craig Waff's essay regarding the first night game in baseball history, an 1880 contest played on a resort beach in Massachusetts that required not only baseball but electrical-engineering skill.

Or it may be provided in any of the several essays detailing the advance and retreat of interracial baseball. One by Jerrold Casway recalls the first meeting of black and white teams, a groundbreaking 1869 contest. John Husman sketches the story of Bill White, who a decade later became the first black person to take the field in an actual National League game. Yet within another decade, as described by Peter Mancuso in an essay unfolding in Newark, New Jersey, the game's "color line" had taken hold.

In a handful of instances, it is not certain whether the events described in this book even took place. Such is the nature of record-keeping in 19th Century baseball. Did Cap Anson become the first player in baseball history to record 3,000 hits in September of 1897? Did Jim Galvin become the first 300-game winner in September of 1888? Did the first game in an enclosed ballpark actually take place in Camac Woods in Philadelphia in July of 1860? Did Paul Hines really record the game's first unassisted triple play in May of 1878? Read the essays and judge for yourself. One honest answer to all these questions is "we may never be sure."

Other essay topics are more certainly grounded in fact, but may be viewed as quirky. Do you know which was the first team to go "worst to first"? Which All-Star game was played at the site of one of the seven Wonders of the World ... and why? Which pre-Civil War team made the first "road trip"?

The 100 essays comprising this book, written by more than 40 experts on various aspects of 19th-century baseball, enlighten dozens of moments with the potential to fill in similar "knowledge gaps." They have been reviewed by an editorial board it was my privilege to chair that consisted of 19th-century experts John Thorn, Craig Waff, Peter Mancuso, Bob Bailey, Jerrold Casway and Bob Tiemann. Len Levin handled copy-editing chores, Cliff Blau provided fact-checking expertise and Mark Fimoff gets credit for the artwork. Irwin Chusid's proofreading put the final polish on the book." I am indebted to each of them for assisting in the process of creating this book.

Special thanks are also extended to archivist Pat Kelly at the Hall of Fame for assistance in locating many of the images that appear in this book, and to senior curator Tom Shieber for helping with some of the identifications. Several auction houses graciously provided photos for this project. Thanks go to Doug Allen of Legendary Auctions, Rob Lifson of REA Auctions, Lou Lipset of Old Judge Auctions, and David Kohler of SCP auctions. Thanks also to John Rogers of The Rogers Archive/The Conlon Collection. A number of private collectors provided images. They include Brian Campf, Jerry Casway, Paul Conan, Clint Cox, David Dyte, Phil Garry, Dennis Goldstein, Doug Goodman, John Husman, Mark Macrae, Jay Miller, David Nemec, Chris Rainey, John Thorn and Erich Wolters. William Wheaton descendant Bruce Marshall allowed us to use an excellent photo of his ancestor. Thanks also to Ronald Shafer for his magical digital restoration of a torn Library of Congress image of Charlie Byrne. Special thanks to Alma Ivor-Campbell for use of the 10-22-1884 scorecard from her collection.

Some of the subjects of these 100 games, such as Bobby Lowe's four-home-run game against Cincinnati, are well-remembered today. Several, such as the 1858 game between Portland, Maine, and the Tri-Mountain team of Massachusetts that brought the "New York" rules to New England, are largely forgotten. Yet collectively these 100 contests laid the foundation for the game we love. That alone makes them well worth remembering.

— *Bill Felber*

Introduction

Modern baseball—the very mention of that hideous phrase will curl the lip of any real historian of the game, and ought to bring a sickly silence upon any who would consider a truncated set of great players, great seasons, great moments. And yet "modern baseball" has attained a broad currency among journalists, announcers, even advanced fans, for whom the term may signify different things. Some will hold that modern baseball begins with the turn of the century in 1901, for no other reason than the march of time. Others will say that modern baseball begins with the first World Series in 1903, ignoring the reality of postseason championships played under that and other names since 1884. Some will hold out for 1920, when Babe Ruth came to New York, hit 54 home runs, and singlehandedly, in an instant, swept out the deadball era. The socially conscious fan will aver that until Jackie Robinson stepped on a big-league field on April 15, 1947, major league baseball was bush league. Others will point to the first year of expansion, 1961, as the dawn of the modern game.

Among those in this Baseball Babel, however, one truth is held in common: the national pastime of the 19th century was a morass of quaint custom, ill-considered rules, unmatchable records, and unconscionable exclusion. Major League Baseball's record keepers, when they proclaim new "firsts" or search the archives to find an appealing nugget for broadcast chatter, dismiss the passé century without a moment's misgiving.

This book, then, stands as something of a corrective. Its title, *Inventing Baseball*, is in part ironic, as the game was not invented but instead evolved. Yet it is a fine title, because baseball continued to change in so many fascinating ways, from the 1840s on, that an air of invention could be said to have characterized the entire era. Not only was baseball's rise and flower unsteady and halting, its status as the nation's game was by no means guaranteed by the creation of what only much later came to be called Major League Baseball. Baseball's fate hung in the balance as the 20th century dawned, following upon a brutal decade of interleague warfare and suicidal cartel practices, and contemporary observers thought that college football or competitive bicycling might surpass it by the dawn of the new century.

Early baseball, however you define or pinpoint it in the years before 1901, was indeed different from the game we see on the field today, yet there can be no doubt that it was baseball. Players in the big-league parks of the 1880s, packed with thousands of paying spectators, knew they were playing the same game that had been staged for free at the Elysian Fields of Hoboken in the 1840s.

Take a football fan of today to a gridiron contest played by the rules of 1890 and he might fairly say that the game and its equipment were so different from the one he knew that it might not seem to be the same game at all. From the size of the players to the shape of the pigskin bladder, from the ban on passing to the restrictions on substitution to the point values accorded to field goals and touchdowns, football reinvented itself, from a low-scoring game of mass momentum and dangerous formations to one of quick strikes and long gains. The same might be said of basketball at the turn of the century—that with the center jump, lumpy ball, and brutal play at the rim, the low-scoring fracas seemed like football without the padding. Yet baseball was always baseball, as Bruce Catton noted in *American Heritage* in 1959:

> The neat green field looks greener and cleaner under the lights, the moving players are silhouetted more sharply, and the enduring visual fascination of the game—the immobile pattern of nine men, grouped accord-

ing to ancient formula and then, suddenly, to the sound of a wooden bat whacking a round ball, breaking into swift ritualized movement, movement so standardized that even the tyro in the bleachers can tell when someone goes off in the wrong direction—this is as it was in the old days. A gaffer from the era of William McKinley, abruptly brought back to the second half of the twentieth century, would find very little in modern life that would not seem new, strange, and rather bewildering, but put in a good grandstand seat back of first base he would see nothing that was not completely familiar.

And that is precisely our point, we several authors of this project, to identify the hundred greatest games before the 20th century, some of them played decades before the idea of league play was even a glimmer in the eye of Harry Wright or William Hulbert. Undertaken by members of the 19th Century Committee of the Society for American Baseball Research, of whom I am proudly one, *Inventing Baseball* provides the intrepid reader with a peephole into a little known and unfairly neglected period of the game, populated not with old heroes, feats and tales but new ones … or, to paraphrase Satchel Paige—ones that ain't never been heard by this generation. Maybe the reader will know King Kelly or Albert Spalding or other men honored today with plaques in the Baseball Hall of Fame, but what of Doc Adams, or Jim Creighton, or Fleet Walker?

Until Bobby Thomson hit "the shot heard 'round the world" on October 3, 1951, most veteran baseball observers believed that another game involving Brooklyn—the victory by that city's Atlantics over the Red Stockings of Cincinnati on June 14, 1870—was the greatest in the game's history. Where it will rank for the reader as he considers the entire panoply of baseball's epic contests cannot be guessed, but this writer, who thirty years ago wrote a book titled *Baseball's Ten Greatest Games* and was constrained by its publisher from dipping into the 19th century, will find it hard not to include that game in his unconstrained top ten.

Roger Angell wrote an essay for the *New Yorker* some decades back in which Smokey Joe Wood, hero of the 1912 World Series, sat in the stands watching a dazzling pitching duel between Yale's Ron Darling and St. John's Frank Viola. "The Seamless Web" he called his piece, to signify that these three great pitchers, separated by seven decades, belonged to the same fraternity, were made from the same fabric, were part of it. The writers in *Inventing Baseball* know that Joe Wood was also part of a tradition into which he entered, one that went back to John Clarkson and Hoss Radbourn, to Asa Brainard, Frank Pidgeon and the legendary Creighton. They were heroes all, those who graced the game in its formative years. They lived and labored in a thrilling period of invention. They made the game we love.

And these men deserve to be recalled by all baseball fans of today in their greatest moments, in the glory of our times as well as theirs. To know that Albert Pujols and Derek Jeter are part of a seamless web with Roger Connor and John Ward makes the experience of today's games richer than merely to compare our stars with those since 1901.

Some of the names and games in this book may seem obscure even to knowledgeable enthusiasts (as fans were called before that term was coined in the 1880s), but the story of baseball has been played out on fields other than those of the National League, and by others than those whose playing records may be found in the encyclopedias (because they played "major-league ball" in the years since 1871). The writers/selectors of these hundred games to follow will have their personal favorites, in some measure reflected by their decision to speak for the editor's assignment of a particular game. But every game reported in this book had numerous advocates and may be commended to your attention.

Editor Bill Felber has charged his crew to select and depict games of historic significance as well as visceral thrills. It would have been easy to choose a hundred cliffhangers, but then we might have overlooked the game that was first to be played before a paid crowd, or the game that for a moment made

Introduction

Fort Wayne the capital of the baseball world, or another in which the forces of good and evil seemed to be pitted against each other (cast in the uniforms of, respectively, Boston and Baltimore) for the National League title of 1897.

I could go on, highlighting more personal favorites or piquant inclusions, but it is time to move on, to read about the first games, or some in the middle, or ones at the end. They are arranged chronologically rather than in any kind of ranking. However, one may dip into this book randomly, as if it were a box of Cracker Jack, and provide oneself with an individualized nonlinear experience.

This is the game we love, we who have compiled this book for you, and the years before 1900 form our favorite period. We may not convince archivists or reporters of Major League Baseball that the early game was as exciting as the one they are covering, but we hope to convince you.

— *John Thorn*

In the Beginning

Olympics of Philadelphia, Pa. vs. Camdens of Camden, N.J.

Camden, N.J.
July 4, 1833

By Richard Hershberger

On Independence Day of 1833, two groups of town ball players from Philadelphia met in Camden, New Jersey.[1] One group was a loose collection of friends who had been playing together in Camden for two years. The other, bearing the classical name Olympic, was formed to hold Fourth of July games.

The 1833 game was not merely a competition. It also had the character of a corporate courtship leading to merger. The two groups joined to form a new organization, keeping the name *Olympic*. The Olympic Ball Club of Philadelphia would go on to be by far the longest-lived club of the early baseball era, playing into the late 1880s. It would long keep its association with the holiday, for many years including a picnic, the singing of national songs, and the reading of the Declaration of Independence by the club's president.

The game of 1833 has been called by some the first known match game of baseball. Others have denied it this status. It certainly lacks the satisfying details of other, later candidates for the honor. We don't know the score, much less have a box score. We can only guess at who the players were. We know the name of one side, but not of the other (nor do we know whether it even had a name). But these are beside the point of the question: Was it a match game of baseball? Or, more precisely, of two questions: Was it a match game, and was it baseball?

"Match game" was a technical term in the 19th century. It denoted a formal competition between two defined sides. In its classic form from the heyday of amateur baseball, a match game was between two clubs. More broadly, the two sides might be selected from neighboring villages or might be students from different classes.

The distinction was that in a non-match game the two sides were selected ad hoc from a single body: two captains choosing sides from the student body of a school, or from the membership of a single club. In a match game the structure of the two sides existed outside of that one game.

This was considered important enough that isolated clubs, with no nearby outside competition, would try to replicate the match-game experience by choosing sides along some arbitrary but objective criterion: fat versus skinny, old versus young, or the especially popular single versus married (usually described as "bachelors versus Benedicts," showing a Shakespearean flair sadly absent from the modern game).

The 1833 game is not quite the classic match game, as only one side seems to have been an organized club. But both sides had an existence outside of that game. This places it well within the range of what could fairly be called a match game.

The second question is trickier: Were they playing baseball? They didn't call it that. They called it "town ball." Later in the 19th century, town ball would come to be understood as an ancestor of modern baseball. Many modern writers still subscribe to this interpretation, but it has serious problems. For one thing, "base ball" is the much older term, being attested nearly a century before "town ball." For another, modern baseball derives from a version played in New York City, where town ball is unattested.

The actual usage of the time was to apply various regional dialectal terms for a family of closely related informal games. The most important of these were base ball, town ball, and round ball. The modern game is known as baseball because it derived from the New York version, in base ball territory. Had the modern game derived from the Philadelphia version, in town ball territory, it would be called town ball today and base ball would be regarded as a quaint name for its predecessor.

– 1 –

The Olympics would switch to the New York game in 1860. New York writers would routinely dismiss the Olympics' claim to seniority by pointing out that before 1860 they were merely a town ball club, not a proper base ball club at all. This perspective may be reasonable when discussing modern baseball, but is anachronistic for the 1830s.

The New York game would have some distinctive features, but the available evidence suggests that these features had not yet developed in 1833. While we know in hindsight that New York was the birthplace of the form of baseball that would displace all others, in the context of 1833 it had no particular claim to special status among the innumerable local variants. So unless we restrict the discussion to modern baseball, this game in Camden is as much baseball as any other of the day.

This might be thought unsatisfying, but it really is in concert with other early baseball firsts. These rarely are so clear-cut as is often imagined. Baseball wasn't really invented in 1839, or 1845, or in any other year one might choose. The Knickerbockers weren't really the first baseball club. The Cincinnati Red Stockings weren't really the first professional club. Any claim to identifying the first professional baseball player is at best an educated guess, and at worst pure speculation.

However we might like pat answers to trivia questions, history rarely works this way. The reality is usually more nuanced, if not confused and obscure. Is the "first match game of baseball" a poorly documented game played between two obscure groups under vaguely understood rules? This fits right in.

Note:

1. The most important sources for the early history of the Olympics are two pamphlets printed by the club: "Constitution of the Olympic Ball Club of Philadelphia (Philadelphia: John Clark, 1838), and Constitution and By-Laws of the Olympic Ball Club of Philadelphia (Philadelphia: Ashmead, 1866). These pamphlets were typical of clubs of all sorts in that era. The 1838 pamphlet includes the club constitution, by-laws, and membership roster. The 1866 pamphlet added to these the contemporary rules of baseball, and most importantly for our purposes a brief history of the club and historical membership roster from its founding to that day.

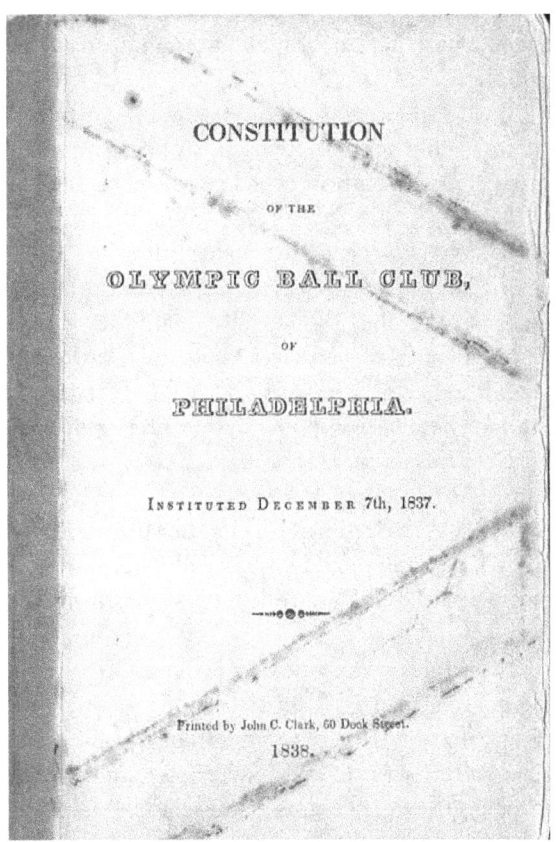

The cover page of a copy of the 1837 Constitution of the Olympics of Philadelphia, one example of a set of early rules governing what was then known as town ball or base ball.

The Legendary Doubleday Game

Two sides of boys

*Phinney Farm along the west side of
Lake Otsego, N.Y.
circa 1840*

By Mark Pestana

By 1905, pitcher-turned sporting goods entrepreneur Albert Spalding was sorely fed up with his friend Henry Chadwick's notions concerning baseball's origins. The British-born sports journalist Chadwick, who had been studying and writing about the game since the late 1850s, pushed Spalding's tolerance to the limit by asserting, in Spalding's *Official Base Ball Guide* for 1903, that our National Pastime had developed from an English game called rounders. Spalding, believing baseball a thoroughly American invention, but lacking proof, decided to remedy the situation by convening a special commission that would examine all evidence and render a definitive answer.

Two years of haphazard information gathering produced a ragged body of data unlikely to ratify either man's theory. But amidst it all, Spalding found something he liked. A 71-year old Denver mining engineer named Abner Graves wrote in 1905 two letters (one to the editor of the Akron, Ohio *Beacon-Journal* and the other to Spalding) recounting how, in his childhood home of Cooperstown, New York, a boy named Abner Doubleday surprised his playfellows one fine day with a concept for a game called "base ball."[1] Spalding must have been overjoyed when he realized that not only had he found an eyewitness account affirming baseball's American origin, but that its purported inventor grew up to be a military hero in the Civil War![2] Lacking anything more substantive or suitable to their inquiry, Spalding and the commission ran with it.

Henry Chadwick passed away only a month after Spalding published his Doubleday blockbuster in March 1908, but there has never been any shortage of challenges to baseball's singular Creation Myth.[3] Elementary fact-checking reveals the future General Doubleday to have been enrolled at West Point at the time of his alleged invention. Graves, we learn, was a man of questionable stability who later shot his wife and died in an asylum. Numerous accounts of earlier baseball activity have since been documented.

There remains a sense, nonetheless, that the old story cannot be *wholly* without substance. Even in the testimony of a great liar, there is usually some kernel of truth. The Doubleday legend may prove of value despite the shortsighted rubberstamping it received from a stacked jury a century ago, and what Abner Graves witnessed by the banks of Glimmerglass surely deserves a second look.

It was sometime in spring and probably in the year 1840 when a certain Abner Doubleday introduced a novel version of ballplay to his youthful peers.[4] It is now known that two persons of that name lived in Cooperstown during Graves's time there, and it is essential to consider both in trying to make sense of the legend.

The "famous" Abner, son of Ulysses Doubleday, had departed for West Point by September 1838 and was unlikely to have been indulging in idle recreation back in Cooperstown at the time in question. But he had a younger cousin, Abner Demas Doubleday, son of Ulysses' brother, Demas. Abner Demas was born about six miles north in Pierstown in March 1829,[5] and so would have been 11 years old in spring 1840.

As for our eyewitness, Abner Graves, he was younger yet, having just turned six in February. It is certainly easier to envision him a playmate to the 11-year-old Doubleday than to the 20-year-old future major general.

Graves recalled "several of the best players of sixty years ago," naming Thomas Bingham, Nelson Brewer, Joseph Chaffee, John Starkweather, and his own cousin John Graves, as well as another Doubleday cousin, John.[6] But perhaps the most significant other participant was Elihu Phinney, whose family had run a printing business in Cooperstown since the 1790s, and lived on a farm about half a mile up the west side of Lake Otsego. Graves specifically cited the Phinney Farm as a favored location for ballgames.[7]

Picture, then, Abner Demas directing a group of these boys, laying out a unique playing field in the meadow at Phinney Farm. Instead of just the two bases—the batter's home and an out-goal to which he ran—used in the hybrid of Old Cat and town ball the Cooperstonians always played, there was now a circuit of four, marked by flat stones set in a diamond shape.[8]

To the disappointment of Abner Graves and the other youngest enthusiasts, this new version of ball did not allow for dozens of boys, all ages and sizes, to swarm about, colliding with each other in pursuit of fly hits. There were now but 11 players on the field at a time, in distinctly-assigned positions.

Four spread symmetrically across the outfield. Five man the infield: one at each base, then two extras within the basepaths—one between first base and second; another between second and third.

In their old town ball, a "tosser" would stand next to home base, throwing the ball straight upward for the batter to strike upon its fall. Doubleday's plan puts this player in the center of the diamond, pitching underhand to the batsman. This necessitates a final fielder, the catcher, to stand behind home base and corral stray pitches.

Whereas, in town ball, every man tallied runs for himself, and the catcher of a fly ball went to bat no matter how many times he might have already batted, participants were now divided into two teams of equal number and bat in predetermined order. The batter must circle through three bases and reach home again in order to tally for his team.

In a holdover rule, "plugging" a runner with the ball was still good for a put-out. But a proviso declaring a batter out if he swings and misses at three pitches was new to the Cooperstown lads.

Abner Doubleday, credited with organizing the legendary first baseball game in Cooperstown in 1839

The frolic in Cooperstown that so impressed Abner Graves was undoubtedly but one of myriad early experiments—variations on a theme of bat and ball and bases. Taking his recollections at face value, however, tells us that the seeds of "The New York Game" were planted in the provinces five years before the Knickerbockers put their rules into writing. Glancing backward to that dim past we have conjured a mental snapshot, depicting a day when our game was very young, very free, and growing with great boyish eagerness toward its maturity.

Notes:

1. The two letters, dated April 3 and November 17, 1905, are printed in David Block, Baseball Before We Knew It: A Search for the Roots of the Game (Lincoln and London: University of Nebraska Press, 2005), pp. 252-256.

2. For more on connections between Spalding and Doubleday, see Philip Block, "Abner and Albert, The Missing Link," Chapter 3 (pp. 32-49) in David Block, *Baseball Before We Knew It*.

3. On the creation and debunking of the Doubleday Myth, see Robert W. Henderson, *Ball, Bat and Bishop: The Origin of Ball Games* (New York: Rockport Press, 1947; reprinted Urbana

and Chicago: University of Illinois Press, 2001), pp. 170-194; David Block, *Baseball before We Knew It*, pp. 32-66; John Thorn, *Baseball in the Garden of Eden: The Secret History of the Early Game* (New York: Simon and Schuster, 2011), pp. 1-24.

4. Graves never pinpointed 1839 as the year of Doubleday's invention. In his first letter on the subject he said it was "either the spring prior or following the Log Cabin & Hard Cider campaign of General Harrison for President." In his second letter he said it was "either 1839, 1840 or 1841." The second letter provides an additional clue. Again referring to President William Henry Harrison, Graves states: "The incident has always been associated in my mind with the Log Cabin and Hard Cider campaign of General Harrison, my father being a Militia Captain and rabid partisan of Old Tippecanoe."

It was not until December 1839 that the Whig Party nominated Harrison as their candidate. It makes little sense that a baseball game in Spring 1839 would be associated in memory with the campaign of a man whose candidacy would not even exist for several more months. Spring 1841 makes perhaps even less sense, for by that time Harrison's campaign was long over and he was, in fact, dead, felled by pneumonia in March. If 1841 were the year, would Graves not have more likely said, "The incident has always been associated in my mind with the death of General Harrison"? The Democrats nominated Martin Van Buren the first week of May 1840, and the presidential contest would have been seen as truly beginning at that time. A New York newspaper titled *The Log Cabin* published its first issue on May 2, 1840. The association of a unique new game with the launching of a military hero's presidential campaign might very naturally have been made in the mind of the young son of a Harrison supporter. In a letter of 1916, Graves did specify 1840 as the date of the first baseball game.

5. Record for Abner Demas Doubleday at www.familysearch.org.

6. Letter of Abner Graves to Beacon Journal of Akron, OH, April 3, 1905.

7. Ibid.

8. All details concerning the manner of ballplay—both of the old "Town Ball" and the new "Base Ball"—are derived directly from the two letters of Abner Graves cited in footnote 1.

The First Recorded Games

Intraclub games between various squads

Elysian Fields, Hoboken, N.J.; Union Star Cricket Club Grounds, Brooklyn, N.Y.; Elysian Fields
October 1845

By John Thorn

Three games between rival clubs were played in October 1845. Any one of these might suffice to refute the longstanding claim that the contest of June 19, 1846 between the Knickerbocker Base Ball Club and the New York Base Ball Club was the "first match game." The last named may still be considered the first that was certainly played by the Knickerbocker rules that were adopted on September 23, 1845, but even this assertion begs several larger questions: (a) were the Knickerbockers the first club to play by written rules; (b) were they truly the pioneer club; (c) were the Knickerbocker and New York clubs distinct, or were they blended, playing on June 19 what amounted to an intramural match like many that the Knickerbockers had played earlier?

This is a big topic, upon which I have written previously and will again. For the purposes of this book, let's focus on October 1845.

The Knickerbockers, recently organized under that name after several years' play at New York's Madison Square and Murray Hill, played their first recorded game on October 6. Although they commenced formal play in brisk weather, the Knickerbockers managed to squeeze in 14 games before shutting down to await April 1846 and the opening of a new season. The scoring for these contests survives in their *Game Book*, held by the New York Public Library and, gloriously, readily available to researchers.

In the first intrasquad game, seven Knickerbockers won by a count of 11–8 over seven of their fellows in three innings. The rules calling for the victor to accumulate 21 runs over as many innings as that might take was, clearly, observed in the breach. Not for a dozen additional years would the rules of baseball require a set number of innings or players to the side, and these were at first settled upon as seven, not nine!

The umpire of this practice game was William Rufus Wheaton, who by his own account had reduced the rules of the Gotham Base Ball Club to writing in 1837. A skilled cricket player, Wheaton came to prefer baseball in the 1830s. His Gothams also went by the name Washingtons, signifying either their primacy among baseball clubs or their possible origin among the butchers and produce vendors of the Washington Market. As the years went by, the Gothams spawned offshoots, including both the New Yorks and the Knickerbockers. In 1887 Wheaton told a reporter for the *San Francisco Examiner*, for a piece titled "How Baseball Began: A Member of the Gotham Club of Fifty Years Ago Tells About It":

> The new game quickly became very popular with New Yorkers, and the numbers of the club soon swelled beyond the fastidious notions of some of us, and we decided to withdraw and found a new organization, which we called the Knickerbocker. For a playground we chose the Elysian fields of Hoboken, just across the Hudson river. ... **We played no exhibition or match games** [emphasis mine], but often our families would come over and look on with much enjoyment. Then we used to have dinner in the middle of the day, and twice a week we would spend the whole afternoon in ball play.

William H. Tucker, who in some unknown measure assisted Wheaton in laying down the Knickerbocker rules, played in 10 of the 14 contests, including the one on October 6, in which he scored three of the losing squad's eight runs. Like Wheaton and other Knickerbockers, he had been a player with the New York Ball Club and maintained a tie to them, indeed playing in two formal matches of the New Yorks with the Brooklyn Club on October 21 and 24 of 1845, a month after he had helped to form the Knicks. In his 1998 history of American cricket, Tom Melville pointed to an even earlier contest between these two clubs, on October 11 (actually October 10), reported in the *New York Morning News*. Research more than a decade later has revealed a somewhat fuller account in the obscure and short-lived newspaper the *True Sun*:

> *The Base Ball match between eight Brooklyn players, and eight players of New York, came off on Friday on the grounds of the Union Star Cricket Club. The Yorkers were singularly unfortunate in scoring but one run in their three innings. Brooklyn scored 22 and of course came off winners.*

Wheaton also umpired the game of October 24, 1845, between New York and Brooklyn, and played in the game of November 10 to mark the second anniversary of the New York Club, which, like the recently discovered Magnolia Ball Club, had commenced play at Hoboken's Elysian Fields in 1843—two years before the Knickerbockers.

Many of the early New York baseballists had cut their teeth on cricket, and this was true of the Brooklyn players as well. In the game of October 21, conducted at the Elysian Fields, the Brooklyn Club (possibly not the same men who had played in the game of October 10, as no box score survives) were originally reported to be the victors once again, but this report proved in error. As was reported the next day, the eight players of the New York club won handily, and did so again in the game of October 24, played at the grounds of the Union Star Cricket Club, opposite Sharp's Hotel in Brooklyn, at the corner of Myrtle and Portland Avenues, near Fort Greene. The scores were, respectively, 24–4 and

William Rufus Wheaton

37–19. On both these occasions the Brooklyn club included established cricketers John Hines, William Gilmore, John Hardy, William H. Sharp, and Theodore Forman. The lineup appears to have been identical for the two games, as the Ayers of October 21 and the Meyers of October 24 may be the same individual, while the other seven men match up.

There is more work to be done with all this, certainly, but the NYBBC anniversary match of November 10, 1845, seems to have much in common with the purported "first match game" of June 19, 1846, while the games of October 1845, particularly the latter two, seem to be true match games between differentiated clubs.

October 24, 1845

New York			Brooklyn		
	Hands out	Runs		Hands out	Runs
Davis	2	4	Hunt	1	3
Murphy	0	6	Hines	2	2
Vail [W.]	2	4	Gilmore	3	2
Kline	1	4	Hardy	2	2
Miller	2	5	Sharp	2	2
Case	2	4	Meyers	0	3
Tucker	2	4	Whaley	2	2
Winslow	1	6	Forman	1	3
	12	37		12*	19

* The "Hands out" total 13 rather than 12, a venerable typo now beyond rectification.

Match Play

Knickerbockers of New York vs. Washington of New York

Field next to Red House, Harlem, N.Y.
June 3, 1851

By John Zinn

Some baseball games are historic even though few details of the contest survive. A case in point is the June 3, 1851, Knickerbocker-Washington game. Although the only surviving information is the line score, the match is remembered because it marked the beginning of ongoing match play.

Before that game, there is no surviving record of a true match game since the famous June 19, 1846, contest between the Knickerbockers and the New York Club, won easily by the latter, 23–1. The 1846 game, which took place at Elysian Fields in Hoboken, New Jersey, has been called the first baseball game, the first documented baseball game, and the first game played by the Knickerbocker rules. Neither of the first two claims is accurate and the third may not be.

In the fall of 1845 the New York Club played three games against a Brooklyn team, losing one and winning two, so the 1846 match was definitely not the first documented baseball game. There is also some basis for believing the earlier New York Club games were played by the Knickerbocker rules or their equivalent since William Wheaton helped write the rules for both the Knickerbockers and the New York Club.[1]

Perhaps more importantly, since there were no repeat performances for five years, the 1846 affair didn't establish match play as an idea whose time had come. Some of this might be put down to reluctance by the Knickerbockers to associate with a club they had left because the Knickerbockers were more "fastidious." However, that is unlikely, because less than two weeks after the 1846 contest, a game was played between two teams, each a mixture of Knickerbocker and New York Club players. Another possibility is after being thrashed 23-1, the Knickerbockers saw no point in competing with a team that never seemed to lose. In addition, since the Knickerbocker Club hadn't been formed to play other clubs, further match play probably wasn't a priority.[2]

Regardless of the reasons for the five-year hiatus, things had clearly changed by 1851. The June 3 match may have been facilitated by a reorganization of the old New York/Gotham/Washington Club into a new Washington Club. The Knickerbockers seem to have taken the impending match very seriously, since by June 2 they had played almost twice as many intrasquad matches as in the same period in 1850.

Somewhat surprisingly, the match was played at the Red House in Harlem instead of Elysian Fields in Hoboken. The most logical explanation is that in the wake of the May 27 riots in Hoboken between immigrant Germans and a Nativist group called the Short Boys, the clubs may have felt it wiser to allow passions to cool before playing at Hoboken.[3]

The running score doesn't indicate which team batted first, but in the early going the Knickerbockers may have wondered whether anything had changed in five years. Washington led 2–0 after one inning, 7–3 after two, and 8–6 after three. The fourth inning marked the turning point, as the Knickerbockers added three aces while blanking the Washington Club.

The more "fastidious" bunch then exploded for five more runs in the fifth and a 14–9 lead, only seven short of the winning score of 21. Scoring was limited over the next two innings and the Knickerbockers led 15–11 as the game went to the eighth inning. This time they were not to be denied, tallying six times for a 21–11 win and sweet, albeit much delayed, revenge.

Unlike the 1846 affair, the game wasn't a one-time thing; a return match took place two weeks later, this time at Elysian Fields. The Knickerbockers prevailed in a much closer, 22–20 game that took 10 innings.[4]

Why was the June 3 match historic? Unlike the 1846 contest, the 1851 game marked the beginning of regular team competition—competition that has continued to this day. Competition is a key word here. To that point the New York/Washington Club not only won its matches, but did so easily. With little prospect of success, other clubs had little incentive to venture beyond intraclub play. Real competition would, however, be much more appealing to both the players and potential spectators. Similarly, there is also a direct path between the rules in 1851 and the rules of today's game. Once regular competition between the clubs became the norm, the rules had to be standardized and modified as necessary—a process that continues.[5]

The Knickerbocker victories also marked one of the first transitions in organized baseball. Before this match, the Washington Club (by whatever name it was called) was the preeminent club. The club had been formed earlier, had effectively spun off the Knickerbocker Club, and appeared to have no peers on the field. But after losing to the Knickerbockers twice in two weeks, in spite of having some of the old guard from 1845–46, the older club was no longer dominant.

In fact, it would be four years before the Washington Club (by then called the Gothams) would defeat its new/old rivals. The 1851 Knickerbocker win was also therefore the beginning of a cycle of change that has continued. When the two clubs took the field on that long-ago June day, the players probably weren't thinking beyond what the game meant to them and their respective teams, but almost regardless of the details, the day was truly historic.[6]

| Knickerbockers | 033 | 350 | 16 – 21 |
| Washington | 251 | 012 | 00 – 11 |

Notes:

1. *New York Herald*, October 25, 1845; Randall Brown, "How Baseball Began," *National Pastime*, 2004, 51-54; Randall Brown e-mail, August 12, 2011

2. John Thorn, *Baseball in the Garden of Eden: The Secret History of the Early Game*, (New York: Simon and Schuster, 2011), 71, 73; Knickerbocker Game Books, June 29, 1846, Albert G. Spalding Collection, New York Public Library; Brown, *How Baseball Began*, Randall Brown e-mail, July 21, 2011.

3. Thorn, *Baseball in the Garden of Eden*, 308-09, reference page 39; Knickerbocker game books, 1850-1851, Albert G. Spalding Collection, New York Public Library (Not all the matches in the Knickerbocker game books are clearly dated, but in 1851, the Knickerbockers played 15 interclub games from April 3 through June 2, the day before the Washington Club match. In 1850, it appears the club had only nine interclub matches through June 1); *New York Tribune*, May 27 and 28, 1851; Randall Brown e-mail, July 26, 2011.

4. Charles A. Peverelly, *Book of American Pastimes*, (New York: 1866), 345.

5. Thorn, *Baseball in the Garden of Eden*, 35.

6. William J. Ryczek, *Baseball's First Inning: A History of the National Pastime Through the Civil War*, (Jefferson, North Carolina: McFarland & Co., 2009), 47; John Thorn e-mail, July 20, 2011.

The Rivalry Begins

Brooklyn all-stars vs. New York all-stars

Fashion Race Course, Flushing, N.Y.
July 20, August 17 and September 10, 1858

By John Zinn

The baseball rivalry between Brooklyn and New York, made famous when the Yankees and Dodgers played six World Series in 10 years, actually dates to 1858, when the presidents of the Brooklyn base ball clubs challenged their New York counterparts to "a friendly match game of base-ball" between selected nines from the two cities. Since the participants were chosen or "selected" from multiple clubs in their respective cities, the matches were, in effect, the first all-star games. Played at the Fashion Course Racetrack near today's Citi Field, the best-of-three series also marked the first New York area contests played on enclosed grounds; in turn this facilitated another innovation, the first documented admission charge.[1]

Drawn almost equally from the Empire, Gotham, Eagle, Knickerbocker, and Morrisania clubs, the New York nine included well-known names such as Charles DeBost and the relatively unknown Harry Wright. In Brooklyn's case, the Atlantics had been the dominant 1857 club, but only three Atlantics started the first game, with the Excelsiors, Putnam, and Eckford also represented. Offensive prowess was apparently a criterion; two-thirds of the Brooklyn starters averaged more than three runs a game in 1857.[2]

A crowd estimated at between 4,000 and 10,000 was in place for the July 20 opener of the series. While newspaper coverage emphasized the "respectable" nature of the attendees, the "baser element"—gamblers and other purveyors of games of chance—were also present.[3]

As the game began, the odds offered by gamblers favored the Brooklyn team. This seemed to be confirmed by the early going. The Brooklynites led 3–0 after one inning, 5–1 after two, and 7–3 going to the bottom of the fourth before New York rallied to tie things at 7–7. Brooklyn briefly regained the lead by scoring four times in the top of the fifth, but New York scored seven times in the bottom of the inning, taking a lead it wouldn't relinquish. New York led 22–18 after eight innings and any hopes of a Brooklyn ninth-inning comeback were quickly dashed by "three brilliant catches" that "did their [Brooklyn's] business."[4]

New York's pitcher, Theodore Van Cott, helped his own cause by scoring four times, with Hoyt (4 runs), Pinckney (3), Benson (3), and Wadsworth (3) also contributing offensively. Future Hall of Famer Harry Wright was, however, shut out. Van Cott threw 228 pitches, incredible by today's standards, but was topped by Brooklyn's Matty O'Brien, who threw 264 pitches in only seven innings. Future Brooklyn great Joe Leggett scored only once and was replaced at catcher after he lost "two balls in succession." Leggett's poor performance led to his removal from the lineup for the rest of the series. Clearly the Excelsiors had fallen from grace as the other two members of the club were also dropped. Two more Atlantics were added for the second contest, including another future star, Dick Pearce, at shortstop. Like Leggett, Harry Wright was dropped from the lineup and didn't appear again in the series.[5]

By the time of the August 17 rematch, some of the excitement had worn off, as evidenced by a somewhat smaller crowd. If there was less excitement, there was even less drama as Brooklyn was in complete charge. A porous New York defense helped. With two out in Brooklyn's first and one run in, two fielding errors followed by some overthrows led to five more runs. With Brooklyn ahead 11–3 after three innings, further overthrows "too numerous to mention" contributed to six more runs for a 17–3 lead on the way to a 29–8 victory.[6]

Not surprisingly, Brooklyn decided to stay with a winning combination after its easy second-game

Game action from the July 20, 1858 match as depicted in the New York Clipper, *July 24, 1858*

victory. The one substitution (Boerum for Masten at catcher) was described as being due to the latter's "unavoidable absence." Masten's loss was described as putting the New York players "in fine feather." For its part, New York made wholesale changes, replacing two-thirds of the second-game lineup. Pitcher Van Cott was replaced by Dick Thorn; Van Cott reported being injured and didn't want to "risk the match."[7]

As in the first two games, Brooklyn took an early lead in the September 10 contest, but New York answered with a seven-run first and led 15-6 after six innings. Brooklyn tallied four times in the seventh to close the gap to five runs, but New York matched that with five of its own in the bottom of the inning. The match ended with a 29-18 New York victory.

New York's optimism about Masten's absence was apparently well-founded, as his replacement allowed eight passed balls.[8]

The immediate result of the Fashion Course games was a New York triumph. As important as the result was at the time, the series had an even more important influence on base ball's long-term development. The public's willingness to pay to watch this relatively new game provided the most tangible proof possible of base ball's growing popular appeal. The matches also marked the formal beginning of one of the most intense rivalries in sports history. Base ball competition between Brooklyn and New York took many forms, but for more than 100 years it provided great passion and drama. The Fashion Course games also marked a transition. While New

York won the series, the Brooklyn teams would dominate the sport for the next decade and more. The difference was more than geographic. For the most part the Brooklyn clubs consisted of workingmen, very different from teams like the Knickerbockers, who were not "from the world of physical toil." To some degree, the 1858 matches were the last hurrah of gentlemanly organizations like the Knickerbockers, Eagles, and Gothams. By winning, the New Yorkers honored their historic contributions. By agreeing to play against men from a different social class, they also contributed to baseball's future expansion and popularity.[9]

Box Score – July 20, 1858

New York	Hands	Runs	Brooklyn	Hands	Runs
Pinckney 2b	2	3	Leggett c	5	1
Benson rf	3	3	Holder 2b	4	2
Bixby 3b	3	1	Pidgeon ss4	1	
DeBost c	3	2	Grum cf	2	4
Gelston ss	4	2	PO'Brien lf	3	2
Wadsworth 1b	3	3	Price 1b	3	–
Hoyt lf	2	4	MO'Brien p	2	3
Van Cott p	2	4	Masten 3b	4	1
Wright, cf	5	0	Burr rf	2	1
Total	**27**	**22**	**Total**	**27**	**18**

Brooklyn   322 042 140 -- 18
New York   012 472 150 -- 22

August 17, 1858

Brooklyn	Outs	Runs	New York	Outs	Runs
Masten, c	3	4	Gelston, ss	2	3
Pidgeon, p	4	3	Pinckney, 2b	2	1
Price, 1b	3	2	Bixby, 1b	5	0
Oliver, 2b	3	3	Marsh, 3b	3	1
M. O'Brien, 3b	5	2	DeBost, c	3	0
Pearce, ss	2	4	Hoyt, lf	3	1
Grum, rf	1	6	Turner, rf	3	1
P. O'Brien, lf	2	3	Davis, cf	4	0
Manolt, cf	4	2	Van Cott, p	1	1
Total	**27**	**29**	**Total**	**27**	**8**

Brooklyn   605 623 421 -- 29
New York   201 000 104 -- 8

Notes:

1. Schaefer, Robert H. *The Great Base Ball Match of 1858: Base Ball's First All Star Game*, pp. 47-66; *Nine: A Journal of Baseball History and Culture*, Volume 14, Number 1, Fall 2005; *Brooklyn Daily Eagle*, July 10, 1858; *Porter's Spirit of the Times*, June 12, 1858. Brooklyn was an independent city until January 1, 1898.

2. Wright, Marshall D. *The National Association of Base Ball Players, 1857-1870*, (Jefferson, North Carolina, McFarland & Co, 2000), pp. 18-27; *New York Clipper*, July 24, 1858; *Brooklyn Daily Eagle*, July 21, 1858; *New York Daily Tribune*, July 21, 1858; *Porter's Spirit of the Times*, June 19, 1858, July 3, 1858.

3. Schaefer, Robert H. *The Great Base Ball Match of 1858*; *Nine*; *New York Daily Tribune*, July 21, 1858; *New York Times*, July 21, 1858; *New York Clipper*, July 24, 1858; *Brooklyn Daily Eagle*, July 22, 1858.

4. *New York Daily Tribune*, July 21, 1858; *New York Times*, July 21, 1858; *New York Clipper*, July 24, 1858.

5. *Brooklyn Daily Eagle*, July 21/August 18, 1858; *New York Daily Tribune*, July 21, 1858; *Porter's Spirit of the Times*, July 24, 1858.

6. *New York Times*, August 18, 1858; *New York Daily Tribune*, August 18, 1858, *Brooklyn Daily Eagle*, August 18, 1858.

7. *New York Times*, September 11, 1858; *Porter's Spirit of the Times*, September 18, 1858.

8. Schafer, Robert H. *The Great Base Ball Match of 1858*; *Nine*; *New York Times*, September 11, 1858.

9. Schaefer, Robert H. *The Great Base Ball Match of 1858*; *Nine*; Ryczek, William J. *First Inning: A History of the National Game Through the Civil War*, (Jefferson, North Carolina, McFarland & Co, 2009), p. 44.

Box Score, 9/10/1858

Brooklyn	Outs	Runs	New York	Outs	Runs
Pidgeon, p	3	3	Gelston, ss	2	5
Manolt, cf	4	1	Wadsworth, 1b	5	2
Grum, rf	2	2	Benson, cf	3	4
M. O'Brien, 3b	4	1	Pinckney, 2b	3	3
P. O'Brien, lf	5	1	Thorn, p	2	5
Price, 1b	3	1	Tooker, rf	2	3
Boerum, c	2	3	DeBost, c	5	2
Pearce, ss	2	3	Burns, lf	2	3
Oliver, 2b	2	3	McCosker, 2b	3	2
Total	**27**	**18**	**Total**	**27**	**29**

Brooklyn   200 202 444 -- 18
New York   700 332 536 -- 29
Umpire – D. Adams, Knickerbocker Club
Scorer for Brooklyn, Mr. Dakum, Putnam Club
Scorer for New York, Mr. Davis, Knickerbocker Club

The New York Rules in New England

Portlands of Portland, Me. vs. Tri-Mountains of Boston, Mass.

*Boston Common, Boston, Mass.
September 9, 1858*

By Casey Tibbitts

Baseball before the Civil War was very much a regional game, focused in the Northeastern United States around local clubs that played by local rules. In 1845 the Knickerbocker Base Ball Club of New York devised one of the first sets of codified regulations, which became known as the Knickerbocker rules. Meanwhile New Englanders played a version of what we now know as the Massachusetts Game, a descendant of town ball and Rounders. Though similar, the two versions had substantial differences.

Fifteen New York area clubs convened in early 1857 and adopted almost all of the Knickerbocker rules as official, making what we call the New York rules. Later that same year, a young baseball enthusiast named Edward G. Saltzman moved from New York to Boston and began promoting this style of play. A former second baseman for the Gothams of New York, a rival of the Knickerbockers, Saltzman soon formed the first club in New England dedicated to playing the New York game—the Tri-Mountains of Boston (named after the three hills that dominated the early Boston skyline).[1]

On May 13, 1858, 10 Massachusetts clubs met in Dedham, Mass., to form the Massachusetts Association of Base Ball Players and to codify their regulations. The Tri-Mountains advocated the adoption of the New York rules but were voted down, and the rules of the Massachusetts Game became official in the region.[2]

The Tri-Mountains could not find another club to face them on the field, so they spent more than a year practicing and playing intrasquad games. No one else in the area played by the New York rules, and no one from New York would make the trip to Massachusetts to oppose them. At last, the Portland Club, Maine's first organized team,[4] agreed to travel to Boston for a match. On September 9, 1858, the two teams met on Boston Common in the first recorded game played in New England under the New York rules. The following day the *Boston Herald* ran this account of the contest:

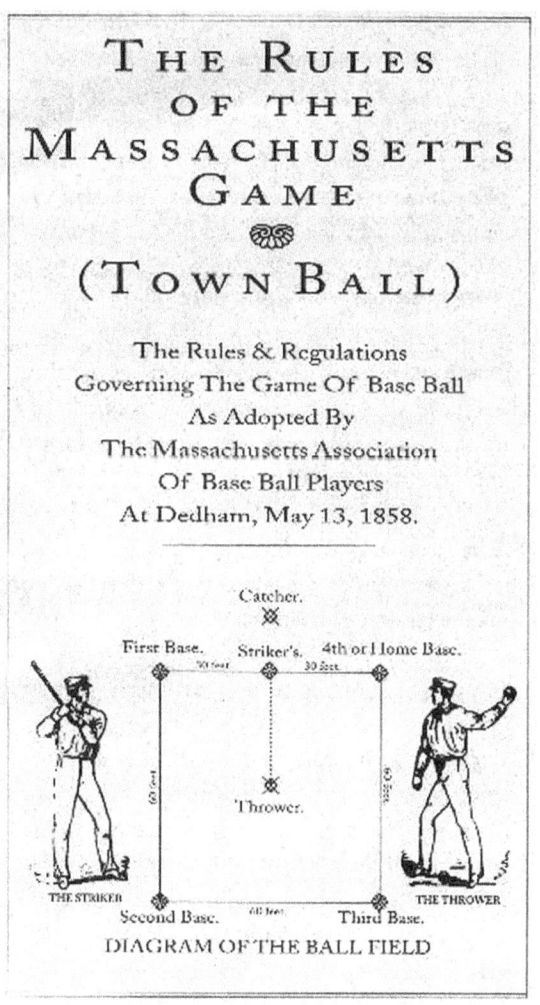

The Massachusetts Game playing field in 1858.[3]

An Interesting Game of Base Ball on the Common —
The Portland Club of Portland, Me., vs. the Tri-Mountain Club of Boston

A very closely contested game of base ball was played on the Common in this city yesterday afternoon, between the Portland Club of Portland, Me., and the Tri-Mountain Club of Boston. The game was that known as the New York game, and the Portland boys won by five runs. The rules of the New York game differ materially from those adopted by the Massachusetts Association of Base Ball Players last fall. The bases are placed at the angles of a rhombus instead of a square, the home base being the position of the striker; provision is made for "foul hits," and the ball is caught on the "bound" as well as on the "fly." The game consists of nine innings instead of one hundred tallies, and the ball is pitched, not thrown.

The playing commenced about three o'clock, the Tri-Mountain Club having the first innings, and the ninth innings of the Portland Club was finished at a quarter to six. ... The playing was witnessed by a large and interested crowd of spectators.[5]

A half-century later, the *New York Times* republished an account of the game and added this note about the contest's final runs:

The finish of the game was highly sensational.

It should be borne in mind that, at that time, a "home run" counted two.

When the score was "tied" for the last time, in the last half of the "ninth," "Capt. Sidney" (who was then thirty years of age, weighed two hundred and thirty pounds, and was a steam-boat captain, in active service, between New York and Portland) went to bat with the bases full and two men out.

The fates allowed him to "knock a long fly," which let the four of 'em around, scoring the five extra runs.[6]

The popularity of the New York game steadily grew in New England, and by September 1859 there were 13 clubs in Massachusetts that played according to those rules.[7] The New York rules continued to spread for a variety of reasons, which brought together teams from all parts of the Union. In 1865 one of the nation's leading sports weeklies predicted the demise of the Massachusetts game and emergence of the New York rules—a prediction that soon proved true:

The National Association or "New-York game" is now almost universally adopted by the Clubs all over the country; and the Massachusetts, and still more ancient style of playing familiar to any school-boy, called "town ball," will soon become obsolete. No lover of the pastime can regret this, as the New-York mode is superior and more attractive in every way; and better calculated to perpetuate and render "our national game" an "institution" with both "young and old America."[8]

Tri-Mountain Club	H.L.	Runs	Portland Club	H.L.	Runs
G. E. Guild, c	1	7	E. N. Robinson, c	6	4
H. F. Gill, 3b	3	6	S. M. Eaton, p	3	5
C. C. Dimon, 1b	1	5	S. Crowell, 2b	3	5
G. F. Goldthwait, 2b	5	0	J. C. Furbish, rf	4	5
F. N. Scott, cf	1	4	G. H. Abbott, lf	2	6
G. Troupe, rf	5	4	J. B. Winslow, 3b	2	5
G. Arnold, Jr., lf	4	5	G. M. Woodbury, 1b	4	5
W. H. Bourne, ss	5	4	Samuel Chadwick, ss	2	7
I. H. Ware, p	2	7	J. M. Knight, cf	1	5
Total		42	**Total**		47
Tri-Mountain	0 5 0 11 13 5 0 7 1 – 42				
Portland	2 0 2 7 9 4 5 10 8 – 47				

H.L. = Hands Lost. Number of balls pitched by Ware, of the Tri-Mountain Club, 143; passed Guild, the catcher, 5; caught on the fly, 2. Number pitched by Eaton, of the Portland Club, 115; passed Robinson, the catcher, 4; caught on the fly, 4.
Umpire – Richard Tower of the Tri-Mountain Club. Scorers – A. P. Margott of the Tri-Mountain Club and C. G. Gammon of the Portland Club.

Notes:

1. Brian McKenna. "Edward G. Saltzman, Baseball Pioneer." www.baseballhistoryblog.com, July 1, 2010.

2. Ibid.

3. "1858 Rules of the Massachusetts Game/Town Ball," www.baseball-almanac.com.

4. Gratwick, Harry. *Hidden History of Maine*, (Charleston, South Carolina: The History Press, 2010).

5. "An Interesting Game of Base Ball on the Common—The Portland Club of Portland, Me. Vs the Tri-Mountain Club of Boston," *Boston Herald*, no. 10,953 (Sept. 10, 1858), p. 2, col. 1, reprinted in Troy Soos. *Before the Curse: The Glory Days of New England Baseball, 1858-1918*, rev. edition. (Jefferson, North Carolina: McFarland, 2006), p 163-164.

6. "A Baseball Story of Long Ago—The Oldest Ball: Note The Difference Bteween the Account of This Game in 1858 and the Victory of the New York Americans Over Washington Yesterday," *New York Times*, vol. 58, no. 18,713, April 25, 1909, p. S-2, cols 3-5.

7. Ryczek, William J. *Baseball's First Inning: A History of the National Pastime through the Civil War*. (Jefferson, North Carolina: McFarland, 2009).

8. *Wilkes' Spirit of the Times*, March 18, 1865.

Caught On The Fly

Excelsiors of South Brooklyn vs. Knickerbockers of New York

Elysian Fields, Hoboken, N.J.
June 30, 1859

By Craig B. Waff

In the May, 29 1859 issue of the *Sunday Mercury*, a weekly New York newspaper that extensively covered the expanding world of base ball playing, an untitled paragraph announced the possibility of a forthcoming game that would be strikingly different from all others played during the past few years: "We have heard it rumored—we do not know with what truth—that the Knickerbocker Club, of this city, will shortly play a match with the Excelsior Club, of Brooklyn, in which they will repudiate catching the ball *upon the bound*." William Cauldwell, the editor of the newspaper, predicted that it would be "an interesting match, but no doubt somewhat tedious."[1] Nevertheless, on June 30, nearly 3,000 spectators gathered at the Elysian Fields in Hoboken, N.J., to watch what a *New York Times* reporter characterized as an "experimental" game "to determine the relative merits of putting out men when fair struck balls were caught on the fly: as contrasted with the rule adopted by the Base Ball Convention, of allowing men to be put out when fair struck balls were caught either on the bound or fly."[2]

The conduct of such an experimental "fly" game had its impetus from a desire in the mid-1850s by the Knickerbockers to change the rules of the game "from the easy mode in which they have hitherto played it."[3] They were particularly uncomfortable with the "bound" out, which counted any ball caught on one bounce as an out.

The desire to update the rules led to the holding of a convention of New York and Brooklyn ball clubs in Manhattan on Feb 25, 1857. The Knickerbockers proposed, according to the *New York Clipper*, abolishing the bound out in order to make the game "more manly and scientific." Other players, particularly younger ones who had only begun playing in the mid-1850s, argued that such a rule change would make the game of base ball "too much like Cricket" and that balls caught on the fly rather than the bound "would hurt the hands more." A compromise proposed by the bound advocates was unanimously adopted. The bound out continued to be permitted under the proposed new rule: "[The striker is out] if a fair ball is struck, and the ball is caught either without having touched the ground or upon the first bound." But as an inducement for players to attempt to catch the ball on the fly, the committee also proposed that "if a man was caught out before the ball touched the ground, that then the players who were running to the different bases, or home, could neither make an Ace nor Base, but had to return to their original position."

Although the Knickerbockers had failed to get the bound out excluded, they nevertheless forbade it during their intra-club practice games. In early 1859, they were finally able to persuade another club, the Excelsiors of South Brooklyn, "between whom and themselves the most cordial sentiments of friendship exists," to play an experimental club-vs.-club game that excluded the bound out. The quality of play during the first half, which had the Excelsiors leading 24–15 after five innings, was sloppy. The *Sunday Mercury* reported, "There was some very bad fielding, and wild throwing on both sides, and on the part of some of the Knickerbocker members, a want of judgment in disposing of the ball, was plainly discernable." The last was perhaps best epitomized in the second inning, when, with one out and runners on second and third, the Knicks right fielder Samuel Kissam caught a fly ball struck by Edwin Russell of the Excelsiors and, "apparently forgetting himself, sent the ball to third base, instead of second (which the lead runner had left and was bound to return to)."[4] The lost out would have terminated the inning without the Excelsiors scoring a run. Instead subsequent strikes by John Holder, Thomas Reynolds, and Harry Ditmas Polhemus brought in four runs.

The fielding noticeably improved in the latter half, however, and the play moved along so crisply that the 26–22 Excelsior victory became the shortest on record in terms of time—two hours and 10 minutes. But while conceding the game was "in spots" very interesting, especially a ninth-inning rally by the Knickerbockers, a skeptical *Mercury* reporter failed to discern any aspects of the game that would make him prefer the new "fly" system:

"We do not think that any balls were caught on the fly that would not have been so caught under the regular rules, but there were several balls lost, which might, perhaps, have been caught upon the bound; and one or two pretty catches were made upon the bound (one by Mr. [James Whyte] Davis) which, of course, did not count. Had the game been one governed by the regular rules of catching, our impression is that it would have been much more pleasing, and certainly shorter by several runs."[5]

In contrast, positive assessments of the "fly" game—probably written by Henry Chadwick—appeared nearly a week later in *Porter's Spirit of the Times* and in the *New York Clipper*.[6] The *Porter's* account found that the experimental "fly" game:

"[W]as such as to satisfy any unprejudiced mind of the superiority, in every respect, of the [fly] method. In fact ... but for the catch on the bound, which so often gives rise to a display in the field unworthy the efforts of the merest tyro, we should certainly claim for base-ball the merit of affording more frequent opportunities for brilliant fielding in one match, than can be had in a dozen cricket matches."

Despite confident predictions in the *Porter's* and *Clipper* accounts that the next convention of the National Association of Base Ball Players would surely eliminate the bound out, that action would not come to pass until December of 1864, when the

The 1859 Knickerbockers (at the left) and Excelsiors (at right):
Identifiable Knickerbockers are Charles DeBost (third from left), Doc Adams (fourth from left), and Harry Wright (sixth from left). The man in the suit standing between the teams may be Dr. Joseph Bainbridge. Identifiable Excelsiors are Harry Polhemus (to the right of the man in the suit), Aleck Pearsall (next to Polhemus), Edwin Russell (fifth from right), John Whiting (third from right), and probably Tom Reynolds at far right.

thinning out of weaker and older clubs finally reduced sufficiently the conservative opposition to a rule change.[7] In the meantime, however, other clubs, inspired by these experimental games, began testing and even regularly playing the "fly" game during the next few years.[8]

Excelsior Club	H.L.	Runs	Knickerbocker Club	H.L.	Runs
Leggett, c	1	5	DeBost, c	3	2
Russell, p	4	3	McLoughlin, p	7	0
Holder, 3b	3	4	Davis, lf	6	1
Reynolds, 2b	2	4	Kissam, rf	5	1
Polhemus, cf	4	1	Stephens, 1b	1	4
Whiting, rf	5	0	Welling, 2b	2	3
Pearsall, 1b	4	2	Wright, ss	0	5
Cole, ss	2	3	Adams, 3b	1	4
Markham, lf	2	4	Morrow, cf	2	2
Total		26	Total		26
Excelsior	345	750	011 – 26		
Knickerbocker	157	203	004 – 22		

Knickerbocker	How Put Out				Excelsior				
	Fly	B'nd	Base	T'tl		Fly	B'nd	Base	T'tl
DeBost	2	4	0	6	Leggett	6	4	0	10
McLoughlin	0	0	1	1	Russell	3	0	2	5
Davis	1	0	0	1	Holder	1	0	1	2
Kissam	1	0	0	1	Reynolds	1	0	1	2
Stephens	1	1	10	12	Polhemus	2	0	0	2
Welling	1	0	1	2	Whiting	1	0	0	1
Adams	1	0	2	3	Pearsall	0	0	3	3
Morrow	1	0	0	1	Cole	0	0	1	1
					Markham	1	0	0	1
Total	8	5	14	27	Total	15	4	8	27

Passed balls: DeBost 10, Leggett 8. HR: Leggett. Umpire: Mr. Bixby. Scorers: Messrs Young and Wenman.

Notes:

1. "Out-Door Sports: Base Ball: Matches to Come Off," *Sunday Mercury*, May 29, 1859, p. 5, col. 4. For previous discussions of the fly-vs.-bound debate, which extend the story through the eventual elimination of the bound out in 1864, see Warren Goldstein, *Playing for Keeps: A History of Early Baseball* (Ithaca and London: Cornell University Press, 1989), pp. 48-53; Andrew J. Schiff, *"The Father of Baseball": A Biography of Henry Chadwick* (Jefferson, N.C. and London: McFarland & Company, Inc., Publishers, 2008), pp. 51-58; and William J. Ryczek, *Baseball's First Inning: A History of the National Pastime Through the Civil War* (Jefferson, N.C. and London: McFarland & Company, Inc., Publishers, 2009), pp. 174-178.

2. "Base Ball: Excelsior Club, of South Brooklyn, versus Knickerbocker Club, of New-York," *New York Times*, vol. 8, no. 2428 (1 Jul 1859), p. 4, col. 6.

3. "The Base Ball Convention and their New Rules," *New York Clipper*, c. February 1857 clipping in Rankin scrapbook, Mears Collection, Cleveland Public Library.

4. "Out-Door Sports: Base Ball: The 'Fly' Game Between the Knickerbocker and Excelsior Clubs," *Sunday Mercury*, 3 July 1859, p. 5, col. 4.

5. Ibid.

6. Both accounts, cited in the next two reference notes, used similar language to encourage the playing of a return game in Brooklyn. The account in *Porter's* stated: "We hope that these clubs will afford our friends, on the other side of the river [i.e., in Brooklyn] an opportunity of judging of the merits of the catch-on-the-fly, by having a return match on the Excelsior grounds, which, in several respects, is favorably located for a fly game. Give us the return match, gentlemen, and as soon as you can." The account in the *Clipper* stated: "We sincerely trust that these excellent clubs will, by a return match on the Excelsior grounds, give our Brooklyn friends an opportunity of witnessing the brilliant play the catch-on-the-fly rule admits of. Play a return by all means, gentlemen, and let us know when, that we may be there to witness a second triumph of our favorite play." Chadwick became the *Clipper's* chief baseball correspondent in June 1857. In at least one earlier instance he internally identified himself as the author of a game account in *Porter's*. An account of a previous Knickerbocker-Excelsior game played on July 8, 1858 reported, regarding post-game activities, that "Our reporter—Mr. Chadwick—was called upon to respond to the toast of 'The Press,' but being somewhat diffident of his oratorical powers, he quietly retreated a moment before the call, having previously deputed the gentleman from the Tribune to respond, which duty he ably performed." Significantly, this same account also included the observation that "The fielding of the Knickerbockers was marked by some excellent catches 'on the fly.' Their opponents seemed to prefer the surer, but less skillful method, of taking the ball on the first bound, a style of catching more suitable to juveniles we think …." "Out-Door Sports: Base-Ball: Great Base-Ball Match in Brooklyn: Excelsior vs. Knickerbocker," *Porter's Spirit of the Times*, vol. 4, no. 20 (July 17, 1858), p. 309, col. 1.

7. "Ball Play: The Base Ball Convention: the Fly Rule Adopted by a Large Majority," *New York Clipper*, December 23, 1864.

8. Other early identified instances of "fly" games include Champion Jr. (NY) vs. Enterprise Jr. (Morrisania), 6 August and early October 1859; Knickerbocker (NY) vs. Empire (NY), August 10 or 11, 1859; Star (South Brooklyn) vs. Knickerbocker (NY), September 13, 1859; Manhattan vs. Oriental, September 29 or October 6, 1859; Excelsior (South Brooklyn) vs. Charter Oak (Brooklyn), June 21, 1860; America (South Brooklyn) vs. Twilight (South Brooklyn), July 7, 1860; Excelsior (South Brooklyn) vs. Putnam (Brooklyn, E.D.), August 4, 1860; Excelsior (South Brooklyn) vs. Knickerbocker (NY), August 25, 1860; Mohawk Jr. (Brooklyn) vs. Nassau Jr. (Brooklyn), October 27, 1860.

Baseball Goes to College

Amherst College vs. Williams College

Field next to Maplewood Young Ladies Institute, Pittsfield, Mass.
July 1, 1859

By Jim Overmyer

Amherst College was founded when Zephania Swift Moore, president of Williams College in Williamstown, in the extreme northwest corner of Western Massachusetts, resigned after a dispute over the school's isolated location. Moore took 15 students with him and started an institution in the town of Amherst, 60 miles to the east. To this day, Williams students and alumni regard those from the upstart Amherst as renegades, "the Defectors of 1821."

This made the two schools fit opponents on July 1, 1859, for the first intercollegiate baseball game. The Williams–Amherst game was played by Massachusetts Rules, a wide-open form of the sport commonly known as roundball, in which all ground was fair, runners could be put out by being hit by a thrown ball, and a single out ended each inning. A game consisted of an indeterminate number of frames, since the winning side would be the first to reach a pre-established score.

This would explain the lopsided 73–32 trouncing Amherst gave Williams, exceeding the agreed-upon 65-run limit during a 10-run 26th inning. But since the innings were all one-out long, the game, which took 3½ hours to play, in one respect pretty much equaled a modern game. There were only two fewer outs recorded than in a modern nine-inning contest.

The challenge match required considerable negotiation, including a June meeting on neutral ground at a small railside town between the two colleges at which representatives worked out arrangements.[1] A neutral site in Pittsfield, 20 miles from Williamstown, was selected. This was not just a game, but a two-day social event that included a banquet and a chess match between the schools. The Williams student body insisted on the chess match on July 2 to provide "a trial of mind as well as muscle."[2]

In a nice touch, the game site was next to the Maplewood Young Ladies Institute, a finishing school. The Maplewood girls turned out in great numbers, the first clue to their interest being "a silken flag suspended from the balcony of the Institute … intimating that bright eyes would look on the contest."[3]

The Amherst student body had been playing ball for at least a year.[4] Although Williams men had also been playing, Amherst was clearly better prepared. Williams baserunners enthusiastically ran themselves into avoidable outs (half of their 26 outs occurred on the basepaths, against only seven for Amherst), and "in passing in, they threw too wildly, each where he pleased."[5] In other words, the Williams outfielders missed the cutoff man many times.

The performance of the leadoff batter, Amherst senior James Claflin, was a tipoff to that team's edge in experience. He hit a first-inning home run on a "back hit," a tricky variation in which a batter would swing backwards with the flight of the pitched ball, put it into play to the rear, where there were few fielders, and run the bases, since there was no foul territory under Massachusetts rules.

Williams actually scored nine runs in the second inning, but Amherst came back with eight in the third and never then trailed, putting the game away with 12-run bursts in the fourth and 16th innings.

The "science" of batting order formation undoubtedly hadn't been developed yet, but Amherst, possibly by sheer chance, had its lineup stacked for maximum production. Its first four hitters, Claflin, Edward Pierce, Sam Storrs, and Frank Tower, scored 26 "tallies" and accounted for only four outs, while

Williams' first four made 15 outs and produced only five runs.

Amherst's "thrower," Henry Hyde, a sophomore, pitched a complete game with such gusto that a rumor began circulating among the spectators that he was actually a "ringer" of sorts, the college's blacksmith, since "nobody but a blacksmith could throw in such a fashion for three-and-a-half hours."[6]

Amherst's account of the game provided exact specifications for its ball (2.5 ounces in weight and 6.5 inches in circumference) and estimated the Williams ball at about the same.[7] A modern-day baseball weighs at least twice that and is about 50 percent larger around. Mathematics and physics dictate that a present-day ball is harder than the balls used in Pittsfield that day. While that was good for the baserunners who were put out by being hit by throws, it would have cut down on the long ball and strong throws from fielders.

Both teams were feted that evening by their Pittsfield hosts, where the Williams players presented their game ball as a trophy to the Amherst team. Both balls are still displayed, side by side, in a glass case at Amherst. The next day Amherst, with Claflin as one of its three players, also won the chess match, with Williams resigning on the 48th move.

Almost all of the 26 collegians playing in the first game went on to graduate from Amherst, Williams, or some other school. Claflin, the only man to participate in both the baseball and chess competitions, went into education and wound up a high-school principal and state representative in Chicago. Pierce, the first of the three productive hitters behind him, eventually became city administrator and police chief in New Orleans.[8]

The Civil War was just over history's horizon as the young men played that day, and at least 11 of them served the Union cause as officers or doctors before war's end. The Williams starting thrower, Robert Edes Beecher, a nephew of the famous abolitionist preacher Henry Ward Beecher, became a lieutenant colonel in the Union Army.[9]

One player from each side died in the war. Henry Gridley of Amherst, a lieutenant with a New York

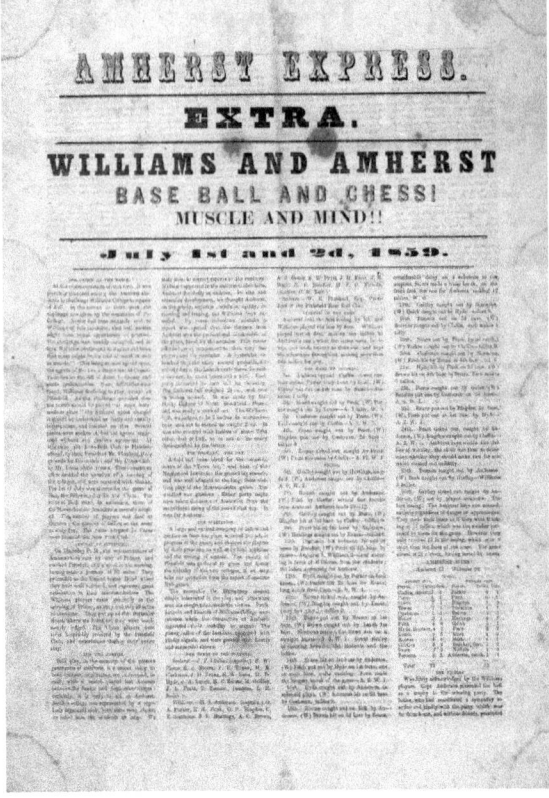

Base ball shares a headline with chess in the July 2, 1859 Amherst Express.

infantry regiment, was shot dead on a Georgia battlefield in 1864.[10] George Alanson Parker of Williams became a naval doctor and died on ship that same year of a fever contracted from sailors he was treating.[11]

Amherst and Williams students continued playing ball, and today they are rivals in the New England Small College Athletic Conference. Along with a third prestigious private college, Wesleyan in Connecticut, they form the Little Three within NESCAC. As the Williams Athletic Department puts it, "There are at least two athletic seasons for each Williams varsity team, the regular season and the Little Three."[12]

Amherst	Tallies	Outs	Williams	Tallies	Outs
Claflin	7	0	Parker	0	4
Pierce	5	2	Fitch	0	5
Storrs	7	1	Blagden	1	5
Tower	7	1	Simmons	4	1
Cushman	4	3	Brown	3	3
Evans	5	4	Hastings	4	1
Fenn	5	0	Quick	3	1
Hyde	4	3	Pratt	2	2
Leach	6	0	Knox	4	0
Roome	5	4	Bush	4	1
Gridley	5	4	Beecher	3	2
Pratt	7	2	Nichols	2	0
Tomson	6	2	Anderson	2	1
Totals	**73**	**26**		**32**	**26**

Notes:

1. *Amherst Express* "extra edition," July 1-2, 1859.

2. Ibid.

3. *Berkshire County Eagle*, July 8, 1859.

4. Cutting, George Rugger. *Student Life at Amherst College, Its Organizations, Their Membership and History* (Amherst: Hatch & Williams,) p. 113.

5. *Amherst Express*.

6. Ibid.

7. Ibid.

8. *Chicago Daily Tribune*, October 2, 1891 (Claflin); Obituary Record of Graduates and Non-Graduates of Amherst College for Academic Year Ending June 20, 1917 (Amherst: Published by the College, 1917), p. 340 (Pierce).

9. *New York Times*, March 29, 1920.

10. Benton, Charles E. *As Seen from the Ranks, A Boy in the Civil War* (New York: G.P. Putnam's Sons, 1902), p. 102.

11. Catalogue of the Sigma Phi. Printed for the Society, 1891, p. 255.

12. www.athletics.williams.edu/The_Little_Three (accessed April 1, 2011).

The Massachusetts Champions

Excelsiors of Upton, Mass. vs. Unions of Medway, Mass.

Agricultural Grounds, Worcester, Mass.
Oct. 11, 1859

By Joanne Hulbert

> HURRAH FOR THE EXCELSIORS!
> *Come my lads and listen*
> *To what I now relate,*
> *How Upton was defeated*
> *By the Champions of the State.*
> *Give ear unto my ditty,*
> *It will contain no lie,*
> *How Medway boys got leave*
> *To sing, Root, Hog, or Die.*

The base ball game played at Worcester on October 11 and 12, 1859 was a rematch, but it was more of a grudge match. The game played the previous July at Ashland with the Medway Unions ended badly, the score 100 to 78, and unfairly according to the Upton Excelsiors. Allegations that gamblers tampered with one or two of the Upton players who were allegedly offered $500 to manage an Excelsior loss—a charge denied—left the "Championship of the State" unresolved in the minds of the Excelsiors and their loyal fans. In order to set things right, repair Upton's reputation, or deny the Medway club any more glory, the Mechanics' club of Worcester offered a $500 prize for the match game to settle the championship.

The Upton Excelsiors Base Ball Club, as was the Medway Union Club, was made up of farmers, storekeepers and clerks who gathered after work afternoons and Saturdays to practice the game once known as round ball and subsequently the Massachusetts game of base ball as codified at the Dedham Convention of 1858. Fourteen players comprised a team, the four bases were arranged in a square and they were marked by four large sticks driven into the ground.

The Upton players were renowned for their skill at catching a base by their hands, swinging around them with force enough to throw themselves completely through the air, and leaping flamboyantly forward to the next base. From the beginning, the Upton club enjoyed a reputation as one of the most prominent ball clubs in Massachusetts.

"Tip" Norcross, as Upton town history records, was the first ball player to introduce the art of sliding to bases in a ball game, and it came about this way: In round ball, as with the Massachusetts game of base ball, "spotting" was allowed and a runner between the bases could be "touched out" with the ball. Norcross started the art of sliding to a base when he saw an opposing player starting to "spot" him and was able to deftly avoid the throw.

Publicity for the game reached all the way from Boston to Springfield, and even caught the attention of the *New York Herald*, which would later report that the game was "witnessed on both days by a large and enthusiastic crowd, among whom were many ladies." A parade that included the two clubs, the Grafton and Worcester clubs, and a huge procession of fans headed up by Fiske's Cornet Band arrived at the Worcester Agricultural Grounds, where a crowd estimated at more than 6,000 spectators bought tickets, while another thousand avoided the admission fee and tried to catch a glimpse of the game from outside the gates.

> CHORUS – *Hurrah for the Excelsiors!*
> *Their science and their skill!*
> *In Ashland, where the game was played,*
> *The Unions got their fill.*
> *They can't compete with Upton,*
> *Our boys do her defy.*
> *Big Pig, Little Pig,*
> *Root, Hog, or Die.*

Every mode of transportation was commandeered to bring people to Worcester, and many walked the 15 miles. Loyalties were evenly divided as all the towns north of Upton, including Worcester and the Brookfields, were solidly for the Excelsiors while towns south of Upton, including Milford, Holliston and Franklin, were solidly with the Medway club. The Upton team arrived in Worcester a day before the game and was kept closely guarded in its hotel. One star player almost didn't get to Worcester in time. He had hay to get in on his farm. When word got out he was not with the club, a man was sent to the farm to get the job done for him.

The game was for 100 tallies, with play commencing at 10 o'clock on the morning of October 11. Upton won the first innings and went out after making one tally. Medway jumped ahead with four tallies. At 12:30, the game stopped while the players had lunch delivered to the grounds from the Bay State House. At the end of the day's play at 5 o'clock, the score was Upton 67, Medway 33.

The game resumed the next day with the Unions making things lively by scoring 10 tallies in one hour's time to Upton's four. Eight innings were played before either team scored again, and the score was Upton 71, Medway 43. After an hour, Upton surged ahead, adding 11 more tallies while Medway was held to only three more. At 2 o'clock, with the score standing at 84 to 55, the players stopped for lunch.

The Excelsiors appeared to have benefitted more from the break, for they scored 16 tallies in less than an hour. The final 100–56 score rewarded them with the $500 prize, the championship of Massachusetts and the victory banner that is still to this day in possession of the Town of Upton. The prize money, the Worcester *Spy* reported, was by previous arrangement divided between the two clubs, the Excelsiors getting $300, and the Unions receiving $200. The Excelsiors also claimed the Championship of the United States, as a "Western club" later refused to play them for a $500 prize.

The Massachusetts *Spy* heaped praise on the Excelsiors. The game had "fully justified the opinion held by many who all along considered the Excelsior Club to be superior in science and skill." It noted rumors that one of their players had been offered $500 to throw the game, but said the offer was "rejected with scorn." And furthermore, "Upton's command of the ball was wonderful. There was something magical in the certainty with which the ball was present at any point where it was wanted. And the Excelsiors are scarcely less admirable as batsmen. Their pre-eminence is fully established; and, henceforth, no one is likely to dispute it with success."

Yes, indeed, magical.

Excelsior banner residing at the Upton (Mass.) Historical Society.

> *Against the odds, in crowd and judge,*
> *Did Upton fight that day,*
> *They won respect from every one*
> *Who came to see them play.*
> *"Excelsior," their motto,*
> *Perfection is their aim,*
> *They're bound to fight another day,*
> *And if they're whipped, Die, Game.*
>   —Anonymous, 1859

The Grand Excursion

Excelsior of South Brooklyn vs.
Champion of Albany, Victory of
Troy, Niagara of Buffalo,
Flour City of Rochester,
Live Oak of Rochester,
Hudson River of Newburgh

July 2, 3, 5, 7, 8, and 11, 1860

By Craig B. Waff

In the spring of 1860, the Excelsior Club of South Brooklyn laid plans for what was termed "a grand excursion," the first extended trip by a baseball team on record.[1] The tour, involving matches in a half dozen cities and towns through upstate New York, would also become a showpiece for the skills of the Brooklyn players, especially pitching phenom Jim Creighton.

The *Troy Daily Whig* interpreted the Excelsior tour as "a crusade through the provinces for the purpose of winning laurels."[2] Regarding the first game, on Monday, July 2, against the Champion of Albany, the 632 observed that the Excelsiors had "pretty well reduced base ball to a science," proving themselves to be "good batters, capital catchers, and their pitching was terrific."[3] That combination led to a 24–6 Excelsior victory. An Albany newspaper reported that Creighton "pitched balls swift as they could be sent from a cannon, and they were most difficult to strike."[4]

Among the more than 1,000 spectators at the Champion-Excelsior game was "an immense delegation of Trojans," that is, players from the Victory Base Ball Club of Troy, the Excelsiors' opponent on the following day. The Victory boys promised that "if they did not beat the strangers this afternoon, they would give them harder treatment than they had experienced at the hands of the Champions."[5] The result was the closest and lowest scoring game of the tour—a 13–7 victory for the Excelsiors, who went ahead with nine runs in the first two innings.

The Excelsior club's desire to visit Buffalo—and for that matter to tour at all—was motivated at least partially by a reason unrelated to the game. The *Buffalo Daily Courier* reported that Excelsior club members had "for years past, been anxious to make a visit to the [relatively nearby] Falls of Niagara, and have desired a challenge from the Niagaras as an inducement to make the tour." The members of the Niagara of Buffalo were eager to oblige, according to the *Courier*, because the club's formation in 1857 and its introduction to the New York Game owed a lot to the enthusiasm of a former Excelsior club member who had relocated to Buffalo.[6]

At 2 P.M. on July 4, the team traveled to Niagara Falls, where they enjoyed a ride "upon one of the finest rivers in the world," saw "the intrepid [French stuntman Charles] Blondin walk" on a tightrope stretched 160 feet above the gorge at the base of the falls (a feat he had first performed in 1859), took "a hurried view" of the falls, and were "hospitably treated" at the prominent Clifton House Hotel on the Canadian side.[7]

On the following day (Thursday, July 5), the clubs met on the Niagara grounds before a crowd of between two and three thousand spectators. The Niagaras correctly anticipated that the Excelsiors would win the game, but they were, according to the Buffalo *Express*, quite surprised and overwhelmed

Excelsiors right fielder and lead-off hitter Asa Brainard.

Franklin Sidway, Niagaras pitcher. He allowed the Excelsiors 50 runs, 24 of them in a single inning.

by the differences that separated the Excelsiors' style of play from their own:

> The manner in which the Brooklyn chaps handled the ball—the ease and certainty with which they caught it, under all circumstances, the precision with which they threw it to the bases, and the tremendous hits they gave it into the long field ... made the optics of the Buffalo players glisten with admiration and protrude with amazement.[8]

By the end of the fourth inning, the Excelsiors had built a 20–6 lead. They scored 24 runs in the fifth inning alone and coasted to a 50–19 final score.

By the end of the game, both pitchers must have been exhausted, as the box score noted that Niagara's Franklin Sidway had pitched 354 balls, while Creighton had delivered 244.[9]

On the following day, the Excelsiors took an eastbound train to Rochester, where on July 7, the two clubs played. Like most of the Excelsior's previous tour opponents, the Flour City club, which had been organized in May 1858, was overwhelmed by the visiting club, this time 21–1. After receiving a telegram announcing the result, *Porter's Spirit of the Times* characterized the result as "the most complete victory on record."[10]

After a day of rest, the Excelsiors returned to ball playing on Monday, when they faced the Live Oak Base Ball Club of Rochester in a game frequently interrupted by rain. The Live Oaks played marginally better than Flour City, but still suffered a 27–9 loss. Then the Excelsiors traveled to Newburgh to play their final tour game, against the Hudson River club.

The first five tour games had been covered entirely by local reporters. For the sixth and last game, however, the weekly *New York Clipper* sent a reporter, almost certainly their base ball editor Henry Chadwick, who responded with a column-long article. He was highly disappointed with the Hudson River grounds:

> *The condition of the ground was not favorable for play, as it is as yet rather rough, and home base heads the field in the wrong direction, the locality in the rear of what is now the 3d base being the most desirous place for the head of the field.*[11]

The reporter observed that the Excelsiors' quality of play was not quite what it had been pre-tour. Nevertheless, the Excelsiors still managed to score 14, 10, and 13 runs in the fourth, seventh, and ninth innings en route to a 59–14 victory.[12]

Finally, on July 12, 11 days after they had departed, the Excelsiors returned home, "somewhat damaged in the way of fingers, and not a little worn out by the fatigue of almost constant travel..."[13] Given that they had traveled nearly 1,000 miles and played six games during this period, it was, according to the *Sunday Mercury*, quite natural to suppose that they must have been pretty well "played out" by the end of their journey.[14]

The Excelsiors had completed what might be considered the first extended baseball road trip—an activity undertaken by all professional clubs since the formation of the National League in 1876. They demonstrated a high-quality style of play that had not been seen before by the upstate clubs. And their string of victories earned them a reputation as one of the best clubs of the nation, worthy of playing against the Atlantics of Brooklyn, universally considered the unofficial "champion" of Greater New York City base ball. Indeed, the skills that the Excelsiors had honed during one of the most intense periods of ballplaying ever attempted may have led to their overwhelming 23-4 victory over the Atlantics only a week after their return.

Champion of Albany vs. Excelsior
July 2, 1860

Champion			Excelsior		
	H.L.	R		H.L.	R
Ferguson, 1b	4	1	Brainerd, rf	3	2
Street, ss	2	2	Russell, ss	6	1
H. Fellows, 2b	3	1	Young, 3b	4	2
Gearley, cf	3	0	Pearsall, 1b	2	4
Armington, 3b	4	0	Writing, 2b	1	5
A. Fellows, cf	4	0	Holder, lf	1	3
Ford, rf	1	1	Creighton, p	5	1
Turner, p	4	0	Polhemus, cf	3	2
Strever, c	2	1	Leggett, c	2	4
Total		6	**Total**		24
Champion	230	100		100 – 6	
Excelsior	371	115		006 – 24	

Notes:

1. "Out-Door Sports: Base Ball: A Grand Excursion in Contemplation," [New York] *Sunday Mercury* [hereafter cited as NYSM], 29 Apr 1860; "Base Ball: A Grand Excursion in Contemplation," *Brooklyn Daily Eagle*, vol. 19, no. 102 (30 Apr 1860), p. 2, col. 5.

2. "A Exciting Base Ball Match," *Troy Daily Whig*, vol. 26, no. 8014 (4 Jul 1860), p. 3, col. 4.

3. Ibid.

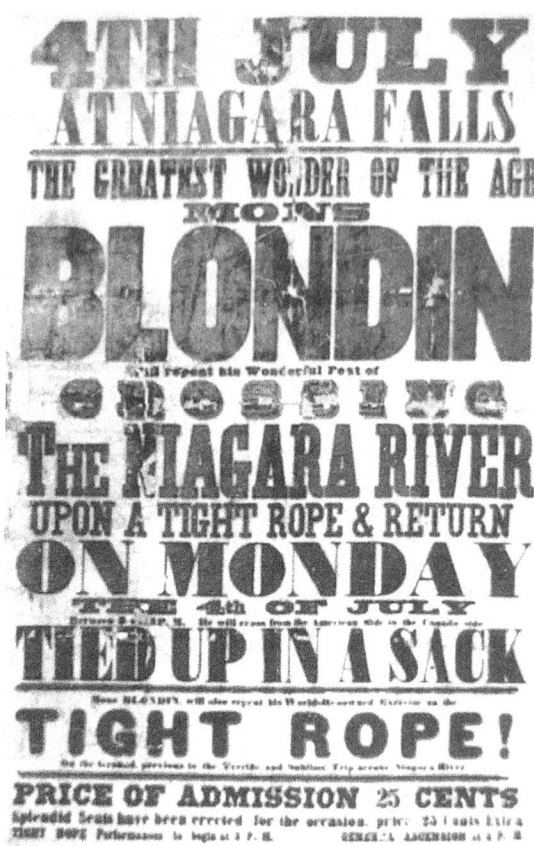

A poster promoting the appearance of French tightrope walker Charles Blondin above Niagara Falls.

4. The quoted remarks, from an unnamed Albany journal, were reprinted in "Out-Door Sports: Base Ball: Excelsior (of South Brooklyn) vs. Champion (of Albany)," *NYSM*, vol. 22, no. 28 (8 July 1860), p. 7, col. 2, and "Out-Door Sports: Base-Ball: Excelsior Base Ball Club," *Porter's Spirit of the Times*, vol. 8, no. 20 (10 Jul 1860), p. 308, col. 3.

5. "Base Ball," *Troy Daily Whig*, vol. 26, no. 8013 (3 Jul 1860), p. 3, col. 5.

6. Ryczek, William J. *Baseball's First Inning* (McFarland, 2009), p. 147, claims that two allegedly former members of the Brooklyn Excelsiors, Joseph B. Bach and Richard Oliver, were instrumental in the genesis of the Niagara club. Bach and Oliver, however, were elected officers of the Excelsior club in November 1857 and remained in the Greater New York City region for the rest of their lives.

7. "The City and Vicinity: Base Ball—Excelsiors and Niagaras," *Buffalo Daily Courier*, vol. 25, no. 157 (4 Jul 1860), p. 2, cols.

4-5; Freyer and Rucker, eds.; *Peverelly's National Game*, p. 57.

8. "Base Ball—Match of the Niagaras with the Excelsior Club of Brooklyn," *Buffalo Morning Express*, vol. 15, no. 4470 (6 Jul 1860), p. 3, col. 1.

9. *Buffalo Commercial Advertiser*, July 6, 1860, as reprinted in *NYSM*, vol. 22, no. 28 (July 8, 1860), p. 7, col. 2. The BCA quotation, but not the pitch count, also appeared in *Porter's Spirit of the Times*, vol. 8, no. 20 (July 10, 1860), p. 308, col. 3, & p. 309, col. 1.

10. "Out-Door Sports: Base-Ball: Excelsior of Brooklyn vs. Niagara of Buffalo," *Porter's Spirit of the Times*, vol. 8, no. 20 (July 10 1860), p. 308, col. 3, & p. 309, col. 1.

11. "Base Ball in Newburgh: Excelsior vs. Hudson River," *New York Clipper*, undated July 1860 clipping in the Mears Collection of the Cleveland Public Library.

12. Ibid.

13. "Out-Door Sports: Base Ball: Excelsior (of South Brooklyn) vs. Hudson River (of Newburg)," *NYSM*, July 15 1860, p. 5, col. 3.

14. Ibid.

No Gentlemen's Game

Excelsior of South Brooklyn vs. Atlantic of Bedford

Putnam Club Grounds, New York, N.Y.
August 23, 1860

By Craig B. Waff

The unofficial concept of a local "champion" among the senior clubs in the Greater New York City region was initially associated with the Atlantic of Bedford club, which by mid-1859 had compiled a seemingly invincible record. The club's last game loss had come at the hands of the Gothams on October 30, 1857, and its only match loss, to the Empires of New York, had occurred in 1855–56.[1]

Although the Atlantics eventually lost, 22–16 to the Eckfords of Brooklyn on September 8, 1859, reporters used the words *champion* and *championship* more frequently in 1860, especially in accounts of games involving the Atlantics.

When the Excelsiors of South Brooklyn challenged the Atlantics in early 1860, the *Brooklyn Daily Eagle* reporter perceived the match as creating "unusual interest," because "it will decide which Club is entitled to the distinction of being perhaps the 'first nine in America.'"[2]

The Excelsior challenge was seen as particularly strong because the club had added pitcher James Creighton and left fielder George Flanley in the offseason, and also because of the Exelsiors' tour through upstate New York, during which they defeated the strongest clubs of Albany, Troy, Buffalo, Rochester, and Newburgh.

The Atlantics, although winning all of their early 1860 games, were perceived as less competitive.[3] This may have been partly due to the absence of Folkert Rapelje Boerum, the team's captain and regular catcher, who had been on an extended trip to Europe since the spring, and to injuries suffered by Matty O'Brien, the regular pitcher, and at least one other unidentified player. These circumstances may help to explain the Excelsiors' 23–4 victory on the Excelsior grounds on July 19.[4]

This apparently spurred the Atlantics, who resoundingly defeated the Mutuals of New York, 34–15, on July 30, and then attained closely contested victories on their home grounds in Bedford over the Excelsiors (15–14 on August 9),[5] the Enterprise (16–14 on August 17), and the Mutuals (26–24 on August 20). Commenting on the last game, the reporter for *Porter's Spirit of the Times* observed, "The playing of the Atlantics, both in fielding and batting, was that superior character which has won for them, for so many years, the right and title to the Base Ball Championship."[6]

On August 21 a *Porter's Spirit* commentator caught the mood of the baseball community in the metropolitan area anticipating the meeting between the Atlantics and Excelsiors: "… The interest and excitement in the trial waxes warmer and warmer, and … it is now generally admitted that it will be witnessed by the greatest gathering of spectators ever assembled on any base ball field."[7]

The size of the expected crowd raised concerns about the playing site. A commentator in *Wilkes' Spirit of the Times* declared for the New York Parade Ground, "a beautiful level field of some thirty acres" with "ground as smooth as a floor" capable of accommodating 20,000 to 30,000.[8]

Instead, club officials settled on the Putnam Club grounds. "There are but poor accommodations [there] for so large a crowd as will be undoubtedly present," the *Eagle* reporter asserted.[9]

On game day at least 15,000 spectators—including, according to the *Eagle*, delegations of ballplayers from Philadelphia, Baltimore, Boston, Albany, Troy, Buffalo, Rochester, Poughkeepsie, and other cities—converged on the Putnam grounds, a large police force keeping them off the playing field itself.

The 1860 Excelsior Club: Thomas Reynolds, John C. Whiting, James Creighton, Harry D. Polhemus, Aleck T. Pearsall, Edwin Russell, Joseph B. Leggett, Asa Brainard, and George Flanley.

In the fifth inning, with the Excelsiors leading 8–4, a fateful sequence of events began. Dickey Pearce reached first base after catcher and team captain Joe Leggett missed a foul tip and second baseman John Holder muffed a grounder. Charles Smith then made a "splendid strike" to left field that scored Pearce and enabled Smith to reach second base. Archie McMahon followed with a grounder to left field which, though fielded well by third baseman John Whiting, allowed Smith to score, McMahon eventually reaching second. One out later, McMahon ran to third, being ruled safe and then out when his hand came off the base. The New York-based *Sunday Mercury* reported that umpire R.H. Thorn's "righteous decision raised a perfect howl among the outsiders," who "began calling 'Not out!' in a very boisterous manner, and indulging in other insulting expictives [expletives?] against the umpire, and the captain and members of the Excelsior nine."[10]

The *New York Clipper* reporter (most likely Henry Chadwick) identified the troublemakers as members of "the betting fraternity." McMahon's extended dispute of the umpire's call, in Chadwick's view, encouraged the rowdy behavior.[11] At that point, Leggett "distinctly proclaimed" that he would pull his players off the field if the behavior continued.

The rowdiness briefly diminished, but resumed more strongly during the sixth inning. With one out pitcher Matty O'Brien missed Leggett's ball both on the fly and the bound, and his brother Peter's throw from shortstop to first narrowly missed retiring Leggett. Creighton then sent a ball toward Peter O'Brien, who threw it to second baseman John Oliver to put Leggett out. Oliver's throw to first, however, was missed by John Price, and allowed Creighton to reach base safely. "The rowdy spirit of the crowd again began to display itself still more forcibly," Chadwick wrote. "So insulting were the epithets bestowed on the Excelsiors, that Leggett decided to withdraw his forces from the field."

According to the *Sunday Mercury* reporter, Leggett offered the game ball to the Atlantics. Matty O'Brien objected and stated a desire to continue, but the Excelsior captain remained adamant about not playing. He did, however, consent to O'Brien's proposal to call the game a draw.

The wisdom of Leggett's action was much debated in the New York press. Chadwick believed Leggett "acted wisely," but was disappointed that the Atlantics did not support him, "As that was the only method of putting a stop to the outrageous conduct of the low gambling set that were present on the occasion." On the other hand, an anonymous writer calling himself "Home Run" contended that Leggett lacked sufficient cause to pull his men when "the field was clear, the rope was perfect around its entire extent, and every player could exhibit as perfect play as he was capable of."[12]

Thorn conceded that neither club "won" the game "inasmuch as it was brought to an abrupt termination by influences outside of the parties interested in the match." But he argued that because the stoppage of the game was not by mutual consent, he had to declare "according to the rules" that the Excelsiors had forfeited the game to the Atlantics. The debate on the outcome continues to this day.

Atlantic			Excelsior		
	H.L.	Runs		H.L.	Runs
Pearce, c	1	2	Russell, 1b	2	1
Smith, 3b	1	2	Flanley, lf	1	2
McMahon, cf	3	0	Whitney, 3b	2	1
P. O'Brien, ss	2	0	Polhemus, cf	1	2
Pricem, 1b	3	0	Bramand, rf	2	1
Oliver, 2b	1	1	Reynolds, ss	3	0
Hamilton, rf	0	1	Holder, 2b	2	0
Joe Oliver, lf	2	0	Leggett, c	3	0
M. O'Brien, p	3	0	Creighton, p	1	1
Total		**6**	**Total**		**8**

Atlantic	121	02 – 6
Excelsior	501	20 – 8

Umpire – Mr. Thorn of the Empire club.
Scorers – For Atlantic, George R. Rogers; for Excelsior, W.H. Young

Notes:

1. Waff, Craig B. "1860.60 Atlantics and Excelsiors Compete for the 'Championship,' July 19, August 9, and August 23, 1860," *Base Ball: A Journal of the Early Game*, vol. 5, no. 1 (Spring 2011), 139-142.

2. "City News and Gossip: Base Ball—The Excelsiors," *Brooklyn Daily Eagle*, vol. 19, no. 165 (July 13, 1860), 3.

3. In an account of a game played against the Putnams of Brooklyn on June 29, the *Brooklyn Daily Eagle* reporter observed that "the Atlantics were far below their proverbial style of play." The *New York Clipper* reporter likewise observed a few weeks later that "this season the general play of the [Atlantics] has not been as good as that of last year, and we have noticed occasionally of

A woodcut from New York Illustrated News depicts the Excelsior vs. Atlantic contest that took place on July 19, 1860. The uniforms and caps of the team on the field match the Excelsiors, so it is reasonable to presume that the pitcher is James Creighton, and that Joe Leggett with his long sideburns is catching. The flag beneath the Excelsior flag is consistent with that of the Brooklyn Yacht Club which had just built a new clubhouse adjacent to the Excelsior base ball grounds. The ship "Jersey Blue" is seen docked in the background. It had been involved in a ship collision on January 7, 1860 leading to a famous lawsuit.

late, a perceptible falling off in the ability that has hitherto been characteristic of their play." Only the Putnam game had been competitive, and thus "a relaxed state of discipline has been induced that has had an unnerving effect." See "City News and Gossip: Base Ball—Atlantic vs. Putnam," *Brooklyn Daily Eagle*, vol. 19, no. 155 (June 30, 1860), 3; "Excelsior vs. Atlantic: The Match for the Championship," *New York Clipper*, vol. 8, no. 14, 108.

4. For accounts of the game, see "City News and Gossip: Base Ball—Excelsiors vs. Atlantic," *Brooklyn Daily Eagle*, vol. 19, no. 171 (July 20,1860), 3; "Base Ball: Excelsior vs. Atlantic—The Excelsiors Victorious—The Champion Club Beaten," *New York Times*, vol. 9, no. 2755 (July 20, 1860), 8; "Excelsior vs. Atlantic: The Match for the Championship," *New York Clipper*, vol. 8, no. 14 (July 21, 1860), 108; "Out-Door Sports: Base Ball: Match between the Champion Clubs," [New York] *Sunday Mercury*, July 22, 1860, 5; "Out-Door Sports: Base-Ball: Excelsior vs. Atlantic—The Excelsior Victorious—The Champion Club Beaten," *Porter's Spirit of the Times*, vol. 8, no. 22 (July 24, 1860), 340; "Base Ball—Excelsior vs. Atlantic," *Spirit of the Times*, vol. 30, no. 25 (July 28, 1860), 304; "Grand Match of the Season: Excelsior vs. Atlantic," *New York Clipper*, vol. 8, no. 15 (July 28, 1860), 116; "Out-Door Sports: Base Ball: Match between the Excelsior and Atlantic Clubs," *Wilkes' Spirit of the Times*, vol. 2, no. 21 (July 28, 1860), 331.

5. For accounts of the game, see "Base Ball: Grand Ball Match at Bedford," *Brooklyn Daily Eagle*, vol. 19, no. 189 (August 10, 1860), 2; "Out-Door Sports: Base Ball," *New York Times*, vol. 9, no. 2773 (August 10, 1860), 8; "Out-Door Sports: Base Ball: Return Match Between the Atlantic (of Bedford) and the Excelsior (of South Brooklyn), [New York] *Sunday Mercury*, August 12, 1860, p. 5; "Out-Door Sports: Base-Ball: Atlantic vs. Excelsior," *Porter's Spirit of the Times*, vol. 8, no. 25 (August 14, 1860), 388;"Grand Base Ball Match: The Atlantics Victorious: Excelsior vs. Atlantic," *New York Clipper*, vol. 8, no. 18 (August 18,1860), 141; "Out-Door Sports: Base Ball: Atlantic of Bedford vs. Excelsior of Brooklyn," *Wilkes' Spirit of the Times*, vol. 2, no. 24 (August 18,1860), 378.

6. "Out-Door Sports: Base-Ball: Atlantic vs. Mutual," *Porter's Spirit of the Times*, vol. 8, no. 27 (August 28, 1860), 420-21.

7. "Out-Door Sports: Base-Ball: Excelsior vs. Atlantic," *Porter's Spirit of the Times*, vol. 8, no. 26 (August 21, 1860), 408.

8. "Out-Door Sports: Base Ball: Grand Base Ball Match—Atlantic vs. Excelsior," *Wilkes' Spirit of the Times*, vol. 2, no. 26 (September 1, 1860), 405.

9. "Base Ball: Matches to Be Played: Atlantic vs. Excelsior," *Brooklyn Daily Eagle*, vol. 19, no. 198 (August 21, 1860), 2; "Base Ball: Atlantic vs. Excelsior," *Brooklyn Daily Eagle*, vol. 19, no. 199 (August 22, 1860), 3.

10. "Out-Door Sports: Base Ball: Atlantic vs. Excelsior—The Conquering Match," [New York] *Sunday Mercury*, August 26, 1860, 5. The quoted passage may contain the first specific use of the term sliding to describe that aspect of the running game. *Paul Dickson's The Dickson Baseball Dictionary*, 3rd ed. (New York: Norton, 2009), 787-788, cites an 1866 newspaper article for "1st use."

11. "Ball Play: Third Grand Match at Base Ball: The Game Broken Up by Rowdies: A Drawn Game: Excelsior vs. Atlantic," *New York Clipper*, vol. 8, no. 20 (September 1, 1860), 154.

12. "Out-Door Sports: Base-Ball: Excelsior vs. Atlantic—Game Broken up in a Row—Card from the Umpire—Letter from 'Home Run'," *Porter's Sprit of the Times*, vol. 8, no. 27 (August 28, 1860), 420.

13. Thorn defended his position in a letter to the editor that appeared in numerous newspapers, e.g., "Out-Door Sports: Base-Ball: Excelsior vs. Atlantic—Game Broken up in a Row—Card from the Umpire—Letter from 'Home Run'," *Porter's Spirit of the Times*, vol. 8, no. 27 (August 28,1860), 420; R.H. Thorn, Umpire, "Out-Door Sports: Base Ball: Decision of the Umpire," *Wilkes' Spirit of the Times*, vol. 2, no. 26 (September 1, 1860), 405; "Ball Play: Third Grand Match at Base Ball: The Game Broken Up by Rowdies: A Drawn Game: Excelsior vs. Atlantic – the Umpire's Decision," *New York Clipper*, vol. 8, no. 20 (September 1, 1860), 154.

The First Enclosed Ballpark

Olympics of Philadelphia vs. St. George of Philadelpha

*St. George's Cricket Club Grounds,
Camac Woods, Philadelphia, Pa.
July 24, 1860*

By Jerrold Casway

Determining the first enclosed baseball field is a matter for debate. A significant criterion for inclusion is whether the playing site was adapted from another recreational venue such as a race track, fairgrounds, cricket pitch, skating rink, or a parade field. Candidacy should be solely based on whether the grounds were specifically erected and intended for baseball games where admission was charged.

One of the most frequently suggested candidates was the Union Grounds in Williamsburg, New York, across the East River from Lower Manhattan. The site was developed by a Brooklyn businessman and politician, William Cammeyer. He seemingly was influenced by an 1858 all-star series played at the Fashion Race Course in what is now Flushing Meadows, Queens. Motivated by this innovation, Cammeyer in 1861 purchased the site and built an ice-skating rink that he intended to turn into a baseball field. A year later, he drained, leveled, and sodded the grounds and converted the site from an ice rink to an enclosed ballfield. The site covered six acres and was surrounded by a "broad fence six or seven feet in height." The grounds had a "commodious clubhouse" and roofed seating for women spectators. On May 15, 1862, without admission fees, he hosted a game between the all-star players from the playing field's three tenant teams, the Eckford, Putnam, and Constellation clubs.[1]

The grounds were distinguished by a three-story pagoda in deep center field that lit up and decorated the winter skating pond.

The question is whether the Union Grounds is a candidate for hosting the first enclosed baseball game. We cannot overlook how the field was a converted ice rink that reverted to its original purpose when the ball season was over. There was also the matter of having a large alien structure in the outfield that had no place in baseball. Finally, the site was widely known as the Union Baseball and Cricket Grounds.

Another candidate, Capitoline Grounds, was sometimes confused with the Union Grounds. This field, in nearby Brooklyn, rivaled Cammeyer's site. But Capitoline Grounds was primarily an ice-skating area that was used for an enclosed baseball game almost two years (May 15, 1864) after the Union Grounds All-Star contest.[2] In the nation's capital, the Nationals of Washington enclosed their pioneering grounds with a 10-foot fence in 1867.[3]

Philadelphia, too, had candidates of its own. One of the city's oldest ballplaying sites was in South Philadelphia, at 11th and Wharton. The Wharton Parade Square, in the shadow of the Moyamensing Prison, was used for baseball and town ball in 1859, but it was not enclosed until 1871. Another pioneering site, the Jefferson Square Parade Grounds, was located at 25th and Masters Streets, across from the city's reservoir. As early as 1863, ballgames were played on these grounds. The field had a clubhouse and wooden bleachers, but the site was not enclosed until 1865.[4] East of this playing field, on 18th Street, was the Mercantile Grounds, which had been fenced in by 1865. The celebrated home of the early Athletics of Philadelphia at 17th and Montgomery Avenue had enclosing fences the following year.[5] Four blocks east, at Camac Woods, was the best candidate for being the first enclosed ballfield.

This site, at 12th and Berks Streets, was part of a popular public park, noted for its manicured lawns and sumptuous strolling gardens. In September

1859 part of these grounds was prepared as a cricket pitch for the All-England Cricket exhibition series. The soon-to-be St. George's Cricket Grounds was resurfaced, leveled, and enclosed by a "broad fence." Wooden stands were erected for 1,500 spectators and benches surrounded the playing area. After the English cricket series the enclosed grounds attracted local baseball clubs. The original fence was raised and modified. A wooden clubhouse was built and "Barlow board benches" were set up for female spectators. Admission fees of 25 cents were frequently charged. On Tuesday, July 24, 1860, the Olympics of Philadelphia played the St. George baseball team. Using New York rules, the Olympics won, 25–17.[6]

Although Camac Woods (St. George's Cricket Ground) was originally intended for the cricket exhibition series, the site was renovated and turned into an enclosed baseball facility that charged admission. The Olympics game, as a result, was the most qualified candidate for being the first game played in an enclosed site set up for baseball.

Notes:

1. *Brooklyn Eagle*, May 16, 1862; Gershman, Michael. *Diamonds; The Evolution of the Ballpark* (Boston, 1993), pp. 11-3; Seymour, Harold. *Baseball: The Early Years* (New York, I, 1960), 48-9.

2. Philip Lowry, *Green Cathedrals* (New York, 2006), pp. 34-5; *New York Herald*, August 15, 1865.

3. David Voigt, *American Baseball* (Norman, Oklahoma: University of Oklahoma Press, 1966) p. 19.

4. Lithograph of Mercantile grounds by T. Sinclair, c. 1865 in Historical Society of Pennsylvania. Picture of Olympic Club House, c. 1865 in Library of Baseball Hall of Fame; Peverelly, Cahrles. *The Book of American Pastimes* (New York, 1866), p. 479; *Philadelphia Inquirer*, October 31, 1865, January 27, 1871; *Sunday Press*, May 6, 1866; *Sunday Item*, March 11, 1894.

5. Jerrold Casway, "At the Old Ball Game," *Temple Review*, Spring 1992, pp. 22-3. Painting of Athletics-Atlantics game, October 22, 1865 in Library of Baseball Hall of Fame.

6. Jerrold Casway, "Camac Woods in Philadelphia," *Nineteenth-Century Notes*, Fall 2008, pp. 1-3; Jerrold Casway, "At the Old Ball Game," *Temple Review*, Spring 1992, pp. 19-22. Peverelly, op. cit., p. 410 & p. 474. Clipping in Campbell Collection, HSP, Vol. 64, 143-4. North American, October 11, 1859; *Philadelphia Public Ledger*, October 13, 1859; *Philadelphia Press*, October 14, 1859; *Sunday Dispatch*, January 28, 1872.

The Grand Excursion, Part II

Excelsior of South Brooklyn vs. Excelsior of Baltimore
Excelsior Grounds, Baltimore, Md.;

and Picked Nine of Philadelphia
Camac Woods, Philadelphia, Pa.
September 22 and 24, 1860

By Craig B. Waff

Following the success of their July 1860 swing through upstate New York—the first "road trip" in baseball history—the Excelsiors of South Brooklyn booked a second such trip during September, their destination this time being the cities of Baltimore and Philadelphia.

That excursion got underway on Friday evening, September 21, when the Excelsior players and other club members left the Jersey City depot for an overnight train ride to Baltimore. Although they arrived at the President Street railroad station at 4 A.M., they were greeted by a committee of Baltimore Excelsiors, who escorted them, in one of Barnum's four-horse carriages, to Guy's Monument House hotel.

After settling in their rooms, they and their hosts all sat down at 9:30 to enjoy a splendid breakfast at the hotel. Following a reception that allowed "the admirers of the game and friends of the club" to meet the visitors, they were taken by carriage to various places of interest in the city.

According to the *New York Clipper*, the Brooklyn players were supported in every way possible: "Every attention it was possible to bestow upon them being given them by the gentlemanly members of the Baltimore Excelsiors. Indeed, from the time of their arrival to their departure not a cent's expense were they allowed to incur."

At 1 P.M., an hour before the start of the game, the visiting players gathered on Holliday Street, where a city car "gaily decked with flags and drawn by four horses" transported them to the local team's grounds at the corner of Madison and Northern Avenues, near Mr. Hartzell's Park House.

More than 3,000 spectators had already assembled on the grounds, including many "blooming belles of Baltimore." The sight of the latter so transfixed players Asa Brainard, John Whiting, and Thomas Reynolds that Captain Joe Leggett had to forcibly call their attention to preparation for the game. The pre-game practice of the visitors made it clear to the local team that they had a major challenge ahead of them. The *Baltimore Republican* reported, "The ball passed from one to the other with great precision, and seldom was it allowed to slip through the fingers of any of them. This little exhibition made it manifest that the Baltimore Club would learn a few new points before the game closed."

As he had during the upstate New York tour, pitcher Jim Creighton immediately bewildered the locals. "Mr. Beam, of the Baltimore nine, a very fine batter usually, led off, but he was hardly prepared for the swift, lightning-like balls which Creighton began to favor him with," a correspondent reported. "He struck once without effect, and looked astonished; he struck again, and missed, and looked surprised; again he made an ineffectual stroke at the ball, and gave up his bat, apparently in wonder and admiration of the performance of the pitcher."

As the pre-game practice indicated, the Brooklyn Excelsiors were equally dazzling in their fielding, making not only three double plays, but also a spectacular triple play. The latter came in the sixth inning, when Creighton switched positions with left fielder Ed Russell. According to the *Sunday Mercury*:

> *"Mr. Shriver ... was at the bat, while Sears occupied the third base, and S. Patchen (substitute for Hazlett) was on the second base. As Shriver struck the ball, both Sears and Patchen ran from their bases — pausing somewhat to witness the fate of the ball, which Creighton*

was after. ... By one of the handsomest backward single-handed catches ever made by Creighton, he took the ball on the fly, and instantly, by a true and rapid throw, passed the ball to Whiting, who caught it, and threw it as quickly to Brainerd, on the second base, before either Sears or Patchen had time to return to their bases, thus putting three hands out 'in a jiffy.' But there was more yet in the ball; for Brainerd hardly received it from Whiting before it was on its way from his hands to Pearsall, who caught it in his own steel trap style, and made all the motions necessary to put out another hand, if there were any 'lying around loose.'"

Edwin Russell: Excelsiors' usual left fielder took a turn on the mound during the southern road swing.

Jim Creighton: From left field, his backhand catch initiated the first triple play presently on record.

The batting of the visitors was similarly dominant, generating outbursts of 6, 6, 7, 12, and 13 runs in the first, fourth, fifth, sixth, and eighth innings en route to a 51–6 victory. After the final out, a scrub match was played for a while, and then a group of 50 people sat down to a sumptuous dinner, "served up in the French style," at Guy's Monument House. After various toasts, the group adjourned at around 11 P.M.

The Brooklyn Excelsiors departed the following afternoon on the 6 P.M. train and arrived four hours later in Philadelphia. After a stay overnight at the Continental Hotel, they spent the morning visiting various objects of interest. By this time, however, the busy schedule was taking its toll. The *Sunday Mercury* reporter observed: "They felt somewhat fatigued and worn out, by travel, the loss of sleep, and other exertions, and were not in as good order as they could have wished, to contend with the picked players who were to be brought against them."

The situation was made worse when the Excelsiors players were obliged to walk quite a distance to the playing field at Camac Woods. The Philadelphia players, picked from the Equity, Olympic, Hamilton, Athletic, and Winona clubs, were also somewhat ill-prepared, having had no time to practice together. Thus the game, which resulted in a 15–4 victory for the Excelsiors, involved play on both sides that was "very creditable, but not so spirited on the part of the Excelsiors as in the Baltimore match." The *Baltimore Republican* reporter mentioned as "having excited our 'special wonder,' the daring, almost reckless catching of Leggett, and the swift, even pitching of Creighton," while the *Sunday Mercury* noted that the Philadelphians were quite as much "taken down by Creighton's peculiar pitching, as were the Baltimoreans."

After the game, all of the players traveled to Schuylkill Falls, where they enjoyed a catfish supper, with appropriate fixings. At 11 P.M. the Excelsiors boarded the "owl train" and arrived back home at daylight.

Excelsior vs. Baltimore, Sept. 22, 1860

Brooklyn			Baltimore		
	H.L.	Runs		H.L.	Runs
Pearsall	3	6	Beam	4	0
Russell	3	6	Mitchell	3	1
Whiting	5	4	Orem	1	1
Leggett	2	7	Sears	3	1
Creighton	3	6	Hazlett	3	1
Brainard	2	6	Shriver	4	0
Flanley	4	5	Woods	3	0
Polhemus	2	7	Williams	2	2
Reynolds	3	4	Pitmam	4	0
Total		51	**Total**		6
Brooklyn	6 3 1	6 7 (13)	1 (12) 2 – 51		
Baltimore	0 0 1	0 1 1	1 2 0 – 6		

The POW game

Game between captured Union soldiers

*Salisbury Prison Camp,
Salisbury, North Carolina
July 4, 1862*

By Patricia Millen

The ballfield was surrounded by stately oak trees, sweet-water wells, and handsome brick buildings, and lined by a wooden fence. The weather was mild when the inmates took to the playing field on the Fourth of July in 1862. Otto Boetticher was there. A 45-year-old military artist and lithographer originally from Prussia, he operated a studio in New York City before enlisting in the 68th New York Volunteers at the start of the Civil War in 1861.

Boetticher, a captain, was captured and spent time in Libby prison in Richmond, Virginia, before he was shipped to the Salisbury Prison in North Carolina in the summer of 1862. It is his print "drawn from nature" and published by Sarony, Major, and Knapp in color in 1863 that captured life in the prison at Salisbury and the baseball games that were played in the pastoral surroundings for a few brief seasons before the prison became unbearable.[1]

For months Salisbury was the "most endurable prison," with only 600 inmates who were allowed to "exercise in the open air." They were comparatively well fed and treated kindly, recalled former inmate Willard W. Glazier in 1866.[2] Before the great influx of prisoners arrived at Salisbury in October of 1864, the prison population remained consistently low. The old cotton factory rested on 16 acres and was renovated by the Confederate government in 1861 to house 2,500 inmates, deserters, civilian prisoners, and Negro prisoners of war. Men were allowed "liberty of the yard"[3] and many of the captured soldiers enjoyed afternoon and evening games of baseball.

"Took a little walk in the evening and watched some of the officers play ball," wrote 23-year-old prisoner Charles Gray, a Union Army doctor, in May 1862. Gray wrote frequently of the games in his diary. "A good state of cheerfulness, thanks to the open space is fairly prevailing. Ball play for those who like it and are able…"[4]

Gray and other observers watched the match games between the captured Union prisoners and other inmates. A soldier from Rhode Island, William Crossley, who arrived at Salisbury in March 1863, recalled a baseball game played by recently transferred prisoners from New Orleans and Tuscaloosa, Alabama:

> *And to-day the great game of baseball came off between the Orleanists and Tuscaloosans with apparently as much enjoyment to the Rebs as the Yanks, for they came in hundreds to see the sport, and I have seen more smiles to-day on their oblong faces than since I came to Rebeldom. … The game was a tie, eleven each but the factory fellows were skunked three times, and we but twice."*[5]

It can be surmised that the "factory" boys were possibly the Confederate guards from the factory-turned-prison or captured soldiers held in the prison barracks. By the time this game took place, Captain Boetticher had been exchanged for a Confederate captain in September of 1862.

On holidays during the Civil War, sport became a common diversion for soldiers as they attempted to forget the hardships, danger, boredom, and homesickness of wartime life. Accounts show that soldiers marched in St. Patrick's Day parades, ran footraces on Thanksgiving, and held shooting and boxing matches. Regiments challenged each other to football and baseball games and snowball fights on Christmas—substituting sport for traditional holiday observances.

On July 4, 1862, at Salisbury prison there was music, a reading of the Declaration of Independence, sack races and footraces along with a greased-pig-catching contest and a baseball game.[6] It is unclear if this is the game featured in Otto Boetticher's rendering, although it is altogether possible. The image shows a well-worn, diamond-shaped playing field, hundreds of fans in the bucolic prison yard and prisoners who even appeared to don makeshift red uniforms!

Confederate Chaplain Adolphus Magnum, who visited Salisbury in 1862, wrote of the celebration on the Fourth of July to include a blindfolded wheelbarrow race and described a dress parade and ball play on the prison grounds:

> ...the officers among the prisoners came out and presented a truly beautiful scene in their recreation. A number of the younger and less dignified ran like schoolboys to the play ground and were soon joining in high glee in a game of ball. Others ... sat down by side with the prison officials and witnessed the sport.[7]

Salisbury prisoner Josephus Clarkson, a ship chandler's apprentice from Boston, wrote of the impromptu ballgames that took place and of the lengthy debates over whether to play by town-ball rules (in which "plugging" or putting runners out by hitting them with the ball was allowed) or by the New York rules:

> "Since many of the men were in a weakened condition, it was agreed to play the faster but less harsh New York rules which intrigued our guards. The game of baseball had been played much in the south, but many of them (the guards) had never seen the sport devised by Mr. Cartwright."[8]

Lithograph of "Union Prisoners at Salisbury, North Carolina," drawn by Major Otto Boetticher.

It is unclear how long Clarkson spent at Salisbury, but the inmates he described were failing in health. As the war dragged on, it was unlikely that the prison yard at Salisbury saw anything but deprivation. By 1864 the prison population had risen to more than 10,000 and hundreds of men died daily of starvation and illness. Most of Salisbury was burned to the ground when the war ended in 1865; a national cemetery is now close by.

After the war some historians promoted baseball as a healing tool to reinforce a new sense of union. A grand game of baseball was indeed played at Salisbury on July 4, 1862. It is unclear whether the game in Boetticher's print was an illustration of this game or a composite of many he remembered while imprisoned there. The print does illustrate, however, that baseball was a uniting force for both armies during and long after the Civil War.

Notes:

1. *An Album of Civil War Battle Art*, 1998, p. 97.

2. Glazier, W. *The Capture, The Prison Pen and the Escape*, 1866, p. 303-304.

3. Sumner, Jim. "POWs Collected RBIs in Civil War Prison Camp," *Baseball America*, 1997, p. 51.

4. Sumner, Jim. "Baseball at Salisbury Prison Camp." *Baseball History*, 1989, p. 20.

5. Ibid.

6. Brown, Louis. *The Salisbury Prison: A Case Study of Confederate Military Prisons*, 1980, p. 136.

7. Sumner, Jim. "Baseball at Salisbury Prison Camp," 1989, p. 22.

8. Twombly, Wells. *200 Years of Sport in America*, 1976, p. 71.

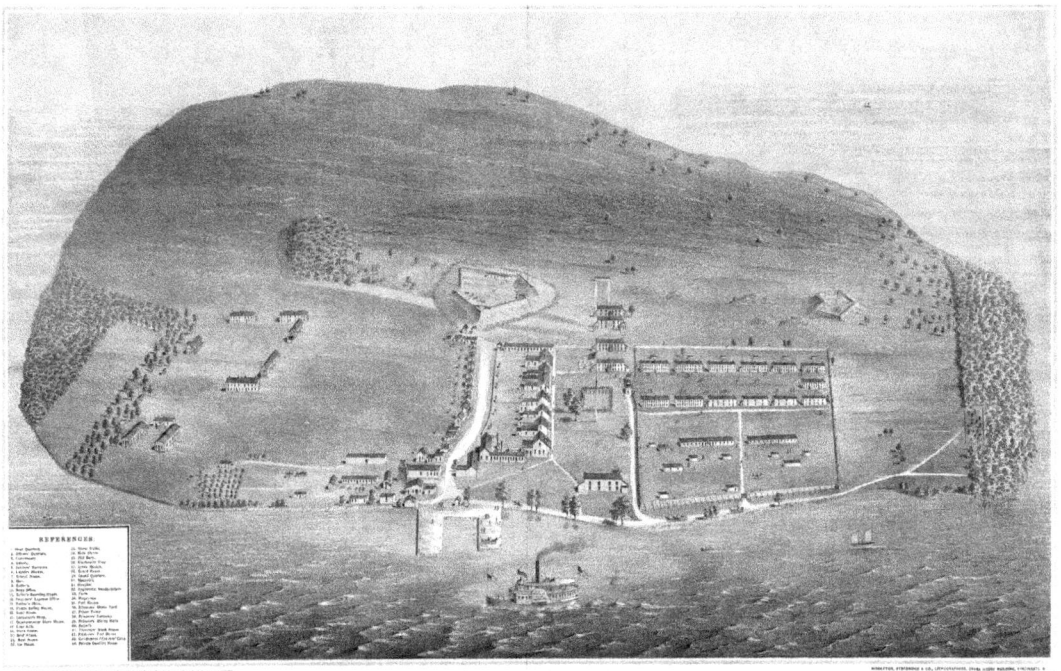

Lithograph of "View of Johnson's Island, Near Sandusky City, O." drawn by Edward Gould.

The "Silver Ball" Game

Atlantics of Brooklyn vs. Eckfords

*Union Grounds, Brooklyn, N.Y.
September 18, 1862*

By Craig B. Waff

By 1862, the unofficial title of "champion" senior club in the Greater New York City region was being regularly applied to the Atlantics of Brooklyn, a team that compiled a series of match wins against other clubs that extended back to 1856.[1] Under the existing "challenge" system, a new "champion" would be crowned only after a club won a match series of games against the reigning champions—at the time, the Atlantics.

One major challenge that the Atlantics faced in 1860, from the Excelsiors of South Brooklyn, is described in another article in this volume.[2] The Atlantics faced one additional serious challenger in 1860—the Eckfords, who were undefeated in 13 contests. The two teams played a series of three games on successive Mondays, the Atlantics prevailing 20–11 in the decisive game.

A general feeling appeared to exist in early 1861 that the challenge system (and particularly the champion's ability to control which challenges to accept) limited the number of teams that could compete for the title. Such a feeling may have prompted the Continental Club of Brooklyn to propose a new way of determining a champion in early April 1861. It called for teams to be paired by lot in a series of games leading to a home-and-home, best-of-three final.[3]

The idea was quickly doomed by the start of the Civil War, which left several teams short of players. But although the proposal was abandoned, the prize that it had intended to award the ultimate winner—a finely engraved "champion silver ball"—resurfaced as a topic of discussion in 1862.[4] In its June 21 issue, the *Brooklyn Eagle* announced, in an article and an advertisement, that "the champion Atlantics and the celebrated Eckfords," representing the Eastern and Western districts of Brooklyn, had agreed to play a series of games at the new enclosed Union Skating and Base Ball Grounds in Brooklyn. Admission would be 10 cents, and the entire proceeds would go to the U.S. Sanitary Commission, for the benefit of sick and wounded soldiers. In addition, the Continental Club announced that it would suitably update its silver ball for a trophy to the winner.[5]

The first game was played on Friday, July 11. Although the game attracted an audience estimated at between 3,000 and 4,000, the *Eagle* reporter deplored the decision by many of them to view the

Future sporting goods manufacturer Al Reach contributed to the Eckfords' offense.

game from the high banks surrounding the enclosure, thus significantly diminishing the contribution the proceeds could make toward the Sanitary Commission. The Eckfords won the first game, 20–14, the *Eagle* reporter attributing the loss to the play of the Atlantics, which it described as "only tolerable and hardly excusable from such players."[6]

The Eckford victory increased interest in the return game, which was played, despite intermittent showers, without delay on the same field on Friday, July 18. The total crowd was estimated to be as high as 8,000—once again split nearly in half between those inside the enclosure and outside on the surrounding banks. They saw a complete reversal of fortune. The fielding of the Atlantics was "up to the mark" and "throughout very fine" (according to the *New York Times*), while the Eckfords, according to a *New York Clipper* reporter, "played a very poor game, the poorest in fact that they have ever played." The final score was 39–5.[7]

The split required the playing of a third game at the Union Grounds. Although Andy Mills had pitched ably for the Eckfords in the first two games, the club delayed the third game until Joe Sprague, its regular pitcher in the early part of the season, returned from a three-month hitch in the Union Army. The two-month delay allowed an unprecedented interest in the game to develop, as is evident in this *Clipper* account of pre-game activity:

> *For an hour or more before the time appointed for commencing the game, all the avenues leading to the grounds were occupied with streams of people proceeding to witness the match, every car on the routes that passed near by being crowded to excess with passengers. ... At a very moderate estimate, there must have been, by 4 o'clock, at least 10,000 people in and around the grounds.*[8]

Joe Start: two stolen bases after single to left field.

The Atlantics scored single runs in the first two innings. The first resulted from shortstop Tom Devyr's mishandling of a ball hit by Peter O'Brien, followed by a hit to right field by brother Matty O'Brien, who made it all the way to third. The second resulted from a hit to left field by Joe Start, who subsequently stole both second and third bases, and scored on a wild throw by catcher Waddy Beach to Andy Mills, now playing third base.

The Eckfords came back with five runs in the second. With left fielder Fred Crane playing deep, Peter Spence safely hit in front of him. He scored when Al Reach sent a hit to right field that Mace muffed enough to enable Reach to reach second base. (The player identified as "Mace" may actually be F.S. Massey, who had played earlier for two Brooklyn teams, Osceola and the Exercise Club, which absorbed the Osceolas in 1859.) After Beach lined out to Pete O'Brien, Joe Sprague hit a "hot one" to third baseman Charlie Smith, whose throw to first failed to beat Sprague. Reach attained third on a passed ball, then Devyr hit a "splendid" grounder to right that allowed him to reach third and both Reach and Sprague to score. Devyr held that base while J. Smith sent a "skyer" that managed to drop between Charley Smith and the two O'Briens, but he scored as Andy Mills grounded out to Charley. Harry Manolt then hit a ball sharply back to pitcher Matty O'Brien, who failed to catch it on the bound. Peter O'Brien then threw the ball wildly to first, enabling Manolt to reach first and Smith to score.

The Eckfords added another run in the third and two more in the fourth, building their lead to 8–2. They scored no more that day, but the Atlantics failed to take advantage, adding only one late run. As the innings wore on, the *Clipper* reporter noted,

Charlie Smith

"The Atlantics expected to make that rally that has hitherto brought them out of many a tight spot in their matches, but somehow or other they did not succeed."

The Eckfords' 8–3 victory gave them the three-game match. Besides attracting the largest audience to a base ball game to that date, it marked the first changeover of "champions" in the New York City region.

Atlantic	H.L.	Runs	Eckford	H.L.	Runs
Smith, 3b	4	0	Mills, 3b	3	1
Pearce, c	4	0	Manolt, lf	2	0
P. O'Brien, ss	3	1	Campbell, 1b	6	0
M. O'Brien, p	1	1	Spence, cf	2	1
Crane, cf	3	0	Reach, 2b	2	2
Mace, rf	3	0	Beach, c	5	0
Oliver, 2b	4	0	Sprague, p	2	1
Start, 1b	2	1	Devyr, ss	3	1
Chapman, lf	3	0	Smith, rf	2	2
Total		3	Total		8
Atlantic	110	000	010 - - 3		
Gotham	951	120	000 - - 8		

Fielding	Fly	B'nd	Base	T'tl		Fly	B'nd	Base	T'tl
Smith	4	1	0	5	Mills	2	1	1	4
Pearce	1	3	0	4	Manolt	0	0	0	0
P. O'Brien	0	0	1	1	Campbell	0	0	8	8
M. O'Brien	0	2	0	2	Spence	1	2	0	3
Crane	3	1	0	4	Reach	1	0	1	2
Mace	1	0	0	1	Beach	0	3	0	3
Oliver	0	0	0	0	Sprague	1	1	0	2
Start	1	0	9	10	Devyr	2	1	0	3
Chapman	0	0	0	0	Smith	0	0	0	0
Total	10	7	10	27	Total	7	8	10	25

How Put Out	Fly	B'd	1_2_3	F'l		Fly	B'd	1_2_3	F'l
Smith	1	0	3_0_0	0	Mills	0	0	2_0_0	1
Pearce	1	1	2_0_0	0	Manolt	0	0	1_0_0	1
P. O'Brien	1	0	1_0_0	0	Campbell	2	0	3_0_0	1
M. O'Brien	0	1	0_0_0	0	Spence	2	0	0_0_0	0
Crane	2	1	0_0_0	0	Reach	0	1	0_0_0	1
Mace	0	0	1_0_0	1	Beach	1	0	3_0_0	1
Oliver	1	0	0_0_1	2	Sprague	0	1	0_0_0	1
Start	0	1	0_0_0	1	Devyr	1	1	0_1_0	0
Chapman	1	1	1_0_0	0	Smith	0	1	0_0_0	1
Total	7	5	8_0_1	4	Total	6	4	9_1_0	7

Passed balls—Beach 3, Pearce 1.
Struck out – Mace 1, P. O'Brien 1.
Fly catches missed – Beach 1, J. Smith 1, Pearce 1, P. O'Brien 1, M. O'Brien 2, Smith 1.
Bound catches missed – M. O'Brien 1.
Left on bases – Mills 1, Manolt 3, Spence 3, Reach 1 Sprague 1, J. Smith 1, Smith 1, Chapman 1, M. O'Brien 2, Crane 1, Mace 1, Start 1.
Time of game – Two hours and fifteen minutes.
Umpire – E. Brown of the Mutual.
Scorers – Messrs Grum and Moore.

Notes:

1. Craig B. Waff, "1860.60 Atlantics and Excelsiors Compete for the 'Championship,' July 19, August 9, and August 23, 1860," *Base Ball*, vol. 5, no. 1 (Spring 2011), 139-142

2. Research by Craig B. Waff.

3. "City News and Gossip: Base Ball Season," *Brooklyn Daily Eagle* [hereafter cited as BDE], vol. 20, no. 78 (April 3, 1861), p. 3, col. 1.

4. The presentation of the game ball by the losers to the winners of a game was a tradition in early base ball and was even specified in rules formulated by the NABBP in 1857. Peter Morris, *A Game of Inches: The Stories Behind the Innovations That Shaped Baseball: The Game Behind the Scenes*, (Chicago: Ivan R. Dee, 2006), 293. Clubs would often write the results (that is, who won and who lost, the final score, and the date on which the game was played) on the ball itself, and some even publicly displayed such trophies. The customs and formalities regarding challenges and game balls were discussed in various question-and-answer correspondences that appeared in the New York-based *Sunday Mercury* newspaper in at least 1859 and 1860. For some samples, see Robert Tholkes, "'Your Valuabal Paper': Baseball Correspondence in the Sunday Mercury, 1859-1860," *Base Ball*, vol. 4, no. 1 (Spring 2010), 44-58, esp. 53-56. The pre-engraved ball that was being offered by the Continental Base Ball Club of Brooklyn, however, was clearly a significant step above the normal trophy game ball. A subsequent *Eagle* article described the ball as being of "exquisite texture, large, and beautifully manufactured." On its face initially was the inscription "Presented by the Continental B.B. Club to the Champion of the Prize Series, 1861" and a "finely executed" drawing below that represented a ballfield while a game was in progress. On the reverse was a scroll with the engraving "The Continental Prize Series" over a drawing of base ball implements (*"Base Ball: Relief for the Sick and Wounded—A Silver Ball Match," BDE*, vol. 21, no. 147 (June 21, 1862), p. 2, col. 5).

5. "Base Ball: Relief for the Sick and Wounded—A Silver Ball Match," *BDE*, vol. 21, no. 147 (June 21, 1862), p. 2, col. 5; "Grand Silver Ball Match Presented by the Continental Club" (advertisement), *BDE*, vol. 21, no. 159 (July 7, 1862), p. 3, col. 5, "Special Notices" section of classified ads, and reprinted in

several subsequent issues prior to the playing of the game.

6 The most detailed accounts of the game were reported in "Ball Match for the Aid of the U.S. Sanitary Committee—Ball Players Patriots—Eckford vs. Atlantic—The Champions Defeated!," *BDE*, vol. 21, no. 164 (July 12, 1862), p. 2, col. 6., and "Out-Door Sports: Base Ball: Grand Match for the Champion Silver Ball: Atlantic vs. Eckford, of Brooklyn: Eckford Club Victorious," [New York] *Sunday Mercury*, vol. 14, no. 27 (July 13, 1862), p. [xx], col. 1. The game was also briefly reported in "Atlantic vs. Eckford," *New York Clipper*, undated July 1862 clipping in Mears Collection, Cleveland Public Library.

7 The most detailed accounts of the game were reported in "Great Base Ball Match: Second Contest for the Champion Silver Ball: Atlantic versus Eckford—The Atlantic Club Victorious," *BDE*, vol. 21, no. 172 (July 22, 1862), p. 2, cols. 5-6, and "The Grand Match for the Championship: The Atlantics the Victors: Atlantic vs. Eckford," *New York Clipper*, undated July 1862 clipping in the Mears Collection, and "Out-Door Sports: Base Ball: Return Match for the Champion Silver Ball: Atlantic vs. Eckford," [New York] *Sunday Mercury*, vol. 14, no. 29 (July 27, 1862), p. [xx], cols. 1-2. A brief account appeared in "Brooklyn News: Base Ball Match: Atlantic Club vs. Eckford Club," *New-York Times*, vol. 11, no. 3378 (July 22, 1862), p. 8, col. 5.

8 The most detailed accounts of the game were reported in "Great Base Ball Match: The Contest for the Championship: Eckford vs. Atlantic: Eckford Victorious—Score 8 to 3: Deciding Contest for the Championship and the Continental Silver Ball—Proceeds for the Benefit of the Sanitary Commission—Immense Assemblage Present—Presentation of the Silver Ball &c.," *BDE*, vol. 22, no. 223 (September. 19, 1862), p. 2, col. 4; "The Grand Match for the Championship: The Eckfords Victorious and the Champions: A Fine Contest and a Remarkably Small Score; A Fair Field and No Favor Shown," *New York Clipper*, undated September 1862 clipping in the Mears Collection; and "Out-Door Sports: Base Ball: The Grand Match for the Championship: Eckford vs. Atlantic—Eckford Victorious," [New York] *Sunday Mercury*, vol. 14, no. 37 (September. 21, 1862). A brief account appeared in "Base Ball," *New York Times*, vol. 11, no. 3429 (September. 19, 1862), p. 3, col. 1.

Atlantic	Outs	Runs	Eckford	Outs	Runs
Smith, 3b	4	0	Mills, 3b	3	1
Pearce, c	4	0	Manolt, lf	2	0
P. O'Brien, ss	3	1	Campbell, 1b	6	0
M. O'Brien, p	1	1	Spence, cf	2	1
Crane, cf	3	0	Reach, 2b	2	2
Mace, rf	3	0	Beach, c	5	0
Oliver, 2b	4	0	Sprague, p	2	1
Hart, 1b	2	1	Devyr, ss	3	1
Chapman, lf	3	0	Smith, rf	2	2
TOTALS	27	3	TOTALS	27	8
Atlantic	110	000	010 – 3		
Eckford	051	200	000 – 8		

Umpire – E Brown of the Mutual.
Scorers – For Atlantic, G.W. Moore. For Eckford, J. Green

The Martyrdom of Jim Creighton

Unions of Morrisania vs. Excelsiors of Brooklyn

Excelsior Grounds, Brooklyn, N.Y.
October 14, 1862

By Richard Bogovich

He has been called baseball's first superstar, its first professional, and a pitching innovator. James Creighton is also central to one of baseball's earliest legends. It stems from the game in Brooklyn on Tuesday, October 14, 1862, when his Excelsiors hosted the Unions of Morrisania and won, 13–9.

The contest itself wasn't noteworthy, as reflected in the *Brooklyn Eagle*'s confession that its report was "very brief," squeezed by other news.[1] The legend is that during the game Creighton swung so mightily while hitting a home run that the swing caused a serious abdominal rupture. However accurate that is, he suffered for a few days at home after that game and died on the 18th. He was only 21.

The *Eagle* wrote about Creighton's death at length, and the *New York Times*, which said he was "extensively known as an expert base ball player," echoed the *Eagle*'s statement that Creighton died as "the result of internal injuries sustained while playing a match on Tuesday last."[2] Creighton's death was also announced in such papers as the *Boston Daily Advertiser*, the *Public Ledger* in Philadelphia, the *Sun* in Baltimore, Virginia's *Alexandria Gazette*, and the *Milwaukee Daily Sentinel*. The *Advertiser's* account called Creighton a "well known base-ball player" and specified that he "burst a blood-vessel in striking at a ball," though without specifying the result.[3]

Creighton was buried at Brooklyn's Green-Wood Cemetery. A few years later, the *Eagle* wrote that visitors to his grave would "see a very neat and pretty marble shaft, bearing all the emblems of the Base Ball field, and the name James Creighton. It was erected in conjunction by the Excelsior and Union Clubs." The paper also provided this account of Creighton's fateful at-bat: "Hannegan was pitching for the Union, and Creighton was at bat. Hannegan was joking with Jim, and told him he would strike out. Creighton had struck twice, and in making a third attempt at a ball struck with such great force and immediately fell down. After a while he felt no more uneasiness, and played the balance of the game."[4]

James P. Creighton, Jr. was born in Manhattan to James and Jane Creighton on April 15, 1841. His mother died when he was eight years old. A decade later Creighton was playing for the Niagaras of Brooklyn when he had his first chance to pitch. Soon thereafter he switched to the opposing team, the Star Club, and in 1860 he joined the Excelsiors. He impressed during the team's ground-breaking tour that season, which included a leg through Philadelphia and Baltimore to Washington.

Jim Creighton

One account of Creighton's final game appeared in *Sporting Life* on April 13, 1887, when it reprinted a letter from an unnamed "Old Timer" to St. Louis's *Republican*: "Creighton's death occurred from the rupture of his bladder, which occurred while he was pitching for the Excelsiors against the Unions of Morrisania. I was a kid at the time, and was a spectator of the match. Creighton played out the game, although I think he changed positions and went out into the field to play during the last two or three innings. Some of my companions averred that they heard his bladder burst, but if they did they did not say anything about it at the time, and it was not generally known until the next day that the celebrated pitcher was injured."[5]

Henry Chadwick wrote a rebuttal in his regular column the next issue: "I saw Creighton play in a cricket match at Bedford, on the outskirts of Brooklyn, as a member of the St. George Club, in a game with the Willow Club eleven in 1862, and in that match, in making a very hard effort to hit a leg ball, Creighton unknowingly ruptured himself. Not being aware of the serious injury he sustained on the occasion, he very unprudently engaged in a base ball match with the Excelsiors, of Brooklyn, against the Unions, of Morrisania, and he had not pitched long in the game before he had to retire from his position from pain. On that occasion Creighton said that he had strained himself playing cricket. He went home early that day from the ball match, and the next thing I heard of him was that he had died from the neglected injury he had received in the cricket match; in other words, from a severe rupture."[6]

In recent years some baseball historians have speculated that shortly after Creighton's death influential baseball figures, led by the Excelsior club's president, Dr. Joseph B. Jones, attempted to shift blame to cricket, its rival then for "national pastime," so that baseball wouldn't be viewed as dangerous. If there was such a plot, it didn't blossom. By 1887, when Chadwick weighed in, there was no need for excuses.

A contrary accusation is that Creighton's death from hitting a home run was quickly fabricated to

Pioneering cricket and baseball reporter Henry Chadwick.

enhance baseball's popularity. "Dying while hitting a long home run is a great story, it's just not true," said Tom Shieber, senior curator of the National Baseball Hall of Fame, a few years ago.[7] Shieber's search of original sources found no homer by Creighton in that fateful game. Still, the home-run myth was probably popularized, if not started, almost half a century later by Creighton's teammate, John Chapman. In Alfred Spink's 1910 book *The National Game*, Chapman was quoted as saying, "I was present at the game between the Excelsiors and the Unions of Morrisiana [sic] at which Jim Creighton injured himself. He did it in hitting out a home run. When he had crossed the rubber he turned to George Flanley and said, 'I must have snapped my belt,' and George said, 'I guess not.'"[8] Despite many authors questioning this legend, it still shows up in print to this day presented uncritically.

Overlooked in this saga is the remainder of James Creighton's father's very sad life. In little more than a decade after 1862, Jim Creighton, Sr. also buried a daughter, Mary, a grandchild, and another son,

John. They are all buried near James Senior's wife and namesake.

Excelsior	H.L.	Runs	Union	H.L.	Runs
Creighton, 2b	0	4	Dunell, 1b	3	1
Brainard, p	4	3	Nicholson, 2b	2	2
Masten, c	3	0	Abrams, c	3	0
H. Brainard, 3b	3	1	Hyatt, ss	2	1
Flanly, ss	3	1	Hannegan, p	1	2
Russell, 1b	2	1	Collins, cf	2	1
Young, rf	1	2	Albro, 3b	2	1
McKenzie, lf	2	1	VanHorn, rf	2	0
Cook, cf	3	0	F. Durrell, lf	1	1
Total		13	**Total**		9
Excelsior	333	301	000 - - 13		
Union	112	041	000 - - 9		

Passed balls – Abrams 2, Nicholson 4, Masten 6, Rurrell 4.
Struck out --- Van Horn 2, Albro 1.
Fly catches missed – Abrams 1, Hannegan 1, Masten 1, Creighton 1.
Put out at 1st base – Excelsiors 4 times, Unions 3 times.
Bound catches missed –Brainard 1, McKenzie 1.
Left on bases – Abrams 1, Hannegan 1, Masten 1, Creighton 1,
Put out at home base – Collins by Brainard, Cook by Nicholson.
Fly catches made – A Brainard 1, H Brainard 1, Masten 3, McKenzie 1, Abrams 3, Durell 2, Hannegan 1, Collins 1, Hyatt 1, Nicholson 1.
Time of game – 2:00.
Put out on foul balls – Excelsiors 7 times, Unions 6 times.

Umpire – P. Johnson of Charter Oak.

Notes:

1. "Base Ball," *Brooklyn Eagle*, October 15, 1862, p. 2

2. "Brooklyn News," *New York Times*, October 20, 1862 (see subheading "Death of a Base Ball Player").

3. *Boston Daily Advertiser*, October 22, 1862, p. 2.

4. "Our National Game," *Brooklyn Daily Eagle*, September 16, 1865, 2. The *Eagle*'s first use of "struck" was merely to mean "swung," implying that Bernie Hannegan had in fact attained a strikeout.

5. "Creighton's Death," *Sporting Life*, April 13, 1887, p. 7.

6. "Chadwick's Chat," *Sporting Life*, April 20, 1887, 5. Creighton did star in a cricket match for New York's St. George Club against Brooklyn's Willow Club on October 9, 1862, just five days prior to the Excelsiors' game against the Morrisania nine.

7. Wayne Coffey, "Daily News Sports Hall of Fame Candidates," *New York Daily News*, June 18, 2006.

8. Alfred H. Spink, *The National Game* (St. Louis: The National Game Publishing Co., 1910), p. 128.

The First Fixed Game

Mutuals of New York vs. Eckfords of Brooklyn

Elysian Fields, Hoboken, N.J.
September 28, 1865

By Philip H. Dixon

The crowd at Elysian Fields in Hoboken, New Jersey, assembled early and eagerly on September 28, 1865, under sunny skies to watch a baseball game between the Mutuals of New York and the Eckfords of Brooklyn. Although the Eckfords and Mutuals were both considered to be among the premiere clubs of the time, on this day the Mutuals were favored. Elysian Fields was situated across the river from Manhattan. Most of the attendees traveled across the Hudson River by ferry from New York City. A crowd of 3,000–4,000 was estimated.[1]

The game began around 3:20 P.M. The Mutuals jumped out to a 3–0 lead and at the end of four innings led, 5–4. The play on both sides was praised as being of the highest quality. Regarding the Mutuals, the *New York Times* observed in its game account the next day that the "Mutuals led off at the bat in handsome style, and backed it up with excellent fielding, the first four innings being splendidly played and closely contested on both sides, no finer having been seen this season."[2]

Then, as the Eckfords came to bat in the bottom of the fifth inning, the tenor of the game changed dramatically. "In the fifth innings, however, the Mutuals fell off in their play considerably … over-pitched balls, wild throws, passed balls, and failures to stop them in the field marked the play of the Mutuals to an unusual extent, it being the only poorly-played innings of the game," the *Times* recounted.[3] The Mutuals surrendered 11 runs in the fifth inning, ultimately losing by a score of 23–11.

John Snyder, the Eckfords center fielder, led off in the fifth and was safe on an error by third baseman Edward Duffy. The next two batters made hits, and a run scored on a passed ball by Mutuals catcher William Wansley. Two hits later, another

The 1864 New York Mutuals. Players in uniform as identified on the photo (names in bold participated in the 9-28-1865 game): 1-**Zeller** 2-Goldie 3-Harris 4-**William Wansley** 5-**Brown** 6-Ward 7-**Thomas Devyr** 8-**Patterson** 9-**McMahon**.

runner scored on a throw by Wansley to third base that Duffy "failed to attend to in time."[4] After an out, Charles Mills, the Eckfords catcher, had a hit to left field and scored when neither the Mutuals' second baseman nor center fielder could catch Wansley's throw to second base. The Eckfords proceeded to pile on several more runs. By the end of the fifth inning Wansley had accumulated two missed catches and six passed balls. He also had four wild throws. Third baseman Duffy was charged with two wild throws and three "failures to stop the ball." McMahon, the right fielder, replaced Wansley as catcher for the final four innings.

Before and during the game, gamblers circulated among the crowd, offering changing odds as the game progressed. At first, the Mutuals were heavy favorites. But as the game progressed and the Mutuals' sloppy performance in the fifth inning erupted, the odds sharply shifted. The New York Herald described the scene:

> "When the players first assembled the confidence in the Mutuals led to odds in the betting in their favor of one hundred to sixty; from that the betting went to eighty, ninety, and at last even, the excitement and interest increasing as the game progressed. It was soon evident that the Eckfords were outfielding their adversaries and equaling them at the bat; and when this fact became apparent the betting changed to odds in favor of the Eckfords, a large amount of greenbacks being invested by the friends of both parties."[6]

After the game the Mutuals president, New York City Coroner John Wildey, charged Wansley with "willful and designed inattention" during the game. Any remaining doubts about what had transpired were soon dispelled when the Mutuals shortstop, Thomas Devyr, provided a written confession to the club, explaining his participation with Wansley and Duffy in the scheme to throw the game. He wrote:

Ed Duffy, one of the players banned along with Devyr and Wansley.

> "Between eleven and twelve o'clock on the morning of the match, I was going toward the ferry, ready to go over to the ground, when I met Wansley, Duffy and another man in a wagon. Bill pulled up and asked where I was going. I told him I was going down toward the ferry and that I was going over to the ground in about an hour. He says, "Do you want to make three hundred dollars?" I say I would like to do anything for that. He says, "You can make it easy." I asked how. He says, "We are going to 'heave' this game, and will give you three hundred dollars if you like to stand with us. You need not do any of the work, I'll do all that myself and get all the blame.""[7]

Wansley told Devyr that his and Duffy's participation in the scheme was merely to convince the gambler providing the money that there were sufficient participants to ensure its success. The three received $100 before the game, of which Devyr got $30.[8]

Devyr, Wansley, and Duffy were banned at the next convention of the National Association of Baseball Players. Less than two years later, the Association's Judiciary Committee dismissed the complaint against Devyr "on account of lack of legal proof of his collaboration with Wansley."[9] The consensus appears to have been that Wansley was the organizer and primary culprit, and that the younger and naïve Devyr merely went along. In September 1868 the Mutuals unilaterally reinstated Duffy, which set off an administrative battle, the procedural history of which would be too lengthy to include in this account. The end result was that Duffy was reinstated.

And, by the National Association convention in 1870, so was Wansley.[10]

Mutuals	O	R	Eckford	O	R
Brown, 2b	1	4	Menalt, lf	3	4
Zeller, lf	2	1	Zettlein, p	3	2
Patterson, cf	5	1	Fox, 3b	5	1
Duffy, 3b	2	2	Swandell, rf	5	1
Hunt, 1b	3	0	A. Mills, 2b	1	5
Harris, p	4	0	Thomas, ss	2	4
Wansley, c	5	0	Kline, 1b	4	1
Devyr, ss	3	1	C. Mills, c	1	2
McMahon, rf	2	2	Snyder, cf	3	3
Mutuals	3 0 1	1 3 0	0 1 2 – 11		
Eckford	0 2 1	1 11 1	0 5 2 – 23		

Notes:

1. *New York Herald*, September 29, 1865

2. "Out-Door Sports: The National Game: An Exciting Contest at Hoboken – Another Defeat For the Mutual Club – The Ex-champion Eckfords the Victors." *New York Times*, vol. 15, No. 4372, September 29, 1865, p. 8, col 3.

3. Ibid.

4. "The Championship Contests: An Exciting Game at Hoboken, Defeat of the Mutuals by the Eckfords." *New York Clipper*, October 7, 1865. *The Clipper* contains the most detailed play-by-play account of the game.

5. Ibid.

6 *New York Herald*, September 29, 1865.

7. "'Hippodrome' Tactics in Base Ball: How To Heave a Game." *New York Clipper*, November 11, 1865; reprinted in Dean A. Sullivan, compiler and ed., *Early Innings: A Documentary History of Baseball*, 1825-1908 (Lincoln and London: University of Nebraska Press, 1995), pp. 49-53.

8. Ibid.

9. *New York Clipper*, May 18, 1867.

10. Ryczek, William J. *When Johnny Came Sliding Home* (Jefferson, North Carolina: McFarland & Company, Inc., 1998). This book contains a thorough discussion of the struggles of baseball's governing bodies with respect to the discipline of the three men.

Lipman Pike's Home Run Record

Alerts of Danville vs. Athletics of Philadelphia

*Athletic Grounds, Philadelphia, Pa.
July 16, 1866*

By Jerrold Casway

On July 16, 1866, the Athletics of Philadelphia played a ballgame at 17th and Montgomery against the Alerts of Danville, Pa. On this intensely hot and humid afternoon, Lipman Pike played third base and set a standard for home runs in a single game. Many stories of that game recorded that Pike hit six home runs, but the actual number was five. The source of this mistaken figure was his 1893 obituaries. This account was accepted and perpetuated by latter-day historians, despite the box score and contemporary reports of the game.[1]

What was remarkable about this feat was the nature of the baseball used for the game, the spacious, irregular shape of the playing field, and Pike's size. The ball Pike struck was not the "dead ball" of later decades, but a livelier ball that was often used for an entire game. After a few innings the ball's condition was not suitable for power hitting. The playing field had an irregular shape with spacious power alleys that sprawled from 300 to about 400 feet in center field.[2] Batting ninth, the 21-year-old left-hander in his first year with the Athletics stood only 5-feet-8 and weighed 158 pounds. Years after his playing days were over, fans still talked about the batting prowess and long-distance slugging of the "Iron Batter." Another Pike feature that contributed to his notoriety was his Jewish faith.

Pike's father was a refugee from Holland who settled in New York among the Dutch Jewish merchant families. Born in 1845, the second of five children, Lipman grew up in Brooklyn. Against their father's wishes, he and his older brother, Boaz, played baseball. By 1865 Lipman was good enough to be invited to play for the renowned champions of the National Association, the Atlantics of Brooklyn. He was 20 years old when he appeared in his first game for the Atlantics. The following year Pike made a career move and joined the Atlantics' major rival, the Athletics of Philadelphia, who lured him by paying him $20 a week.[3] The year before he signed with the Athletics, the club leased a new playing ground from the city and outfitted it. Located between 15th and 17th and Montgomery and Columbia Avenues, this irregularly shaped field was the Athletics' home site until 1871. The grounds were formerly a bivouac and staging area for the Union Army. Here soldiers and workmen for a natural history museum, the Wagner Free Institute, played pick-up ball games. The first regular sanctioned game was played on May 12, 1865.[4]

Lipman Pike: His five-homer game in 1866 has never been equaled.

Pike's first season with the Athletics (1866) was marked by historic contests with the Atlantics of Brooklyn. Record crowds attended each game. The first game drew over 30,000 spectators, and the crowds were so dense that it had to be called after one inning. Between the next two Atlantic contests Pike and the Athletics played the Alerts. In this contest Pike used his remarkable speed to beat out long hits that soared to gaps in the spacious center field, a distance of about 400 feet. His other home runs were lofted over 290 feet, clearing a seven-foot-high fence bordering Columbia Avenue in right field. In all the Athletics stroked 12 home runs and won the game 67–25.[5]

Not much attention was given to Pike's great game. There were no bold headlines or commentaries about his feat. It was reported merely as another victory for the Athletics. The Athletics finished their National Association schedule with a 23–2 record. But Pike's tenure in Philadelphia was tenuous. Questions were raised about the loyalty and reliability of paid professional ballplayers.[6] As a result, he and other professionals were purged from the team. In 1867 Pike found himself playing for Association teams in New Jersey and New York.

By the time he ceased full-time play a dozen years later, Pike had won four home run titles and set the professional National Association career record for home runs. He was also fourth in RBIs. Despite all of that, Lipman Pike would always be known for what he accomplished in his first full year as a professional ballplayer on the sweltering afternoon of July 16, 1866.

Umpire – W. Osterhelt of West Philadelphia Base Ball Club. Scorers – Messrs Senseman and Benson. Passed ball – Fields 3, Kleinfelder 4. Home runs – Dorsey 1, Kleinfelder 1, McBride 2, Reach 2, Dockney 1, Pike 5, Berkenstock 1. Time of game - 3:10. Fly catches – Alert 11, Athletic 10. Out on bases – Alert 12 times, Athletic 6 times. Out on fouls – Alert 5 times, Athletic 12 times.

Notes:

1. *New York Clipper*, July 28, 1866; *Sunday Mercury*, July 22, 1866. The six home run story originated in obituary columns. *Sporting Life*, October 21, 1893, and *The Sporting News*, November 11, 1893.

2. See J. Casway, "At the Old Ball Game," *Temple Review*, Spring 1992, pp. 21-3. Also see images in Baseball Hall of Fame of Athletics-Atlantics, October 22, 1866, No. 63; *Harper's Weekly*, November 18, 1865.

3. *Sporting Life*, October 21, 1893; *New York Clipper*, July 9, 1881, August 25, 1866; *Sunday Item*, October 22, 1893; *The Sporting News*, November 11, 1893.

4. Unpublished biographical article on Lipman Pike that will appear in J. Casway, *Culture and Ethnicity of Nineteenth-Century Baseball*, "Before Hank Greenberg There Was Lipman Pike," p. 3.

5. *New York Clipper*, July 28, 1866; *Sunday Mercury*, July, 22, 1866.

6. Ryczek, W. *When Johnny Came Sliding Home* (Jefferson, North Carolina: McFarland Publishing, 1998), pp. 107-8; Chadwick Scrapbooks, 1866; *Sunday Mercury*, May 27, 1866, November 11, 1866; January 22, 1871; *New York Clipper*, August 25, 1866.

Alert	HL	R	Athletic	HL	R
Dorsey, p	3	4	Kleinfelder, c	5	7
Clinton, lf	3	3	McBride, ss	3	8
Gideon, 2b	2	3	Reach, 2b	4	8
Fields, c	4	2	Wilkins, rf	1	9
Halbeck, ss	2	2	Berkenstock, 1b	2	8
Prevost, 1b	4	2	Dockney, cf	3	7
Emory, cf	2	4	Rayburn, p	5	5
Herme, 3b	3	4	Gaskill, lf	3	7
Wilson, rf	4	1	Pike, 3b	1	8
		25			67

Alert	3	2	4	0 0 0	0 6	(10)	– 25	
Athletic	2	0	(10)	(11) 3 4	(20)	(16)	1	– 67

Money Ball

Athletic of Philadelphia vs. Atlantic of Brooklyn

Athletic Club Grounds, 15th and Columbia, Philadelphia, Pa., October 1, 22, 1866; Capitoline Grounds, Brooklyn, N.Y. October 15, 1866

By Eric Miklich

The Brooklyn vs. New York All-Star series held in Flushing during the summer of 1858, the first to charge the spectators admission, had proved that the public was willing to pay to watch important and high skill-level baseball. That series led clubs to take strong measures to obtain the best players so they could derive the most return on their investment. The October 1866 series between the Athletics of Philadelphia and the Atlantics was, to that point, the culmination of enticing players, arranging tours, promoting matches between top clubs, and charging the public, all to maximize profit.

The first game of the series was to be played on October 1 at the Athletics' grounds at Columbia Avenue and 15th Street. Crowds began gathering downtown early on the day of the game, with newspapers reporting the advance sale of 8,000 tickets at 25 cents apiece, 2½ times the normal 10-cent charge.[1] There were reports of speculators offering the team as much as $5 for reserved seats, anticipating that they could resell them at a profit, only to be turned down by Athletics management.[2] For perhaps the first time, 5-by-4-inch printed fold-over scorecards were handed out. Betting was extremely heavy and the hometown club was slightly favored. Bets estimated to total $5,000 were placed.[3]

While 8,000 ticket-holding spectators would have been a manageable crowd, Philadelphia was unprepared for what actually developed by game time. Another 22,000 to 32,000 people showed up, causing chaos inside and outside the grounds. Preston Orem later described housetops for blocks around the playing grounds, trees, fences, and other prominences all "covered with a dense mass of human beings."[4] There were more people outside the playing field than inside, and those on the field were crammed together, constantly jostling for a view.

The Athletics, batting first and therefore striking a fresh ball, scored on consecutive home runs by pitcher Dick McBride and second baseman Al Reach. In the bottom of the first inning, the Atlantics had Charles Smith on third base and Joe Start on first base with one "hand" out when the excitement overtook the crowd. "Crane was next to bat, but before he had a chance to strike the game was stopped to allow the crowd to be cleared from left field," the *New York Times* correspondent reported.[5] Triggering the commotion was a scuffle between a fan and the police.[6] For about half an hour, efforts to push back the crowd failed, and eventually the game had to be called.[7]

Officials decided to reschedule the contest for October 15 at the Capitoline Grounds in the Bedford section of Brooklyn.

Capitoline Grounds, home of the Atlantics in 1865, seemed better suited to crowd control than the grounds in Philadelphia. It was "bounded on three sides by board fences and on the fourth side by a high stretch of gate work running parallel with the road leading to the highway and the cars."[8] No tickets were sold in advance for this match, reported the *New York Tribune*, which added that spectators arriving on game day should have their quarters ready, as no change would be made. Seven entrances were manned by 18 ticket-takers,[9] proprietors Reuben S. Decker and Hamilton A. Weed wanting to ensure that they collected from all those who entered that historic day.

The spectators began arriving before 10 A.M. for the scheduled 2 o'clock match. The 4,000 available seats were quickly filled and by 11 A.M., possibly as many as 20,000 had encircled the playing grounds.

Employing burly policemen was paramount in retaining order, which was Brooklyn's priority. Inspector John S. Folk ensured that the debacle in Philadelphia would not be repeated. He and 152 captains, sergeants, officers, and patrolmen from 10 precincts arrived at the grounds at 11 A.M. to maintain order.[10] Even though the spectators encircled the field, not one incident was reported.

The Athletics tied the match 11–11 in the fifth inning, but the Brooklyn club scored 16 runs over the last four innings and won 27–17.

The match itself failed to achieve the status of one of the greatest played in baseball's infancy. But the event was without question the greatest day of baseball in North America to date. No game had attracted so many to Capitoline Grounds, required as large a police presence and produced the amount of attendance revenue, estimated at more than $1,000.

The Athletics made it known that Philadelphia police would be represented generously to maintain order at the October 22 return match. They had a fence erected around the field, at the cost of $1,500. They also reduced the number of spectators to a relatively minuscule 4,000. To make certain that a substantial profit was made and perhaps to cover the expenses, the Athletics charged $1 per ticket, an extraordinary amount for baseball in 1866 and four times what had been charged for the first contest.

Between 2,500 and 5,000 spectators paid for the game, the *Times* also reporting that "all the surrounding houses, trees, high ground and vehicles were crowded with spectators making the scene one of great animation."[11]

Woodcut depicting the Atlantics and Athletics from Harpers Weekly, *November 3, 1866. Most of the Atlantics were drawn from a known team photo making their identifications obvious. Identifying the Athletics has proven more difficult.*
Athletics c1866 (top): *Unidentified, Unidentified, Lip Pike (possibly), Wes Fisler, Unidentified, Dick McBride, Al Reach (possibly), Unidentified, Unidentified.*
Atlantics c1866 (bottom): *Unidentified, Tom Pratt, Unidentified, Dickey Pearce, Joe Start, Charlie Smith, Jack Chapman, John Galvin. Seated, Fred Crane.*

Game action from the October 16, 1866 match between the Atlantics and Athletics at the Capitoline grounds in Brooklyn, appearing in Frank Leslie's Illustrated Newspaper, *November 3, 1866.*

The contest was even through four innings, at nine runs apiece. This time it was the Athletics' turn to enjoy a blowout as they outscored the Atlantics 22-3 in the next three innings, taking a commanding 31-12 lead. As the Atlantics batted in the top of the eighth, the rain began to fall heavily, forcing the umpire to call the match at 4:45 P.M. The build-up had again been more exciting than the match.

Immediate allegations of the Atlantics lying down to ensure a third payday were abundant. These were not cynical views. Simply based on the financial take from the two-plus matches, the bare minimum that the two clubs were to share was $7,000. A third and deciding match would have easily pushed the coffers to more than $10,000.

But before splitting the gate receipts, the Athletics had to account for the $1,500 it cost to erect the fence around their playing field. They also accounted for the fact that they paid all of the traveling expenses of the Atlantics to Philadelphia, and that the Atlantics did not do the same for them.[12]

The Bedford club, however, insisted on their share being based on the gross amount. The resulting stalemate ruined the momentum that the two previous matches achieved in terms of money-making ability, spectator interest, and the declaration of an undisputed NABBP Champion. The games did prove that high-level baseball was a viable business and, simply based on that thought, it is unconscionable that the two would not allow a third match.

October 15, 1866
Capitoline Grounds, Bedford, New York

Atlantic	O	R	Athletic	O	R
Pearce, ss	4	2	Klienfelder, rf	3	1
Smith, 3b	2	4	McBride, p	4	2
Chapman, lf	3	3	Reach, 2b	2	3
Crane, 2b	2	4	Wilkins, ss	3	1
Start, 1b	1	6	Berkenstock, 1b	5	0
Pratt, p	4	2	Dockney, c	3	2
Ferguson, rf	5	2	Sensenderfer, lf	5	1
Galvin, cf	2	3	Fisler, cf	1	4
Mills, c	4	1	Pike, 3b	1	3
Totals	**27**	**27**	**Totals**	**27**	**17**
Atlantic	041	421	834 – 27		
Athletic	023	330	321 – 17		

Umpire – Mr. George H. Flanly of the Excelsior Club.
Scorers – Messrs. Monk and Benson.
Time of game – 3:00.
Fly Catches – Galvin 3, Mills 2, Chapman 2, Smith 1, Crane 1; total, Atlantic-9. Berkenstock 4, Reach 2, Fisler 1, Dockney 1; total, Athletic – 8.

Out on Foul Balls – Atlantics 9 times; Athletics 6 times.
Passed Balls – Mills 4; Dockney 11.
Left on Bases – Atlantic 6; Athletic 7.
Home Runs – Start 1; Dockney 1.

**Box score complied from *Brooklyn Daily Eagle*, October 16, 1866, p.2, and the *New York Times*, October 16, 1866.

October 22, 1866
Columbia Avenue and 15th Street,
Philadelphia, Pennsylvania

Atlantic	O	R	Athletic	O	R
Pearce, rf	3	1	Klienfelder, 1b	2	4
Smith, ss	3	1	McBride, p	3	4
Start, 1b	2	2	Reach, 2b	1	6
Crane, 2b	2	2	Wilkins, ss	2	2
Chapman, lf	1	2	Gaskill, cf	2	2
Galvin, cf	2	1	Dockney, c	5	2
Pratt, p	3	1	Sensenderfer, rf	2	4
Ferguson, 3b	2	1	Fisler, cf	0	5
Mills, c	3	1	Pike, 3b	4	2
Totals	**27**	**27**	**Totals**	**21**	**31**
Atlantic	024	310	2 – 12		
Athletic	101	75(12)	5 – 31		

Umpire – Mr. Theodore Bomeisler of the Eureka Club of Newark (New Jersey).
Scorers – Messrs. Mulliner and Benson.
Time of game – 2:35.
Fly Catches – Mills 3, Ferguson 3, Galvin 2, Crane 2, Start, Pratt; total, Atlantic–12. Reach 2, Dockney 2, Fisler, Pike, Sensenderfer; total, Athletic – 7.
Fly Catches Missed – Mills 4, Galvin 2; total, Atlantic – 6. Gaskill; total, Athletic – 1.
Out on Foul Balls – Atlantics 5 times; Athletics 4 times.
Passed Balls – Mills 12; Dockney 4.
Left on Bases – Atlantic 5; Athletic 8.
Home Run – Fisler.

**Box score complied from *Baseball 1845-1881 From Newspaper Accounts*, p.56; *New York Daily Tribune*, October 23, 1866, p.8, and *New York Times*, October 23, 1866.

Notes:

1. Orem, Preston D. *Baseball 1845-1881 From Newspaper Accounts*, p. 52.

2. Ryczek, William. *When Johnny Came Sliding Home* (Jefferson, North Carolina: McFarland & Company, Inc., 1998), p. 95.

3. Ibid.

4. Orem, p. 52.

5. *New York Times*, October 2, 1866, p. 1.

6. Ryczek, p. 95.

7. *New York Times*, op. cit., loc. cit.

8. Orem, p. 53.

9. *New York Tribune*, October 5, 1866, p. 8.

10. *New York Times, Brooklyn Daily Eagle*, October 16, 1866.

11. *New York Times*, October 23, 1866.

12. Ryczek, p. 96.

The Most Important Game in Baseball History?

Washington Nationals vs. Forest Citys of Rockford

Dexter Park, Chicago, Ill.
July 25, 1867

By John Thorn

After the famous tour of the Brooklyn Excelsiors in 1860, which took them as far north as Canada and as far south as Baltimore, the outbreak of the Civil War quashed any thought of new junkets. Then, in baseball's boom year of 1867, the Washington Nationals, a club that had formed prior to the war, announced a trip unlike any thus far attempted. Their notice published in the *Clipper* read:

> The famous Washington club will start upon their proposed Western trip on the 10th [of July], visiting and playing friendly games with the leading clubs of Columbus, Cincinnati, Louisville, Indianapolis, St. Louis, and Chicago, reaching the latter place on the 24th. ...

The Washington club was in fact not yet famous, but wished to become so. It had played only five match games in 1865, welcoming clubs from Philadelphia and Brooklyn to play on the lot behind newly installed President Andrew Johnson's White House.

Although the 1866 Nationals won 10 games against five defeats, they by no means ranked alongside the Atlantics, Athletics, Mutuals, or the champion Unions of Morrisania, led by handsome young George Wright, the coming baseball hero of the age.

In 1867 the Nationals strengthened themselves with additional recruits, giving each a patronage government job, and somehow persuaded Wright to join them too. Although the players were nominal amateurs, there can be no doubt of their uniformly professional status. The club president listed Wright's place of employment as 238 Pennsylvania Avenue, at that time an open field.

During the three weeks of their Western tour, the Nationals made a show of maintaining their amateur status by refusing payments of any kind, even declining reimbursement for travel expenses. These, of course, were covered by their employers, who had graciously permitted them to abandon the desks at which they had seldom been seen anyway. The aim of the National Club directors in going out on tour was not pecuniary gain but social *éclat* and pride of place: The Western farmers had been getting a bit chesty about their brand of baseball and, it was thought back East, needed a slap of reality at the hands of an experienced ballclub.

Al Barker

The Nationals prepared for their trip with easy triumphs over local cupcakes until they journeyed to Cincinnati to play the Red Stockings on July 15, in a battle of two unbeaten nines. Leading up to the match with the Nationals, the 1867 edition of the Cincinnati Base Ball Club—already popularly named Red Stockings—had drubbed four local clubs. After initially holding their own against the Nationals, the Reds ultimately were humiliated by a count of 53–10.

After crushing the Red Stockings and five other patsies, the Nationals headed for Chicago for highly anticipated games against that city's best, the Excelsiors and Atlantics, named in emulation of Brooklyn's finest clubs. The Forest Citys of Rockford had already played the Excelsiors twice that year, losing narrowly each time, and thus ceded the state championship. All the same, the Rockford boys were given the consolation prize of an invitation to Chicago to play what amounted to a warm-up game against the Nationals on Thursday the 25th at Dexter Park. On the following Saturday the Nationals would defeat Rockford's nemesis, the Excelsiors, by a score of 49–4; on Monday the Washington nine would trounce the Atlantics by 78–17.

The "corn crackers" of Rockford were led by novice pitcher Albert Spalding, not yet 17 years of age. Four decades later he recalled:

Frank Norton

> *I experienced a severe case of stage fright when I found myself in the pitcher's box, facing such renowned players as George Wright, [Frank] Norton, [Harry] Berthrong, [George] Fox, and others of the visiting team. ... A great lump arose in my throat, and my heart beat so like a trip-hammer that I imagined it could be heard by everyone on the grounds. I knew, also, that every player on the Rockford nine had an idea that their kid pitcher would surely become rattled and go to pieces as soon as the strong batters of the Nationals had opportunity to fall upon his delivery.*

There were several interesting plays in the game, as noted in the contemporary press. In the third inning Al Barker of Rockford "went to his base on a ball which dropped from the bat." Sounds like a bunt, doesn't it? Yet the "baby hit" is thought today to have been invented by Tom Barlow some years later. In the sixth inning George Wright "took the bat and by a splendid stroke to center field made a home run." As Spalding recalled:

> *(T)he Forest Citys had by this time gotten pretty well settled and their stage-fright had disappeared, yet none of us even then had the remotest idea that we were destined to win the game over such a famous antagonist. The thought or suggestion of such a thing at that stage would probably have thrown us into another mental spasm.*

Novice pitcher and later influential sporting goods magnate Al Spalding.

At this psychological moment, Col. Frank Jones, President of the National Club, rushed up to George Wright, who was about to take his position at the bat, and said, in a louder voice possibly than he intended:

"Do you know, George, that this is the seventh innings and we are six runs behind? You must discard your heavy bat and take a lighter one; for to lose this game would be to make our whole trip a failure." Col. Jones' excited manner plainly indicated his anxiety.

George Wright

This incident inspired the Rockfords with confidence and determination, and for the first time we began to realize that victory was not only possible, but probable, and the playing of our whole team from that time forward was brilliant.

Rockford and Spalding held their six-run lead, emerging victorious by a score of 29–23. There had been upsets before in baseball's brief history, but never one on this scale. The Nationals broke up after the season, but even in defeat their Steinbrennerian squadron had supplied the model for how baseball might succeed as America's game.

Put on yer coats, put on yer coats, das all!

Uniques vs. Excelsiors of Philadelphia

Satellite Grounds, Brooklyn, N.Y.
Oct. 3, 1867

By Irv Goldfarb

"Championship" is often a fluid concept when applied to 19th-century contests. But no match had that title attached to it as arbitrarily as the game that took place on the Satellite Grounds of Brooklyn on October 3, 1867. As a matter of fact, the term by which experts categorize the game today, "The First Colored Championship" really tells only a fraction of the story.

One-third of it, to be exact. When the Excelsiors, a fine black base ball team from Philadelphia arrived in New York that Thursday morning, they were warmly received by what the *New York Herald* characterized as "… a delegation of gentleman of the colored persuasion…" Following a fife-and-drum-led parade and various "sumptuous" entertainments, the team was escorted over to Brooklyn to face the Uniques, a black team representing the Williamsburg section of the borough.

It was the *Brooklyn Daily Times* that labeled this contest "the colored championship of the United States" and claimed that it had been the "…theme of conversation for some time between colored gentleman…"

The match, believed to be the first ever played between black clubs in an enclosed grounds, boasted the largest crowd seen at the field that season, according to the *Brooklyn Daily Union*, with half of the spectators white males. Also in attendance, the *Union* reported, were "… a large number of the gentle demoiselles of darkydom… (who) … by their expressive and readily distinguishable smiles, cheered the dusky heroes in their noble endeavors."

The Excelsiors, by all accounts, were the superior team, some observers going so far as to put them on a par with the best of the white Philadelphia clubs. The home-standing Uniques, meanwhile, were described by the Tribune as "second-rate opponents."

Once the contest got underway, attention focused on the umpire, Mr. Patterson, a black arbiter from the Bachelor Club of Albany. Disputes over his decisions were frequent and led both clubs to engage in various histrionics. In the next morning's Herald, a reporter indentified as Kelly described this plea from the captain of one of the squads following a call that seemed particularly unfair to his side: "Put on yer coats, put on yer coats, das all", he was said to have yelled. Kelly found the game: "… rendered remarkably lively by such interludes…"

Participants included an unidentified Brooklyn pitcher who, according to Kelly, "jerked the ball most palpably…" (Was he perhaps throwing an early version of a curve?) When taken to task over his unorthodox delivery, Kelly reported that the hurler "struck a position and exclaimed, 'jis dry up; you fellers pitch jis the same…'"

The contest continued through seven innings until the Philadelphia team claimed it was too dark to see the ball. As the visitors were leading 42–37 at the time, this naturally led to another disagreement.[1] No "colored darky is a gwine to take deat yere ball out o' Wimsburg," Kelly characterized one Brooklynite as declaring. But, he added, they were finally persuaded to admit defeat, "and the game terminated in most delicious confusion." The *Brooklyn Daily Union* however, was not so easily amused. "The contest was in no respect credible to the organizations," it contended.

The Excelsiors and their contingent ferried their way back to New York in triumph, scheduled to return the next day to take on a second black Brooklyn team known as the Monitor. The next morning's *Times* hyped this event, but included a warning: "It is to be hoped that the scenes that characterized the first game for the 'Colored Championship of the United States' will not be repeated. Act like men, and set an example to the 'white trash,'" they chided.

But the game did not take place as scheduled.

Newspaper accounts of Saturday, the 5th, report that the Philadelphia team never arrived, with the *Times* speculating on a possible cause: "The … manner in which their game with the Unique club was played … doubtless deterred them from visiting the 'Burgh yesterday."

On October 25, however, a game was played on the Satellite Grounds, pitting the Uniques against the Monitor. This match-up seemed a perfect contest between natural rivals, but according to a couple of sources, it might have been more than that, with the *Tribune* trumpeting this game as actually being the third match of a "round-robin": "The Monitors are the gentlemen who, on the return of the Philadelphians from their Albany trip avenged their brethren (the Uniques) by a handsome victory." The *New York Herald* agreed, stating that since the Philadelphia club had beaten the Uniques on October 3 and the Monitor had defeated Philadelphia in a follow-up contest, this game would be for the true "colored championship."

But though box scores and game stories exist for the other two contests, no post-game reports can be found of the Philadelphia-Monitor meeting. For whatever reason, the papers that covered the other two games ignored this "middle" contest, so we can only look at the subsequent Uniques-Monitor match for what it was: the first recorded meeting between the two most prominent black base ball clubs in Brooklyn.

According to the *Daily Times*, this game was "credible at first" with the Monitor holding a 7–6 lead after 4 ½ innings, but due to some "very bad muffing" on the part of the Uniques, the Monitor piled up 42 runs over their final four at-bats, winning 49–17.

Did this win solidify the Monitor as the "Colored Champions of the United States"? Or was the best black team still the Excelsior club of Philadelphia? Like the term "Championship," the hazy history of early baseball is not so easily codified. It would not be until the formation of Professional Negro Leagues decades later, that true Colored Champions could be officially crowned.

Notes:

1 The *New York Tribune* saw the end of the game differently, reporting the final score as 37-24 after six innings, the runs scored in the seventh not counting due to the game being called. Since other sources have included a box score showing the score as 42-37, however, the *Tribune*'s reporter must have assumed that the game was "officially called" after six.

Candy Cummings Debuts the Curve

Excelsiors of Brooklyn vs. Harvard College

Jarvis Field, Cambridge, Mass.
October 7, 1867

By Mark Pestana

One of the oldest, most venerable weapons in the pitcher's arsenal is the curveball. Various have been the claimants to its paternity, but the weight of the evidence falls upon a wispy fellow named William Arthur Cummings, known to posterity as Candy, a term of high approbation at the time of his rise to fame.

Growing up in the crucible of baseball that was Brooklyn in the 1850s and '60s, Cummings first fixated upon the mechanics of objects curving in flight at the age of 14: "In the summer of 1863 a number of boys and myself were amusing ourselves by throwing clam shells and watching them sail along … turning now to the right, and now to the left. … All of a sudden it came to me that it would be a good joke on the boys if I could make a baseball curve the same way."[1]

Four years of secretive experimentation and practice, with tantalizingly inconsistent results, ensued. Meanwhile, Candy climbed through the ranks of Brooklyn baseball, joining the powerful Excelsior club in 1866. The following spring he replaced Asa Brainard as the team's main pitcher. It was near the close of 1867 when his long woodshedding came to fruition.

Consecutive losses to the Keystones of Philadelphia and Lowells of Boston on October 2 and 4 may have hinted to the Brooklyn ace that it was time to pull the rabbit out of his hat. But the decisive impetus came in the form of a hard-hitting catcher named Archie Bush.

Long before facing Candy Cummings, Archibald McClure Bush had been tested on a real battlefield, having entered service in the Civil War in October 1863, just shy of his 17th birthday.[2] After the war ended in 1865, Bush played with the Knickerbocker club of his hometown, Albany, New York. Still but a teenager, he entered prestigious Phillips Academy, a prep school in Andover, Massachusetts, in the fall of 1865,[3] and is credited with organizing their first official baseball team.[4]

A sparkling career at Phillips Andover came to a sudden, ignominious end in May 1867 when Archie and a fellow senior cut classes to attend a ballgame in Boston and were summarily expelled.[5] Undeterred, Bush crammed over the summer for Harvard's exams and won admittance for the fall term.[6] He debuted with the Harvard first nine on September 21, homering and picking off a runner who had carelessly strayed from second base.[7]

Jarvis Field was Harvard's new athletic grounds,

Archie Bush

in use for only about four months when the Excelsior club met the collegians there on October 7, 1867. A small clubhouse sat a hundred feet behind home plate, the spectators' seats forming a semicircle extending from either end of the clubhouse. The seating capacity was at least 5,000.[8]

Harvard scored a run in the first inning; Bush, batting fifth, likely made his initial plate appearance then. Cummings faced him with some trepidation, as he would confess to *The Sporting News* in 1892: "I was afraid of his prowess with the bat."[9] So it was that the 120-pound hurler decided to unleash his secret weapon. Here is his own clinical description:

> "Snapping the ball with a wrist movement and getting it to spin through the air caused an air cushion to gradually form around the ball, gradually throwing the sphere out of a true course and turning it in the direction of the least resistance."[10]

The result?

> "When he struck at the ball it seemed to go about a foot beyond the end of his stick. I tried again with the same result, and then I realized that I had succeeded at last."[11]

Here was affirmation for the long years of preparation.

> "A surge of joy flooded over me that I shall never forget.... I said not a word, and saw many a batter at that game throw down his stick in disgust. Every time I was successful I could scarcely keep from dancing with pure joy."[12]

A unique victory, with longstanding implications, had been won. But this day's battle was not to go the Excelsiors' way, for the pitch was still not fully harnessed:

> "There was trouble. ... I could not make it curve when I wanted to. ... With a wind against me I could get all kinds of a curve, but ... the ball was apt not to break until it was past the batter."[13]

The Excelsiors trailed 3-1 by the end of the fourth. They "batted fairly" but their opponent's infield formed "an impenetrable wall, against which ground balls were struck in vain."[14] The college boys found enough pitches to their liking and heaped on 15 runs in the last four innings. The final score was 18-6 in Harvard's favor.

Nonetheless, one may glean some trace of Cummings' triumph. In two games before and two games after the Excelsior match, Bush tallied 23 runs, seven homers, and only nine outs; against Cummings: four outs and one run.

Cummings persevered and in due time mastered the magical pitch. He averaged 31 wins in his four (1872–75) National Association seasons and placed in the top 10 in strikeouts in all six of his NA and National League campaigns. These impressive statistics and, of course, his curve discovery, secured him a place in the Baseball Hall of Fame.

And what of the man who induced the first competitive curveball to be propelled plateward—the slugger who so spooked Candy Cummings that the spindly hurler finally unveiled his mystery pitch?

Archie Bush should have been a star in the major leagues as he had been in prep school and college, but in fact, he did not enjoy even the brief professional career of his adversary. Graduating from Harvard in the spring of 1871, he umpired two early season National Association games in Boston. Before year's end he was employed with the Troy Car Works, a railroad car manufacturer. He married Margaret Boyd of Albany in October 1877 and the couple embarked on a honeymoon cruise to Europe. In December, with his wife already pregnant with a son, Archie Bush died of typhoid pneumonia in Liverpool, four weeks after turning 31.[15]

Excelsior	O	R	B	Harvard	O	R	B
Tracy, R	3	1	3	Sprague, M	3	3	2
Buckland, 3	1	2	3	Smith, 3	4	2	4
Clyne, M	2	0	0	Hun'll, P	3	1	3
Cummings, P	4	0	1	Bow'ch, L	5	0	1
Lennon, S	4	0	0	Bush, C	4	1	2
Jewell C	4	0	0	Ames, 2	3	3	2
Thompson, 1	3	1	0	Shaw, 1	1	4	5
Hall, L,	3	1	2	Wil'd, S	3	2	3
Hawley, 2	3	1	1	Mealey, R	2	2	3
	6	10			18	26	
Excelsior	001	000	410 - 6				
Harvard	110	105	208 - 18				

Home Run: Hall 1.
Fly catches: Jewell 4, Cook 1, Hall 3, Hawley 2, Total by Excelsiors 10. Smith 1, Hunnewell 1, Bowditch 1, total by Harvard 3.
Foul bound catches: Excelsior 9, Harvard 3.
Umpire: Mr. Flagg, Harvard club. Scorers: Messrs C.J. Holt and H.L. Dehon.

Notes:

1. Cummings, William Arthur. "How I Pitched the First Curve," *Baseball Magazine*, August 1908, p. 21.

2. Eighth Report of the Secretary of the Class of 1871 of Harvard College (Boston: Press of Rockwell and Churchill, September 1896), p. 27.

3. Harrison, Fred. "Athletics For All," at http://www.pa59ers.com/library/Harrison/Athletics02.html.

4. "Nine Inductees Selected for Athletics Hall of Honor," May 7, 2010, at http://www.andover.edu/About/Newsroom/Pages/NineInducteesSelectedforAthleticsHallofHonor.aspx

5. Fuess. Claude M. *An Old New England School*, Chapter XIV, at http://www.ourstory.info/library/5-AFSIS/Fuess/school5.html. The ballgame in question was most likely that of Wednesday, May 15, between Harvard and Lowell of Boston. See also "Abby Locke's Splendid Days: A Teenager's Diary in 1860s Andover" at http://andoverhistorical.org/blog/.

6. Fuess, p. 271-274.

7. *The Harvard Advocate*, Cambridge, Massachusetts, October 8, 1867, Vol. IV, No. 1, p. 10.

8. King, Moses. *Harvard and Its Surroundings* (Boston: Franklin Press: Rand, Avery, and Company, Boston, 1878), p.45.

9. "Curved Balls," *The Sporting News*, February 20, 1892.

10. Murnane, Tim. "First Master of the Curve Ball," *Boston Daily Globe*, January 14, 1906, p. SM3.

11. *The Sporting News*, February 20, 1892.

12. Cummings, p. 21-22.

13. Cummings, p. 22.

14. *The Harvard Advocate*, p. 25.

15. Eighth Report of the Secretary of the Class of 1871 of Harvard College.

A Cunning Play Saves the Streak

Cincinnati Red Stockings vs. Mutuals of New York

Union Grounds, Brooklyn, N.Y.
June 15, 1869

By Greg Rhodes

Tuesday dawned gray and damp in New York City. But the sun broke through in the early afternoon, warming the streets and the spirits of the sporting public, which had long anticipated the day's match between the reigning champions of baseball, the Mutuals of New York, and the interlopers from the West, the Cincinnati Red Stockings.

The Red Stockings, the best club west of the Alleghenies, had still to prove their mettle against the powerhouse clubs of the East. The 1868 Red Stockings compiled a 36–7 mark, but all their losses came against clubs from Philadelphia, Washington, and New York. After the National Association of Base Ball Players changed its rules to permit professionalism, the leadership of the Cincinnati Base Ball Club decided to employ an all-salaried nine for the 1869 season, with the expressed hope of being able to defeat the top Eastern clubs. No other team took up the mantle of professionalism in 1869, thus making the Red Stockings the first professional nine, all players under contract with a stipulated salary (and in turn required to pledge themselves to temperance).

The Red Stockings signed several top players, including George Wright, the younger brother of Red Stockings captain Harry Wright. George was the best shortstop in America, and the strongest batsman: the 19th-century version of Honus Wagner. In addition the Red Stockings featured veteran pitcher Asa Brainard; Fred Waterman, the leading third baseman in the country and the only Cincinnatian on the squad; first baseman Charles Gould; and one unproven youngster, 20-year-old right fielder Cal McVey. At 34, Harry Wright was the established leader, a respected captain, the center fielder and the primary relief pitcher.

The Red Stockings had begun their month-long tour of the East on May 31, and won their first 10 matches before arriving in New York City. Although this was just one game held in the early weeks of the season, it drew the kind of attention one would see today for a postseason game. In part this was because teams did not play each other that often, and this was especially true of a team from as far away as Cincinnati. This was likely to be the only visit the Red Stockings would make to New York, perhaps the only time they would play the Mutuals, unless the Mutuals traveled west (which they did late in the season, but that game had not been scheduled as of June). The game also drew considerable betting interest. "Thousands of dollars" had been wagered on the game, estimated one writer.

At 1:30 P.M., a contingent of Mutual club officials called on the Red Stockings at their hotel and escorted them to the ballpark in elegant carriages. The game was played on the Union Grounds, a large enclosed field in Brooklyn: "The grounds are beautiful, being sodded all over, grass short," wrote a Cincinnati correspondent. "Flags of all nations were floating to the breeze from jackstaffs on different club-houses, and the scene was one of brilliancy." The attendance, diminished by the gray weather, was estimated at 4,000–7,000.

The Mutuals featured several established stars, including outfielder John Hatfield, who had played for the Red Stockings in 1868. Hatfield had signed with Cincinnati for 1869, but also signed with the Mutuals, and he was dismissed from the Red Stockings for this duplicity. His conduct so irritated the decorous Harry Wright that Wright still held a grudge on the eve of the match. He urged his team to not only beat the Mutuals, but in particular to keep Hatfield from scoring a run.

The Red Stockings won the toss and chose to bat last. Back in Cincinnati, baseball enthusiasts gathered around newspaper offices and other establishments that posted regular bulletins on the game's progress. The Red Stockings scored single runs in the first and third innings. But the bulletins seemed to be in error for the Mutuals. In this high-scoring era of rough fields, no gloves, and heavy hitting, teams usually tallied dozens of runs. But on this day the bulletins came in with zero after zero for the Mutuals. Brainard's pitching and sure fielding by the Red Stockings held them scoreless for the first seven innings. Other than their two early runs, the Cincinnati boys were whitewashed as well by the New York pitcher, Wolters.

The Mutuals finally broke through in the eighth with one run. Then they scored the tying run in the ninth and seemed poised for more with runners on first and second and none out. But third baseman Waterman and shortstop Wright pulled off a clever play. Waterman deliberately dropped a fly ball (no infield-fly rule then) and threw to Wright, who had anticipated Waterman's play and rushed to cover third. Wright then threw to second to complete a threat-ending 5-6-4 double play.

With one out in the bottom of the ninth, the Mutual third baseman made a wild throw on Brainard's liner, and Asa wound up on third. He scored moments later on a passed ball, and the victory was the Reds'. The crowd broke onto the field, but the rules of the day required the inning to be played out in full. Once order was restored, Cincinnati scored one more tally, making the final score 4–2.

The game was immediately hailed as the greatest ever played. The crisp play of both teams and the novelty of the low score marked it as truly memorable. "The best played game on record," said the *New York World*. "The most remarkable game on record," gushed the *Sun*. The *Cincinnati Gazette* reporter sent home this dispatch: "We are tossing our hats tonight and shaking each other by the hand. We are the lions ... because we have beaten the Mutuals, and because the game was the toughest, closest, most brilliant, most exciting in base ball annals."

And for Harry Wright, it was especially sweet. The duplicitous John Hatfield did not get a hit, and did not score a run.

Telegrams awaited the boys when they returned to their hotel, including this from "The Citizens of Cincinnati": "The streets are full of people, who give cheer after cheer for their pet club. Go on with the noble work. Our expectations have been met." The noble work continued. The Red Stockings completed their conquest of New York clubs the next two days with victories over the Atlantics and Eckfords, then swept the Philadelphia and Washington nines and returned to the Queen City on July 1 having won all 20 games on the Eastern tour.

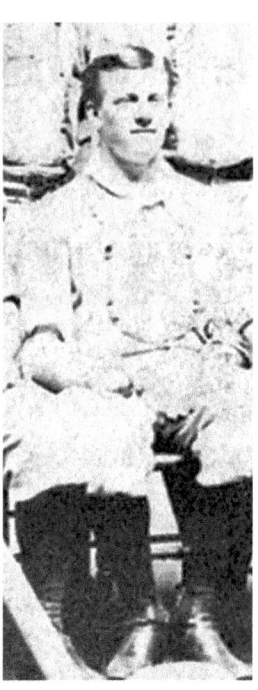

John Hatfield of the Mutuals, the object of Harry Wright's scorn.

Cincinnati	O	R	Mutuals	O	R
G. Wright, ss	4	1	C. Hunt, lf	4	0
Gould, 1b	4	0	Hatfield, 2b	4	0
Waterman, 3b	2	1	E. Mills, 1b	2	0
Allison, c	2	0	R. Hunt, cf	2	1
H. Wright, rf	4	0	Swandell, 3b	2	0
Brainard, p	3	0	C. Mills, c	4	0
Leonard, lf	3	1	Eggler, ss	3	0
Sweasy, 2b	2	1	Wolters, p	3	0
McVey, cf	3	0	McMahon, rf	3	1
	27	4		27	2

Innings	1	2	3	4	5	6	7	8	9	
Mutuals	0	0	0	0	0	0	0	1	1	- 2
Cincinnati	1	0	1	0	0	0	0	0	2	- 4

(O=Outs, R=Runs)

Unbeaten, but Tied

Haymakers of Troy vs. Cincinnati Red Stockings

Union Grounds, Cincinnati, Ohio
August 26, 1869

By Greg Rhodes

By August 1869 the Cincinnati Red Stockings had become the top baseball club in the country. Not only were they undefeated, but the novelty of their all-salaried status, their distinctive uniform style with the long red socks, and the triumphs over all the top Eastern clubs had made them the center of attention in the sporting press.

A handful of the Eastern clubs that the Red Stockings played on their long June tour had traveled west that summer to take on the Red Stockings (and other teams in the Midwest), and the Cincinnati boys had taken their measure. They defeated visitors from Washington, Syracuse, and New York City. But the game that was most anticipated was scheduled for Thursday, August 26, when the Unions of Lansingburgh, New York (now a part of Troy), better known as the Haymakers, invaded the Queen City for one game.

A week before the match the club ran newspaper ads saying, "The Haymakers are Coming." Such a warning was probably wise, given the notorious crowd that accompanied the visitors. Charges of bribery, fixing games, gambling, and ungentlemanly behavior dogged the Lansingburgh team. "The Haymakers, while strong players, are not of good reputation," warned the *Cincinnati Commercial* on the eve of the match.

Yet the staid and sober management of the Red Stockings, led by club president Aaron Champion and captain Harry Wright, agreed to host the Haymakers on their home grounds. The championship race, as it was in this era, was often abused by clubs that refused to play contenders, sometimes even failing to show up for scheduled matches. Champion and Wright wanted no taint or imputation of cowardice to besmirch the glory of the Red Stockings, so the invitation was accepted, the match scheduled and heavily advertised.

Some anticipated problems. The *Commercial* warned the Cincinnati faithful to remain calm and not soil the reputation of the Red Stockings during the match, even if the play of the Haymakers or the decisions of the umpire riled them. Crowds, especially in the East, "get to acting outrageously at times and start to hissing," the newspaper's correspondent asserted. "We sincerely hope nothing of this kind will occur at base ball games in this city."

Cincinnati's hotels swarmed with visiting and local baseball men on the eve of the game. The lobbies and private rooms at the Gibson House, where the Haymakers stayed, were the "scene of great animation." Betting was reported to be very

The undefeated 1869 Cincinnati Reds (clockwise from upper right): Asa Brainard, Charlie Sweasy, Andy Leonard, Charles Gould, Harry Wright, Doug Allison, George Wright, Cal McVey, Fred Waterman.

heavy, and rumors swirled that some of the Cincinnati players had been approached to fix the game. The most prominent backer of the Haymakers, Congressman John Morrisey, had a $17,000 bet on his club, according to the whispers floating about the city.

By noon the streetcars were jammed and pedestrians filled the streets heading to Union Grounds, the Red Stockings' park in the city's West End. The temperature neared 90, but a breeze brought some comfort. By game time, the baseball correspondent for the *Cincinnati Commercial*, Henry Millar, estimated the crowd was 10,000. Although the club put up temporary seats for an additional 2,000 spectators, standees were a dozen deep, and carriages stood in a line in foul ground stretching all the way into right field against the fence. After the teams warmed up on the field for a few minutes, John Brockway, an experienced umpire, tossed the coin; the Haymakers won the toss and sent the Red Stockings to the bat.

The Red Stockings gave up six runs in the bottom of the first, mainly due to some heavy hitting and dropped fly balls by outfielders Andy Leonard and Cal McVey. The rumor mill ground on. Were the Red Stockings on the take? Was pitcher Asa Brainard in cahoots with the New Yorkers? But the Cincinnati nine answered those questions in the top of the second with 10 runs.

The scoring continued at a fierce pace, and by the end of the fifth inning, the boards showed each team with 17 runs. Millar wrote that he had "never witnessed such an overwhelmingly excitement-soaked crowd." McVey led off the sixth inning for Cincinnati and sent a foul ball spinning back to Haymaker catcher Bill Craver. The batter was out if the catcher caught the ball in the air or on the first bounce. The ball hit the ground, and Craver lunged, scraped the ground with his hand, and finally held the ball up. "How's that?" he shouted at the umpire. Brockway ruled that it had bounced twice. It was obviously a close call. Two Cincinnati reporters sitting at a table on the field could not agree whether Craver had caught it fairly.

The play seemed to have little consequence. No

Troy's Bill Craver: Did he really catch that foul ball?

one was on base. McVey was the first batter in the sixth. The Haymakers had just scored four times in the fifth, and seemed to be giving the Red Stockings all they could handle. But the president of the Haymaker club, a man named McKeon, charged onto the field to argue the call with Brockway. Perhaps sensing that the Red Stockings, who were noted for late-inning hitting and scoring, seemed likely to take control of the game, McKeon was looking for an excuse to end the match and protect his associates' bets. After a brief conversation with the umpire, McKeon waved his players off the field.

Despite the newspaper's admonition, the crowd began hissing. Brockway ordered the Haymakers to remain on the field. "It's none of your damned business," shouted McKeon, and the Haymakers boarded the carriage for the ride back to the hotel, the taunts and jeers of the spectators filling the air.

The umpire waited a few minutes, then climbed on a chair and announced to the crowd that the match was over and that he was awarding victory to the Red Stockings. Champion refused to give the visitors their share of the gate money (which he did turn over the next summer). The local and national newspapers were full of denunciations of the Haymakers' behavior. The victory was later declared a tie by the governing body of the day, the National Association of Base Ball Players, although the rules did call for a forfeit if one team was prepared to play and the other failed to take the field. Thus ended the only game the Red Stockings did not win outright that season. They eventually stretched their unbeaten streak to 57 games. They did not play the Haymakers again in 1869.

Cincinnati	O	R	Haymakers	O	R
G. Wright	1	2	McAtee	2	2
Gould	2	2	M. King	1	2
Waterman	2	2	Powers	3	1
Allison	2	2	Fisher	3	1
H. Wright	1	3	Flynn	2	2
Leonard	1	3	Craver	1	3
Brainard	2	1	S. King	1	3
Sweasy	2	1	Bellan	2	2
McVey	2	1	Bearman	0	1
Cincinnati	0 (10) 2	1 4	– 17		
Haymakers	6 7 0	0 4	– 17		

Inter-racial Baseball

Pythians of Philadelphia vs. Olympics of Philadelphia

Olympics Grounds, 25th and Jefferson, Philadelphia, Pa.
September 3, 1869

By Jerrold Casway

Frederick Douglass said no city was more prejudiced against colored people than Philadelphia.[1] The black inhabitants of Penn's City of Brotherly Love after the Civil War numbered 22,185, representing 4 percent of the population. Only Baltimore had more black residents.

Leading Philadelphia blacks understood how education and community associations could further their advancement. A focal point of this movement was the city's only black high school, the Institute for Colored Youth, later renamed the Banneker Institute. In addition to a rigorous curriculum, the Institute supported a number of athletic organizations.[2] An esteemed graduate, later teacher/principal of the school, was Octavius Catto. An experienced cricket and town ball player, Catto became the shortstop and captain of the Institute's baseball team. Known as the Independent ball club, Catto's team by the spring of 1866 became one of the leading black ball teams in the city. Later that summer, because a large number of the Institute's players were affiliated with the Knights of Pythias Lodge, the team was renamed the Pythians.

The colored community of Philadelphia had more than a passing interest in baseball. They followed both white and black local ball clubs. In 1867 the "Pyths," as they were sometimes called, strengthened themselves by recruiting players from other black teams. Under Catto's captaincy the team played 13 games in 1867. They went 8–3, and two games have no known results. One white reporter was so impressed by the Pythians, he described them as a "well behaved gentlemanly set of young fellows ... [who] are rapidly winning distinction in the use of the bat."[3]

Despite their successes, in October 1867 Catto and his teammates got a dose of reality when they applied for admission to the Pennsylvania Association of Amateur Base Ball Players. Despite being nominated by E. Hicks Hayhurst, the vice president of the Athletics ball club and the presiding president of the Association's convention, the Pythians were denied access because of race and were compelled to withdraw their application.[4]

This rejection was not indicative of the Pythians' relationship to Philadelphia's white baseball establishment. Catto's club scheduled games at white-controlled ball fields and had accounts with the A.J. Reach Sporting Goods Company.[5] These relation-

Octavius Catto

A woodcut depicting the shooting of Catto.

ships encouraged Catto to believe that social and political acceptance could be promoted by competing against "our white brethren" on the field of play.[6] But there is no record that any game between white and black teams had been played to that date, and white clubs had mixed feelings about playing a black ball club. They believed that if they won, it would be expected, and if they lost their prowess would be called into question. One columnist even posed the question of whether "negroes" made better players then white men. The response was that colored players were better at "whitewashing, and in hot weather they play a stronger game."[7]

In 1869 the Pythians' challenge was accepted by Philadelphia's oldest ball club, the Olympics, whose town ball tradition went back to 1832. Thus for the first time on record, white and black teams took the field against one another. It appears that the decision to set this game up was based on two factors. Both the Olympics and the Pythians needed the revenue drawn from gate receipts. The Olympics had not played in two months [July 15] and had just undergone a restructuring of the ball club. Team morale and revenue were affected by these actions. If the "novelty" of a game against a local black team was a factor then the game would primarily be a financial decision.[8] The same considerations influenced the Pythians. A game against the Olympics would acknowledge their existence and sustain their treasury. The Olympics also required that the contest would be played at their home field at 25th and Jefferson. Despite these conditions, this controversial match needed mediation. The key figure in the negotiations was Col. Thomas Fitzgerald, the founding president of the Athletics of Philadelphia and the owner and publisher of Philadelphia's *City Item* newspaper. Fitzgerald loved baseball and used his newspaper to promote the city's teams. He also championed equality before the law in his *City Item* editorials. Once the game was set in motion, he agreed to serve as the game's umpire.

As expected a large and enthusiastic crowd assembled on Friday, September 3. It was the largest crowd to see an Olympics game since they played the Red Stockings of Cincinnati on June 19. A number of policemen patrolled the enclosure. They kept the game orderly until the last inning when spectators broke through the restraining ropes. At 2:45 P.M. the game began and the Pythians took a 3–1 lead after the first inning. In the top of the second the Olympics scored eight runs and never again gave up the lead. Catto's team was "blanked" in three innings and to everyone's astonishment the Olympics were held scoreless in their half of the seventh. John Cannon pitched for the Pythians and young Len Lovett threw for the Olympics. Lovett was only 17 years old and had just been recruited to be the Olympics' pitcher. The final score was 44–23. The game took three hours and 10 minutes to play.

The *Philadelphia Inquirer* said the Pythians "acquitted themselves in a very creditable manner."[9]

A return match was set for October 11 to be played at the Athletics field at 17th and Columbia. There is, however, no record that the game was ever played. The Pythians did go against Fitzgerald's white *City Item* ball club on the 16th at the Athletics field. Fitzgerald's three sons actually played in this game, which the City Item team lost 27–17. Another scheduled game against the white Masonic club of Manayunk had no published results.[10]

Although the Pythians played ball through 1871, their schedule was greatly reduced. Racial tensions were heightened by the passage of the 15th Amendment to the Constitution giving male Freedmen the vote, and leaders such as Catto were preoccupied with political matters. It is also possible that white-operated ball fields were intimidated by the possibility of racially-inspired violence. When Octavius Catto was gunned down on October 10, 1871 during race riots spurred on by the local mayoral elections the gains made between the races on the "field of green" did not look so substantial.

Notes:

1. Weigley, R. "The Border City in the Civil War, 1854-1865," *Philadelphia: A 300 Year History* (Philadelphia, 1982), p. 386.

2. Casway, J. "Philadelphia Pythians," *The National Pastime*, No. 15 (1995), p. 120-1; Casway, J. "Octavius Catto and the Pythians of Philadelphia," *Pennsylvania Legacies*, May 2007, Vol. 7, No. 1, p. 5-7; Silcox, H. "Nineteenth-Century Black Militant: Octavius Catto, 1831-1871," *Pennsylvania Magazine of History and Biography*, January 1977, p. 55-8.

3. Casway, "Catto and Pythians," *Legacies*, p. 7; Casway, "Pythians," *National Pastime*, p. 121.

4. *Sunday Mercury*, July 21, 1867.

5. See letters, contracts, and bills of sale in Gardiner Collection, at the HSP.

6. Catto to Dr. McCullough, August 12, 1869 in ibid.

7. *Sunday Mercury*, September 20, 1868.

8. Ibid., December 12, 1869.

9. *Philadelphia Inquirer*, September 4, 1869; *The Playing Ground*, October 2, 1869, p. 637.

10. *Sunday Mercury*, August 18, 1869; September 12, 1869; September 18, 1869; October 10, 1869.

The Atlantic Storm

Cincinnati Reds vs. Atlantics of Brooklyn

*Capitoline Grounds, Brooklyn, N.Y.
June 14, 1870*

By Greg Rhodes

"Friend Chadwick," Harry Wright addressed the esteemed baseball authority and sports journalist Henry Chadwick in a pre-season letter updating the condition of Wright's Red Stockings team. The success of the undefeated Red Stockings in 1869 had sparked national interest in the club's fortunes. Wright, the captain of the team, was confident his nine, which returned every starter from 1869, would continue to dominate the other top clubs:

> "I have the players here now in far better form than they were this time a year ago. They are all members of the gymnasium here, and exercise daily.... I think, when we go East this season we will be able to play a game or games of ball that will keep our reputation."

The Red Stockings ended the 1869 season undefeated in 57 games. They began 1870 with an extended Southern tour into New Orleans. After defeating several area nines back home in Cincinnati, the winning streak reached 71 games. But the stiffest competition was still in the East and it was there the Red Stockings would run the gauntlet.

As in 1869, the Cincinnati club organized a long road trip, beginning in Cleveland on May 31, and ending with a match in Washington, D.C. on June 28. After defeating the Cleveland boys, they moved through upstate New York and into Massachusetts. The traveling correspondent from the *Cincinnati Commercial* noted that the famous Red Stockings attracted "great attention in the streets," and created "much excitement along the route and in the cities." The Red Stockings arrived in New York on June 12, their winning streak at 80 games.

Not everyone treated them so warmly there. The *New York Herald* criticized the club for dictating such harsh financial terms that New York clubs were forced to raise ticket prices to a minimum of 50 cents. But the Red Stockings directors believed the New Yorkers would pay. They were right. More than 7,000 turned out the next day to watch Cincinnati easily defeat the elite New York club, the Mutuals, 16–3. After the victory, the papers predicted another unbeaten Eastern tour for the invaders from the West. The next day, the Red Stockings played the Atlantics of Brooklyn, a team they had defeated soundly in 1869, 32–10.

The *New York World* described the pre-game

A July 2, 1870 Harpers Weekly *illustration of the game between the Atlantics and Red Stockings.*

scene at the Capitoline Grounds in Brooklyn that Tuesday afternoon:

> "Little urchins shouted, 'score cards, names and positions of both nines,' all the way from Fulton Ferry to Bedford, and all Brooklyn seemed awake to the event of the day. Stores were deserted, boys who could not obtain permission to leave school played hooky, and hundreds who could or would not produce the necessary fifty-cent stamp for admission looked on through cracks in the fence, or even climbed boldly to the top, while others were perched in the topmost limbs of the trees, or on the roofs of surrounding houses."

By game time between 12,000 and 15,000 spectators were on the grounds, many thousands standing in a semi-circle that stretched deep into the outfield. The Atlantics appeared in their traditional uniform of long dark blue pants and white shirts with an "A" on the front, and the Red Stockings, in their white uniforms and long red hose, tipped their caps as they came onto the field to acknowledge the polite applause of the spectators.

Seven members of the Atlantics were holdovers from the 1869 team; the main addition was George Zettlein, a powerful pitcher the Red Stockings had never faced. The Red Stockings edged out to a 3–0 lead, but sloppy fielding by third baseman Fred Waterman, first baseman Charles Gould and second baseman Charlie Sweasy let the Atlantics take the lead, 4–3, after six innings. In the top of the seventh, George Wright quieted the big crowd with a single that drove in two runs, and the Red Stockings reclaimed the lead, 5–4. The Atlantics tied the score in the eighth, 5–5, and that is where it stood after nine full innings.

The rules of the era did not dictate extra innings unless one captain wished the game to continue. Harry Wright could well have taken the tie, and kept the unbeaten string alive, and that is what the umpire and the Atlantics captain Bob Ferguson assumed would happen. The umpire left the field, and Ferguson's Atlantics headed to their clubhouse. But Harry engaged Ferguson in discussion about continuing. Ferguson seemed content to accept the tie, but Harry persisted. Finally, the umpire was recalled, the players returned, and the game resumed.

The Red Stockings were out in order in the top of the 10th; the Atlantics mounted a rally in the bottom of the inning. With two on and one out, George Wright moved to catch a short fly ball. But instead he let it bounce, and with no infield fly rule yet written, he easily started a double play. In the 11th, the Red Stockings appeared to have won the game with a two-run rally. But the Red Stockings' ace pitcher, Asa Brainard, now seemed to tire. With one on and no outs, Joe Start, the Atlantic first baseman, lined a ball far over Cal McVey's head in right field. The ball rolled into the crowd, where, by most accounts, an exuberant spectator jumped on McVey's back. McVey shook him off and returned the ball to the in-

JOE START. First-baseman.
Joe Start

field. One run scored and the batter reached third. The Red Stockings finally got an out, but then Ferguson singled home the tying run, and Zettlein followed with another hit, putting runners on first and second. And then came the play that ended the streak.

George Zettlein

George Hall, the Atlantics' center fielder, bounced a ball to George Wright, a sure double play, but George's throw sailed by Sweasy, and Ferguson, running hard from second, scored the winning run.

"The yells of the crowd could be heard for blocks around and a majority of the people acted like escaped lunatics," wrote the *New York Sun* correspondent. The Red Stockings quickly boarded their omnibus and left the grounds, upset at the loss, but gracious in defeat. No one made an issue of McVey's tussle with the spectator; the boys understood that the Atlantics had beaten them squarely. If the streak had to end—and surely it did—this was the way it should have happened: hard fought, stirring rallies, lead changes and extra innings. Club President Aaron Champion summed it up in a telegram back to Cincinnati: "The finest game ever played. Our boys did nobly, but fortune was against us. Eleven innings played. Though beaten, not disgraced."

Cincinnati	R	H	O	A	E	Atlantics	R	H	O	A	E
G Wright, ss	2	3	2	4	0	Pearce, ss	2	3	1	2	0
Gould, 1b	0	0	9	0	1	Smith, 3b	2	2	2	0	1
Waterman, 3b	0	2	3	4	2	Start, 1b	3	3	14	0	0
Allison, c	1	3	5	0	3	Chapman, lf	0	0	2	0	0
H Wright, cf	0	1	3	0	0	Ferguson, c	1	2	4	0	3
Leonard, lf	0	0	2	0	0	Zettlein, p	0	1	2	1	0
Brainerd, p	2	2	0	1	3	Hall, cf	0	1	3	0	0
Sweasy, 2b	2	3	7	5	3	Pike, 2b	0	1	3	6	1
McVey, lf	0	0	2	0	0	McDonald, rf	0	1	2	0	2
Total	7	14	33	14	12		8	14	33	9	7

Cincinnati 201   000   200   02 – 7
Atlantics   000   202   010   03 – 8
Umpire - Charles Mills. Time – 3:00.

The First "Chicago" Game

Mutuals of New York vs. White Stockings of Chicago

*Dexter Park, Chicago, Ill.
July 23, 1870*

By Richard Bogovich and Mark Pestana

Given the powerhouse teams that represented the Windy City in the 1870s and '80s, one might assume that the quaint jargon signifying that a team had been "Chicagoed" stems from some unfortunate nine suffering a walloping at the hands of one of those mighty clubs.

The truth is quite to the contrary. The term actually stems from a game played on July 23, 1870, when Chicago's National Association entry became the first team ever held scoreless in a National Association championship contest.

During the previous autumn, moneyed interests in Chicago pooled assets to assemble a team that would rival the Red Stockings of Cincinnati. Essentially a "picked nine" of all-stars lured away from prominent teams including the Eckfords, Athletics, and Haymakers, the White Stockings won their first 31 games. On an early summer tour of the East, they suffered their first losses, one of them a 13–4 embarrassment at the hands of the Mutuals in New York on July 6.

The Chicagoans surely looked forward to revenge when the Mutuals came west to play them later in the month, and most fans assumed they would get it, as indicated by the betting line. That line made the White Stockings two-to-one favorites. Torrid heat kept attendance to around 6,000 as the two teams faced off at Chicago's Dexter Park on July 23, a Saturday.[1]

The Mutuals scored an unearned run in the first off pitcher Mark Burns, whom Chicago had plucked from Fordham's Rose Hill club just after the 13–4 defeat.[2] New York's Rynie Wolters, who had beaten Chicago a fortnight earlier, faced only nine White Stocking batters through the third inning.

Chicago got a man as far as second base in the fourth, but mounted a genuine threat only in the fifth. Right fielder Clipper Flynn led off with a base on balls. After Fred Treacey flied out to Dave Eggler in center field, Levi Meyerle garnered Chicago's first safe hit, Flynn advancing to second. But when catcher Bill Craver flied out to Patterson in left, the Mutuals outfielder found Flynn straying and fired to second for a double play to end the inning.

The New Yorkers turned up the heat in the top of the sixth. Wolters tripled past Ned Cuthbert in left, then hits by Swandell and Eggler and heads-up run-

LEVI S. MEYERLE,

Chicago star Levi Meyerle was one White Stocking victim of the embarrassing defeat at the hands of the Mutuals.

ning on a couple of miscues by Craver behind the plate brought three runs across.

Opening Chicago's half of the inning, Treacey lofted a long one to left, but was put out on a great one-handed catch by Patterson. The *Tribune* said the outfielder caught the ball "in one hand while running backward, making a catch as rare as angels' visits." Meyerle scorched a grounder past Hatfield and reached for the second time. Next up was Craver, who grounded to Nelson at third to start what looked like a double play. Hatfield forced Meyerle, but his relay to first missed the target and Craver wound up at third. But Chicago's best scoring chance yet went for naught as Burns popped out.

After a scoreless seventh inning, the Mutuals put up another three runs in the top of the eighth, thanks to four hits and an error by shortstop Charlie Hodes. In the bottom of the inning, Cuthbert and Flynn reached base, but the former was caught stealing and the latter was stranded by Treacey and Meyerle.

In the ninth, the White Stockings gift-wrapped a pair of runs for the Mutuals via three errors, two passed balls, and a wild pitch. Only a Hodes-to-Wood-to-McAtee double play prevented the damage being greater. Facing a 9–0 deficit, the *Tribune* said the White Stockings "seemed to have given up"[3] as they took their last chance in the bottom of the ninth. Craver, Burns, and McAtee were all retired on infield flies.

Rather than credit Wolters, whom, it noted "other clubs have batted … severely," the *Tribune* blamed impatience by Chicago batters for "the terrible defeat," adding, "What sane individual … would have

The 1870 Mutuals. Back row: Candy Nelson, Phonney Martin, Marty Swandell, Dave Eggler. Front row: Everett Mills, John Hatfield, Charlie Mills, Rynie Wolters, Tom Patterson.

incurred the risk of an examination before a commission of lunacy, by admitting the rare possibility, much less by uttering the prediction?"[4] The *Spirit of the Times* declared the outcome more surprising than any that had come before it. "When the Red Stockings beat the Unions of Morrisania without letting them get a run, it was regarded as a wonderful performance, but that exhibition has been completely eclipsed by the White Stockings receiving similar treatment at the hands of the Mutual nine," it said.[5]

Newspapers in many other cities also reacted with shock and mockery, some judging that Chicago's vaunted "$18,000 Nine" had been proven a horrible investment. The *New York Herald* appears to have been the first newspaper to use the term "Chicagoed" to indicate being held scoreless, doing so on July 27.[6] Two days later, the *Cincinnati Commercial Tribune* predicted that "'Chicagoed' will hereafter be used to indicate a blank score, instead of the less elegant term whitewashed."[7] After Cleveland beat the mighty Mutuals on July 29, the *Cleveland Plain Dealer* quipped: "The Mutuals were 'Chicagoed' six times, the Forest Citys, five."[8] Before long, newspapers in several other cities, including Chicago's own *Tribune*, had adopted it.

When Albert Spalding began publishing his annual guides a few years later, he always included a tabulation of "Chicago games." That and its adoption by the era's pre-eminent sportswriter, Henry Chadwick in the *New York Clipper*, gave it life into the 20th century.

Yet notwithstanding the facts of the term's origins, confusion occasionally surfaced. In the late 19th century, *The American Slang Dictionary*, compiled by James Maitland, perpetrated the most common misimpression: that the term honored a Chicago achievement rather than a failure. "Some years ago Chicago had a base-ball club which met with phenomenal success," Maitland wrote, explaining that "other competing clubs which ended the game without scoring were said to have been 'Chicagoed.'"[9] This reverse explanation occasionally lingers to today.

Mutual	AB	R	H	E	White Stockings	AB	R	H	E
Hatfield, ss	4	1	1	1	McAtee, 1b	4	0	0	0
Eggler, cf	2	3	1	1	Hodes, ss	3	0	0	0
Patterson, lf	4	1	1	1	Wood, 2b	2	0	0	0
Nelson, 3b	4	1	2	2	Cuthbert, lf	3	0	0	1
E. Mills, 1b	3	0	0	0	Flynn, rf	2	0	1	0
Martin, rf	4	0	0	0	Treacey, cf	4	0	0	1
C. Mills, c	4	0	0	0	Meyerle, 3b	3	0	1	0
Wolters, p	1	2	2	1	Craver, c	3	0	0	0
Swandell, 2b	3	1	1	1	Burns, p	3	0	0	0
	29	9	8	7		27	0	2	2
Mutual	100	003	032 – 9						
White Stockings	000	000	000 – 0						

Umpire - N Bouse of Cleveland. Scorers - Messrs Thacher and Dougan. Time of Game - 2:10.

Fly catches - Hatfield 5, Eggler 2, Patterson 5, E Mills 1, Martin 1, C Mills 2, Total 16. Hodes 1, Wood 1, Cuthbert 2, Treacey 2, Total 6.

Notes:

1. "The National Game," *Chicago Tribune*, July 24, 1870, p. 4.

2. Burns has gone without a first name in almost every source of information about baseball games circa 1870; his first name was provided by the *New York Times* on June 12, 1871 ("St. John's College Nine as Tourists"), quoting an announcement by St. John's College of Fordham that he had returned as their Rose Hill club's top pitcher. Burns was one of two Rose Hill players pressed into service for one game in May of 1870 by the Unions of Morrisania against the Athletics, and that figured into his first game with Chicago being played under protest by the amateur Star club of Brooklyn. Burns was released by Chicago after one month.

3. "The National Game," *Chicago Tribune*, July 24, 1870, p. 4.

4. Ibid.

5. *Spirit of the Times*, July 30, 1870, p. 372 (referring to the Reds' 14 – 0 win on June 15).

6. "The National Game," *New York Herald*, July 27, 1870, p. 5.

7. *Cincinnati Commercial Tribune*, July 29, 1870, p. 8.

8. *Cleveland Plain Dealer*, July 30, 1870, p. 3

9. Maitland, James. *The American Slang Dictionary* (Chicago: R. J. Kittredge & Co., 1891), p. 64.

The Birth of the NA

Mutuals of New York vs. White Stockings of Chicago

Dexter Park, Chicago, Ill.
November 1, 1870

By Bob Tiemann

Modern sports fans take for granted that a champion will be crowned at the end of each season. But in baseball in the 1860s, the nominal championship changed hands in the same way in which modern boxing crowns are transferred: when a challenger unseated the titleholder in direct competition. The one difference back then was that the champ had to lose a "home and home series" (or two out of three games, if necessary). These series were usually played over the course of several weeks with other games interspersed. In this manner the "championship" was passed among the Atlantics of Brooklyn, the Unions of Morrisania, the Mutuals of New York, and the Eckfords of Brooklyn from 1867 through 1869. All of these titular champs were from the New York City area, and through artful scheduling they managed to avoid putting the title on the line against other clubs. Even the undefeated 1869 Red Stockings of Cincinnati were denied a chance to hold the title.

A new contender, the Chicago White Stockings, had entered the professional arena in 1870, with a high-salaried squad dubbed "The $18,000 Nine." After a somewhat disappointing start, the club began to win regularly. They won their first meeting with the mighty Red Stockings on September 7, having already defeated the current champion Atlantics, and headed east with a chance to claim the championship pennant. Cynics in Chicago declared that "while Chicago may play better baseball, New York can play other games better,"[1] and predicted that the Mutuals would be allowed to win the Atlantics' title before the Chicago club arrived. Sure enough, the Mutes beat the Atlantics on September 15, and although Chicago swept its four games versus the Eckford, Mutual, Atlantic, and Athletic clubs, the team returned home frustrated. But in order to strengthen their dubious championship claim, the newly crowned Mutuals scheduled a trip to Chicago and Cincinnati, giving the White Stockings another chance.

The Chicago game was played on an unseasonably warm November 1. The Mutuals picked Tom Foley as umpire from among the locals available. Although all the runs were aided by walks and errors, the game was relatively well-played and went into the eventful ninth inning with Chicago leading 7–5.

Just three putouts from victory, the jittery White Stocking infield flubbed three straight chances, allowing the Mutes to load the bases. A passed ball and a run-scoring groundout tied the game, much to the chagrin of the vast crowd of seven or eight thousand. After a second out raised the home rooters' hopes, the Mutuals sent them plunging with six straight safe hits, making it an eight-run inning. With a 13–7 lead "the Mutuals were jubilant and danced about the field with ill-concealed delight. Victory could not be wrested from them at so late a junction, they seemed to think."[2]

But they had not counted upon a determined foe backed by a partisan umpire. Up to this point the White Stockings had been given seven bases on balls, as opposed to none for the Mutuals. Now the Chicago batsmen simply refused to swing at pitches, relying on umpire Foley to give them their bases. Clipper Flynn led off, waited patiently, and was awarded his base on balls, much to pitcher Rynie Wolters' irritation. The next two batters were also awarded first base "on very questionable called balls."[3] With the bases now loaded, Ed Pinkham surprised Wolt-

Tom Foley

ers by swinging and lining a hit to left-center, sending two men home. Ed Duffy came through with a fair foul over third base that plated another. Pinkham and Duffy tried a double steal, and a wild throw allowed one man to score and the other to reach third. Duffy soon crossed the plate after a passed ball. The score was now 13–12, with the crowd roaring for more. Bub McAtee stood at the plate like a statue and refused to offer at any pitches. Having already appealed to the umpire, Wolters stopped and asked McAtee where he wanted the ball, all to no avail. After more than a dozen pitches, Wolters threw down the ball and refused to allow the farce to continue any further. Mutual captain Charles Mills called his men in and, despite all appeals, would not continue. The sun was setting, the excited crowd broke onto the field, and umpire Foley called the game, not as a 9–0 forfeit but as a 7–5 Chicago victory through the last completed inning.

The Windy City celebrated its team as champions, but it was a hollow triumph. The correspondent to the *New York Clipper* summed it up thusly:

> *"No one would be more delighted than I to see the Chicagos the champions, but were I asked my unbiased opinion as to how the Mutuals came to lose the game they had so handsomely in hand, I should reply, '"Out umpired."'*[4]

In the same issue of the *Clipper*, sports editor Henry Chadwick headlined the question, "Who Are the Champions for 1870?" He added, "If we have been asked the question once this week we have been asked fifty times, and from the position of things we find it a rather tough question to solve."[5]

The muddled question of baseball's championship was among the first issues addressed when the professional teams gathered in New York to form their own organization in March 1871. There the plan was adopted to award the championship at the end of the season to the team having won the most games among the contenders. This would entitle the winning club to fly the championship pennant for the entire following season. This, of course, made the 1871 National Association season the first "pennant race."

Mutual	O	R	H	TB	Chicago	O	R	H	TB
Hatfield, ss	4	1	1	1	McAtee, 1b	3	2	1	1
Eggler, cf	3	2	1	1	Wood, 2b	2	1	1	2
Patterson, lf	3	3	1	2	Cuthbert, cf	4	1	0	0
Nelson, 3b	4	1	1	1	Flynn, rf	2	1	0	0
C. Mills, 1b	4	1	1	1	Treacey, lf	4	1	0	0
Martin, rf	3	2	0	0	King, c	2	1	1	1
Wolters, p	2	1	3	4	Meyerle, 3b	3	2	1	1
Higham, 2b	2	2	3	4	Pinkham, p	2	1	1	1
	2	3	1	1	Duffy, ss	3	2	2	2
	27	13	12	15		25	12	7	8
Mutual	000		030	028 – 13					
Chicago	300		300	105 – 12					

Bases on called balls – Chicago, 10. Bases on errors – Chicago, 13; Mutual, 9. Left on bases – Chicago, 6; Mutual, 4. Flys caught - Cuthbert, 3; Duffy, 2; Flynn, 2; Treacey, 1; total, Chicago, 8. C. Mills, 2; Nelson, 2; Patterson, 4; Eggler, 1; total, Mutual, 9. Flys missed – Treacey, 1; Cuthbert, 1; Hatfield, 1; C. Mills, 1; Patterson, 1. Foul flys caught – King, 3; Patterson, 1; Nelson, 1; C. Mills, 1; Foul bounds – King, 3; Flynn, 1; C. Mills, 2. Passed Balls – King, 3; C. Mills, 3. Struck out – Pinkham, 1. Put out of bases – McAtee, 6; Wood, 1; E. Mills, 3; Higham, 1; Hatfield, 1. Assisted by – Wood, 5; Pinkham, 3; Duffy, 3; Hatfield, 1; Nelson, 2; C. Mills, 1. Umpire – Tom Foley, of the Rockford Forest Citys. Scorers – J.M. Thatcher and J.G. Pangborn. Time of game – 2:30.

Notes:

1. Orem, Preston D. *Baseball (1845-1882) From the Newspaper Accounts* (Altadena, 1961), p. 118.

2. *Chicago Tribune*, November 2, 1870.

3. *New York Clipper*, November 12, 1870.

4. Ibid.

5. Ibid.

Other Sources:

Chicago Evening Mail

Association Ball

Forest City of Cleveland vs. Kekionga of Fort Wayne

*Kekionga Base Ball Grounds,
Fort Wayne, Ind.
May 4, 1871*

By John Thorn

On the rainy evening of March 17, 1871, delegates from 10 professional baseball clubs met at Collier's Rooms in New York City, an upstairs saloon run by 32-year-old character actor James W. Collier at the corner of Broadway and 13th Street, just across from Wallack's Theatre, where he frequently trod the boards. The clubs had come together at the invitation of the Mutuals to establish a new professional National Association, based largely upon the rules and regulations of the amateur organization from which they had just departed.

Of the 10 clubs present that evening, eight would plunk down the mandatory $10 to join: the already established Athletics (Philadelphia), Mutuals (New York), Olympics (Washington), Haymakers (Troy), White Stockings (Chicago), two Forest City clubs (Rockford and Cleveland), plus Harry Wright's newly founded Red Stockings of Boston. The Eckfords of Brooklyn and Nationals of Washington sent delegates to the meeting, but held tight to their wallets and did not join the new National Association for play in 1871. The Atlantics of Brooklyn, who might have been expected to join, did not send a delegate, deciding to retain so-called amateur status.

In the days that followed, a surprising ninth club came across with the dues: the Kekionga of Fort Wayne, Indiana, named for the Miami Indian settlement around which Fort Wayne grew. In the Miami language, Kekionga meant "blackberry patch." Woefully uncompetitive against the big clubs in its previous seasons, they had lost two games to the unbeaten Cincinnati Red Stockings of 1869 by scores of 86–8, and 41–7, then took a 70–1 pasting in the following year. Yet now the Fort Wayne hayseeds declared themselves a fully professional nine, based on their having picked up, in August 1870, several stranded players from the Maryland Club of Baltimore, which had run out of funds while playing in Chicago. The star of the Marylands had been diminutive pitcher Bobby Mathews, who would now pitch for the Kekiongas. Eleven days after the meeting at Collier's Rooms, the Kekionga directors dispatched George J. E. Mayer—the club's secretary, catcher, and captain in 1870—to New York to acquire additional professional players, which he did.

The National Association of Professional Base Ball Players launched its inaugural season with a single game on May 4, 1871. The Forest City of Cleveland, a strong club led by Jim "Deacon" White, came to Fort Wayne to play the revamped

Deacon White of Cleveland.

Kekionga, none of whose players had yet cut much of a figure in the baseball world except Mathews, who was only 19. Mayer had given up his position in the nine to Billy Lennon, a stronger catcher he recruited from the Marylands of Baltimore via the Mohawks of New York.

In what the Fort Wayne correspondent to the *Chicago Tribune* called "the finest game on record in this country," Mathews shut out the visiting Forest Citys by 2–0 in a game in which there were no errors by Cleveland and only three by Fort Wayne, a marvel in those days of bare hands and rutted fields. Moreover, the low score was unprecedented among top-level clubs, the previous "model game" being the victory of the Cincinnati Red Stockings over the Mutuals by a score of 4–2 on June 15, 1869.

The outcome was also a great upset. The *Cleveland Herald* had written of their darlings beforehand: "The Forest Citys left yesterday for a brief Western tour. The first club that they are expected to slaughter is the Kekiongas, of Fort Wayne, which little job is to be performed this afternoon. If the Kekiongas play half as bad as their name sounds, they will be awful tired tonight. Kekionga! Ugh! Big Injun!"

The day after the game, the same newspaper felt compelled to report:

> *There were ten very badly surprised young men at Fort Wayne last evening, not to speak of some others who remained in Cleveland. The ten went out to Indiana to begin the slaughtering for 1871, but what little slaughtering there was happened to be on the other side.*

Because of threatening weather, only 200 spectators witnessed this historic game at Fort Wayne's Grand Dutchess ballpark. According to a report in the *Cincinnati Gazette*, play was finally stopped by rain after the top of the ninth inning had been concluded, depriving the Kekiongas of their completed final at bat. However, a *Fort Wayne Daily Gazette* box score supplied a complete play-by-play indicating that each side had recorded 27 outs.

Bobby Mathews, recently moved from Baltimore to pitch for Fort Wayne.

After a scoreless first inning, the Kekionga broke through for a run in the bottom of the second. Lennon led off with a double. Tom Carey lifted a fly to center, where Cleveland's Art Allison made a running one-hand grab, "The finest fly catch ever made, he falling and rolling over two or three times." Ed Mincher also was retired, but Joe McDermott singled to bring Lennon home. The Kekionga added a run in the fifth, needless as it turned out. Each club registered only four hits.

"The Cleveland boys were well satisfied with the result," reported the *Cincinnati Gazette*, "and that they are recorded as playing the finest game in the country." For the citizens of Fort Wayne, however, this glorious victory turned out to be very nearly the club's high water mark. After winning three of its next four contests, the Kekionga went 1-11; despite winning two games at home in late August, it chose to disband on that relative high note."

The First Pennant Race

Chicago White Stockings vs. Athletics of Philadelphia

Union Grounds, Brooklyn, N.Y.
October 30, 1871

By Bob Tiemann

When the professional clubs met to form their own association in March of 1871, they resolved to scrap the old system of passing the "championship" from the nominal titleholder to a successful challenger and replace it with a season-end championship awarded to the best team. The winning club would then have the right to fly a "championship streamer" until the end of the following season. This made the 1871 season of the National Association baseball's first pennant race. No club was more desirous of this change than the Athletic Club of Philadelphia, which had a strong team led by pitcher and Captain Dick McBride and had been denied a shot at the championship several times in the past five years.

Rules were adopted requiring contending teams to send in an entry fee before May 1, with championship games to be played before November 1. Each club was to play each other contender in a "best three in five games" series, with "the first games played to be the championship series unless otherwise stated in writing" (meaning each club could claim no more than three victories in each series). The club "winning the greatest number of games" in these series would be declared champion by the National Association's championship committee. In case of a tie, the committee would examine the records of the tying teams and award the pennant to the team "with the best average in championship contests" (i.e., with the best winning percentage).[1]

It was widely assumed that one team would win all its series and therefore have the most wins and be champion. But as that first season neared its end, the Boston Red Stockings had lost their series against the Chicago White Stockings, the White Stockings had refused to play the Haymakers of Troy and had split their first four games against the Athletics of Philadelphia. The Athletics, meanwhile, had lost their series against Boston. The situation was further complicated by the Great Chicago Fire of October 8, which destroyed the White Stockings' ballpark and the homes of most of its players. The White Stockings, desperate for cash, decided to play in Troy after all, splitting two games, before arranging to finish their series against the Athletics at the neutral Union Grounds

Chicago's 1871 National Association team (clockwise from top left): Fred Treacey, Joe Simmons, Ed Pinkham, Bub McAtee, Marshal King, Tom Foley, E. P. Atwater, Charlie Hodes, Ed Duffy. Center top: Jimmy Wood. Center bottom: George Zettlein.

in Brooklyn on October 30. Although there were still unresolved questions concerning some games, the most reliable figures showed Boston with 22 wins and 10 (or maybe 9) losses, the Athletics with 21 wins and 7 (or 9) losses, and Chicago with 19 wins and 8 losses.

Neither team was at full strength. The Athletics arrived without second baseman Al Reach and center fielder John Sensenderfer, necessitating several shifts in positions. Wes Fisler was moved from first base to second, George Heubel came in from right field to first, and utilityman George Bechtel was stationed in center. Veteran Tom Pratt was on the card to play in right field, but he was also absent, forcing the captain, Dick McBride, to press 40-year-old Nate Berkenstock, a well-known Philadelphia amateur, into service. This "Old Reliable" veteran did some outstanding fielding in the only professional action of his career. The Chicago squad was also short, since neither third baseman Ed Pinkham nor outfielder/change catcher Mart King had made the trip east. Young Mike Brannock played third base, and although the scorecard listed "Pinkham" at second base, Captain Jimmy Wood was there at his usual station. The White Stockings had lost their uniforms in the fire and each man wore a different set of borrowed shirts, pants, socks, and hats for this game.

Although the *Philadelphia Press* wrote that "no other event in the baseball world has attracted so much attention as this (game),"[2] only about 600 fans were in attendance despite favorable weather. The game "in all respects, was one of the best of the season," and "the pitching was the finest ever seen on the grounds and elicited appreciative applause and comments even from the veteran Chadwick."[3]

McBride lost the toss, and the Athletics made the first blank, followed by the White Stockings. In the second inning Fisler opened with a safe hit and moved around on a dropped third strike, an infield out, and a wild pitch. After another zero for Chicago,

The 1871 Philadelphia A's of the National Association (clockwise from top left): Al Reach, Fergy Malone, Dick McBride, Levi Meyerle, John Radcliffe, George Bechtel, George Heubel, Count Sensenderfer, Ned Cuthbert, Wes Fisler.

Nate Berkenstock, an old amateur, came through for the A's

Ned Cuthbert scored in the third inning, reaching when his hot shot to shortstop was muffed, advancing on a single to short left by McBride, and scoring when pitcher George Zettlein threw past first base after fielding a grounder.

Nicknamed "The Charmer" because of his deceptive changes in speed and his ever-present smile, Zettlein settled down and blanked the Athletics through the next three innings. But McBride was pitching even better ball, his speed handcuffing the Chicago hitters. With the aid of two fine catches by Berkenstock, the Philadelphians led 2-0 through six innings. A hit up the middle by Levi Meyerle, a two-baser to left by Bechtel, and a useful ground out by Cuthbert added one to the Athletic ledger in the seventh inning. One-base hits by Fisler, Heubel, and Meyerle brought in another run in the eighth.

As the game entered the ninth inning, the possibility of a "Chicago" game (i.e., a shutout) piqued interest. However, the White Stockings avoided a whitewash when Zettlein was able to reach second base on a double error and was allowed to score while the next two hitters were disposed of at first base. When Fred Treacey flied out to Berkenstock, ending the game as a 4–1 Athletic victory, "The assemblage broke forth in one wild shout which was very generally joined in by the Philadelphia players."[4]

"The whip pennant belongs to the Quaker City," the *Philadelphia Press* crowed, and "all festive Philadelphians will congratulate themselves."[5] As expected, three days later the National Association's Championship committee ruled favorably about some disputed games and ended with a toast to Athletic president James N. Kerns ("To the president of the championship club"), who in turned raised his glass to the team's captain and proposed "the health of Jonathan Dickson McBride."[6] After half a decade of frustration, Dick McBride and the Athletics were finally, definitively champions.

Athletic	O	R	H	PO	A	Chicago	O	R	H	PO	A
Cuthbert, lf	3	1	2	3	0	McAtee, 1b	4	0	0	9	0
McBride, p	5	0	1	0	1	"Pinkham," 2b	3	0	1	6	5
Radcliff, ss	4	0	1	1	4	Treacey, lf	4	0	1	5	0
Malone, c	4	0	1	7	1	Duffy, ss	3	0	0	1	2
Fisler, 2b	1	2	3	4	1	Simmons, rf	3	0	1	1	0
"Pratt," rf	4	0	0	3	0	Foley, cf	4	0	0	0	0
Heubel, 1b	3	0	2	6	0	Bannock, 3b	2	0	1	2	2
Meyerle, 3b	1	1	3	2	1	Hodes, c	3	0	0	3	0
Bechtel, cf	2	0	2	1	0	Zettlein, p	1	1	2	0	0
	27	4	15	27	8		27	1	6	27	9
Athletics	011		000		110 – 4						
Whi.Stockings	000		000		001 – 1						

Runs earned – Athletic 2, White Stockings 0. First base by errors – Athletic 3, White Stockings 2. Left on bases – Athletic 7, White Stockings 3. Run out – Athletic 1. Out of third strike – Athletic 2. Fair flies taken – Athletic – Cuthbert 2, Radcliff 1, Fisler 1, "Pratt" 3, Meyerle 1, Bechtel 1 – 9; White Stockings – "Pinkham" 5, Treacey 4, Duffy 1, Bannock 1 – 11. Foul flies taken – Athletic – Cuthbert 1, Malone 2, McBride 1 – 4; White Stockings – Treacey 1, Bannock 1 – 2. Foul bounds taken – Athletic – Malone 5; White Stockings – Hodes 1.
Umpire – M. Swandell, Esq., Atlantic Base Ball Club
Time of game – 1:35.

Notes:
1. *New York Clipper*, March 25, 1871.
2. *Philadelphia Press*, October 31, 1871.
3. Ibid.
4. *New York Herald*, October 31, 1871.
5. *Philadelphia Press*, October 31, 1871.
6. *New York Clipper*, November 11, 1871.

New Game in the Old Country

U.S. teams tour England

July 30 through August 26, 1874

By John W. Bauer

It has been stated that America and England are two countries separated by a common language. The countries are also separated by a common love of bat-and-ball games. Baseball and cricket were part of the American sporting scene in the middle of the 19th century. English cricketers toured America on occasions. English-born Harry Wright, the celebrated ballplayer and skilled cricketer, was included among those wishing to take baseball to England.

In January 1874 Albert Spalding, then a pitcher for the Boston Red Stockings, traveled to England as an emissary of the Boston club and the Athletics of Philadelphia. Boston and the Athletics were the preeminent baseball clubs of that time. With letters of introduction, Spalding secured an audience in London with the renowned Marylebone Cricket Club. He sought assistance in arranging a series of baseball exhibitions and offered the prospect of Anglo American cricket matches as further enticement. With the support of the Marylebone Cricket Club, the Red Stockings and Athletics agreed to play baseball among themselves and also to combine to play cricket against English clubs.

The players arrived in Liverpool on July 27, 1874. Harry Wright attempted cricket instruction aboard the ship. His brother, Red Stockings shortstop George Wright, was considered adept at cricket, and younger brother Sam was brought along specifically for his cricket expertise. Boston and the Athletics played their first game on July 30 at Edgehill, the grounds of the Liverpool Cricket Club. Before a crowd of about 500 the Athletics outlasted Boston, 14–11, in a 10-inning affair. A smaller gathering saw Boston win, 23–18, on July 31. The apparent lack of interest disappointed the tourists, but lackluster promotion was blamed.[1] The teams traveled to Manchester for a match at the Old Trafford Cricket Grounds[2] on August 1. About 2,000 greeted the Americans, who treated the crowd to a 13–12 affair won by the Athletics. Before the match the Americans explained the manner of setting up the field and treated the spectators to an exhibition of throwing and catching.[3]

After the match in Manchester, the Americans traveled to London where they were feted by the Marylebone Cricket Club. Before a bank-holiday crowd of 5,000 on August 3, Boston routed the Athletics, 24–7, on the hallowed Lord's Cricket Ground. The game featured several home runs, as did other matches on the tour, partly on account of the solid hits getting past fielders on the hard cricket grounds of England. Despite the rout and errors in the field, the British press complimented the fielding skills of the ballplayers.[4] The Americans also endeavored to play their hosts in cricket over August 3 and 4. Throughout the tour, the Americans were granted a considerable advantage of players (often 18 or more Americans against 11 or 12 English) when they met English opponents in cricket. In challenging Marylebone, the advantage helped the Americans claim a 107–105 win.

Prince's Club hosted the Americans at their grounds in Chelsea on August 6–7. On the eighth the teams played at Old Deer Park, adjacent to the Kew Gardens. The grounds formed a basin that resulted in a sharp descent as batters ran for first base.[5] After a delay because of a thunderstorm, the Americans met the Richmond Cricket Club in a 22-versus-13 cricket match that concluded early in deference to baseball. The 2,000 spectators watched Dick McBride shut out the Red Stockings through seven innings. Boston managed to score late, but the Athletics claimed an 11–3 win.

The Americans spent August 10 and 11 at the Crystal Palace in London, "situated in a midst of

A scene from Harper's Weekly, *September 5, 1874, depicts action at Lord's Cricket Grounds in London on August 3, 1874, as the Red Stockings defeated the Athletics 24–7 before a crowd of 5,000.*

a grove of noble trees."[6] Despite the idyllic setting, rain suspended the first game in the seventh inning, Boston claiming a 17–8 win. The Red Stockings scored six runs in the first inning and eight in the third in gaining an early lead they never relinquished. On the 11th the Athletics hit Spalding hard, so much so that Harry Wright relieved the Red Stockings ace. Wright fared little better and the Athletics won, 19–8.

The Surrey Cricket Club hosted the Americans on their last London exhibition, at Kennington Oval on August 13–14, after which the tour left London for Sheffield. Playing cricket at Bramall Lane, now the stadium site for the Sheffield United Football Club, the Americans won 130–88 in a match started on the 15th and ended on the 17th. On those same days, Boston defeated the Athletics by scores of 19–8 and 18–17. After the matches in Sheffield the Americans returned to Manchester.

On August 20 the Americans faced the Manchester Club in cricket at Old Trafford. After the Americans batted their first innings, cricket play was suspended for a baseball game won by the Athletics, 7–2. The cricket match resumed the next day with the Americans achieving a 126-run victory. Afterward, several Manchester Club players joined the Americans in a scratch game but the English were without success in scoring.

The trip concluded in Dublin, Ireland. After an initial rain-induced delay, the Americans and the Irish commenced a cricket match on August 24, but suspended the game for baseball. Boston defeated the Athletics, 12–7. The next day the Americans completed their cricket program with a win of 165 runs to 78, and the Athletics defeated Boston, 15–4. On the 26th, the final day of competition on the tour, a combined nine of Red Stockings and Athletics faced a team made up of six from the Dublin Cricket Club supplemented by George Wright pitching and Harry Wright catching. Even with the Irish nine allotted five outs per inning, the Americans won, 12–6. Afterward the Americans played a scratch game among themselves. With the conclusion of the tour, the Americans returned home aboard the Abbotsford, arriving in Philadelphia on September 9.

The tour interrupted the National Association season. At the time of their departure Boston and the Athletics were first and second, respectively, in wins. Their absence allowed the Mutuals to win enough games to make the stretch run a three-team fight. In the end the Red Stockings won their third straight National Association pennant, with the Mutuals second and the Athletics third.

The tour was not the financial success its promoters had hoped it would be. The clubs lost money on the venture. Time would prove what was assumed then: Americans remained true to their baseball and the English to their cricket. According to the *Philadelphia Inquirer*, "The experience will probably be sufficient to deter Americans proficient in athletic games and sports hereafter endeavoring to show the English people what they can do."[7]

Notes:

1. There was some suggestion that Liverpool was not fertile ground for sporting exhibitions, with even cricket not attracting as much interest there as elsewhere in England. *New York Herald*, August 2, 1874.

2. The Old Trafford Cricket Ground, located near the Manchester United FC stadium bearing the same name, remains in use today and serves as the home of Lancashire County Cricket Club.

3. *New York Times*, August 3, 1874.

4. *New York Times*, August 4, 1874.

5. *Boston Journal*, August 24, 1874.

6. Ibid.

7. *Philadelphia Inquirer*, September 11, 1874.

The First No-Hitter

Princeton vs. Yale

Hamilton Park, New Haven, Ct.
May 29, 1875

By Richard Bogovich

"Hurrah! Hurrah! Hurrah! Tiger! Hish! Boom! Ha!" According to the *New York Sun*, that cheer "peculiar" to Princeton erupted from its triumphant team after the Yale players' own gracious cheer in tribute to their collegiate foes after having been subjected to the first no-hitter in the history of organized ball. It's not clear, however, whether any East Coast sportswriters at the time or even the ballplayers themselves understood the historical significance of Princeton's "signal victory."[1]

This major milestone was reached on May 29, 1875, by 18-year-old Joe Mann, the pitcher for the visiting Princeton team at Hamilton Park in New Haven, Connecticut. The final score was Princeton 3, Yale 0.

Joseph McElroy Mann was born in New York City on July 13, 1856, to the Rev. Joseph Rich Mann and the former Ellen Thomson. The Rev. Mann graduated from Princeton Seminary in 1848 and for seven years during the 1860s he was pastor of the Second Presbyterian Church in Princeton. One of the Manns' four other sons was George Williamson Mann, who played on Princeton's baseball team before young Joe, mostly at shortstop.

Joe Mann appeared in a few Princeton box scores in 1873, though as an infielder. He became the school's regular pitcher in 1874, and it was actually his work *before* the no-hitter that garnered much of the fame he experienced later in life. That's because, later in the century, many sources gave Mann considerable credit for popularizing the curveball, with some even suggesting that he developed the pitch of his own accord.[2] By late May of 1875, Mann's teammates had already been exposed to his ability to dominate an opposing nine.

According to the *New York Times*, a Mr. Rogers of Staten Island was supposed to serve as umpire for the game in New Haven but failed to appear, so Frank Dunning of Princeton was selected. The paper characterized the crowd as "large" and said the defensive highlights "were two flying balls (caught) by Duffield, of the Princetons, in the fourth inning, and corresponding foul catches by Woods."[3] A 1901 book, *Athletics at Princeton*, echoed praise for Duffield's running catches in left, adding that Moffat did likewise at second base. Denny, as Mann's catcher, was among those players mentioned as having played faultlessly. However, errors in the first and second innings kept Mann from a perfect game.[4] According to a much later *New York Times* account, Yale's runners both reached base "through a battery error,"[5] so if Denny played flawless defense, the errors were Mann's.

As historic as it was, few other remarkable details of the game were provided. This wasn't even a case of a pitcher whose dominance manifested itself in a gaudy number of strikeouts, though one of the few sources, besides box scores, for a full picture of how Yale's batters were retired, was a letter to the *New York Times* in 1900 by a classmate of Mann's. Though the writer heaped praise on Princeton's pitcher, he wrote that "Mann struck out only one Yale man, five Yale men went out on foul flies, two on foul bounds (then allowed), and eight on fair flies, four of which were hit to left field, as the result of the out-curve. The other men went out on in-field plays. …"[6]

Yale apparently didn't grouse about the umpiring, but one rationalization surfaced quickly: that Yale's batters "were caught napping by the use of a Reach ball, which is a little smaller than the regulation size."[7] Did Yale choose that ball, or did the home team not provide one? Regardless, later research suggested that Reach was one of two models of ball accepted as regulation in 1875, the other being Peck and Snyder's Dead Red. Those two balls were required to have the same weight and dimensions.[8]

Neither Princeton nor Yale had a campus newspaper until 1876 and 1878, respectively, but fans of baseball in New York were able to read about Yale's defeat in the *Times* and the *New York Herald* a day or two after it happened. However, neither paper noted that Yale had been held hitless. The detailed box score in the *Herald* included a column for base hits, but its brief article on the game made no mention of Yale's total hits.[9]

It took quite a while for the significance of a no-hitter to sink in, much less that Mann's was a historic first. Still, in the wake of Mann's dominant performance, some big-time ballplayers, namely John Radcliffe, Bill Boyd, Chick Fulmer, Billy Barnie and Bob Ferguson, reportedly made a point to observe and study Mann at work, if not insist on batting against him.[10] Sadly, by the time Mann graduated in 1876 he had pretty much blown out his arm. In fact, according to one of Mann's two sons, he overextended himself demonstrating his pitching for those professionals.[11]

After graduating, Mann worked for the *New York World* until 1883, then spent three years with the Presbyterian Board of Foreign Missions before working more than three decades for the publisher Charles Scribner's Sons in New York. In 1883 he married Fannie Benedict Carter, and they had two sons, both of whom went on to graduate from Princeton and practice law.

Mann died on November 17, 1919, about two years after his wife. In the two decades before his death he was able to enjoy some overdue fame. He loomed large throughout *Athletics at Princeton* in 1901 (the primary source of the box score)[12] and in 1908 he was one of the two featured speakers at an alumni association event honoring that spring's baseball team.[13] Recognition beyond Princeton included being the tenth person featured in a series that ran in the *Pittsburgh Press* in 1911 under the banner, "Notable Figures in Baseball"[14] and being featured in a quarter-page article in *Sporting Life* in

The 1875 Princeton Tigers baseball team. Joe Mann, author of the first recorded no-hitter, is seated at left in the photo.

1916. The latter concluded with the author expressing pleasure to note that Mann still played baseball with his two boys, and at some point had regained the ability to pitch fastballs and curves.[15]

Princeton	R	H	O	PO	A	Yale	R	H	O	PO	A
Moffat, 2b	0	1	3	1	1	Hotchkiss, cf	0	0	3	1	0
Laughlin, ss	1	0	3	2	4	Morgan, rf	0	0	4	0	0
Walker, cf	0	2	3	0	0	Knight, 2b	0	0	3	3	2
Campbell, 1b	0	0	4	11	0	Avery, p	0	0	3	0	4
Woods, 3b	0	0	4	3	3	Bigelow, 3b	0	0	2	1	0
Karge, rf	0	1	3	0	0	Jones, 1b	0	0	3	11	0
Mann, p	1	2	2	1	2	Maxwell, c	0	0	3	8	2
Denny, c	1	2	5	2	0	Smikth, lf	0	0	3	2	0
Duffield, lf	0	0	3	4	0	Wheaton, ss	0	0	3	1	4
	3	8	27	27	12		0	0	27	27	8
Princeton	100		000	020 – 3							
Yale	000		000	000 – 0							

Bases on errors – Princeton 2, Yale 2. Time – 1:40. Umpire – F. Dunning, Princeton '76. Scorers – T.W. Harvey, Princeton, W.S. Kenney, Yale.

Notes:

1. "College Men at the Bat," *New York Sun*, May 31, 1875, p. 1.

2. For example, three letters to the editor on the subject, including one from Mann himself, appeared in the *New York Times* on June 10, 1900, with a late rebuttal appearing on September 29.

3. "Base-Ball," *New York Times*, May 30, 1875.

4. Presbrey, Frank and Moffatt, James Hugh. *Athletics at Princeton: A History* (New York: Frank Presbrey Company, 1901), p. 103.

5. "Distinguished Pitchers," *New York Times*, July 29, 1915.

6. W.J. Henderson, an 1876 Princeton graduate, wrote one of the letters to the *New York Times* that appeared on June 10, 1900.

7. *New Haven Palladium*, May 31, 1875.

8. Grayson, Harry. "Curve Developed 73 Years Ago." *Portsmouth Herald* (NH), May 19, 1948, p. 10.

9. "The National Game," *New York Herald*, May 30, 1875, p. 12.

10. In fact, on August 8, 1898, the *New York Times* said that Mann struck out the first four of these. It was Henderson (see note 6) who listed Ferguson, along with the other four, in his letter to the *Times* in mid-1900.

11. Grayson, *Portsmouth Herald*, May 19, 1948.

12. Presbrey and Moffatt. *Athletics at Princeton: A History*, especially p. 29-32, 83-84, and 94-108.

13. "Smoker for Baseball Men," *The Daily Princetonian*, October 15, 1908, p. 1.

14. Aulick, W.W. "Notable Figures in Baseball," *Pittsburgh Press*, January 13, 1911, p. 26.

15. Davis, Parke H. "Mann First Curve Pitcher," *Sporting Life*, April 22, 1916, p. 6.

The Unbeatable Red Caps

Boston Red Caps vs. St. Louis Red Stockings

*Red Stocking Base Ball Park, St. Louis, Mo.
June 3, 1875*

By Bill Nowlin

The best winning percentage the New York Yankees ever enjoyed was .714 in their 110–44 1927 world championship season. The Yankees would have had to improve to 139–15 to match the .899 winning percentage the Boston Red Caps (71–8) held at the end of the 1875 season. It was as good a year as any team has ever had.

Boston won every one of its 37 home games, and went 34–8 on the road. The Red Caps started the season with a 26–0–1 record, not losing a single game until June.

Boston's dominance in 1875 was no surprise, for the team had won National Association championships in 1872, 1873, and 1874 with a cumulative record of 134 wins and only 42 losses. The Red Stockings possessed four future Cooperstown selectees—catcher Jim "Deacon" White, outfielder Jim O'Rourke, pitcher Al Spalding, and shortstop George Wright—in the starting nine. A fifth Hall of Famer, George Wright's brother Harry, was the manager. Much of the rest of the Boston lineup—notably second baseman Ross Barnes and first baseman Cal McVey—were considered among the game's elite.

The streak began with a 6–0 Opening Day shutout at home against New Haven. The Red Stockings outscored the Washington Nationals 54–7 in a three-game series, and by May 11 they were 11–0, Spalding having won all 11. Their other pitcher, Jack Manning, didn't start a game until the 12th game of the season—but he won, too. On May 27 in front of 5,000 people in Philadelphia, the Red Caps' win streak finally ended in a 3–3 tie.[1]

Boston beat the Mutuals of New York May 28–29, the latter their 24th win against the lone tie. Few of the games had been close. To that point, Boston had scored 288 runs and allowed only 74. Al Spalding was 22–0 and already a 20-game winner.

The team headed out by train to St. Louis, to play the Brown Stockings on June 2. Spalding won 10–3 in front of 6,000 who flocked to Grand Avenue Park. The *Boston Globe* headline the next morning ran in Latin: BOSTON OMNIA VINCIT (Boston Conquers All).

Spalding planned to pitch the next day against the other St. Louis team, the Red Stockings (also known as the Reds), who figured to be easy. It was their first, and only, year in the National Association, and they had played just nine games, winning just two of them. Even within St. Louis itself, the Reds were the second team. The Brown Stockings, also playing their first season, were the local favorites, eventually finishing fourth at 39–29. The St. Louis Reds would wind up 10th at just 4–15.

Al Spalding, star pitcher for Boston, had just beaten the St. Louis Brown Stockings.

The 1875 St. Louis Brown Stockings of the National Association: 1 - Ned Cuthbert, 2 - Joe Battin, 3 - Charlie Waitt, 4 - Unidentified, 5 - Lip Pike, 6 - George Bradley, 7 - Unidentified, 8 - Herman Dehlman, 9 - Unidentified, 10 - Dickey Pearce, 11 - Bill Hague, 12 - Unidentified, 13-Jack Chapman.

Charlie Sweasy, a 27-year-old second baseman who doubled as the Reds manager, selected right-hander Joe Blong to face Spalding. Blong got a rough greeting. Boston scored three runs on three St. Louis errors and a McVey double in the top of the first.

The Red Sox (so the St. Louis team was dubbed in the Boston papers—the *Globe*, *Herald*, and *Advertiser*) scored one in the second and another in the third. But Boston put up a fourth run in the top of the fourth, and added a decisive four more in the top of the fifth. Barnes singled and O'Rourke drove a hard-to-handle ball through third baseman Joe Ellick. Andy Leonard tripled, McVey singled, and Spalding doubled. The Reds came back with two of their own in the bottom of the inning on three hits and had the bases loaded with one out. But George Wright's fielding produced a force out at home plate, and a second force out halted the rally. Boston added a run in the sixth, St. Louis one in the eighth, and then Boston put up a final run in the top of the ninth that made the score 10–5. Boston had run its record to 26–0.

Spalding was far from his best. The Bostons were outhit for just the second time all year, 13–12. The correspondent for the *Advertiser* wrote that while Boston prevailed, "it was not by any very brilliant display at the bat or in the field." They'd won the game "by their superior base-running and the many errors of their opponents."[2]

Those errors mounted up, with Boston making six of them (three by Spalding) and St. Louis committing 16. St. Louis catcher Silver Flint made six all by himself. There were so many errors that the on-scene accounts differ. The *St. Louis Republican* box score claimed Boston had committed seven errors and the Red Sox had committed 19, with just one earned run by each team. The *Daily News* had eight Boston errors and 14 by St. Louis.

Boston catcher White had no errors, but did have to leave his position in the sixth inning after injuring his thumb. He didn't leave the game; his finger was "straightened and tied up in a rag" and he moved to right field the following inning.[3]

Crowd estimates ranged between 1,000 and "at least" 2,000 reported by the *Republican*. That newspaper conceded that interest might have been lessened because "[I]t was looked upon as a foregone conclusion that the Bostons would achieve an easy victory." The newspaper added that "the 'striplings' … gave them a good game."[4] The *Daily News* described the losers as "not nearly so badly defeated as they themselves expected to be."

The win boosted Spalding to 24–0 for the season. He eventually won 54 games in the 79-game schedule, if one can call it a schedule when some of the games were really arranged as the weeks passed by.

Despite Spalding's staggering statistics in wins and losses, Boston's success was primarily due to offense. Their .321 team batting average ranked far above the second-place Athletics at .290, who were in turn well above the .260 average shared by the Chicago White Stockings and Hartford. Boston also led in on-base plus slugging, .737 to .677 for the Athletics. The team 1.87 ERA was good enough to rank fourth in the league. Boston's .870 fielding average ranked third.

The Red Caps (with catcher White in a hospital) finally lost on June 5, the Brown Stockings defeating Spalding 5–4. The *Advertiser* headline read: THE BOSTONS MEET A WATERLOO AT LAST.

After the 1875 season, Spalding, White, Barnes, and McVey all signed on with the Chicago White Stockings in the new National League—and won the 1876 pennant. Playing a 66-game season, Spalding was 47–12, with a 1.75 ERA. Barnes hit for a .429 average.

| Bostons | 300 | 141 | 001 | – 10 |
| Red Sox | 001 | 020 | 010 | – 5 |

Runs Earned – Bostons 4, Red Sox 2
First Base on Errors – Bostons 7, Red Sox 6
Base Hits – Bostons 12, Red Sox 16

Notes:

Thanks to Maurice Bouchard, Dwayne Isgrig, and Jeff Kittel.

1. Boston was 22-0 when they saw the May 24 game end in a tie. But it wasn't a fair tie. Boston scored three runs in the top of the 10th, taking a 6-3 lead. The first two Athletics hit safely in the bottom of the 10th, but then a play happened on which accounts differ. Boston argued that Cap Anson had shoved second baseman Barnes and should be ruled out for interference. Umpire William

Cal McVey

McLean agreed, and so did the Athletics after some discussion. As Anson was leaving the field, he "made some remarks" and the umpire walked off the field. The crowd flocked onto the field and play was impossible, so McLean called the game – rather than forfeit it – and it reverted to the tie it had been at the end of nine. *Boston Herald*, May 28, 1875.

2. *Boston Advertiser*, June 4, 1875. Perhaps unsurprisingly, accounts vary from newspaper to newspaper. The *Daily Times* box score, for instance, showed 12 hits for each team and had St. Louis scoring its first run in the first inning, not the second.

3. The quotation about the treatment of the finger comes from the *Daily Times*. Bill Ryczek offers a note from the *New York Clipper* of June 12, 1875, which says that White subsequently had to be hospitalized for a week. "McVey is a fine catcher, but not Jim White – for James stands alone," declared the *Clipper*. The book *Blackguards and Red Stockings* by William J. Ryczek (Wallingford, Connecticut: Colebrook Press, second printing 1999) provides an invaluable history of the National Association.

4. The *St. Louis Daily Times* cited the size as 2,000. A good source dedicated to 19th century St. Louis baseball is Jeff Kittel's site http://thisgameofgames.blogspot.com.

The "Model" Game

Hartford vs. Chicago

23rd Street Grounds, Chicago, Ill.
June 19, 1875

By David Arcidiacono

The *Chicago Tribune* called it "The Most Brilliant Contest in the History of the Game." Sportswriter Henry Chadwick, an ardent supporter of low-scoring "scientific" games, labeled it "the model game." Other news reports called the June 19, 1875, contest between Hartford and Chicago the "most extraordinary" and "most remarkable" game ever played.

For years baseball games had been dominated by offense. From 1871–74 the average number of runs in a National Association game was 19. Double-digit scores were common. The 1875 season was different. That year the league batting average plunged nearly 20 points from the previous season and total runs per game were down to 12. The 1875 season also featured the first 1–0 game in history, won by Chicago over the St. Louis Red Stockings on May 11. Ten days later Hartford duplicated the feat, beating the New Mutuals of New York by the same score.

Although scoring was down, no one had witnessed a pitching duel like the one the 3,000 spectators at Chicago's 23rd Street Grounds saw that Saturday afternoon. The drop in offense in 1875 was due in part to the growing prevalence of the curveball and Hartford had one of the first and best curveball pitchers in the box, William Arthur "Candy" Cummings. At the start of the year, the *Hartford Post* noted that Cummings "seems to have improved in his peculiar style of delivery over last year, and that wonderful curve will bother the heavy batters of opposing nines this year as it has before." Veteran fastballer George Zettlein pitched for Chicago in this first meeting of the season between the two teams.

The game started unremarkably. Hartford and Chicago managed some baserunners—Hartford would leave seven men on base for the game, Chicago eight—but no runs crossed the plate. Hartford loaded the bases in the third inning but failed to score.

The Chicago crowd believed the slightly built Cummings (5-feet-9, 120 pounds) would falter against the bigger Zettlein, who outweighed him by 40 pounds. To their surprise, Cummings continued to shut out the White Stockings. Hartford nearly broke the scoreless streak in the eighth inning when, for the second time in the game, the visitors loaded the bases. But Chicago's Scott Hastings, who had played for Hartford in 1874, saved the game with a great running catch in right field on a hit by Tom Carey. In an unprecedented development, the game remained scoreless through the entire nine innings. The two previous 1-0 games had both ended after nine innings.

The Chicago crowd was in a frenzy as the extra frames began. In the top of the tenth Hartford threatened again. An error and a hit put Jack Remsen on second base and Ev Mills on first with no outs. The end of the scoreless streak seemed imminent. Tommy Bond grounded to shortstop, where John Peters alertly threw to third to force out Remsen. Harmless infield popups by Doug Allison and Jack Burdock ended the threat. Chicago went down in order in the bottom of the 10th.

Paul Hines was Chicago's leading hitter in 1875.

In the top of the 11th Cummings reached first on an error by Chicago first baseman Jim Devlin. Tommy York then stroked a hard-hit line drive to Peters at shortstop. He snared the ball and tagged Cummings to complete a double play.

Hastings opened the Chicago 11th with a single. Devlin then grounded to Bob Ferguson at third base for what looked like a sure double play. Fergy threw to second baseman Burdock for the force out, but when Burdock attempted to turn the double play, he threw wildly into the stands, allowing Devlin to scamper all the way to third base. Although no newspapers reported it, Cummings recalled in an interview with the *Hartford Courant* in 1913 that the throw actually hit Hastings as he ran from first to second, causing the ball to carom into the stands.

With Devlin standing on third and only one out, the dangerous Paul Hines stepped to the plate. Hines would lead the White Stockings in batting in 1875 with a .328 average. Cummings later recalled, "The man at bat was a good hitter and I was trying my best to have him hit to center field. Instead the ball was hit to left and right away I knew it was all over. I ran behind the catcher to back him up, but knew it was useless, for the man in left field [Tom York], while he could throw home, invariably sent the ball far over the catcher's head." York caught the fly ball cleanly and Devlin broke from third. As Cummings had anticipated, the ball sailed over the catcher's head, and Cummings gathered it in. "When at last Devlin galloped from third base across the home-plate every pair of lungs exerted themselves to the utmost, and stamping and clapping of hands were added to the vocal uproar," the *Chicago Tribune* reported. As was the custom, the inning was finished with a base hit by Glenn and a fly out to right field by Peters.

The 1875 Hartford club of the National Association. Back: Jack Remsen, Tom York, Candy Cummings, Tommy Bond, Bill Harbidge. Front: Doug Allison, Everett Mills, Bob Ferguson, Tom Carey, Jack Burdock.

Cummings, who later called this "the best game I ever pitched," declared: "Had that run been shut off, there is no telling how long that game would have lasted."

Chicago	R	B	P	A	E	Hartford	R	B	P	A	E
Higham, C	0	0	5	0	2	Allison, C	0	2	8	0	0
Hastings, rf	0	1	3	1	0	Burdock, 2b	0	1	4	2	1
Devlin, 1b	1	1	8	1	1	Carey, ss	0	0	1	4	3
Hines, cf	0	2	1	0	0	Cummings, p	0	0	0	0	1
Glenn, lf	0	1	3	0	0	York, lf	0	0	6	0	0
Peters, ss	0	2	2	3	0	Ferguson, 3b	0	0	2	2	0
White, 3b	0	0	3	1	2	Remsen, cf	0	1	5	0	1
Zettlein, P	0	0	5	1	0	Mills, 1b	0	2	6	0	0
Miller, 2B	0	0	3	4	1	Bond, rf	0	1	1	1	0
	1	7	33	11	6		0	7	33	9	6
Hartford 000	000	000	00 – 0								
Chicago 000	000	000	01 – 1								

Total Bases on Hits – Chicagos, 8: Hartfords, 8. First Base on Errors - Chicagos, 5: Hartfords, 3. Left on Bases - Chicagos, 8: Hartfords, 7. Wild Pitch – Cummings, 1. Passed Balls - Higham, 1: Allison, 1. Time of Game – Two hours. Umpire – William McLean, of Philadelphia. Double Play – Peters, 1.

The First Professional No-hitter

Chicago White Stockings vs. Athletics of Philadelphia

Jefferson Street Grounds, Philadelphia, Pa.
July 28, 1875

By Casey Tibbitts

Professional baseball in the 19th century produced many notable firsts and many colorful characters, but rarely were the two combined as they were on July 28, 1875. On that warm midsummer day 21-year-old Joseph Emley Borden, in just his third start for the Athletics of Philadelphia of the National Association, etched his name firmly in the history books by pitching professional baseball's first no-hitter.

In July 1875 the National Association of Professional Base Ball Players, baseball's first professional league, was midway through its fifth and final season. Borden came to the Philadelphia club only because Cherokee Fisher, the team's hard-drinking pitcher, had clashed with team captain Mike McGeary and was released. To fill the hole the club lured away Chicago's George Zettlein, one of the better hurlers in the league. But Zettlein was slow to arrive in Philadelphia, so McGeary was forced to turn to the local amateur teams for an interim solution.[1] He found Borden, whose style John Morrill would later describe as "so entirely different from every one else that nobody could hit him."[2]

Borden agreed to pitch for Philadelphia but only if he was listed in game accounts and box scores as Joseph E. Josephs, evidently to keep his well-heeled family in New Jersey from discovering that he was playing baseball for pay. (He was also known to have played as Joseph Nedrob, Borden spelled backwards).[3]

McGeary agreed, and Borden, now Josephs, joined the club on July 24 for its game against the crosstown rival Athletics at the Jefferson Street Grounds. It was an inauspicious debut, as Borden and the White Stockings lost 11–4 before a crowd estimated at 1,000. Two days later the Chicago White Stockings arrived for the first of two scheduled games, and Borden again was defeated, this time by a score of 5–1.[4]

The clubs squared off again for the series finale two days later, on Wednesday, July 28, and this time Borden's fortunes took a dramatic turn. He defeated the visitors 4–0 and in the process pitched the first no-hit game in the short history of professional baseball. His performance instantly made him a star.[5]

Borden, still known as Joe Josephs, started four more games for Philadelphia. His first two outings after the no-hitter were losses, but he earned his second win of the season with an outstanding 16–0 shutout of St. Louis on August 9, defeating an 18-year-old Pud Galvin. At this point Zettlein arrived and took over the pitching chores. Borden started one last game, on September 2, tying Boston and Albert Spalding 8–8. He left the team with a re-

Joe Borden, author of the first professional no-hitter on record, refused to pitch under his real name.

cord of two wins and four losses in seven starts.[6] But Borden still had two significant games to play.

In 1876 the National Association folded and the National League was formed to take its place. Harry Wright moved his champion Boston team into the new league, but in the process lost Spalding to Chicago. To fill the void created by the defection of his star pitcher, he signed Borden to an unheard-of three-year contract at the princely sum of $2,000 per season. Local sportswriters immediately hailed him as Spalding's successor and dubbed him "Josephus the Phenomenal."[7]

On April 22, 1876, Borden, now playing under his real name, beat Philadelphia 6–5 in the first game in National League history, making him the League's first winning pitcher (see companion entry).[8]

The following month Borden narrowly missed out on yet another first when Boston defeated the Cincinnati Red Stockings 8–0, with Borden allowing only two hits. The official scorer that day was O.P. Caylor, whose practice it was to count bases on balls as hits. In 1950 historian Lee Allen researched the game and argued that the hits had actually been walks, and that Borden should have been credited with the National League's first no-hitter. It remains uncertain how Caylor actually scored the game.[9]

Borden started 18 of Boston's first 19 games in 1876 before showing signs of arm soreness and fatigue. He yielded the box for five starts, then returned for five more. On July 15 he pitched an embarrassing 15–0 loss to Chicago and Spalding.[10] Frustrated with his performance, Wright dropped Borden, still only 22, from the team. His final totals for the year were 11 wins and 12 losses in 24 starts.[11]

Since Borden was still under contract, the club put him to work taking tickets, cutting the grass, and mending the fences, hoping he would quit and void the agreement. But he went about his new job cheerfully, and the club bought him out at the end of the season.[12] He later found work stitching baseballs, and was erroneously reported to have died in the Johnstown Flood of 1889.[13] In fact he passed away in 1929 at the age of 75, his name firmly written in baseball lore as the man who pitched professional baseball's first no-hitter.

Phil.	R	H	PO	A	Chicago	R	H	PO	A
Murnane, 1b	0	1	13	0	Higham, c	0	0	5	2
McGeary, 2b	1	1	5	4	Devlin, 1b	0	0	13	0
Addy, rf	1	2	0	0	Hines, cf	0	0	2	0
Meyerle, 3b	1	2	0	0	Glenn, lf	0	0	3	0
Snyder, c	0	0	4	1	Peters, ss	0	0	0	7
Fulmer, ss	0	0	0	4	Miller, 2b	0	0	1	2
McMullin, cf	0	0	3	0	Golden, p	0	0	2	1
Josephs, p	0	0	1	2	Warren, 3b	0	0	1	0
Treacey, lf	1	1	1	0	Bielski, rf	0	0	0	0
	4	7	27	11		0	0	27	12
Chicago	0 0 0				0 0 0 – 0				
Philadelphia	1 2 0				0 0 0 1 0 0 – 4				

Runs earned – None. First base on errors – Chicago 4, Philadelphia 1. Umpire – N.E. Young. Time – 1:35.

Notes:

1. Nemec, David and Zeman, David. *The Baseball Rookies Encyclopedia* (Brassey's, 2004).

2. Spalding, A.G. *Spalding's Official Base Ball Guide for 1896* (American Sports Publication, 1896).

3. Cook, William A. *The Louisville Grays Scandal of 1877: The Taint of Gambling at the Dawn of the National League* (McFarland, 2005).

4. www.retrosheet.org, 1875 Philadelphia White Stockings Regular Season Game Log

5. Nemec and Zeman, op. cit.

6. www.retrosheet.org, 1875 Philadelphia White Stockings Regular Season Game Log

7. Kaese, Harold. *The Boston Braves, 1871-1953* (University Press of New England, 2004).

8. Westcott, Rich. *Philadelphia's Old Ballparks*. (Temple University Press, 1996).

9. Cook, op. cit.

10. www.retrosheet.org, 1876 Boston Red Caps Regular Season Game Log

11. www.baseball-reference.com, Joe Borden statistical summary

12. Tuohey, George V. *A History of the Boston Base Ball Club* (M. F. Quinn & Co., 1897).

13. Cook, op. cit.

A New Age Begins

Boston Red Caps vs. Philadelphia Athletics

Athletic Grounds, Philadelphia
April 22, 1876

By John Zinn

It is perhaps fitting that the National League played its first game in Philadelphia, 100 years after the country was born in the same place.

As with the nation itself, the new league's founding fathers had multiple agendas. While ostensibly providing a solution to the National Association's many ills, Chicago owner William Hulbert, the driving force behind the National League, was hardly a disinterested party. Hulbert had raided the rosters of the Boston and (Philadelphia) Athletics clubs in violation of National Association rules, and feared that the acquisitions would be canceled. Rather than risk such sanctions, he launched a preemptive strike under the guise of solving the old league's problems.[1]

Although Hulbert raided the Athletic and Boston rosters, he wanted both clubs in the fledgling league. This was especially true of the Boston Red Stockings, managed by Harry Wright with his brother George starring at shortstop. The new league's leadership was less enthusiastic about the Athletics, but needed a team in Philadelphia.

The inaugural contest took place on Saturday, April 22, 1876 at the Athletics' grounds at 25th and Jefferson, which had been improved at an estimated cost of $10,000.[2] A crowd of about 3,000 was on hand in "favorable" weather. Although the new league was committed to prohibiting gambling, at least two news accounts showed that there was no shortage of betting going on.[3]

Boston scored the new league's first run in the second inning, largely due to a bad throw by Ezra Sutton, the A's third baseman. However, "fine hits" by the Athletics' George Hall and Bill Coon tied the game in the bottom of the inning.

Boston struck again in its next at-bat, scoring twice on hits by Jim "Orator" O'Rourke and Tim Murnane, aided by a defensive lapse in the Athletic outfield. Good hitting and baserunning by Andy Leonard and George Wright added another run for the visitors in the fifth for a 4–1 advantage. While Boston built its lead, pitcher Joseph Borden set the Athletic club down in order in the third, fourth, and fifth innings. In the home sixth, however, Coon, Hall, and Wes Fisler led a rally that tied the score at 4–4.

Although the next two innings were scoreless, neither team lacked for opportunities. The home team had baserunners in both innings, but couldn't score. Boston had even more chances, but was also turned away, especially in the eighth because of "a pretty double play." Perhaps not surprisingly for an opening game, injuries became a factor. Sutton's "rheumatic arm" led to his being moved to right field, with Bill Fouser going to second and Levi Meyerle to third.

Future Hall of Famer Jim O'Rourke.

Boston had its own injury problems as catcher Tim McGinley's eye was almost closed by a foul tip, but "pluckily" he stayed in the game.[4]

As the game headed to the ninth local newspapers described the excitement as "continuing at fever heat." The "pretty double play" turned by the Athletic infield in the eighth proved to be a two-edged sword. Under the rules of the day the first Boston batter in the ninth was the player hitting after the runner who was put out on the bases for the third out. That allowed Murnane and Harry Schafer to bat again. Both came through with base hits and scored through "desperate baserunning" when Fouser, the Athletics' new second baseman, couldn't field Jack Manning's hit.

The visitors took a two-run lead into the bottom of the ninth, but the Athletic club wasn't finished. Lon Knight doubled, stole third, and scored on Force's out to Bill Parks in left. Then Parks couldn't handle David Eggler's "difficult chance," putting the tying run on second. Fisler hit a foul ball that McGinley, playing with one eye, somehow caught. Down to one last out, the Athletics got a reprieve when Boston third baseman Schafer muffed Meyerle's grounder. That brought up Sutton, the "weak spot of the Athletics in this game." He managed only a "feeble hit" back to the pitcher, who retired him at first.[5] The Bostons were 6–5 winners.

While the game featured plenty of misplays and only three of the 11 runs were earned, the new league's opener couldn't have been more dramatic. Newspaper accounts agreed that defense and baserunning were the keys to Boston's victory. The Athletic club didn't have to wait too long for revenge, routing Boston two days later, 20–3.[6]

Although the large crowd and competitive opening game had gotten the National League off to a good start, there was plenty of uncertainty ahead. The Philadelphia team didn't survive the season, refusing to incur the impending financial losses of the last Western trip and being expelled from the league. It would be six years before major-league baseball returned to Philadelphia.

The baseball futures of the players in that first game varied tremendously. One-third were out of

Tim McGinley: His eye injury hampered Boston in the inaugural game.

the major leagues after 1876, including Tim McGinley, who stayed in that first game so heroically. The extreme case was Boston outfielder Bill Parks. His first National League game was his last major-league appearance. At the other extreme were George Wright and O'Rourke, who would be elected to the Hall of Fame. Murnane went on to a long and distinguished career as a sportswriter. Athletics outfielder George Hall participated in the league's first scandal in 1877 as a member of the Louisville club. Yet somehow, and sometimes in spite of itself, the new league was there to stay.[7]

Bostons	R	H	PO	A	E	Athletics	R	H	PO	A	E
G Wright, ss	2	1	2	2	0	Force, ss	0	1	0	4	1
Leonard, 2b	0	2	0	4	1	Eggler, cf	0	0	4	1	1
O'Rourke, cf	1	2	0	0	0	Fisler, 1b	1	3	14	0	1
Murnane, 1b	1	2	8	0	0	Meyerle, 2b	1	1	3	2	1
Schafer, 3b	1	1	1	0	1	Sutton, 3b	0	0	0	1	2
McGinley, c	1	0	8	0	3	Coon, c	2	2	1	2	3
Manning, rf	0	0	4	0	0	Hall, lf	0	2	1	0	0
Parks, lf	0	0	3	0	1	Fouser, rf	0	0	3	1	2
Borden, p	0	0	1	1	1	Knight, p	1	1	1	3	2
	6	8	27	7	7		5	10	27	14	13

```
Bostons    012 010 002 – 6
Athletics  010 002 001 – 5
```
Earned runs – Athletics 2, Bostons 1. First base on errors – Athletics 3, Bostons 6. Base on balls – Bostons 2, Athletics 1. Umpire – William McLean. Time of game – 2:05.

Notes:

1. Thorn, John. *Baseball in the Garden of Eden: The Secret History of the Early Game* (New York: Simon & Schuster, 2011), p. 159.

2. MacDonald, Neil W. *The League That Lasted: 1876 and the Founding of the National League of Professional Base Ball Clubs* (Jefferson, North Carolina: McFarland & Co, 2004) p. 28-29; *Sunday Mercury*, February 20, 1876.

3. *Philadelphia Inquirer*, April 24, 1876; *Boston Journal*, April 24, 1876; *New York Clipper*, April 29, 1876; Thorn, p. 162.

4. *Boston Journal*, April 24, 1876; *New York Clipper*, April 29, 1876.

5. *Boston Journal*, April 24, 1876; *New York Clipper*, April 29, 1876.

6. *Boston Globe*, April 24, 1876; *Philadelphia Inquirer*, April 25, 1876; *Boston Journal*, April 24, 1876; *New York Clipper*, April 29, 1876

7. Thorn, p. 164-65; www.retrosheet.org.

Wearin' of the "Grin"

Hartford Dark Blues vs. St. Louis Brown Stockings

*Grand Avenue Park, St. Louis, Mo.
July 15, 1876*

By Parker Bena

Since 1876 marked the US Centennial, it was only fitting that a man given the name of George Washington should play a starring role in that summer's events.

This George Washington—his surname was Bradley—wasn't a politician but a baseball pitcher. On July 15, 1876, less than two weeks after the Centennial observance took place in Philadelphia and less than three weeks after George Armstrong Custer met his doom at Little Bighorn, Bradley became the first pitcher in National League history to throw a no-hit game.

Granted, it was a young National League history at that point. Only the previous February, Chicago businessman William A. Hulbert had gathered together a group to form what would become the National League of Professional Base Ball Clubs.

Bradley pitched for the St. Louis Brown Stockings, and he accomplished his pitching feat against the Hartford Dark Blues at Grand Avenue Park in St. Louis. In two previous meetings that week—one of them coming on his 24th birthday—Bradley had already shut out the Hartfords, both times besting the man who was his pitching opponent again on the 15th, Tommy Bond. Described as a perpetually happy fellow, Bradley was rarely called George or George Washington by those who knew him, but more commonly "Grin." By whatever name, Bradley entered the game in the midst of an amazing streak that would extend to 37 consecutive shutout innings.

His teammates gave Bradley the only run he would need in the top of the first inning. With one out, catcher John Clapp drove a clean single to center, reached third on a wild throw by Bond, and scored on Mike McGeary's fly ball.

Bradley's duties were made more challenging by his teammates' lack of fielding support. The Brown Stockings committed eight errors that day, the first coming in the opening inning when shortstop Dickey Pearce threw badly to first on a groundball by Jack Burdock. A passed ball sent Burdock to second, but he died at third base.

The Browns added another run in the second. Right fielder Joe Blong's one-out single got things going, and he took second on left fielder Tom York's slow fielding. Bradley hit a grounder that should have been played by first baseman Everett Mills, but Mills let the ball slip between his legs, allowing Blong to trot home

Over the next 7½ innings, Bradley and Bond matched each other goose egg for goose egg, Bradley overcoming sloppy fielding to hold his two-run edge. St. Louis threatened twice. In the third John Clapp doubled to left with one out. He died at second as Mike McGeary popped up to Jack Burdock at second and Lip Pike sent a liner to York in left for the third out. In the sixth Pike beat out a grounder to Burdock at second. He stole second, but got no farther as Joe Battin went down on strikes for the third out.

Going into the eighth inning, the Browns still led 2–0 and Bradley's consecutive scoreless innings streak had reached 25. Despite the no-hitter being intact, a lapse of control presented Hartford with a golden opportunity to score in its half of the eighth. The frame started out with Tom York reaching first on a base on balls. He was sacrificed to second, and made it to third on a wild pitch. There he remained as catcher Bill Harbridge grounded to McGeary at short, who threw it to Dutch Dehlman at first. Inning over. Threat over. Golden opportunity wasted for the Hartfords.

The St. Louises went quietly in their half of the ninth, leaving Hartford one final opportunity. Jack Remsen grounded to Dickey Pearce at short for the first out, but Battin muffed Burdock's groundball for the Brown Stockings' eighth error of the game. Dick

Higham was the next man up for the Hartfords and he hit a shot to Battin at third, who caught it and doubled Burdock off first to end the game. Grin Bradley now had his no-hitter and his place in baseball history.

For a while, it looked as though Bradley was going to secure yet another place in baseball history in his next start, three days later against Cincinnati, also at Grand Avenue Park. He was perfect through seven innings and took another no-hitter into the ninth.[1] Center fielder Charley "Baby" Jones broke up that opportunity with a double. Jones scored on a hit by catcher Amos Booth, and although the Brown Stockings won 5–1, Bradley's scoreless innings streak ended at 37. That mark stood until Christy Mathewson tossed 39 straight scoreless innings for the New York Giants in 1901.[2]

Pitching virtually every game, as was the custom of the time, Bradley won 45 games that season for the Brown Stockings, who finished second in the new league, six games behind the champions from Chicago. His 1.23 earned-run average was the lowest in the league, although the profusion of fielding errors made behind him (and behind all pitchers in those days) gave that statistic less importance than it has today.

Bradley never approached the same performance levels after 1876. Signing with Chicago in 1877, he started 44 games, but won just 18 and saw his ERA climb to 3.31, the highest among pitchers with at least 20 starts. He remained in the big leagues for six more seasons, but usually as a sort of a spare part, winning 75 games but losing 83. After one season with Philadelphia in the American Association, he closed his big-league career pitching for Cincinnati in the 1884 Union Association and worked in the minors until 1890. He became a Philadelphia police officer after his baseball career ended and was retired on a pension when he died in Philadelphia on October 2, 1931.

No-hit pitcher George Bradley with fellow members of the 1876 St. Louis Browns: 1 - Joe Blong, 2 - George Bradley, 3 - Herman Dehlman, 4 - Joe Battin, 5 - John Clapp, 6 - Tim McGinley, 7 - Lipman Pike, 8 - Mike McGeary, 9 - Dickey Pearce, 10 - Denny Mack, 11 - Ned Cuthbert.

But if his career as a whole was undistinguished, Bradley certainly distinguished himself by heading a list that is now well into the 200s – the roster of major-league pitchers who have thrown a no-hitter. It was exactly the sort of accomplishment the game might have expected from somebody named George Washington in the summer of '76.

St. Louis	R	H	PO	A	E	Hartford	R	H	PO	A	E
Cuthbert, lf	0	0	2	0	0	Remsen, cf	0	0	3	0	0
Clapp, c	1	3	3	0	3	Burdock, 2b	0	0	3	0	0
McGeary, 2b	0	0	3	5	0	Higham, rf	0	0	1	0	0
Pike, cf	0	1	1	0	0	Ferguson, 3b	0	0	2	1	0
Battin, 3b	0	0	2	3	1	Carey, ss	0	0	0	3	0
Blong, rf	1	1	0	0	0	Bond, p	0	0	0	0	1
Bradley, p	0	0	0	3	1	Yorke, lf	0	0	3	0	1
Dehlman, 1b	0	1	16	0	1	Mills, 1b	0	0	11	0	1
Pearce, ss	0	0	0	3	2	Harbridge, c	0	0	4	3	1
	2	6	27	14	8		0	0	27	7	4

St. Louis   110 000 000 – 2
Hartford   000 000 000 – 0
Runs earned – None.
Time of game – 1:50.
Umpire – Mr. Daniels, of Hartford.

Notes

1. thisgameofgames.blogspot.com/search/label/George%20Bradley

2. thisgameofgames.blogspot.com/search/label/George%20Bradley

The Double Shutout

Syracuse Stars vs. St. Louis Brown Stockings

Sportsman's Park, St. Louis, Mo.
May 1, 1877

By W. Lloyd Johnson

"The Grandest Game ever played," Henry Chadwick called it. Chadwick's reference was to the 15-inning scoreless tie between the independent Star club of Syracuse and the National League's Brown Stocking club of St. Louis played at old Sportsman's Park in St. Louis on May 1, 1877.

The game drew national recognition to the Stars, a very good nine that featured Patrick Henry "Harry" McCormick, a local stud pitcher. But the Syracuse club's usually thrifty board of directors had also cast a wider net to attract talent. That included catcher-outfielder Pete Hotaling, an Ohioan picked off the Ilion, New York, independent club; second baseman Jack Farrell, signed off the Princeton, New Jersey, town team during an Eastern road trip; first baseman Alex McKinnon, picked up on the same road trip from an amateur Boston squad; and left-handed third baseman Hick Carpenter, who joined the Stars when his hometown Ithaca, New York, club disbanded in 1876. Outfielder Mike Mansell, one of three Auburn, New York, ballplaying brothers, joined the Stars on his way to the big leagues. Newcomers in 1877 included a veteran of dubious reputation, English-born Dick Higham, a future umpire who would be expelled from that profession for crookedness. Big Jim Clinton, a former major leaguer, was the change pitcher, and outfielder. Billy Geer was the son of one of the founders of the Central City Base Ball Club of Syracuse, a nine that battled the fabled Cincinnati Red Stockings of 1869. Geer's career was cut short because of lack of talent and accusations that he was an arsonist.

The Stars, all bachelors, were very young to be playing such a high caliber of ball. Yet they stayed together for four shining years as Syracuse defeated all comers with slick fielding, timely hitting, and steady headwork from the pitcher's box.

From the St. Louis Brown Stockings' point of view, the game was scheduled to fill an off day and make some money. It turned out to be a monumental turning point in baseball history as well as one garnering coast-to-coast publicity. The game elevated pitcher Fred Nichols to top-line status. It also told St. Louis club directors that, as good as their team was, it could not beat a nine viewed as being from the baseball backwaters.

This was surprising because the Browns had success at the game's top levels. Behind star pitcher George Washington Bradley, they had competed for the National Association's upper division in 1875, and during the first year of the National League, 1876. In 1877, however, Bradley left to join the Chicago White Stockings, and St. Louis struggled to reach mediocrity.

The team's best player, shortstop Davy Force, was in the middle of what would become a 22-year career. He had started as an under-the-table pro with the Olympic club of Washington in 1867, bouncing from one team to another until his contract-jumping became the focal point of the reserve clause, after which Force settled down with the Buffalo Bisons. Third baseman Joe Battin would in time wind up in Syracuse, playing for the 1888 International Association pennant-winning Stars. He would proclaim on that occasion, "I've been in baseball for twenty years and this is my first champion-

Infielder Davy Force was a star for St. Louis in 1877.

ship." Jack Remsen, one of the last players to wear a full beard, manned center field. Another Brownie known to the Stars was left fielder Mike Dorgan, who had played catcher with them in 1876.

Ironically, Dorgan had played a role in Syracuse pitcher McCormick's development. During the previous season Dorgan worked with McCormick to perfect the curveball that Harry had learned at a clinic held after the Watertown, New York, tournament in 1875. Fred Goldsmith and Candy Cummings were both there and both stayed after to teach the young McCormick the finer art of the "crooked" pitch. That winter McCormick practiced in Dorgan's apartment (Dorgan was married to a Syracuse woman), where the two devised a rope contraption that simulated the strike zone. Dorgan was probably responsible for scheduling this exhibition game.

The "Grandest Game Ever Played" was boring by high-scoring standards, but in the day it featured "heavy batting, splendid fielding, and universal brilliancy of play." The Stars were baffled by Nichols, managing to hit only eight fly balls to the outfield in 15 innings. Most hits were grounders to the infield. Five Stars reached base because of errors while only two batters made safe hits.

Never before had two clubs played so long without scoring. While the Stars struggled, the Brownies swatted seven base knocks and reached first four more times on errors. The Browns spent most the game popping up McCormick's curveballs to catcher Higham. The closest either team got to scoring came in the eighth inning, when Syracuse center

1877 Syracuse Stars: The player at left in back is not positively identified. The two figures to the right in the back row are Hick Carpenter and Pete Hotaling. Seated from left to right we have Harry McCormick, Alex McKinnon, Jim Clinton, Dick Higham and Al Hall. The two players in front are Billy Geer and Jack Farrell.

fielder Hotaling made a nifty catch and throw to nip the speedy Force, who was trying to score on an outfield fly.

The 0–0 game took a back seat two weeks later when Harvard University and Manchester of the International Association battled to a 24-inning, 0–0 tie, in which no ball was hit into the outfield after the fourth inning. The slosh fest featured a softer ball, known as the "mush." These two games showed that a harder ball would be necessary to expand baseball as more and faster nines took to the playing field. By the next year, L.H. Mahn would introduce a much denser ball that would be accepted by both the National League and the International Association. The Spalding company then produced an even harder ball that became the standard for the International Association midway through the 1878 season.

As a footnote, the Mahn Ball collection at the Baseball Hall of Fame likely consists of the International Association balls that were abandoned when Spalding introduced its much harder ball to the league in midseason 1878.

Syracuse Stars	R	1b	TB	PO	A	E	St. Louis Browns	R	1b	TB	PO	A	E
Higham, c	0	1	2	17	1	2	Dorgan, lf	0	0	0	1	0	0
Geer, ss	0	0	1	5	3	0	Clapp, c	0	0	2	10	2	2
McKinnon, 1b	0	0	0	6	1	1	McGeary, 2b	0	1	1	3	5	0
Mansell, lf	0	1	1	6	0	0	Battin, 3b	0	0	0	2	2	0
Clinton, rf	0	0	0	0	1	1	Force, ss	0	2	3	1	5	0
Hotaling, cf	0	0	1	3	1	0	Remsen, cf	0	2	5	5	2	0
Farrell, 2b	0	0	1	5	2	0	Croft, 1b	0	2	4	21	0	0
McCormick, p	0	0	1	1	7	0	Blong, rf	0	0	0	2	1	0
Carpenter, 3b	0	0	0	2	0	0	Nichols, p	0	0	0	0	6	4
TOTALS	0	2	7	45	16	4	TOTALS	0	7	15	45	21	6

Syracuse	000	000	000	000	000	– 0
St. Louis	000	000	000	000	000	– 0

Umpire – George S. Ward

Gray Outcomes

Louisville Grays vs. Hartford Dark Blues

Union Grounds, Brooklyn, N.Y.
August 20, 1877

By Bob Bailey

Baseball's difficulties with gambling have a long if not distinguished history. From the early days of professional teams, the presence of gamblers at the various baseball grounds selling pools and taking bets caused second thought among fans and owners about the honesty of play on the field. The pronouncements of the founders of the National League in 1876 included platitudes about protecting the game and the fans from the evils of gambling.

In 1877 the year-old league was faced with a major test of its willingness to back up those platitudes: a pennant-throwing scandal. Through early August, the Louisville Grays had built a four-game lead over St. Louis with a 27–13 record. On August 17, with about 20 games to go, Louisville started an East Coast road trip. The first eight games were against Hartford (playing home games in the more lucrative location of Brooklyn, New York) and Boston. The Louisville nine went 0-7-1 before losing two of three in Cincinnati on its way home.

The Grays returned home in second place, seven games behind Boston. John A. Haldeman, a baseball writer for the *Louisville Courier-Journal*, saw something suspicious in the team's play. Haldeman had very good access to team officials, because his father, Walter Haldeman, was the majority owner and president of the Grays.

Through the younger Haldeman's efforts, it came out that three Louisville players—pitcher Jim Devlin, outfielder George Hall, and substitute Al Nichols—were in league with gamblers to throw games. Also drawn into the scandal due to his earlier gambling run-ins with baseball officials was shortstop Bill Craver. All four were ultimately banned from Organized Baseball for life.

Popular history holds that the four players arranged for Louisville to tank the season during the Eastern trip, giving the pennant to Boston. But evidence of this is hard to come by. The Louisville-Hartford game of August 20 at the Union Grounds in Brooklyn illustrates the difficulty.

Devlin was in the box for Louisville, as he was for every inning during the 1877 season. With one out and a man on first in the top of the first inning, Craver muffed a soft toss from second baseman Joe Gerhardt. Instead of hitting into an inning-ending double play, Hartford scored an unearned run. Errors of all kinds were not uncommon, so pointing to Craver's muff as evidence of a fix is problematic.

With the score unchanged in the top of the fourth, Hartford's Joe Start singled to right and took second on a passed ball. Bob Ferguson then sent a slow grounder to Craver, who tried to catch Start going to third. But his low throw was muffed by Bill Hague, who was charged with the error. Start scored

George Hall: Insisted he never threw a league game, but was expelled with Devlin, Craver and Nichols.

Jimmy Delvin: Louisville pitcher was one of four players thrown out of baseball for crookedness.

Hartford's second unearned run on a grounder to second. With two outs in the fifth, Hartford reached Devlin for a double and a run-scoring single to make the score 3–0.

As Louisville came to bat in the sixth, the Grays had collected just one hit off Hartford pitcher Terry Larkin. Outfielder Bill Crowley singled with one out, went to second on a passed ball, and moved to third on Juice Latham's single. On the play, Jim Holdsworth overthrew third and Crowley came home to make the score 3–1. Latham was advanced to third with two outs, but Hall sent a routine grounder to first to end the inning. Hartford bunched three hits each in the seventh and ninth to score two more runs, Louisville finishing with a total of four singles and a 5–1 loss.

The play of Craver and Devlin may look suspicious, with Craver contributing to a pair of Hartford runs and Devlin not looking like the 27-game winner he was at that stage of the season. But that's only because we know the end of the story. Did Devlin ease up in the game or even in all the games on the road trip? Earned runs in the 19th century are difficult to tease out of some box scores, but we do know that Devlin allowed an average of 5.05 runs (earned and unearned) per game before the start of the Eastern trip. During that trip he allowed an average of 4.75 runs per game. During the final 10 games of the season, he allowed an average of 3.77 runs per game. No obvious statistical evidence of any funny business there. But that is the problem with assessing an individual's effort in any single game, or his contribution to a loss.

Throughout the investigation of the pennant race, Devlin and Hall maintained that they never threw a league game. But Hall's confession makes it appear that they did contribute to a 1–0 loss to Cincinnati on September 6. Otherwise, both players maintained that they only took money to lose exhibition games. Al Nichols didn't say anything. He took his release and faded out of the major-league picture. Craver loudly insisted on his innocence, but having been involved in earlier game-throwing behavior, he was pretty much ignored by the National League leadership.

There was another problem for a team trying to win (or lose) a pennant in 1877: Nobody knew where they stood in the standings. The Cincinnati club had started the season, disbanded, and reappeared later with new owners. The status of games played against Cincinnati was open to question. So newspapers ran several sets of standings. The *Courier-Journal* had a table in many editions including games against the original Cincinnati club; a table including all Cincinnati games regardless of ownership; and a table ignoring all Cincinnati games. In early September Louisville was either tied with Boston, half a game behind, or a game and a half ahead.

In December the National League decided to toss out all Cincinnati games. Modern references include all the Cincinnati games, thus giving Boston a seven-game lead over second-place Louisville. But the lead shrinks to three games when following the league's 1877 decision.

That Devlin, Hall, and Nichols threw games in 1877 seems unquestioned. Craver's role is more difficult to determine. But Boston's 20–1 record from August 17 to the end of the season may have swayed the standings beyond what the Louisville Four did.

Three In One?

Boston Red Caps vs. Providence Rhode Islanders

Messer Street Grounds, Providence, R.I.
May 8, 1878

By Kathy Torres

The baseball game played on May 8, 1878, between Providence and Boston would not have been considered one of the 100 greatest games of the 19th century except for one enduring and still controversial question: Did Providence center fielder Paul Hines, in the eighth inning of this match, achieve the first unassisted triple play in major-league baseball? Or was it a misunderstanding encouraged by the publicity-seeking Hines that eventually grew into a myth?

In an essay titled *The Unassisted Triple Play*,[1] Don Meyer defines an unassisted triple play as occurring "when a defensive player makes all three outs in one continuous play without any other teammate touching the ball."

The game was played at the Messer Street Grounds in Providence in front of 4,500 fans. In the earliest report of the game, printed in the *Boston Evening Transcript* the next day, Hines is credited with a "triple play" only, with no mention of its being unassisted: "In the eighth inning there was great excitement, when, through errors of the Providence club, O'Rourke scored and Manning and Sutton were on bases. Burdock struck a fly—just beyond Carey—which Hines caught after a long run, ran to third base and put out Manning and threw to second, putting out Sutton and making a triple play." Providence won the game, 3–2. However, the story in the *Providence Journal* the next day reported that "Manning and Sutton proceeded to the home plate," meaning that both rounded third.

According to 1878 rules, if both players passed third base, they would have been out when Hines stepped on the bag, and the play would have indeed been unassisted. Arthur Irwin was quoted in an 1897 book, *A History of the Boston Base Ball Club*, as saying, "The greatest play I ever saw was made by Paul Hines. ... he caught a low fly ball behind the shortstop on a full run, continuing on to third base where he put out the two men ... from second and third bases, making the treble play unassisted."

On August 24, 1902, the *New York Times* wrote that "it was not until the fall of 1888 that the public was informed (through a magazine article) that (an unassisted triple play) had been accomplished." Apparently the claimed achievement was soon contradicted by Providence second baseman Charles Sweasy. The *Times* quoted him as stating: "I assisted Hines in making the triple play mentioned so largely in the public prints. The ball was struck by Burdock to short left field. Hines started for it on a dead run, and succeeded in catching it, but nearly stumbled.

Charlie Sweasy: The Providence second baseman claimed credit for assisting Hines's unassisted triple play.

Regaining his feet, however, he kept on running to third base, reaching that station before Manning could return, thereby putting Manning out. Sutton, who had reached third, seeing Hines coming with the ball, started back to second. Hines touched third and started to catch Sutton; but, Sutton being a good sprinter, Hines saw that he could not catch him, and threw the ball to me at second base in time to catch Sutton before he reached it." The rules did not require Hines to throw to Sweasy to put Sutton out. Did he do it just to be certain?

The question was visited again in the May 1947 issue of *Baseball Digest*, which said that former Boston first baseman Tim Murnane, later a baseball writer in Boston, was "the first to bestow this honor upon Hines." The article said, "Some years later the claim was disputed by George Moreland and an investigation proved Murnane to have been in error. ... Providence was leading, 3-0, when an eighth-inning error gave Boston a score, putting Manning on second with Ezra Sutton on first and none down. Blackie Burdock, Boston's famous second baseman, hit a fly to deep short. Hines went after it like a deer, nailed the ball on a 35-yard run and kept on going to third, tagging Manning, who had overrun the bag, and then throwing to Sweasy at second to catch Sutton for a triple play."

So, is it a debunked myth or a disputed accomplishment? Was it simply the product of the fuzzy memories of old teammates and/or Hines's desire for public acclaim? While the early reporting seems to establish that it was indeed an unassisted triple play under the rules of the time, and that Hines' unnecessary throw to second merely confused the issue, the debate lives on, in part because of the very rarity and extreme difficulty of the unassisted triple play. There are more perfect games on record than unassisted triple plays. So, no matter where fans of baseball history stand on the question, it's still fun to talk about.

Paul Hines: More than 130 years after it happened, his remains one of the most controversial fielding plays in baseball history.

	R	B	TB	PO	A	E
Providence						
Higham, r.f.	1	1	1	2	1	0
York, l.f.	1	1	1	1	0	0
Murnane, 1 b.	0	0	0	9	1	2
Hines, c.f.	0	1	1	4	1	0
Carey, s.s.	0	0	0	1	1	1
Hague, 3 b.	1	1	1	3	1	0
Nichols, p.	0	0	0	0	7	2
Allison, c.	0	3	4	6	1	1
Sweasy, 2 b.	0	0	0	1	3	1
	3	7	8	27	16	7
Boston						
G. Wright, s.s.	0	2	2	0	2	0
Leonard, l.f.	0	0	0	0	0	3
O'Rourke, c.f.	1	1	2	1	0	0
Manning, r.f.	0	0	0	1	0	1
Sutton, 3b	0	0	0	0	2	1
Burdock, 2b	1	0	0	4	4	0
Morrill, 1b	0	0	0	12	0	1
Bond, p.	0	2	2	0	10	0
Snyder, c.	0	0	0	9	1	6
	2	5	6	27	19	12

Providence 100 000 110 - 3
Boston   000 000 011 - 2

Two-base hits - Allison, 1; O'Rourke, 1. First base on balls - Bostons, 1. First base on errors - Providence, 4; Bostons, 5. Balls called - On Nichols, 26; on Bond, 22. Strikes called - Off Nichols, 13; off Bond, 18. Double plays - Burdock and Morrill. Triple play - Hines and Sweasy. Time - 2h 45m. Umpire - J.A. Cross of Providence.

Notes:
1. http://www.vfcc.edu/aboutVFCC/?p=showthinkAboutIt&id=190

Farewell to Old-style Ball

Syracuse Stars vs. Buffalo Bisons

Buffalo Park, Buffalo, N.Y.
September 14, 1878

By W. Lloyd Johnson

On September 14, 1878, more than 3,000 screaming supporters shoved into the old Buffalo ballpark at Niagara and Rhode Island Streets to watch their beloved Bisons battle the league-leading Stars of Syracuse. At stake was the International Association pennant. In the 6-by-6-foot pitching box were the league's two best, future Hall of Fame member James "Pud" Galvin for Buffalo and Patrick Henry "Harry" McCormick, curveball specialist, for the Stars. The umpire in charge was known to be a Buffalo homer, C.W. Nichols.

The game climaxed a season-long four-team pennant battle involving the defending champion London (Ontario) Tecumsehs and the Uticas. The "shining orbs," as one nameless newspaper writer called the Stars, won 22 of their first 25 games. One of the losses had been a forfeit to Auburn when the Stars left the field complaining of poor umpiring. Another loss, to the Tecumsehs, occurred when backup hurler Jimmy Macullar took the box instead of McCormick.

After a slow start, Buffalo reeled off 14 straight wins during a homestand. Bison detractors, namely the Stars, asserted that Buffalo victories were aided by weird calls from their favorite umpire, Nichols. Earlier in the season, the Bisons had actually uncovered a crooked umpire, George Campbell, who lived in Syracuse, but did his dastardly work in a Rochester-Buffalo contest. After the *Buffalo Express* wrote about Campbell's work, he sued the paper for slander but never appeared for trial. Rochester had won the disputed contest, 16–3, in Buffalo, causing hometown fans to lose a small fortune in bets on the game. Disgruntled losers mobbed Campbell, but quick and decisive action by two large policemen saved the arbiter, and the pennant race continued.

Founded by Candy Cummings and James A. Williams and called an "interloper" league by baseball historian Harold Seymour, the International Association, in its second season in 1878, resembled the old National Association, with loose scheduling and cheap entry fees. But until breaking apart in 1880, it was considered the rival of the National League. The International Association was a precursor of the Eastern and International Leagues of today. In the 21st century, four International Association cities, Buffalo, Rochester, Syracuse, and Columbus, were in the International

Hick Carpenter: The Syracuse third baseman would be a regular at that position throughout the 1880s.

The Buffalo Bisons won a late-season showdown against Syracuse to claim the 1878 International League pennant. In 1879, both teams would advance to the National League. Back: Tom Dolan, Dick Allen, Bill McGunnigle, Pud Galvin. Middle: Bill Crowley, Dave Eggler, Steve Libby, Chick Fulmer, Denny Mack. Front: Davy Force, Trick McSorley.

League, including the two franchises that battled for the 1878 pennant.

Buffalo stalwarts were Galvin and shortstop Davy Force, who was at the midpoint of a long career. Five players on the squad received Clipper prizes, emblematic of the best player at his position. They were shortstop Force, first baseman Steve Libby, pitcher-manager Bill McGunnigle, outfielder Joe Hornung, and pitcher Galvin. While all of the 1878 Bisons would play in the major leagues, the season belonged to Galvin. The soon-to-be-portly hurler tossed 900 innings in 101 games that season, winning 72 games and losing 25. Pud pitched 96 complete ones with 17 shutouts. He had a 10–5 record against National League teams. Buffalo was so strong that the team joined the National League in 1879 and remained for seven years.

The Stars' collision with Buffalo climaxed a meteoric, four-year rise that had placed an unknown, backwater nine into the ranks of the establishment. The club was aided by a mythological record of winning every game and doing it with a reckless abandon that few towns had ever seen. All bachelors, the club featured left-handed third baseman Hick Carpenter, for whom the term "hot corner" would be coined; McCormick, who learned the art of the curveball from inventors Cummings and Goldsmith; second baseman Jack Farrell, who would star for Providence's National League team; and first baseman Alex McKinnon.

A strange, paralyzing malady suffered by McKinnon and his 1879 contract-jumping fueled the practice of blackballing and the establishment of the reserve clause. Star outfielders Pete Hotaling and Mike Mansell patrolled the outer gardens with the reserve pitcher. Mansell was one of three Auburn brothers who would play major-league ball. Catcher Mike Dorgan became a manager in the National League and with McCormick married sisters in Syracuse's social affair of the 1879 year.

The 1878 Stars formed the best nine ever to wear Syracuse flannels. The next year the franchise would join Buffalo in entering the National League intact, where McCormick would become the only pitcher to hit a home run in the first inning of a 1–0 shutout and the team would win a court judgment against a building owner who placed bleachers on top of his edifice that overlooked the left-field fence of the Stars' Newell Park.

The importance of the International Association championship game lay in its play on the field; it was not the last game of the season, nor was it the game that clinched the pennant for Buffalo. Even so, every fan of the pennant race that year knew that the winner of the game would win the league. Aided by the umpire, Buffalo wasted no time in scoring runs, scoring frequently in the first two innings and taking the decision, 9–1.

In a larger sense, the game symbolized the "last hoorah" of the old regime, under which players were in control of the league, local umpires made calls that benefited local teams, and teams interpreted league rules for themselves. The Stars went to the International Association winter meetings determined to alter the result of the pennant race by claiming two more late-season victories over the disbanded Rochester nine. The directors of the Association threw out the Stars' claim, awarded the championship banner to Buffalo, and then watched the National League snatch its two best teams.

The previous year had been the worst in National League history, but the ascension of Buffalo and the Stars demonstrated that it was on its way to recovery. Buffalo's directors wanted out because they lost $279 in 1878. They wanted the assurance of success that they thought the other league offered.

The National League also learned how to deal with rivals, lessons that were applied four years later when the American Association was created.

Syracuse Stars ace Harry McCormick was roughed up by the Bisons.

The National League took in John B. Day, owner of the American Association's New York Metropolitans, as owner of the National League's New York franchise, and within a few years Day had sold the Mets.

The ruthlessness that the National League displayed with the International Association doomed the "good old days" of laissez faire baseball business practices. The "loose play" of the International Association left the professional leagues and became a staple of outlaw leagues and barnstorming teams.

	AB	R	H	PO	A	E
Syracuse						
Hotaling, cf	4	0	0	0	0	1
Farrell, 2b	4	0	2	3	2	3
Carpenter, 3b	4	0	1	0	3	0
McKinnon, 1b	4	0	1	9	0	1
McClure, c	4	1	1	11	3	3
McCormick, p-rf	4	0	1	3	3	2
Mansell, lf	4	0	0	1	0	1
Derby, rf-p	3	0	1	0	9	3
Macullar, ss	3	0	0	0	3	0
	34	1	7	27	23	14
Buffalo						
Crowley, c	4	1	1	7	0	0
Allen, 3b	5	1	1	0	0	0
Eggler, cf	5	1	3	2	0	0
Libby, 1b	3	1	1	7	0	0
Galvin, p	4	0	0	3	3	2
Fulmer, 2b	4	2	1	2	4	1
Hornung, lf	4	3	0	2	0	0
Mack, rf	4	0	0	2	0	0
Force, ss	3	0	1	2	1	0
	36	9	8	27	8	3

Lee Richmond's No-hit Debut

Chicago White Stockings (NL) vs. Worcesters (NA)

*Agricultural Fairgrounds, Worcester, Mass.
June 2, 1879*

By John R. Husman

When the National Association's last place Worcester club sent a collegian out to pitch against the National League leading Chicago White Stockings in an exhibition game, it sounded like a mismatch. The result bore out that presumption … but it was the Chicagoans who were over-matched.

Lee Richmond, a 22-year-old left-hander from the Brown University team, not only shut out Cap Anson's proud White Stockings, 11–0, that afternoon in Worcester, he did so without allowing a hit. That makes Richmond's debut arguably the most remarkable by any pitcher against a big-league team.

The exhibition—common in those days as teams on long road trips tried to generate revenue during off days on their league schedule—was played at the Worcester Agricultural Fairgrounds, also known as Driving Park, the home field of the Worcester nine. About 500 spectators attended, most doubtless drawn by the chance to see such stars of the only major league then in existence as Anson, Abner Dalrymple, George Gore, and Ned Williamson.[1]

At the time of the game, Chicago stood 14–1 and led the National League by four games over Providence. The White Stockings had won eight consecutive league games with the last six coming against Boston. Worcester, just 5–13, was in last place in the nine-team National Association, then a minor league.

In an effort to invigorate his club, Worcester manager Frank Bancroft brought in three new players for their first professional game and "materially reinforced his nine."[2] Richmond was the star left-hander of the Brown University nine. Also making their debuts that day were Richmond's catcher at Brown, W. H. Winslow, and infielder Arthur Irwin.

Initially, Richmond had no interest in challenging the National League leaders. Walter F. Angell, Richmond's classmate and lifelong friend, later wrote that Richmond had received several telegrams from Bancroft asking Richmond to pitch, one of which Angell saw Richmond open. "He handed it to me with the comment that of course he could not go; but his college catcher Winslow came along and persuaded him to take chances and change his mind, Winslow agreeing to go with him and play as catcher." Angell

Lee Richmond as he looked while pitching for Brown University.

recorded.³ Those "chances" involved the cutting of classes and recitations to make the Worcester trip. Richmond and Winslow were each paid $10 and expenses for the game. According to the *New York Tribune* it was the need for a pair of pants that induced Richmond to turn professional. Because "Winslow figured that he would need a new pair of trousers and the $10 would help foot the bill, he induced his battery mate to go for friendship's sake."⁴

Despite never having appeared in anything more than a college game, Richmond dominated the afternoon. He walked lead-off batter Dalrymple and then retired the next 21 Chicago batters in order in the game, which was shortened to seven innings due to rain. Richmond struck out eight and did not allow a ball to be hit out of the infield.⁵ All of Richmond's strikeouts came against Chicago's four left-handed batters, Dalrymple (1), Gore (3), Orator Shafer (3), and Bill Harbridge (1).

The Worcester defense played errorless ball. "Tricky" Nichols did good work at short, Arthur Irwin made two brilliant plays at third, and first baseman Charlie Bennett made what was described as "a remarkably fine foul catch."⁶

The Worcester offense garnered 12 hits, good for 20 bases, off Chicago pitcher Frank Hankinson. Steve Brady hit the game's first pitch for a triple and was promptly driven in by Lon Knight's single.⁷ No one knew it at this stage but that was all the runs the Worcesters would need. They went on to score a total of three in the top of the first inning. Worcester had three singles, two doubles, and a triple as they batted around in the fifth to score four times and ice the game. The final score was 11–0. Brady had four hits on the day.

Those who didn't see the game had a hard time believing the result. The next day's *Worcester Evening Gazette* reported that "the progress of the game was … bulletined as usual, but the crowd who watched the black board were inclined to believe that there was some misplacement of figures…"⁸

Richmond's success was primarily due to his skill. But he also had a couple of other advantages. The first was the Chicago batters' unfamiliarity with him. It also helped that he was left-handed, for the NL featured only one left-handed pitcher at the time, Bobby Mitchell, and he pitched infrequently. Chicago's four left-handed hitters found making contact with Richmond's deliveries especially difficult. Further, Richmond had pitches that were unusual. He utilized a "peculiar set of curves that he had evolved. Instead of throwing curves that broke in and out his ball broke upward or downward. His jump ball was one of the biggest successes of the period, while his tantalizing drop greatly resembled the far-famed 'fade-away' employed by Christy Mathewson of the Giants."⁹

The Chicagos and Worcesters met in another exhibition game later that same season, on September 18. The result was much the same with Richmond shutting out the Chicagos 7–0 in an eight-inning game. The Chicagos held the lead in the pennant race until August 14 and then fell all the way to fourth place, 10½ games behind the league champion Providence Grays. Richmond proved to be a "franchise player" for the Worcesters in leading them to a 19–23 record and solid fourth-place finish in the National Association.

Abner Dalrymple: His leadoff walk was the only blemish on Richmond's record that day.

George Gore: White Stockings stalwart struck out three times against the collegian.

He had another no-hitter later in the year, won his major league debut, and totaled 47 wins (amateur and professional) for the season. The outstanding play of the Worcesters following the acquisition of Richmond propelled the city into the National League in 1880.

	AB	R	H	TB	PO	A	E
Worcester							
Brady, 2b	5	2	4	6	1	2	0
Knight, rf	5	1	1	1	0	0	0
Bennett, 1b	2	2	1	3	12	0	0
Sullivan, cf	4	0	0	0	0	0	0
Bushong, lf	4	1	2	3	0	0	0
Richmond, p	2	1	1	3	0	8	0
Winslow, cf	3	1	2	3	6	2	0
Irwin, 3b	3	2	1	1	1	2	0
Nichols, ss	3	1	0	0	1	4	0
	31	11	12	20	21	18	0
Chicago							
Dalrymple, lf	2	0	0	0	0	0	0
Gore, cf	3	0	0	0	2	0	1
Anson, 1b	3	0	0	0	6	0	0
Shafer, rf	3	0	0	0	2	0	0
Peters, ss	2	0	0	0	1	2	2
Quest, 2b	2	0	0	0	0	1	2
Hankinson, p	2	0	0	0	0	6	3
Williamson, 3b	2	0	0	0	4	1	0
Harbridge, cf	2	0	0	0	6	0	3
	21	0	0	0	21	10	11

Worcester 301 340 0 – 7
Chicago 000 000 0 – 0

Runs earned: Worcesters 5. Three-base hits: Brady, Bennett, Richmond. Two-base hits: Winslow, Bushong. 1st on errors: Worcesters 1, Chicagos 0. 1st on balls: Worcesters 5, Chicagos 1. Left on bases: Worcesters 5, Chicagos 1. Struck out: Dalrymple, Gore 3, Shafer 3, Harbridge, Knight, Sullivan, Nichols 2. Balls called on: Richmond 56, Hankinson 111. Strikes called off: Richmond 14, Hankinson 12. Strikes missed off: Richmond 23, Hankinson 23. Fouls struck off: Richmond 11, Hankinson 21. Double play: Williamson. Time of game: 2:10. Umpire: William McLean of Philadelphia.

Notes:

1. *Worcester Evening Gazette*, June 3, 1879.
2. *Providence Daily Journal*, June 3, 1879.
3. Walter Angell, letter to editor of the *Boston Post*, August 18, 1925.
4. "Richmond's Debut In Professional Baseball," *Brown Alumni Monthly*, 1910-1911, from the *New York Tribune*.
5. *Chicago Tribune*, June 3, 1879.
6. *Worcester Daily Spy*, June 3, 1879.
7. *Worcester Evening Gazette*, June 3, 1979.
8. *Worcester Evening Gazette*, June 3, 1979.
9. "Richmond's Debut In Professional Baseball," *Brown Alumni Monthly*, 1910-1911, from the *New York Tribune*.

The Cameo of Bill White

Cleveland Blues vs. Providence Grays

Messer Street Grounds, Providence, R.I.
June 21, 1879

By John R. Husman

An answer commonly given to the question of who was the first black man to play major-league baseball is still Jackie Robinson in 1947. Knowledgeable baseball people know that Robinson was preceded by the Walker brothers, Moses and Welday, for Toledo in 1884. Recent research, led by SABR's Peter Morris, has uncovered evidence of still earlier African American participation in the major leagues. Morris's detective work reveals that William Edward White, a former slave, had a one game career for the National League's Providence Grays on June 21, 1879.

White had come north from his native Milner, Georgia, to attain his education.[1] He was a student at Brown University and a member of the school's crack baseball team, which had just claimed the college championship of 1879.[2] He was, no doubt, known to the professional club that shared the same city and ballpark and which had faced the Brown nine in several early-season games that year. When the Grays' regular first baseman, "Old Reliable" Joe Start, "broke the second finger on his left hand"[3] during the Grays game of June 19, White was pressed into service as his replacement. Though he played well, he was replaced, in turn, by Jim O'Rourke, the Grays' regular right fielder, for the remainder of Start's absence.

The Grays were a very strong club that included future Hall of Famers O'Rourke, player-manager George Wright, and John Ward, and stood second to Chicago in the National League standings in what would be a pennant-winning season for the Rhode Island team. The Clevelands rested in the cellar on White's career day. After falling behind early, Providence rallied for a 5–3 win as the 19-year-old Ward notched one of his 47 victories that season.

For his part, Bill White "played first base in fine style."[4] The *Providence Journal* wrote of his play at first base in the game, "White, first baseman of the University Nine, occupied that position for Providence, and it is needless to state that he was as expert and effective, as ever, catching some widely-thrown balls with great ease. He was apparently cool and collected throughout and will be a valuable substitute for the unfortunate [injured Joe] Start."[5] The *Providence Morning Star* commented on his offense and the support of his Brown University teammates, "The Varsity boys lustily cheered their favorite at times, and howled with delight when he got a safe hit in the ninth inning, as they also did his magnificent steals of second in that and the fifth inning."[6] He had a single in four at-bats and the two stolen bases, scored a run, and played errorless ball, recording 12 putouts.

The *Providence Journal* article, discussing the upcoming series with Boston, wrote that "White has been engaged to cover first in the series."[7] This did not come to pass and, for reasons undetermined except by speculation, William Edward White never again played in the major leagues.

He did continue to play for Brown through the fall 1880 season and subsequently left school without graduating.

Peter Morris has determined that White was indeed partially African American by identifying him, in federal census records, as the mulatto son of Andrew J. White, a white man, and Hannah White, his mulatto domestic servant.[8] Confirmation was found when Morris examined Andrew White's will of 1877 and found that William Edward White, Anna Nora White, and Sarah Adelaide White were "the children of my servant Hannah."[9] He stipulated that William and a sister "now at school in the North" be able to complete their education."[10]

Bill White, whose 1879 appearance for Providence made him the first black to play in a major league game, played on Brown University's 1879 championship baseball team. White is sitting directly behind the man in the suit holding the bat.

Other than census reports, no known contemporary record made after White moved north contains reference to his race. These records include those at Brown University and newspaper accounts of the Grays' game in which he played. In the 1880 Federal census he identified himself as a 19-year-old white student born in Georgia and living in Providence.

Research by W. Zachary Malinowski, a *Providence Journal* investigative reporter, has shown that White attended the Friends Boarding School in Providence before enrolling at Brown. Malinowski found an undated White record there that included a Chicago address for him. Morris did follow-up work and found White in Chicago in both the 1900 and 1910 federal censuses where, in each case, White again declared his race to be white.

By the retroactive application of genetic rules, William Edward White is the first known black man to play major-league baseball. Within his society, however, he was not. He played baseball and lived his life as a white man. If White, who was also of white blood, said he was white and he was not challenged, he was white in his time and circumstances.

	AB	R	H	TB	PO	A	E
Providence							
O'Rourke, rf	5	0	1	2	0	0	0
Hines, cf	5	0	1	2	2	0	0
McGeary, 2b	5	1	1	1	3	6	3
Wright, ss	4	1	0	0	2	6	2
York, lf	4	1	1	1	1	0	0
Brown, c	4	0	0	0	7	1	2
Hague, 3b	4	1	1	1	0	1	0
Ward, p	4	0	0	0	0	7	0
White, 1b	4	1	1	1	12	0	0
	39	**5**	**6**	**8**	**27**	**21**	**7**
Cleveland							
Phillips, 1b	5	1	1	1	9	0	3
Eden, rf	4	1	1	3	0	0	0
Glasscock, 2b	4	0	0	0	4	3	1
Gilligan, c	4	1	2	2	5	2	5
Carey, ss	4	0	1	1	1	4	0
Warner, lf	4	0	1	3	1	0	0
Allen, 3b	4	0	0	0	1	3	1
Mitchell, p	4	0	0	0	1	6	1
McCormick, cf	4	0	1	1	5	0	0
	37	**3**	**7**	**11**	**27**	**18**	**11**

Earned runs—Providence, 1; Cleveland, 1. Two-base hits—O'Rourke, Hines. Three-base hits—Eden, Warner. First base on balls—O'Rourke, Wright, York, Glasscock. First base on errors—Providence, 8; Cleveland, 4. Double plays—Wright, McGeary, and White; Carey, Glasscock, and Phillips. Passed balls—Brown, 2; Gilligan, 3. Wild pitch—Mitchell. Umpire, J.J. Egan, Boston. Time - 2:15

Notes:

1. Fatsis, Stefan. "Mystery of Baseball: Was William White Game's First Black?" *Wall Street Journal*, January 30, 2004, p. 1.

2. Richmond, J. Lee. "Beating Harvard and Yale in Seventy-nine," *Memories of Brown* (Brown Alumni Magazine Company: Providence Rhode Island, 1909), p. 364.

3. *New York Clipper*, June 28, 1879, p. 107.

4. Ibid.

5. Malinowski, W. Zachary. "Who was the first black man to play in the major leagues?" *Providence Journal*, February 15, 2004, p. A-1.

6 Ibid.

7 Ibid.

8 United States Federal Census. Year: 1870; Census Place: Pike, Georgia; Roll: M593_169; Page: 234A; Image: 474; Family History Library Film: 545668

9 Fatsis.

10 Ibid.

11 *New York Clipper*, June 28, 1879, p. 107.

Baseball Perfection

Cleveland Blues vs. Worcester Brown Stockings

Agricultural Fairgrounds, Worcester, Mass. June 12, 1880

By John R. Husman

"The most wonderful game on record."[1] That's how contemporary newspaper reports described the no-run, no-hit, no-man-reach-first-base 1–0 triumph by Worcester's Lee Richmond over Cleveland. Although the term itself wouldn't be created for more than a quarter-century, it was the first "perfect game" ever pitched.[2] Actually, the "perfect" label was applied to one aspect of the game: the Worcester fielding. "Richmond was most effectively supported, every position on the home nine being played to perfection," reported the next day's *Worcester Daily Spy*.[3]

The National League game was played on Saturday, June 12, 1880, at the Worcester (Massachusetts) Agricultural Fairgrounds, also known as Driving Park, and was the second game of a three-game series. The Ohio team came to town in third place, just a half-game behind the upstart Worcesters. Both teams were far behind runaway leader Chicago. In the first game of the series, on Thursday the 10th, Richmond and Worcester had shut out Cleveland, 5–0, the clubs swapping positions in the standings.

A 23-year-old left-hander in his first full season, Lee Richmond was a busy man both on and off the field that week. In fact, his activities prior to his perfect game made the outcome all the more unlikely. Besides being the Worcesters' front-line pitcher, he was wrapping up his college studies and was scheduled to graduate from Brown University in Providence, Rhode Island, 40 miles down the road from Worcester, on June 16. Richmond skipped Worcester's Friday exhibition game with Yale University, returning instead to Providence for Brown's graduation festivities. His classmate, Walter Angell, recorded Richmond's activities while in Providence in a scrapbook:

> I met them (Thursday night) at the depot … and rode out to the Messer St. ball grounds in a carriage. …We returned at midnight. Next day was Class Day. Richmond went to the Class Supper at Music Hall. He was up all night. He took part in the usual ball game about 4:50 Saturday morning; went to bed about 6:30; took the train for Worcester at 11:30. …[4]

On Saturday Richmond and Cleveland's Jim McCormick were matched in what became a classic duel. McCormick was outstanding, giving up three hits and one unearned run while striking out seven

Lee Richmond

and walking one. Richmond, batting second in the order, got the first hit, in the fourth but was erased on a double play. Shortstop Art Irwin led off the fifth with a single. Catcher Charlie Bennett followed with a walk. Then Art Whitney hit a comebacker to McCormick, who threw to second only to see second baseman Fred Dunlap drop the ball. Alertly, Irwin rounded third and kept right on running. Dunlap recovered but threw home wildly for his second error on the play, allowing Irwin to score. McCormick allowed only one more baserunner. Dunlap was an unlikely source for decisive defensive miscues; he was considered a fine fielder. "I used to think Dunlap was the greatest defensive second baseman in the world," Richmond later said of him.[5]

As good as McCormick was, Richmond was even better. Of the 27 batters Richmond faced, only two hit fair balls beyond the infield and one of these resulted in a gem-saving play. Leading off the fifth inning, Cleveland first baseman Bill Phillips slapped a Richmond left-handed delivery into right field for an apparent base hit. Lon Knight, the Worcester right fielder and team captain, fielded the sharply hit ball and fired to first in time to retire Phillips.

The game was delayed by rain for about five minutes with one out in the bottom of the eighth inning. Richmond then finished the game with the aid of sawdust that he used to dry the ball before every pitch.[6] Richmond struck out five in the one-hour, 26-minute game.

The 700 people in attendance also witnessed what might have been the first instance of platooning. Richmond, the game's first regular left-hander, had been in the league for only about six weeks. Cleveland had not yet seen him, but already the Clevelands knew that right-handed batters might have an edge against the left-handed heaver.[7] Because of this, the Cleveland team changed its batting order against Richmond. Immediately before and after the Worcester series, Cleveland's left-handed hitters, Orator Shafer, Pete Hotaling, and Ned Hanlon, were second, third and fourth in the lineup. For the June 10 game against Worcester, Shafer was dropped to fourth, Hanlon to seventh, and Hotaling to ninth.

For the games of June 12 and 14 Shafer dropped to the number five slot, Hanlon moved to the ninth position, and Hotaling was removed from the lineup. In addition, switch-hitting in order to face the pitcher from the opposite side was employed as a strategy in this game. The *Cleveland Leader* reported in its June 10 edition, "Hotaling in today's game will bat right-handed. ..."[8] Game accounts do not reveal whether Hotaling did turn around against Richmond. Nonetheless, the seed was planted for using the strategies of switch-hitting and platooning that are integral in today's game.

Cleveland won the series' final game, 7–1, on Monday, McCormick defeating Richmond. By season's end, the 23-year-old rookie had won 32 games and lost an equal number as his team finished in fifth place. But the notoriety of pitching professional baseball's first perfect game went with Richmond throughout his life. He remarked of it, "I can remember almost nothing except that my jump ball and my half stride ball were working splendidly and that Bennett and the boys behind me gave me perfect support."[9]

	AB	R	H	TB	PO	A	E
Worcester							
Wood, lf	4	0	0	0	0	0	0
Richmond, p	3	0	1	1	0	6	0
Knight, rf	3	0	0	0	1	1	0
Irwin, ss	3	1	2	2	2	3	0
Bennett, c	2	0	0	0	8	0	0
Whitney, 3b	3	0	0	0	1	2	0
Sullivan, 1b	3	0	0	0	14	0	0
Corey, cf	3	0	0	0	1	0	0
Creamer, 2b	3	0	0	0	0	4	0
	27	1	3	3	17	16	0
Cleveland							
Dunlap, 2b	3	0	0	0	4	2	2
Hankinson, 3b	3	0	0	0	0	0	0
Kennedy, c	3	0	0	0	9	1	0
Phillips, 1b	3	0	0	0	7	0	0
Shaffer, rf	3	0	0	0	2	0	0
McCormick, p	3	0	0	0	0	8	0
Gilligan, cf	3	0	0	0	1	0	0
Glasscock, ss	3	0	0	0	0	2	0
Hanlon, lf	3	0	0	0	1	0	0
	27	0	0	0	24	13	2

Cleveland 000 000 000 – 0
Worcester 000 010 00x – 1

Runs earned, 0; first base on errors, 0; first base on balls, Worcesters 1; left on bases, Worcesters 2; struck out, Richmond 2, Corey 2, Sullivan, Wood, Bennett, Shaffer, Hanlon, Dunlap, Phillips, Glass-

The pictured score sheet documents the details of professional baseball's first perfect game. It was retained by Lee Richmond until his death in 1929 and was one of two nearly identical such sheets passed on to the author following Mrs. Richmond's death in 1971. It is a copy made by George O. Ward, M. D., who was a resident of Worcester at the time of the game and thereafter and, presumably, the maker of the original.

cock; balls called, on Richmond 44, McCormick 79; strikes called, on Richmond 9, on McCormick 15; wild pitches 0; double plays, Glasscock, Dunlap, and Phillips. Time - 1:26; umpire, Bradley. Attendance: 700
Game delayed by rain in eighth inning

Notes:

1. *Sunday Herald* (unidentified clip in J. Lee Richmond file, National Baseball Library, Cooperstown, New York); *Cleveland Leader*, June 13, 1880.

2. Dickson, Paul. *The Dickson Baseball Dictionary* (New York: W.W. Norton Company, Inc., 2009,), p. 630.

3. *Worcester Daily Spy*, June 14, 1880.

4. Letter from Walter Angell to the Editor of the *Boston Post*, August 18, 1925, p. 2.

5. Mayer, Ronald A. *Perfect!* (Jefferson, North Carolina: McFarland & Company, Inc., 1991), p. 17.

6. *Worcester Daily Spy*, June 14, 1880.

7. "Richmond's Debut In Professional Baseball," *Brown Alumni Monthly*, 1910-1911; from the *New York Tribune*.

8. *Cleveland Leader*, June 10, 1880.

9. Spink, Alfred H. *The National Game* (St. Louis: National Game Publishing Co., 1910), p. 155.

Perfection Revisited

Buffalo at Providence

June 17, 1880

By John R. Husman

Two perfect games within a week defies all odds. But that is exactly what happened when John Montgomery Ward pitched professional baseball's second such game just five days after his antagonist, Lee Richmond, had thrown the first just 40 miles away. Ward's game came on June 17, 1880, and was not duplicated until Cy Young did it for Boston in an American League game in 1904. The next three were also pitched by American Leaguers (including Don Larsen's perfect game in the 1956 World Series). No National Leaguer matched it until Jim Bunning turned the trick in 1964.

Providence was destined to finish second in the 1880 National League race. The Grays played at a fine .619 clip, but finished 15 games behind Chicago, which had a sizzling .798 winning percentage. Buffalo, the victim of Ward's perfect effort, finished seventh, ahead of only Cincinnati and playing less than .300 baseball. The teams may have been a bit mismatched that day, but the pitchers were not. Ward and Buffalo's Pud Galvin were both destined for the Hall of Fame, the only such players on the field. Galvin was young, at 23, and already a proven winner, but just coming into his own as an established star. Ward, even younger at 20, had won 47 games for Providence in 1879 and was destined to notch 39 wins that season. Galvin was a good pitcher on a bad team while Ward was a good pitcher on a good team.

The starting time for the Thursday contest, played at Providence's Messer Street Park, was moved to 11 A.M. to avoid conflicting with boat races scheduled in Providence that afternoon. The ploy was successful, as a fine weekday crowd attended the game. *The New York Clipper* summarized Ward's effort:

A young John M. Ward. He was only 20 when he dazzled Buffalo in Providence in June of 1880.

Ward pitched so effectively that not one safe hit was made off him while the entire field backed him up with perfect play. The result of this united work was that not one of the Buffalos reached first base in the entire nine innings, thus equaling the extraordinary Worcester-Cleveland contest on June 12.

Of note is the usage of the descriptors "perfect play" and "united work." Though the term "perfect game" had not yet been coined, the observer and writer recognized that the then rare errorless play and teamwork made the unblemished game possible. A Providence newspaper commented on fine defensive play in support of Ward: "Hines playing in his position [center field] was remarkably fine, catching balls that looked good for two-base hits. Peters [shortstop] made some wonderful stops." The paper also commented on the hazard of being an unprotected catcher in 1880. "Rowe and Crowley changed positions in the middle of the fourth inning, on account of Rowe splitting his finger in trying to catch a foul tip." Rowe's treatment for his injury was to be sent to right field where he was, ostensibly, to heal. Providence prevailed, 5–0 (of course), and the game story was top and center on the front page of the *Providence Daily Journal* the next day:

... (E)ighteen hundred admirers of the national sport, who pronounced the fielding and batting exhibition of the champions excellent in every respect, [the Grays were the reigning National League pennant winners] as not one of the players of the visiting club were able to secure a safe hit off of Ward's delivery, and not even allowing in the whole nine innings a man to reach the first bag without being put out.

Certainly such a game cannot be pitched on demand but perhaps Ward's effort was especially intense as he had an opportunity to equal his rival's performance of five days earlier. Ward and Lee Richmond knew each other well. Richmond had pitched

James "Pud" Galvin was the hard-luck Buffalo pitcher who was bested by Ward.

for Brown University, located in Providence. He and his Brown team faced the Providence professionals numerous times in exhibition games. Richmond never beat Ward as an amateur, but the tables were turned when Richmond pitched for money. He beat Ward when he made his major-league debut in September of 1879 and twice more that fall while pitching for Worcester. The following spring, with Richmond again an amateur pitching for Brown, Ward prevailed in two meetings. But then, after Richmond turned professional for a final time, he beat Ward and Providence in four of six meetings before their perfect efforts.

In his book *Perfect!*, Ronald Mayer wrote that "there was little love lost between these two rival pitchers. ... Ward had a habit of hitting Richmond. Of course Richmond would retaliate whenever given the opportunity. And the bitter grudge lasted throughout their baseball careers." It is at least an oddity that these two frequent opponents would both accomplish, within days of each other, a pitching feat not even thought of previously.

7. As stated by baseball-reference.com/bullpen/John_Ward: "While later baseball histories call him Monte frequently, he was not known by that name when he played. This appears to be an error on the part of historians."

8. *Providence Daily Journal.*

	AB	R	H	TB	PO	A	E
Providence							
Paul Hines Cf	5	0	2	2	2	0	0
Joe Start 1b	5	1	1	3	14	0	0
Mike Dorgan Rf	5	0	2	2	0	0	0
Emil Gross C	5	0	0	0	5	1	0
Jack Farrell 2b	4	3	3	4	0	2	0
John Ward P	4	0	1	1	2	6	0
John Peters Ss	4	0	1	1	0	6	0
Tom York Lf	4	0	2	4	3	0	0
George Bradley 3b	4	1	1	3	1	4	0
Totals	**40**	**5**	**13**	**20**	**27**	**19**	**0**
Buffalo							
Bill Crowley rf,c	3	0	0	0	3	0	0
Hardy Richardson 3b	3	0	0	0	0	1	0
Jack Rowe c,rf	3	0	0	0	4	1	1
Oscar Walker Lf	3	0	0	0	3	0	1
Joe Hornung 2b	3	0	0	0	2	3	0
Denny Mack Ss	3	0	0	0	3	3	1
Dude Esterbrook 1b	3	0	0	0	10	0	0
Tom Poorman Cf	3	0	0	0	2	0	1
Pud Galvin P	3	0	0	0	0	5	0
Totals	**27**	**0**	**0**	**0**	**27**	**13**	**4**

Providence   010 100 111 – 5
Buffalo   000 000 000 – 0

Runs earned, Providence, 2; three-base hits, Start, York, Bradley; two-base hits, Farrell; first base on errors, Providence 1; left on bases, Providence 7; struck out, Hines, Gross, Crowley, Richardson, Rowe, Mack, Poorman, Galvin (2); passed balls, Crowley 1; wild pitch, Galvin 2; balls called, on Ward, 58; on Galvin 52; strikes called, off Ward 15; off Galvin 10. Time - 1:50. Umpire, Daniels.

Notes

1. According to baseball-reference.com, 201,156 regular-season major-league games have been played from 1871 through 2011. Using those numbers and the 19 perfect games pitched through 2011, a perfect game would occur on the average of once every 7.24 years or 10,587 games.

2. *New York Clipper*, June 28, 1879, p. 109.

3. Ibid.

4. Ibid.

5. Ibid.

6. Meyer, Ronald A. *Perfect!* (Jefferson, North Carolina: McFarland & Company, Inc., 1991), p. 23.

Night Baseball

R. H. White & Co. vs. Jordan Marsh & Co.

Sea Foam House, Nantasket Beach, Hull, Mass.
September 2, 1880

By Craig B. Waff

Today many major league baseball games are played under artificial illumination. In the first few decades of "base ball" playing, however, games were often curtailed due to darkness. The increasing number of electric lighting systems being installed in the late 1870s made experimentation with artificial illumination at ball games almost inevitable.

The first known such experiment occurred during the evening of Sept. 2, 1880, when two teams, mostly employees from the dry-goods firms R. H. White and Company and Jordan Marsh and Company, played a nine-inning game on the back lawn of the Sea Foam House, a hotel near Nantasket Beach in Hull, Mass.

At that time, the prevailing means of nighttime artificial illumination was gas. But various electrical lighting firms were created to challenge the monopoly of the gas companies. The Boston-based Northern Electric Light Company, perhaps desiring a venue where thousands of people might be able to view a sample of the potential of their lighting equipment, erected at the beach three wooden towers 500 feet apart in an equilateral triangle. Each was 100 feet high, and mounted upon each of these was a circular row of 12 electrical lights "of the Weston patent." Each light had an estimated 2,500 candle power; thus, the light of 90,000 candles was concentrated within a limited territory. The company used three "Weston machines," undoubtedly dynamos, to generate "a motive-power of 36 horses," that is 36 horsepower.[1]

The mention of "Weston" equipment is an indication that the lighting apparatus involved was not incandescent lamps (invented by Thomas Edison a year earlier in 1879 and in which a filament gives off light when heated to incandescence by an electric current), but rather the electric arc lamps (electrical lamps that produce light by an arc made when a current passes between two incandescent electrodes surrounded by gas) and electric dynamos developed by Edward Weston. In 1873 he established the Harris & Weston Electroplating Company in partnership with George G. Harris, and in the same year he developed his first dynamo (a machine used to convert mechanical energy into electrical energy) for electroplating. Two years later, Weston patented what he called the "rational construction of the dynamo," which enabled him, so he claimed, to increase its efficiency from 45 percent to more than 90 percent.

The New England Weston Electric Light Company was possibly a collaborator, perhaps with the idea that playing a base ball game under artificial illumination might bring added attention to its equipment. But it certainly had in mind a market much more extensive than just ball fields. The *Boston Herald* noted, "The design of the exhibition was to afford a model of the plan contemplated for lighting cities from overhead in vast areas, the estimate being that four towers to a square mile of area, each mounting lights aggregating 90,000 candle power, will suffice to flood the territory about with a light almost equal to mid-day."

Reporters at the game assessed that the amount of lighting was insufficient for good ball play. Although reporting that the lights, with one single slight flicker, "burned steadily and brilliantly all evening" between 8 and 9:30 P.M., the *Herald* observed that "on account of the uncertain light, (resembling that of the moon at its full,) the batting was weak and the pitchers were poorly supported." The historian Preston Orem summarized accounts in several Boston newspapers to conclude, "The light was quite imperfect and there were lots of errors made. The players had to bat and throw with caution. For the spectators the game had little interest as only the movements of the pitcher, in general, could be discerned, while the course of the ball eluded the vision of the watchers. ... None of the reporters believed the idea to be at all practical."[2]

The game ended in a 16–16 tie after nine innings, with further play precluded by the desire of the players to catch the last ferry boat back to Boston. What the electric companies involved officially concluded from the experiment is not known. But *The Boston Evening Transcript* concluded that "if the projectors of the experiment wish to convince the public that they can shed light enough over a city from elevated stands to allow people to sit in their houses and pursue their ordinary evening occupations without gas, candle or lamp light, more light still will be necessary."[3]

Arc-lamp outdoor lighting from a system of high towers, known as moonlight towers, did become briefly popular in the 1880s and 1890s in several cities in the United States and Europe. But the numbers of such towers decreased as incandescent electric street lighting became more common.[4]

The contemporary accounts of the Nantasket Beach night game make no mention of individual participating players, which may have been deliberate. In 1909, nearly 30 years after it was played, an anonymous correspondent, stating that he had been the "Official Scorer" of the game, wrote to the *New York Sun* newspaper and claimed that "at almost the last moment the two firms mentioned [for an unspecified reason] forbade their employees taking part, so it was played *sub rosa*." The ban by the companies, according to the correspondent, made it "inexpedient [for him] to mention any names of players, as some of them may still be employed in these establishments, although a number of players were recruited from the various jobbing houses in the dry-goods trade."

Northern Electric did reward the players and officials for their efforts with a fine post-game supper (probably in Boston), of which the Sun correspondent had "the most vivid remembrance."[5]

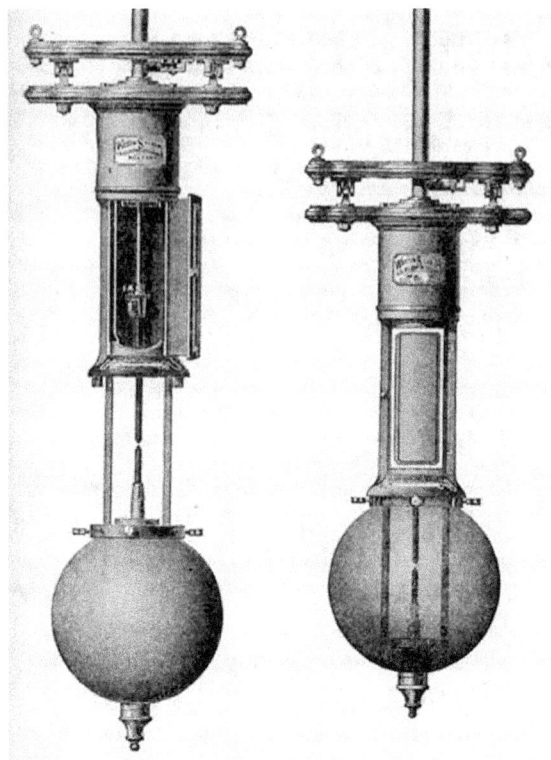

The Weston arc lamp, opened and closed.

U.S. patent drawing of the Weston arc lamp.

Notes:

1. "Electric Lights in a Cluster," *New York Times*, vol. 29, no. 9045, September 4, 1880, p. 3, col. 7, reprinted from the *Boston Herald*, September 3, 1880. The *Herald's* account was also reprinted in *The Annual Register: A Review of Public Events at Home and Abroad, for the Year 1880*, new series, vol. 122 (London: Rivingtons, 1881), p. 88.

2. Orem, Preston. *Baseball 1845-1881 From the Newspaper Accounts* (Altadena, Calif.: Self-published, 1961), p. 342.

3. The passage is quoted in the Appendix item "September 2, 1880: The Latest Yankee Notion" p. 176-177 in Troy Soos, *Before the Curse: The Glory Days of New England Baseball, 1858-1918*, rev. ed. (Jefferson, N.C., and London: McFarland & Company, 2006).

4 For a lengthy, illustrated account of these structures, see the Wikipedia article "Moonlight tower."

5 The passage from the letter to the *Sun* by "Official Scorer" was reprinted in William Shepard Walsh, *A Handy Book of Curious Information* (Philadelphia and London: J. B. Lippincott Company, 1913), p. 107.

George Gore's Theft Spree

Providence Grays vs. Chicago White Stockings

Lake Front Park, Chicago, Ill.
June 25, 1881

By Jerry Grillo

The Chicago White Stockings were the most powerful team in the early National League, winning six pennants in the circuit's first 11 seasons (1876, 1880–82, 1885–86).

They did it under the shrewd front-office guidance of Albert Spalding, and with a Stone Age version of Murderers' Row that included Hall of Famers Adrian "Cap" Anson and Mike "King" Kelly, and one of the 19th century's great sluggers, Abner Dalrymple. Dalrymple was considered so dangerous at the plate in his prime that he became the first player to be intentionally walked with the bases loaded.

Then there was center fielder George "Piano Legs" Gore, one of the era's most valuable players, who was on seven pennant winners, all in the 1880s. On June 25, 1881, he did something truly extraordinary, running into the record book as the first player to steal seven bases in a game. (Only Billy Hamilton, in 1894, has matched the feat.)

Gore was a complete ballplayer. He hit for average, sometimes for power (he was the second person to smack five extra-base hits in a game), he could field, and he could throw.

He could also run really, really well.

Gore finished his 14-year career with more runs (1,327) than games played (1,310), reflecting the sturdy legwork of a player who earned his nickname because of superhero-shaped calf muscles.

In 1880 Gore led the National League in batting (.360). His average took a nosedive in 1881 (he finished at .298), but he was an artist at getting on and around the bases, and that Saturday game in June, a 12–8 win over the visiting Providence Grays, was probably his masterpiece.

According to the *Chicago Daily Tribune*, about 2,000 fans saw an offensive outbreak that "was full of action and at all times interesting. ... Chicago won by virtue of superiority in every point of play, but notably so in base-running. Gore's performances in this respect were something phenomenal."[1]

Gore reached base five times in five plate appearances, had three solid singles and a walk, scored five runs, and generally made life really stressful for the Providence battery, pitcher Bobby Mathews and catcher Emil Gross. Gore stole second base five times—or every time he reached base—and stole third twice.

At the time, stolen bases were not part of the official statistical records in the National League, but the *Tribune* nonetheless noted that Gore had set "a record which as a whole has probably never been equaled in a League game."[2]

The game itself wasn't a thing of beauty: "The contest was characterized by numerous errors in fielding," the *Tribune* reported. The teams combined to make 14 errors (10 by the Providence club). There were three passed balls (all by Gross), and only one of Chicago's dozen runs was earned.[3]

At the time the White Stockings were in the midst of their longest winning streak of the season (eight games) and hottest stretch (they went 18–3 from June 4 though July 13). Gore's record-setting performance came in the second of a three-game set at home against Providence, during which Chicago outscored the Grays 39–20.

As the two teams took the field for Saturday's game, Chicago was in first place with a three-game lead over the second-place Buffalo Bisons, and Providence was in last place, one win behind Cleveland.

Chicago took a 3–0 lead in the first. Batting second, the left-handed-swinging Gore reached on either an error or a fielder's choice, stole second, and scored on Anson's double. He had base hits in the second, fourth, and sixth innings—subsequently stealing bases and scoring each time. Those helped Chicago build a 10–4 lead through six innings.

Gore walked in the eighth and scored on Ned Williamson's two-run triple to give Chicago a 12–4 lead. Providence scored its last four runs in the top of the ninth on four hits and a wild pitch.

National League rules banned Sunday baseball at the time, so the two teams finished their three-game set on Monday, a 19–12 Chicago victory.

After the series the Grays turned their fortunes around, posting the best record in the league for the stretch run (35–17–1). That included a change in field managers, with outfielder Tom York replacing second baseman Jack Farrell. It was Charles "Old Hoss" Radbourn's rookie season, and he led Providence with a 25–11 record.

Chicago went 33–18 after the Providence series to finish 56–28, winning the pennant by nine games over the second-place Grays. It was a familiar pattern—Chicago won three straight pennants, 1880–82, and Providence finished second each time.

And Gore? He kept on running wild, and not just on the basepaths. Anson considered Gore one of the best players of the era, and even included him on his list of all-time greats, but claimed, "Women and wine brought about his downfall." Gore was suspended from the 1885 World Series for drunkenness, and a year later Chicago sold him to the New York Giants because of all the drinking and cavorting. He helped New York win two pennants.

In his 14 major-league seasons, Gore led the league in runs scored in 1881 (86) and 1882 (99), then scored 100 or more runs a season for seven of the next nine years and is one of the most prolific run scorers of all time (1.02 runs per game). He batted .306 for his career with a .386 on-base percentage, and led the league in walks three times in an era when pitchers stood only 45 (then 55½) feet away.

Ironically, Gore never "led" the league in stolen bases—the National League didn't start keeping official records on the statistic until 1886. He stole 23 bases that year, a career-high 39 the next, and is credited with 170 stolen bases for his career. But Gore always will be remembered for the day he swiped seven in one game.

The 1881 National League-champion Chicago White Stockings: 1 - Cap Anson, 2 - Silver Flint, 3 - Ned Williamson, 4 - Joe Quest, 5 - Fred Goldsmith, 6 - Mike Kelly, 7 - Abner Dalrymple, 8 - Larry Corcoran, 9 - George Gore, 10 - Tom Burns, 11 - Andy Piercy, 12 - Hugh Nicol.

Chicago	AB	R	H	E	Providence	AB	R	H	E
Dalrymple, LF	5	3	1	0	Hines, 2B	5	1	3	2
Gore, CF	4	5	3	1	Start, 1B	5	1	1	0
Kelly, RF	5	1	2	0	Farrell, CF	5	1	1	3
Anson, 1B	4	2	2	0	York, LF	5	1	1	0
Williamson, 3B	4	1	2	0	Ward, RF	5	1	1	1
Burns, SS	5	0	1	0	McClellan, SS	4	2	1	1
Goldsmith, P	4	0	1	1	Gross, C	4	0	2	1
Flint, C	4	0	2	2	Mathews, P	4	0	0	0
Quest, 2B	4	0	1	0	Denny, 3B	4	1	3	2
	39	12	15	4		41	8	13	10

Providence	000	202	004 –	8
Chicago	320	302	02x –	12

Earned runs: Chicago, 1; Providence, 4; Two-base hits: Anson, Flint, Hines, Start, McClellan; Three-base hit: Williamson; Base on balls: Gore, Anson, Williamson; First base on errors: Chicago, 6; Providence, 5; Left on base: Chicago, 5; Providence, 1; Struck out: Start, Farrell, Mathews, Ward, Dalrymple; Passed balls: Gross, 3; Wild pitches: Mathews, 1; Goldsmith, 1; Time - 2:15; Umpire: Foghorn Bradley

---

Notes:

1. *Chicago Daily Tribune,* June 26, 1881.

2. Ibid.

3. Ibid.

Mullane vs. Reccius for 18 Innings

Akrons vs. Eclipse of Louisville

Central Park, Louisville, Ky.
June 26, 1881

By Richard McBane

For sheer head-to-head doggedness, few pitching matchups in baseball history can match the exhibition contest waged between Akron's Tony Mullane and The Eclipse of Louisville's John Reccius on a Sunday in June of 1881.

The independent professional baseball club of Akron, Ohio, had its start in 1879 when it chalked up a 17–3 record, with two of the losses coming late in the season to Cleveland's National League entry. The Akrons posted a 19–12–1 record against substantially stronger competition in 1880, including a 1–9 record against National League opponents. The single victory was a solid 4–3 victory in September over Cap Anson's Chicagos, the League champions.[1]

Heading into the 1881 season, the reputation of the Akrons was such that the National League arranged its schedule so as to give every club open dates in Cleveland to be filled with exhibition games against the Akrons. In fact, the *Cleveland Leader* newspaper called them "... the strongest non-league club in the country."[2]

But when the team departed for Louisville in late June to play four games with the Eclipse, its prospects looked bleak. The strength of the team made it difficult to find local opponents, and it had fared badly against the National League teams, dropping all five of those games. It took to the road with only six wins and six losses. It would be "reorganized," or, perhaps, disbanded on its return.[3]

The Eclipse, which would join the American Association in 1882, was a solid, experienced semi-pro club led by Louis Rogers "Pete" Browning and Fred Pfeffer, both destined for productive major-league careers. Browning, then just 20 years old, was still three years short of acquiring the original Louisville Slugger bat. He went on to win two American Association batting titles and a third in the Players League. Pfeffer, a Louisville native, played 16 major-league seasons as a sure-handed second baseman, mostly in an era when fielders were still gloveless.[4]

In all, seven members of the 1881 Eclipse club eventually played in the majors. At the same time, of the 19 players who played all or part of 1881 season with the Akrons, 14 played in either the American Association or the National League in 1882. Chief among these were Bid McPhee and Tony Mullane. McPhee, a second-base counterpart to Pfeffer, spent his entire 18-year major-league career with Cincinnati, during which he led his league in double plays in 11 seasons and in fielding average in eight seasons. Mullane was both talented and strong-willed, and his ego frequently led him into conflicts with management. Nevertheless, in 13 major-league seasons he racked up 284 victories, including five 30-win seasons in his first five full seasons in the American Association.[5]

All of that was in the future when the Akrons arrived in Louisville for their four-game engagement beginning on Tuesday, June 21. The Eclipse was undefeated at the time, and the fact that the Akrons triumphed 9–1 before a crowd of about 800 at Eclipse Park served as a wake-up call. The following day, with Louisville hosting the Midsummer Encampment of Masonic

Louisville's John Reccius.

Lodges, the game was held at Central Park before a crowd estimated at 7,000. Jimmy Green was the starting pitcher for the Akrons and, as the *Louisville Courier-Journal* reported, "... the home boys got on to Green, and they just batted him all over the field." The Eclipse chalked up an 11–6 victory.[6]

After two days of rest, the Akrons returned the favor in a Saturday game with a 10–6 victory in which the Eclipse was charged with 13 errors. That set the stage for the Sunday game.

Mullane pitched for the Akrons on Sunday and the Eclipse countered with John Reccius. Batting first, the Eclipse took the lead in the second inning when Fred Pfeffer tripled and scored, the game's only run until the bottom of the seventh inning. Then Daniel "Link" Sullivan, Akron's center fielder, singled and scored on two Eclipse errors. The Eclipse took the lead again in the top of the eighth on a run-scoring double by Pete Browning, only to have the Akrons tie it again in the bottom of the inning on errors.

The Eclipse, in fact, was charged with 10 errors for the game, but neither team could score again, although the Akrons came close in the bottom of the 18th inning. Ed Swartwood attempted to score from second on a hard hit by Mullane, but was thrown out at home on what the game report in the *New York Clipper* called "a wonderful throw by Pfeffer from left field." Since Pfeffer played second and the only Louisville outfielder credited with an assist was center fielder Ike Van Burkalow, it is more likely that Pfeffer's "wonderful throw" was a relay of a throw from Burkalow.[7]

The 19th inning was scoreless and the game was then called due to darkness. Mullane and Reccius had each gone the distance. But neither team was content with a tie, so the Akrons remained in Louisville an extra day and a fifth game was played at Eclipse Park on Monday. Mullane and Reccius each started again, but the *Courier-Journal* termed the result "a general disappointment" following Sunday's showing. Reccius was pounded for five runs in the first inning, and the

Akron's Tony Mullane: 19 innings, one run, no decision.

Akrons headed home with a 14–5 victory, as well as three wins, a loss, and the 19-inning tie from their visit to Louisville. It was enough to save the team that was, indeed, "re-organized" when it reached Akron.[8]

Eclipse	T	R	1B	PO	A	E	Akron	T	R	1B	PO	A	E
Sommers, 3b	8	1	2	4	4	0	Sullivan, cf	8	1	3	1	0	1
Burkalow, cf	8	0	2	2	1	0	Swartwood, rf	8	0	2	7	0	0
Browning, ss	8	0	1	0	3	0	Wise, 3b	8	0	3	3	6	0
Reccius, p	8	0	0	1	15	1	Morton, ss	8	0	1	3	6	0
Pfeffer, 2b	8	1	2	6	12	3	Mullane, p	8	1	2	1	16	0
Crotty, c	8	0	1	17	1	2	Maskrey, lf	8	0	2	1	0	0
Zimmerman, rf	7	0	2	4	0	0	McPhee, 2b	8	0	1	5	5	1
McLaughlin, 1b	7	0	2	19	0	4	Green, 1b	8	0	1	24	0	1
Dyler, lf	7	0	0	4	0	0	Kemmler, c	8	0	1	12	3	2
	69	2	12	57	36	10		72	2	16	57	36	5

Louisville 010 000 000 000 000 000 – 1
Akron   000 000 100 000 000 000 – 1
Earned runs - Eclipse, 2. First base on errors - Eclipse 2; Akron, 4. Passed balls - Crotty 4; Kemmler, 1; Struck out - Eclipse 11; Akron 13; Double-plays - Sommers, Pfeffer and McLaughlin; Crotty, Sommers, Pfeffer and McLaughlin; and Reccius, Pfeffer and McLaughlin; Kemmler, McPhee and Green. Two-base hits - Browning, 1, Pfeffer, 1; Swartwood, 1, Wise, 1. Three-base hits - Pfeffer and Wise. Umpire, Thos. Irwin of Cincinnati Ravens. Time - 3:05.

Notes:

1. *Summit County Beacon*, October 29, 1879; Peterjohn, Alvin K., "Baseball in Akron, Ohio, 1879-1881, A Case Study," undated paper in the Akron file at the National Baseball Hall of Fame Library; *New York Clipper*, September 18, 1880, p. 205; *Akron Sunday Gazette*, September 12, 1880.

2. *Summit County Beacon*, Sept. 29, 1880; Peterjohn, op.cit.; Grismer, Karl. *Akron and Summit County* (Akron, Ohio: Summit County Historical Society, undated), p. 229; *Cleveland Leader*, April 27, 1881, July 23, 1881.

3. *Worcester Evening Gazette*, May 14, 1881; *New York Clipper*, May 21, 1881, p. 138; *Cleveland Leader*, May 14, 16, 17, 24, 25, 27, 28, 1881; *Akron City Times*, May 25, June 22, 1881; *Summit County Beacon*, June 22, 1881.

4. Tiemann, Robert L. and Rucker, Mark, eds. *Nineteenth Century Stars* (Society for American Baseball Research, 1989), pp. 19, 102.

5. Ibid., pp. 91, 97.

6. *New York Clipper*, July 2, 1881, p. 233; *Summit County Beacon*, June 29, 1881; *Louisville Courier-Journal*, June 22, and 23, 1881.

7. *New York Clipper*, July 9, 1881, p. 252.

8. *New York Clipper*, July 9, 1881, p. 252; *Louisville Courier-Journal*, June 28, 1881; *Summit County Beacon*, June 29, 1881.

Roger Connor's Grand Slam

Troy Trojans vs. Worcester Brown Stockings

*Riverside Park, Albany, N.Y.
September 10, 1881*

By John R. Husman

Nearly half a century before baseball borrowed the expression "grand slam" from contract bridge,[1] and more than a century before someone first referred to a "walk-off" home run,[2] Roger Connor accomplished both with a single swing of his bat.

Troy, New York, and Worcester, Massachusetts, were at the time members of the National League, the former for four seasons, 1879–82, and the latter from 1880–82. Neither was a serious contender but both were competitive. Both had their best finishes in 1880, with Troy finishing fourth, a game ahead of Worcester. Troy would finish fifth in 1881 just two games out of the first division, while the Worcesters finished last in the eight-team circuit. Worcester's demise was due for the most part to manager Frank Bancroft's departure for Detroit accompanied by key players Art Whitney, Charlie Bennett, Lon Knight, and George Wood.

The two teams met for the 12th and final time of the 1881 season on September 10 in a game that meant little for either. By virtue of sweeping the first five games of the year, Worcester led in the season series eight games to three. Rather than being played at Troy as scheduled, the contest was staged in nearby Albany, perhaps due to the paltry attendance of 200 for the previous day's game, which was played in Troy.

Until the day's final swing, the game itself was unremarkable. The Worcesters held a 7–3 lead going to the bottom of the ninth. The *New York Clipper* described what the Troy lineup then did against left-hander Lee Richmond: "The Troys went to the bat in the last half of the ninth inning, wanting four runs in order to tie their opponents' score. [Mickey] Welch, [Buck] Ewing and [Frank] Hankinson filled the bases on safe hits, [Jake] Evans was retired, [Tim] Keefe was given his base on balls, sending in Welch. [John] Cassidy was the second man out, and then Connor cleared the bases and made a clean home run, thus winning …"[4] The *Worcester Daily Spy* described Connor's hit as "a terrific drive to right."[5] Connor's two-out blow gave his team a stunning 8–7 win.

The account of the game from the *Troy Daily Times* is not complimentary of the day's play and curiously describes Connor's hit only in closing:

Troy's Last Game with Worcester Won By a "Scratch."
The Albany Argus says that the 100 persons who attended Saturday's Troy-Worcester game at Riverside [P]ark saw the most

Roger Connor: The author of the first recorded grand slam home run.

"barbarous base ball" and "funny fumbling" ever seen on the diamond. The errors of the Troys, it says, were more numerous than their hits, and the play was only notable for its lack of life. The [R]uby [L]egs scored five runs in the sixth chiefly on errors, and the Trojans in the last innings made five runs by the "funny fumbling" of Carpenter, the poor pitching of Richmond and the accidental hit of the Megatherian Connor.

There would not be another walk-off grand slam in a three-run game until Babe Ruth duplicated the feat on September 24, 1925.[6]

That Connor would be the first to have such a memorable power-hitting feat seems fitting. He was a robust, 6-foot-3-inch left-handed hitter. And though this home run, only his fifth, came in just his second season in the major leagues, he went on to hit many more. His lifetime total of 138 stood as the career best until it was topped by Babe Ruth in 1921. Though Connor led his league in home runs in only one season, he hit 10 or more seven times for another 19th-century record, and once hit three home runs in a game.[7]

Connor's solid career landed him in the Hall of Fame. Three other members of the 1881 Troys, all also in their second major-league season, have also been enshrined: Mickey Welch, Buck Ewing, and Tim Keefe.

The major leagues' second grand slam was hit just 19 days later. Harry Stovey of the same Worcester club connected on the season's next-to-last day, September 29, against pennant-winning Chicago. Oddly, the pitcher of the first grand-slam ball, Lee Richmond, was on the bases for Worcester at the time.[8]

	AB	R	H	TB	PO	A	E
Worcester							
Dickerson, lf	5	1	2	2	4	1	0
Stovey, 1b	5	0	0	0	5	0	1
Richmond, p	5	0	1	1	0	4	0
Nelson, ss	5	1	1	1	1	6	0
Hotaling, cf	5	2	1	1	2	1	0
Corey, rf	5	1	2	3	1	0	1
Carpenter, 3b	5	1	2	2	1	0	1
Creamer, 2b	5	0	0	0	3	2	0
Bushong, c	4	1	2	2	9	2	1
	44	7	11	12	26	16	4
Troy							
Cassidy, ss	5	2	2	5	1	5	1
Connor, 1b	5	2	2	5	5	0	4
Ferguson, 2b	4	0	0	0	4	1	3
Gillespie, lf	4	0	0	0	2	0	0
Welch, cf	4	1	1	1	1	6	0
Ewing, c	4	1	3	5	7	2	1
Evans, rf	4	0	0	0	2	0	0
Hankinson, 3b	4	1	3	3	3	2	1
Keefe, p	4	1	0	0	2	0	1
	38	8	11	19	27	16	11

Worcester 010 005 001 – 7
Troy 200 010 005 – 8
Earned runs—Troy 5; Worcester 2. Two-base hits—Cassidy, Ewing (2), Corey. Three-base hit—Cassidy. Home run—Connor. Bases on balls—Troy, 2. Bases on errors—Troy 3; Worcester, 8. Struck out—Troy 4; Worcester 4. Left on bases—Troy 4; Worcester 10. Double plays—Cassidy and Connor, Dickerson and Bushong, Nelson, Creamer, and Stovey. Passed balls—Ewing 1. Balls called—Richmond 80; Keefe, 80 Strikes called—Richmond 25; Keefe 35. Umpire, Mr. Higham. Time - 2:25.[9]

Notes:

1. Dickson, Paul. *The Dickson Baseball Dictionary*. (New York: W.W. Norton Company, Inc., 2009), p. 381, dating the term's baseball application to 1929.

2. Dickson, op. cit., p. 909, dating the term to 1988.

3. *Worcester Daily Spy*, September 10, 1881.

4. *New York Clipper*, September 17, 1881, p. 413.

5. *Worcester Daily Spy*, September 12, 1881.

6. "Collecting Home Runs-Ultimate Grand Slams," *Baseball Quarterly Reviews* (Schenectady, New York, 1991)

7. www.baseballhall.org/hof/connor-roger.

8. Bob McConnell, letter to John R. Husman referencing the Tattersall Home Run Log, December 10, 1984.

9. *New York Clipper*, September 17, 1881, p. 413.

The Beer and Whiskey League: Day One

May 2, 1882

By John W. Bauer

The inaugural American Association season opened on May 2, 1882, with teams in six cities: Baltimore, Cincinnati, Louisville, Philadelphia, Pittsburgh, and St. Louis. Events leading to the Association's opening day can be traced to the National League's expulsion of its Cincinnati franchise after the 1880 season. Among the reasons for throwing out the Red Stockings were that the club permitted use of its grounds for semi-pro games on Sundays, charged less than 50 cents admission, and sold alcoholic beverages inside the park. During the winter of 1881–82, the Cincinnati club joined with teams in five other cities to form the American Association.

Allegheny at Cincinnati

About 1,500 people gathered at Cincinnati's Bank Street Grounds for an offensive display that was not decided until Bill Tierney flied out to Allegheny center fielder Charlie Morton with two on and two out in the ninth inning to close out Allegheny's 10–9 victory. The defeat provided a bittersweet homecoming for Red Stockings pitcher Will White, who had been a pitching mainstay of Cincinnati's National League team.

Cincinnati opened the scoring with two runs in the bottom of the first inning. Joe Sommer walked and, after Bid McPhee flied out, Hick Carpenter reached first on an error by Allegheny second baseman George Strief. Catcher-manager Pop Snyder and Dan Stearns hit to left field in successive plate appearances to score Sommer and Carpenter.

In the top of the third Allegheny reversed Cincinnati's advantage with four runs of its own. Billy Taylor's two-run triple started the Alleghenies' comeback. Fielding errors by the Red Stockings al-

Allegheny's Charlie Morton (top) and Jim Keenan (bottom) combined for seven hits in the opener in Cincinnati.

lowed Taylor and Jack Leary to score. But in the bottom of the inning McPhee reached base on a muff and Carpenter and Snyder singled to load the bases. Stearns's double tied the game, then Snyder scored when Allegheny catcher Jim Keenan dropped the ball at home on Tierney's hit. Chick Fulmer reached first when Stearns was out at home, but singles by Jimmy Macullar and White scored Tierney and Fulmer before Sommer's double-play ball ended the inning with Cincinnati ahead 7–4.

Allegheny tied the score in the fifth inning, aided by Morton and Keenan, who would combine for seven of the Alleghenies' 15 hits. The Alleghenies went ahead in the sixth when three Cincinnati errors allowed Taylor to reach base and subsequently score for an 8–7 advantage. The final of those three errors allowed Goodman to reach base, and Morton's hit two batters later scored him for a 9–7 lead. Allegheny added the 10th and winning run in the seventh inning when three straight hits scored Ed Swartwood. In the bottom of the inning, Cincinnati closed the gap to one run when a wild pitch and passed ball contributed to Carpenter's scoring his third run of the day. Trailing by two heading into the ninth, Cincinnati drew within one run when Snyder's one-out hit scored Sommer. Stearns's fly ball moved Carpenter and Snyder into scoring position before Tierney's fly ball to Morton ended the game. Despite just arriving from Boston and showing "promise of good work to come," first baseman Tierney was released that evening.

While the Red Stockings opened the season with a loss, they ultimately proved the strongest club over the course of the 80-game season. Cincinnati assumed first place on June 13, never to relinquish the lead en route to winning the inaugural American Association pennant by 11½ games.

Baltimore at Athletic

The Athletics had fielded a semipro team in 1881, providing continuity in the club's transition to the American Association. Drawing heavily on players with Philadelphia connections, Baltimore hastily assembled its side when the club became a replacement for Brooklyn in March 1882.

Played before 2,500 spectators at Oakdale Park, the game proved a back-and-forth affair. The Athletics opened with a run in the first inning. After Baltimore responded with two in the top of the second, the Athletics tied the score in the bottom half. They moved ahead 3–2 after four, but Baltimore regained the lead with a three-run fifth inning. Baltimore's lead held until three seventh-inning runs allowed the Athletics to take a 6–5 lead.

Baltimore responded with two runs in the top of the eighth from John Shetzline and Charlie Householder. Baltimore's turn at the plate also provided dramatic moments as Athletic catcher Jack O'Brien was knocked unconscious on a foul tip by his Baltimore counterpart, Ed Whiting. To his credit, O'Brien caught the ball before collapsing and resumed play after a delay for treatment. In the bottom of the eighth, the Athletics closed out the scoring with four runs for the final 10-7 tally. While Baltimore threatened in the ninth with two baserunners, the game ended on Whiting's strikeout. Of the 18 players to appear in the game, all but Stricker managed to get at least one hit.

The Athletics also won the next day, pacing themselves to a second-place finish over the course of a season in which they never fell below .500. Baltimore lost eight of its first nine, and was an almost wire-to-wire last-place club.

Eclipse at St. Louis

Behind pitcher Jumbo McGinnis, the Browns opened with a 9–7 win over the Louisville Eclipse at Sportsman's Park.

While striking out seven Eclipse batters in gaining the win, McGinnis also threw six wild pitches. Some responsibility for his wildness was placed on catcher Sleeper Sullivan. McGinnis helped his cause with two hits. Charlie Comiskey, Oscar Walker, and Jack Gleason each contributed two hits and two runs to the Browns' offense, while Walker received mention for three hard-running catches in center field. Gleason, at third base, and rookie Bill Gleason, at shortstop, became the first brother tandem to play

Cincinnati's 1882 American Association champions. Back: Harry McCormick, Phil Powers, Dan Stearns, Bid McPhee. Middle: Hick Carpenter, Pop Snyder, Will White, Chick Fulmer, Joe Sommer. Front: Jimmy Macullar, Harry Wheeler.

in the same infield in the major leagues.

The Eclipse were hamstrung by an inability to string together consecutive hits until the ninth inning. Guy Hecker (4-for-5) and Dan Sullivan (2-for-5 with 3 runs) provided what existed of an Eclipse offensive punch. Third baseman and eventual batting champion Pete Browning suffered through a 0-for-4 afternoon while committing half of the Eclipse's eight errors.

St. Louis also won the next two games between the clubs, allowing the Browns to open the season with a sweep. Over the course of the year, the Eclipse recovered to take nine of the 16 games between the clubs in staking itself to a third-place finish, while the Browns finished fifth.

Sources:

Websites:

www.baseball-reference.com, www.retrosheet.org

Newspapers:

Cincinnati Commercial Tribune, Cincinnati Daily Gazette, Daily Inter Ocean (Chicago), *Philadelphia Inquirer.*

Books:

Nemec, David. *The Beer & Whiskey League* (Guilford, Connecticut: The Lyons Press, 2004).

Nemec, David. *The Great Encyclopedia of Nineteenth Century Major League Baseball* (Tuscaloosa, Alabama: University of Alabama Press, 2006).

Thorn, John. *Baseball in the Garden of Eden: The Secret History of the Early Game* (New York: Simon & Schuster, 2011).

Mullane Goes Both Ways

Louisville Eclipse vs. Lord Baltimores

Newington Park, Baltimore, Md.
July 18, 1882

By Jerry Grillo

You have to wonder what kind of mind-altering substance could have inspired the *Baltimore Sun* to claim that its city's ballclub was "now the equal of some of the best nines" in the American Association.

Seriously? The Baltimores had just lost three straight, had gone 0-for-June, and were planted in the league basement with a 6–30 record as the Eclipse team of Louisville pulled into town for a four-game mid-July series in 1882.

When the Baltimores built a 7–1 lead after three innings of the July 18 series opener, the *Sun*'s hubris did not seem so misplaced. For the fans at Newington Park that Tuesday afternoon, this was a rare sight. But in a few moments they would witness something stranger than a Baltimore lead.

The Eclipse's dashing young pitcher, Tony Mullane, playing his first full major-league season (and en route to the first of five consecutive 30-victory seasons) wasn't used to being bullied this way, certainly not against the likes of the lowly Baltimores.

The right-hander was getting frustrated so he did something no one had ever seen in a big-league game before. He switched pitching hands.

"Mullane, of the Eclipse club, changed hands in the fourth inning and pitched with his left," the Sun reported, retiring the Baltimores, "in good style." Mullane had just become the first ambidextrous pitcher in major-league baseball history.

The 23-year-old Irish-born Mullane was really just beginning an incomparable career as one of the 19th century's dominant pitchers and great characters, a handsome, free-spirited rogue and one of the game's most versatile athletes.

A strong-armed pitcher who completed 468 of the 504 games he started, Mullane had injured his right arm in a distance-throwing contest a few years earlier, so he'd taught himself to throw left-handed. That's why on July 18, 1882, he was capable of giving his self-made sinistrality a test run against a Baltimore team that ranked among the weaker ones in the American Association.

The weakling Baltimores were halfway through a season that would end with a miserable 19–54 record and a team batting average of .207. Oddly, they were actually pretty good in close games, finishing 8–5 in one-run contests. They had a solid rookie outfielder, Tom Brown, who would bat .304 in '82.

The Eclipse was 20–18 coming into the game en route to a third-place finish (42–38–1) in the six-team league. The Eclipse had a superstar rookie outfielder, Pete Browning, who would lead the American Association with a .378 batting average that year (the first of three batting titles for the original "Louisville Slugger"). And they had a soon-to-be-30-game winner in Mullane.

But the Louisville-based team had lost four straight before arriving in Baltimore and seemed ready to roll over again as the home team took a 3–0 lead in the first, highlighted by Brown's two-run triple. They made it 7–0 after two, with Charlie Householder, Doc Landis, Henry Myers, and Charlie Waitt crossing the plate.

Mullane's ambidextrous turn in the fourth may have lit a little fire for the Eclipse, who scored four runs in the fifth, "by heavy batting, aided by wild throwing," the *Sun* reported. And Mullane mostly kept Baltimore off balance, switching back and forth, throwing right-handed to left-handed hitters and lefty to righties.

The Eclipse knotted the score, 8–8, in the eighth on a home run by Guy Hecker.

But in the bottom of the ninth, the Baltimore crowd saw something that was almost as rare as an ambidextrous pitching performance—a home run by first baseman Householder, his only one of the season (he hit four in his career). It was "a tremendous hit over centre-field, nearly to the fence," according to the *Sun*. "He was surrounded by the crowd and received an ovation."

Less than two months later, on September 11, Mullane pitched a no-hitter against the Cincinnati Red Stockings, the first of its kind in the American Association.

But he is still remembered most for switching hands in a game he lost. He was not the last to pitch with both hands, nor was that game in Baltimore the last time he tried. He did it twice more: On July 5, 1892, and again on July 14, 1893, throwing left-handed in the final inning of a 10–2 loss to the Chicago Colts.

He wasn't even the last Louisville pitcher to do it. On May 9, 1888, Elton "Icebox" Chamberlain, a right-hander, threw shutout ball with his left hand over the final two innings of an 18–6 win over the Kansas City Cowboys. (Chamberlain would pitch ambidextrously one more time, for Philadelphia's American Association team in 1891.) Two years after Mullane did it, on June 16, 1884, right-handed Larry Corcoran, pitching for the Chicago White Stockings, became the first ambidextrous hurler in the National League, alternating arms in a 20–9 loss to the Buffalo Bisons.

Only one other player in major-league history is known to have tried since then. On September 28, 1995, Greg Harris, a natural right-hander, pitched lefty to two batters in a 9–7 loss to the Cincinnati Reds. (There are disputed reports that George Wheeler pitched ambidextrously for Philadelphia in the late 1890s.)

But Mullane had set the standard. He wound up with 284 victories in his 13-year career, second all-time in wins among pitchers not in the Baseball Hall of Fame.

Mullane won fame and earned infamy away from the playing field, challenging the reserve clause,

The 1882 Louisville Eclipse: 1 - Leech Maskrey, 2 - Pete Browning, 3 - Tony Mullane, 4 - unidentified, 5 - unidentified, 6 - Dan Sullivan, 7 - Denny Mack, 8 - Guy Hecker, 9 - John Reccius, 10 - Chicken Wolf.

jumping from team to team (he played for eight different clubs), and earning a suspension in the prime of his career (1885), which almost certainly cost him the victories he needed to reach 300. (He also sat out part of another season to protest a pay cut.)

Nicknamed the Count and the Apollo of the Box, Mullane was considered so handsome that teams would schedule Ladies Day when he was pitching. In other ways, however, Mullane was a less attractive figure. In 1884 he pitched for the Toledo Blue Stockings, where his catcher was the African American Moses Fleetwood Walker. Mullane called Walker the best catcher he ever worked with, but also said he disliked blacks and refused to take signals from Walker. So Mullane threw whatever he wanted, without warning, crossing up (and occasionally injuring) Walker and hurting the team in the process.

Mullane played every position except catcher at one time or another. He was also a fine ice skater and boxer, known for putting his pugilistic skills to the test on a ballfield.

There is no record of whether his right cross was better than his left hook, however.

	AB	R	H	PO	A	E
Eclipse						
Browning, 3b	5	2	3	5	3	1
Hecker, 1b	5	2	2	13	0	0
Sullivan, 3b	5	0	0	0	2	2
Wolf, rf	5	0	1	1	0	1
Mullane, p	5	2	2	0	7	0
Maskrey, lf	5	1	2	0	0	0
Reccius, cf	4	1	1	2	0	0
Strick, c	4	0	2	2	1	2
Mack, ss	4	0	0	2	1	1
	42	8	13	25	14	7
Baltimore						
Myers, ss	5	1	1	1	4	0
Whiting, c	5	1	1	7	2	1
Householder, 1b	5	3	2	11	0	0
Brown, rf	4	1	2	2	1	0
Cline, cf	4	1	2	0	0	1
Shetzline, 3b	4	0	0	1	1	1
Pierce, 2b	4	0	1	1	2	2
Waitt, lf	4	1	1	2	0	0
Landis, p	4	1	3	2	4	1
	39	9	13	27	14	6

Eclipse   000 140 030 – 8
Baltimore 340 010 001 – 9
First base on errors – Eclipse 4, Baltimore 3. Earned runs – Eclipse 5, Baltimore 4. Two base hits – Browning, Wolf, Mullane, Cline. Three base hits – Brown, Pierce. Home runs – Householder, Hecker. Double play – Myers, Pierce and Householder. Left on base – Eclipse 7, Baltimore 3. Struck out – Baltimore 3, Eclipse 2. Base on called balls – Eclipse 3. Passed ball – Strick 1. Wild pitch – Landis 1. Time – 1:36.

Radbourn The Slugger

Detroit Wolverines vs. Providence Grays

*Messer Street Grounds, Providence, R.I.
August 17, 1882*

By Edward Achorn

Harry Wright had seen dozens of electrifying games over the years, both as a star player and brilliant manager—leader of the undefeated Cincinnati Red Stockings of 1869 and the mighty Boston Red Stockings of the 1870s.

But moments after the contest of August 17, 1882, ended, Harry told reporters point-blank that it was the greatest baseball game he had ever witnessed.[1]

The game was an 18-inning, 1-0 masterpiece of wily and resolute pitching, gritty catching, and dazzling fielding during the era of barehanded play, when contests of such meticulous beauty were rare. And it was capped by a home run so dramatic that people talked about it for decades.

Some 1,200 fans paid their way into Providence's Messer Street Grounds that hot Thursday afternoon.[2] The third-place Detroit Wolverines, trailing by 4½ games in a still-competitive National League pennant race, were anxious to keep from slipping too far behind the first-place Providence Grays.

They sent out their ace, George "Stump" Weidman, a 21-year-old en route to a career-high 25 wins. Providence manager Wright countered with John Montgomery Ward. Three years earlier, at 19, Ward had led the Grays to the pennant, but his young arm was already showing signs of serious wear, and he was being phased out as the club ace, replaced by the ornery Charles "Old Hoss" Rad-

The 1882 Detroit Wolverines. Back: Charlie Bennett, Joe Farrell, Martin Powell, George Wood, Sam Trott. Middle: Mike McGeary, George Derby, Frank Bancroft, Ned Hanlon, Lon Knight. Front: Stump Wiedman, Dasher Troy.

bourn, who was resting up on this afternoon by playing in right field.

Almost from the start, both clubs knocked on the door. In the fourth inning two Providence throwing errors landed Detroit's speedy Ned Hanlon on second base, and when Martin Powell drove a single to center, Hanlon tore around third for home. But Paul Hines, a graceful fielder who was so deaf he needed an ear trumpet to hear anything, snatched up the ball and fired it to "the Spaniard," the Grays' Latino catcher Sandy Nava, who fell on the sliding Hanlon to retire the runner inches from the plate.[3]

On and on it went, inning after inning: fifth, sixth, seventh, eighth, ninth—still 0–0. That was, in part, because Grays third baseman Jerry Denny was snaring everything that came his way—barehanded, of course. One woman in attendance, noting that Denny seemed to catch the ball even with his knees, suggested he wear an apron.[4]

Nine innings down, a "second game" commenced with the opening of the 10th.[5] "Neither Ward nor Wiedman appeared to have suffered much from the great strain imposed upon their pitching arms," the *Star* observed. In those days, pitchers considered it unmanly to quit before the finish, no matter how many innings it took.

Meanwhile, in downtown Providence, 20 minutes away by horsecar, a throng had gathered around the first-floor window of the *Providence Journal* for telegraphed updates. As inning succeeded amazing inning, hundreds more jammed around the building, following the historic contest with rapt attention.[6]

With two out in the 15th, and a man on third, the Wolverines got a terrific chance to end it. As Hanlon broke for home, Detroit catcher Sam Trott lofted a pitch to deep right field. Radbourn turned and sprinted toward the fence, straining to reach for the escaping sphere. "The ball was over Radbourn's head, and very nearly got by him," the *Star* observed, but Charlie snared it out of the sky with his bare hands, and Detroit was out.

Then it was the Grays' turn. Shortstop George Wright—Harry's brother, nearing the end of a legendary career—hammered a drive to left field. In the corner was a gate, used to admit the posh carriages of

The 1882 Providence Grays. Back: Paul Hines, Jerry Denny, Hoss Radbourn, Jack Farrell. Middle: Tom York, Joe Start, Harry Wright, George Wright, John Ward. Front: Charlie Reilley, Sandy Nava, Barney Gilligan.

well-heeled New Englanders who could, for a fee, park along the outfield fences. The ball scooted through this half-open gate, through a crowd of spectators and into the street, followed closely by left fielder Wood, while Wright tore around the bases. Disappearing for a moment, Wood somehow recovered the ball—whether some accommodating fan tossed it to him is not clear—and heaved it over the gate to third baseman Charlie Bennett. Catcher Trott got it just in time to tag out the luckless Wright. Providence sportswriters contended that veteran umpire George "Foghorn" Bradley should have declared the ball dead once he lost sight of it, returning brother George to third. But the bang-up play at home plate stood, and the Grays got nothing from their first extra-base hit but a heart-stopping out.

On it went … 16th, 17th. Dusk was settling over the smoky city, and workers were already munching their supper. Radbourn, hitless in six attempts to that point, whacked a soaring fly toward the offending gate in left field, now safely shut.

"It was very close to the foul line and high in the air," recalled Detroit second baseman Tom Foster, who lived until 1946, the last survivor of the great game. "George Wood could have caught it if there hadn't been a fence in the way. To me it looked as if it came down foul outside the fence. But the umpire, Foghorn Bradley, waved me away. He said it was a fair ball crossing the fence."[7]

Even Radbourn, a notoriously cantankerous fellow who would enter the Hall of Fame on the strength of his pitching—most notably his astonishing 59 wins in 1884—could not suppress a grin. "It was laughable to see Rad smile as he saw the ball moving over the left field fence," the *Telegram* noted.

The telegraph clicked out the news to the hundreds downtown, setting off "deafening applause."[8] Back at the ballpark, people cheered wildly, filling the air with hats and pouring onto the field. "Everybody shook hands with the members of the nine, with Manager Wright, with their neighbors, and then went out and shook hands with themselves," the *Star* reported.

The *Telegram* called it "the most beautiful base ball game in the history of the League." It was "one long to be remembered by those so fortunate as to be present," the *Journal* added—a sound prediction, because, for years, people talked about the 18-inning scoreless tour de force, broken at last by a clout from the bat of the greatest pitcher of the age.

Detroits	AB	R	H	TB	PO	A	E
Wood, lf	7	0	1	1	3	1	0
Hanlon, cf	7	0	1	1	5	0	0
Powell, 1b	7	0	1	1	21	0	1
Bennett, 3b	7	0	1	2	3	3	2
Trott, c	7	0	2	2	13	1	2
Knight, rf	6	0	0	0	1	1	0
Weidman, p	6	0	1	2	2	9	0
Whitney, ss	6	0	2	2	1	10	3
Forster, 2b	6	0	0	0	2	4	1
	59	0	9	11	51	29	9
Providence	**AB**	**R**	**H**	**TB**	**PO**	**A**	**E**
Hines, cf	7	0	1	1	1	1	0
Farrell, 2b	7	0	1	1	6	9	0
Start, 1b	7	0	0	0	26	0	1
Ward, p	7	0	1	1	0	5	0
York, lf	7	0	1	1	3	0	0
Radbourne, rf	7	1	1	4	1	0	0
Wright, ss	6	0	1	3	2	5	1
Denny, 3b	6	0	1	1	5	11	1
Nava, c	6	0	0	0	9	1	2
	60	1	7	12	53	32	5

Detroits   000 000 000 000 000 000 – 0
Providence   000 000 000 000 000 001 – 1

Umpire – Bradley. Runs earned – Providence, 1. Home run – Radbourne. Three-base hit – Wright. Two-base hits – Bennett, Weidman. Struck out – Providence, 6; Detroits, 4. Base on called balls – Knight. First base on errors – Providence 3, Detroits 2. Double plays – Farrell-Start (2), Denny-Farrell-Start. Passed ball – Trott. Time – 2:40.

Notes:

1. *Providence Morning Star*, August 18, 1882.

2. *Providence Morning Star*, op. cit., reported 1,200. The *Providence Evening Telegram*, August 18, 1882, put the number at "about 1,400."

3. *Providence Morning Star*, op. cit, refers to Nava as "the Spaniard" in its game account.

4. *Providence Evening Telegram*, op. cit, cites the apron quip.

5. *Providence Morning Star*, op. cit., refers to "second game."

6. *Providence Journal*, August 18, 1882.

7. Brandt, Bill. *Do You Know Your Baseball?* (A.S. Barnes and Company, New York, 1947), p. 37.

8 *Providence Journal*, op. cit.

The Innovative Mind of King Kelly

Providence Grays vs. Chicago White Stockings

Lake Front Park, Chicago, Ill.
September 13, 1882

By Bob Tiemann

In his year-end assessment of baseball in 1882, Henry Chadwick asserted that "baserunning gave the Chicago team the League championship in 1880, '81, and '82."[1] This was never more evident than in Chicago's 6–5 victory over Providence in a crucial game played on September 13, 1882.

Chadwick emphasized base stealing in his article but also extolled taking chances in other circumstances. The pivotal play in the game came when Michael "King" Kelly made contact with George Wright at second base, causing a two-run, three-base throwing error. Basepath collisions were rare at that time, and "breaking up the double play" as we know it today was unheard of. Kelly's move created much discussion in later weeks, but it became the norm within the next few years.

The game was the middle one in a clutch three-game sweep of the league-leading Grays by the defending champion White Stockings, part of a 15–1 finish that took Chicago from four wins behind the Grays to three ahead at the end. Chicago's hot streak coincided with a lineup switch reinstating Joe Quest to replace right fielder Hugh Nicol in the ninth spot in the batting order. The young Nicol was a daring baserunner in the White Stocking mold, but could not keep his batting average over .200. Quest, while not much of an offensive threat either, was a fine second baseman, and the move allowed Captain Anson to shift Tommy Burns back to shortstop from second. That steadied the infield defense for the pennant run. After all, Chadwick had begun his assessment by saying, "There is no questioning the fact that base-running, *next to fielding*, has come to be the most important element of success in baseball, it being far more important than batting as batting is carried on nowadays."[2] (Italics added.)

Providence manager Harry Wright had strengthened his team's fielding in mid-June by adding his brother, veteran George Wright, to the roster. The old star had played very little since being the target of the first reserve clause following his pennant-winning stint as Providence's captain and manager in 1879. The layoff had not diminished his fielding

King Kelly: His break-up of a double play attempt led to controversy.

skills, though he batted a woeful .162 in his reprise performance. Relying on the formidable pitching tandem of Johnny Ward and Charlie Radbourn, Harry Wright's team had pulled ahead of Anson's at the end of July and led all through August.

When the Grays arrived in Chicago for their final showdown, they had a 47–26 record with just 11 games to play, while the second-place Whites were 43–28 with 13 games to go. The series opener was a good-fielding, tightly played game (only three fielding errors and one base on balls), won by Chicago, 6–4.

The second game was a wilder affair, featuring dashing baserunning from the start. Chicago lost the toss and batted first, George Gore scoring a run after a single, a steal of second base, an infield out, and a clean hit by Captain Anson. Providence turned the score around with two runs in the second, thanks to heady work on the bases. With men on first and third, Jerry Denny broke for second, and Radbourn stole home just ahead of the return throw from second base. Then, while catcher Silver Flint argued the call on Radbourn, Denny streaked over to third, then trotted home on a single by George Wright. Providence counted another pair in the fifth after a passed ball allowed Jack Farrell and Ward to move into position to score on a single by Tommy York. A passed ball and a wild pickoff throw helped Ned Williamson and Kelly to score in the Chicago sixth.

So the score stood 4–3 in favor of Providence at the start of the eighth inning. An error,

Chicago captain and first baseman Cap Anson.

Chicago's Hugh Nicol was replaced by Quest in right field.

a force out, and a single by Kelly put runners on first and second when Burns grounded sharply to Wright at shortstop. The veteran fielded it cleanly and stepped on second base to force Kelly, but as he continued his motion to throw to first for a double play, Kelly ran almost straight at him. Kelly veered off at the last instant but did make enough contact to cause the throw to soar into the stands. Before it could be retrieved, two men had scored, including the batter Burns, who circled the bases on the error. George Wright looked indignant, but the umpire, William Hawes, was looking at first base and saw no interference.

Quest tripled and scored in the top of the ninth. And Sandy Nava scored in the bottom of the inning on a walk, a passed ball, and error. But with one on and two out, Wright fouled out to make the final score 6-5, Chicago.

Kelly's collision with George Wright was not mentioned in the next day's newspapers, but a few days later Harry Wright wrote a letter to the *Providence Journal* complaining about Kelly's tactics in general and this instance in particular, which Harry viewed as intentional interference. The letter was given wide circulation on the nation's sports pages, setting off a minor brouhaha. Kelly justified his actions by saying that while he would never intentionally injure another player, "I play to win and if I have to employ a few subterfuges to win I cannot help it."[3]

Chicago also won the series finale, 6–2, with Fred Goldsmith pitching a seven-hitter and batting home three runs. The sweep left the White Stockings one win behind in the standings, and they went on to win nine of their final ten to fly past Providence and finish three games ahead in the final standings.

	AB	R	H	TB	PO	A	E
Chicago							
Dalrymple, lf	5	0	0	0	0	0	1
Gore, cf	5	1	1	1	2	0	0
Williamson, 3b	5	1	1	2	0	5	0
Anson, 1b	4	1	3	3	7	0	0
Kelly, rf	4	1	2	2	0	2	1
Burns, ss	4	1	1	1	1	5	1
Corcoran, p	4	0	0	0	0	3	0
Quest, 2b	4	1	1	3	7	0	1
Flint, c	4	0	1	1	0	4	1
	39	6	10	13	27	19	5
Providence							
Hines, cf	4	0	0	0	1	0	0
Farrell, 2b	5	0	1	1	5	8	2
Start, 1b	5	1	3	4	12	0	1
Ward, p	4	1	1	1	1	1	1
York, lf	2	0	1	1	1	0	0
Radbourn, rf	4	1	1	1	2	1	0
Denny, 3b	4	1	1	1	1	1	2
Wright, ss	4	0	2	2	2	4	1
Nava, c	3	1	0	0	2	0	1
	35	5	10	11	27	15	8
Chicago	100	002	021 – 6				
Providence	020	200	001 – 5				

Earned runs – Chiago 3, Providence 1. Reached on errors – Chicago 4, Providence 3. Left on Base – Chicago 4, Providence 7. Two-Base Hits – Williamson, Start. Three-Base Hits – Quest. Bases on Balls – York 2, Nava, Hines. Struck Out – Farrell 2, Nava, Quest. Passed Balls – Flint 2, Nava. Wild Pitch – Corcoran. Double Play – Wright to Farrell to Start. Umpire – W. Hawes. Time – 2:20.
Attendance – 4,061. Runs Batted In – Anson 2, Burns, Dalrymple, Wright, York 2.

Sources:

Periodicals: *Chicago Tribune, Chicago Evening News, Chicago Herald.*

Books: Achorn, Edward. *Fifty-nine in '84* (HarperCollins Publishers, New York, 2010).

Perrin, William D. "Days of Glory," a 1984 SABR reprint of articles originally appearing in the *Providence Journal* in 1928.

Orem, Preston D. *Baseball (1882-1891) From the Newspaper Accounts* (Altadena, California, 1966).

Notes:

1. *New York Clipper*, February 10, 1883.

2. Ibid.

3. Quoted in Edward Achorn, *Fifty-nine in '84*, HarperCollins Publishers, New York, 2010.

The First Meeting of Champions

Cincinnati Red Stockings vs. Chicago White Stockings

Lake Front Park, Chicago, Ill., and
Bank Street Grounds, Cincinnati, Ohio
October 6, 1882

By Jim Farmer

It's hard to imagine big-league baseball without a series at the end of the season that decides which team claims the title of "World Champion." But in the early years of major-league baseball there was only one league, and winning the pennant was the crowning achievement. From 1876 to 1881 the National League reigned as the baseball world's lone major league.

Cincinnati had been represented in the National League from 1876 until 1880. But the league's rules banning beer sales and prohibiting Sunday games were both sore points in that city. When Red Stockings ownership decided to ignore those prohibitions late in the 1880 season, the club's franchise was unceremoniously terminated for 1881.

Cincinnati sportswriter O.P. Caylor, angry at what he considered the National League's arrogance, made a push to bring major-league baseball back to Cincinnati for the 1882 season. He and businessmen from other baseball-deprived cities organized a new major league. The newly formed American Association fielded teams from six cities in its first year: Baltimore, Louisville, Pittsburgh, St. Louis, Philadelphia, and Cincinnati.

The new Cincinnati team was guided by veteran player and rookie manager Pop Snyder. His band of warriors consisted of a healthy mix of veterans and prospects. A handful were familiar faces to Cincinnati cranks. Among those were third baseman Hick Carpenter, pitcher Will White, and outfielders Harry Wheeler and Joe Sommer. All four had played for the National League Reds and were fan favorites. Also on the team was rookie sensation and eventual Hall of Famer John Alexander "Bid" McPhee. Snyder guided his club to a 55-25 record, good for the Association's first pennant, finishing a commanding 11½ games ahead of the second-place Athletics.

Meanwhile, in the National League the mighty Chicago White Stockings captured their third straight pennant, finishing the season with a 55-29 record. The Chicagos were at the peak of their championship run and were loaded with plenty of baseball studs, among them Hall of Famers Cap Anson and Mike Kelly.

At the conclusion of the season the White Stockings and Red Stockings agreed to face each other in exhibition games, the first time in major-league baseball that two pennant winners would meet.

The first of the historic games took place on October 6 at Cincinnati's Bank Street Grounds. Both Anson and Snyder penciled in most of their starters. Snyder excluded himself because he was nursing a sore finger. Phil Powers took over the catching duties. For the Chicagos, Kelly, oddly missing from his

Jimmy Macullar's catch of Cap Anson's ninth-inning line drive snuffed out a late threat.

usual place in the lineup, was replaced by pitcher Larry Corcoran.

The game began shortly after 3 o'clock with 2,700 fans on hand to witness a match full of base hits and exciting defense. Both pitchers hurled great games. The only scoring happened during the sixth inning and, to Chicago's horror, it all belonged to Cincinnati. After the White Stockings successfully retired Wheeler, Carpenter nailed a line drive to center, Ecky Stearns hit safely to right, and Chick Fulmer singled to center field, sending Carpenter home with the game's first run. McPhee, the "handsome gentlemanly second baseman,"[1] slapped a triple, sending the ball between right fielder Hugh Nicol and center fielder George Gore, scoring both Stearns and Fulmer. Chicago's Fred Goldsmith then threw a wild pitch that sent Biddy home for the final run of the inning and the game.

The Red Stockings' Will White held the Chicagos, who had averaged seven runs per game during the season, scoreless. In those days a shutout ballgame was referred to as a "Chicago," an irony that Anson desperately hoped to avoid as the final inning began.

Abner Dalrymple opened that last inning by scratching out a hit to left field. Gore popped out to Wheeler in right before Ned Williamson doubled to right-center. With only one out and runners at second and third, Anson himself stepped up to the plate. But he failed to deliver, hitting a shot that was caught by center fielder Jimmy Macullar. Dalrymple tried to hustle home from third but was caught by Macullar's brilliant throw to catcher Powers for the final out.

Red Stockings fans celebrated with a great cheer, "All yell, and let it be a champion whoop!"[2] for their new baseball club had defeated the champions of the league that snubbed them exactly two years before. The *Cincinnati Enquirer* reported that Anson "looked as glum as a jilted lover."

Riding high from their 4–0 shutout, the Red Stockings entered the second game with high hopes of duplicating their feat from the day before. White was in the box for the Red Stockings again, and Corcoran took over the pitching duties for the White Stockings. Again both pitchers hurled stellar games, but this time two costly errors committed by the Red Stockings in the first inning resulted in the only two Chicago runs of the game, and the White Stockings held on for the 2–0 victory.

Despite the loss in the follow-up game, Cincinnati fans still rejoiced. Their Red Stockings had competed with the best that the National League had to offer.

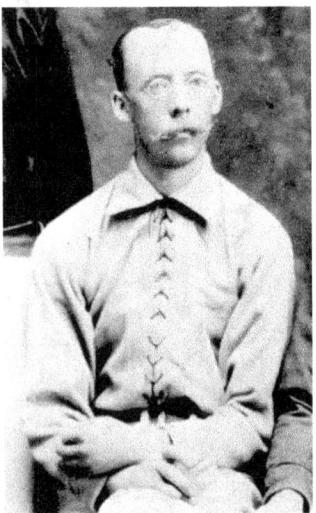

Will White: Pitcher for the pennant-winning Reds.

	AB	R	H	S	PO	A	E
Cincinnati							
Sommer, lf	4	0	0	2	4	0	0
Wheeler, rf	4	0	0	0	4	0	0
Carpenter, 3b	4	1	2	1	2	0	0
Stearns, 1b	4	1	1	0	5	0	1
Fulmer, ss	4	1	2	0	1	4	0
McPhee, 2b	4	1	3	0	4	2	0
Macullar, cf	3	0	1	0	2	1	0
Powers, c	3	0	0	1	5	3	0
White, p	3	0	2	0	0	4	0
	33	4	11	4	27	14	1
Chicago							
Dalrymple, lf	4	0	2	0	4	0	0
Gore, cf	4	0	1	0	0	0	0
Williamson, 3b	4	0	2	0	1	2	0
Anson, 1b	4	0	1	0	15	0	0
Burns, 2b	3	0	0	0	2	5	0
Goldsmith, p	3	0	1	0	1	8	1
Corcoran, ss	3	0	0	1	0	0	1
Nicol, rf	3	0	0	0	1	0	0
Flint, c	3	0	1	1	3	2	0
	31	0	8	2	27	17	2
Chicago	000	000	000 – 0				
Cincinnati	000	004	00x – 4				

Earned runs – Cincinnati 3, Chicago 0. Two-base hit – Williamson. Three-base hits – McPhee, Williamson. Double plays – Carpenter to Macullar to Powers. Left on base – Cincinnati 4, Chicago 3. Wild throws – Corcoran. Balk – Goldsmith. Foul assists – White. Wild pitches – White, Goldsmith. Passed balls – Flint. Attendance – 2,700. Umpire – Pop Smith.

Notes:

1. *Cincinnati Commercial Gazette*. October 7, 1882.

2. Ibid.

Cap Anson vs. Fleet Walker

Chicago White Stockings vs. Toledo Blue Stockings

League Park, Toledo, Ohio
August 10, 1883

By John R. Husman

Future Hall of Famer Cap Anson helped establish the color line.

The beginning of the end of African American participation in Organized Baseball probably dates to an in-season exhibition game less than two decades after the close of the Civil War.

Cap Anson's Chicagos were a model of success on the field, having won the three previous National League titles, and at the time of the game they were in the thick of a battle for a fourth straight. Anson was their very capable leader, a Hall of Fame-bound player and by modern standards an outspoken racial bigot. His views were hardly unique at the time, within baseball or in the country at large, but his prominent position made him a major factor in segregating the game.

Baseball in Toledo was in its infancy, the 1883 season being the city's first. The Toledo catcher was Moses Fleetwood Walker, a mulatto man[1] and the target of Anson's prejudice. Walker was one of just a few black men playing in the minor leagues at the time. His race nearly denied him that opportunity. The executive committee of the Northwestern League met at Toledo's Boody House on March 14, 1883, to consider "a motion ... by the representative from the Peoria, Illinois, club that no colored player be allowed in the league."[2] This action was made specifically to expel Walker. After a bitter fight, the motion was defeated, allowing Walker to play.

Unfortunately for researchers, only one Toledo newspaper containing the game account and the events leading up to it survives. The *Toledo Daily Blade*'s lengthy account is not at all complimentary of either Anson or his team. In fact it is exceedingly supportive of Walker and indicates that the Toledo management came to his defense and suggests that the city did as well. The article is replete with opinion and appeared under several headlines including "Baby Anson and the Color Line."[3] It is repeated here in part:

> Walker, the colored catcher of the Toledo Club ... was a source of contention between the home club and ... the Chicago Club. Shortly after their arrival in the city ... the Toledo Club was ... informed that there was objection in the Chicago Club to Toledo's playing Walker....
>
> Walker has a very sore hand, and it had not been intended to play him in yesterday's game, and this was stated to the bearer of the announcement for the Chicagos. ... Not content with this, the visitors ... declared with the swagger for which they are noted, that

they would play ball "with no d----d nigger." ... (T)he order was given, then and there, to play Walker and the beefy bluffer was informed that he could play or go, just as he blank pleased. Anson hauled in his horns somewhat and "consented" to play, remarking, "We'll play this here game, but won't play never no more with the nigger in."[4]

Toledo's manager, Charlie Morton, had called Anson's bluff, forcing the latter onto the field in order to secure his interest in the day's gate receipts.

Contrasting the Toledo reporting, the *Chicago Tribune*'s brief story contained only basic game information and was not accompanied by a box score. "Ten innings were played today between the Chicagos and the Toledos, and the former barely succeeded in defeating the home nine, securing but one additional run on the extra inning. The score stood 7 to 6 and the home nine felt proud of having succeeded in holding down the league champions to their work."[5]

Toledo secured two moral victories that day. Their manager and team had taken the high road by supporting Walker. Of lesser importance was their play, which forced the powerful Chicago team to extra innings. Most of the Chicago team had been together for several years and included two future Hall of Famers, Anson, the 19th century's best hitter, and colorful catcher King Kelly. The supporting cast included Billy Sunday, who went on to become a noteworthy evangelist.

But Anson made good his bold statement—"won't play never no more with the nigger in."[6] Chicago was at Toledo again in 1884 but this time Walker did not play. The reason is not clear, but Chicago had requested assurance in writing that no black would play any position in the July 25 exhibition game.[7] Toledo's response to this request is not known, but it is known that Walker had not played the previous three games because of injury, nor did he catch again until August 18. Teams featuring Walker and Anson met again in Newark in 1887 with Walker on the sidelines along with his black batterymate, George Stovey.[8] Walker left after the 1889 season, "The last black to play in a highly competitive integrated league"[9] until the arrival of Jackie Robinson in 1947.

Cap Anson was not entirely responsible for baseball's more than half-century of segregation, but he had a lot to do with it. The incident of August 10, 1883, in Toledo certainly brought the issue to the forefront and began an open, blatant, and successful effort to bar black players from Organized Baseball.

Fleet Walker

	AB	R	H	TB	PO	A	E
Toledos							
Barkley, 2b	6	0	2	3	4	7	0
O'Day, 1b	6	0	3	4	12	0	1
Miller, ss	6	0	2	2	0	6	0
Tilley, lf	5	0	1	1	1	1	0
Welch, c	5	2	1	1	6	2	2
Walker, rf	5	1	0	0	2	0	0
Lockwood, cf	5	0	2	2	3	0	1
Moffet, p	5	1	2	2	1	4	1
Morton, 3b	5	2	3	5	1	1	1
	48	6	16	20	30	21	6
Chicagos							
Dalrymple, lf	5	0	2	3	2	0	0
Gore, cf	5	0	0	0	2	0	0
Kelly, c	4	3	1	1	4	2	1
Anson, 1b	5	1	2	3	16	0	0
Williamson, 3b	3	2	0	0	0	6	2
Burns, ss	5	1	4	5	1	4	1
Pfeffer, 2b	5	0	0	0	4	4	1
Goldsmith, p	4	0	0	0	0	5	0
Sunday, rf	4	0	1	1	1	1	1
	40	7	10	13	30	22	6
Toledos	020	002	100	1 – 6			
Chicagos	022	000	010	2 – 7			

Earned runs—Toledos, 2. Two base hits—O'Day, Barkley, Dalrymple, Anson, Burns. Three-base hits—Morton. Left on bases—Toledos, 11; Chicagos, 6. Struck out—O'Day, Miller, Dalrymple, Williamson, Sunday. Bases on called balls—Chicagos, 3. First base on errors—Toledos, 5; Chicagos, 3. Wild throws—Welch 2; Moffit, Williamson, Pfeffer. Passed balls—Welch, 2. Wild pitches—Moffit, 2. Balls called—On Moffit, 90; on Goldsmith, 65. Strikes called—On Moffit, 32; on Goldsmith, 29. Time - 1:55. Umpire—McQuaid.[10]

Notes:

1. Zang, David W. *Fleet Walker's Divided Heart* (Lincoln: University of Nebraska Press, 1995), p. 2.

2. *Toledo Daily Blade*, March 15, 1883, p. 3.

3. *Toledo Daily Blade*, August 11, 1883, p. 3.

4. Ibid.

5. *Chicago Daily Tribune*, August 11, 1883, p. 2.

6. *Toledo Daily Blade*, August 11, 1883, p. 3.

7. Rosenberg, Howard W. "Recapping a Bit of Toledo's History," *The Blade*, November 8, 2006, C 2.

8. Rosenberg, Howard W. "Cap Chronicled-Cap's Great Shame-Racial Intolerance," at www.capanson.com.

9. Zang, p. 61.

10. *Toledo Daily Blade*, August 11, 1883, p. 3.

Grasshopper Snatches the Pennant

Chicago White Stockings vs. Boston Beaneaters

South End Grounds, Boston, Mass.
September 13, 1883

By Mark Pestana

In September 1883 a key late-season series in Boston pitted perennial powerhouse Chicago against a fine nine from Beantown. The Windy City team blew into the Hub holding first place, riding an 11-game win streak and appearing destined for a fourth consecutive National League title. Boston, however, was knocking on the door, a game and a half out, despite having just dropped two of three to the Providence Grays. And the Beaneaters would see to it that their visitors left town with pennant hopes dashed, thanks to a man called Grasshopper.

Chicago's White Stockings fairly owned the League in the 1880s: five pennants and only one finish out of the top three. Led by future Hall of Famers Cap Anson and King Kelly, they fielded a lineup that was a veritable all-star team unto itself. Pitching duties were shared by Fred Goldsmith, a steady 20-game winner, and Larry Corcoran, who topped 30 victories four times between 1880 and 1884.

Boston could not boast the stable of stars that Chicago did, but the Beaneaters were not without stalwart veterans and promising youngsters. Jack Burdock and Ezra Sutton held down infield positions as they had since playing on Boston's 1878 pennant winners, and first baseman-manager John Morrill had done service with the team since the inaugural 1876 season; all three were batting over .300. Twenty-two-year-old pitcher Charlie Buffinton was on his way to a 25-win season … but he was not the ace of the staff.

James Evans Whitney had broken in with Boston in 1881, making an immediate splash by leading the National League in both games won (31) and games lost (33) for a team that struggled to end up at 38–45.

Boston's 1883 National League champions, in a studio pose. Standing: Joe Hornung, Ezra Sutton, Sam Wise, Jack Burdock. Seated: Charlie Buffinton, Paul Radford, Jim Whitney, John Morrill, Mike Hines, Mert Hackett, Edgar Smith.

Possessor of a nickname alternately attributed to the shape of his head[1] and to the way he walked,[2] Grasshopper Jim lasted 10 seasons in the majors, piling up 191 wins along the way. The 6-foot-2, 170-pound workhorse would clock 514 innings and 54 complete games in 1883, and set an NL record for strikeouts with 345. His greatest strength was his control of the strike zone: '83 was the first of three consecutive years he topped all pitchers in strikeout-to-walk ratio.

An audience of close to 3,500 packed Boston's South End Grounds on Monday, September 10, for the series opener. "The interest manifested in the critical situation of the struggle for the league championship was well shown by the large attendance at the base ball grounds," the *Boston Daily Advertiser* reported.[3] Morrill's club, despite committing an embarassing seven errors, evaded disaster thanks to its big right-hander. As the *Advertiser* concluded: "Whitney was the obstacle that (Chicago) could not surmount, and the bats would whistle around that sphere in every exasperating way but the right way."[4] Whitney's line for the 4–2 complete game win: nine strikeouts, three hits, one walk, no earned runs. Goldsmith took the loss.

Now a half-game back of the visitors, Boston sent Whitney to the box again Tuesday, this time to face Corcoran. Cap's men cobbled together a two-run sixth but failed to hold the lead. Boston scored the tying and winning runs in its final at-bat, and Whitney closed with a one-two-three ninth. The nearly 4,000 spectators went home happy; their Beaneaters were now in possession of first place.

On Wednesday the 12th, Whitney patrolled center field, as he usually did when he wasn't pitching, and it was Buffinton's turn to corral Anson's troops. About 2,900 fans stuck around despite a persistent drizzle, and they were rewarded with an 11–2 Boston rout. Goldsmith suffered his second defeat of the series.

Thus the stage was set for the finale on Thursday the 13th. Even with a victory, the White Stockings could not reclaim first place, but they could claw back to within a half-game of the lead and send a message to the Bostonians that they were not entirely down and out, despite a poor three days' showing. The smallest crowd of the four-game set, a handful under 2,000, was attributable to unfavorable conditions. "The weather was rainy and the ground soft," noted the *Chicago Daily Tribune.*[5]

Larry Corcoran: The Chicago ace was done in by one bad inning.

For the White Stockings, Dalrymple's leadoff drive to left in the first was misplayed by left fielder Joe Hornung, landing Abner on second base. Up next came George Gore, who pushed the runner to third with a single, whence he was brought home by Kelly's fly ball. They threatened again two innings later, but with men on second and third with no outs, Hornung and center fielder Paul Radford made fine plays to hold them at bay. Hornung came through again in the fifth, running down a "terrific drive"[6] over his head off Corcoran's bat with a man on.

Boston got all the runs Whitney needed in the third. Catcher Hines, who went 3-for-4 in the game, opened with a double. Radford and Hornung reached via infield errors. With Hines already home, Sutton stepped in next and laced a two-run single. Thus ended the day's scoring. Corcoran was no easy touch; more Bostons made first on errors (seven) than on hits (six). He allowed but one earned run.

The problem for the Windy City men was that Whitney was even better. The four base hits he allowed were scattered and thus largely harmless. His strike-zone mastery was in evidence, as he struck out four while surrendering just a single base on balls. With Chicago mounting a last-gasp challenge in the ninth, fueled by a Buffinton muff and a questionable safe call by the umpire,[7] Whitney fanned Fred Pfeffer to end the affair and notch his 32nd victory.

Hurling three complete games, Whitney had yielded a modest 13 hits, which in turn produced but two earned runs. Only two batters were able to milk him for walks, while 19 went down on strikes. Anson, Kelly, Gore, Pfeffer, and Ned Williamson together mustered a scant three safeties. After the series ended the Beaneaters won nine of their final ten to win the title, but the true turning point came in that series against Chicago, when Grasshopper Jim Whitney held sway over the 19th-century version of Murderers' Row.

Boston	AB	R	H	Chicago	AB	R	H
Hornung, lf	4	1	0	Dalrymple, lf	4	1	1
Sutton, 3b	4	0	1	Gore, cf	4	0	2
Burdock, 2b	4	0	0	Kelly, rf	4	0	0
Whitney, p	2	0	1	Anson, 1b	3	0	0
Morrill, 1b	4	0	1	Williamson, 3b	4	0	0
Wise, ss	3	0	0	Burns, ss	4	0	0
Buffinton, rf	4	0	0	Pfeffer, 2b	4	0	0
Hines, c	4	1	3	Flint, c	3	0	0
Radford, cf	3	1	0	Corcoran, p	3	0	1
	32	3	6		33	1	4

Boston   003 000 000 – 3
Chicago 100 000 000 – 1

Earned runs – Boston 1. Two-base hit – Hines. First base on balls – Whitney (2), Wise, Anson. First base on errors – Boston 7, Chicago 3. Struck out – Morrill, Wise (2), Buffinton, Hines, Burdock, Whitney, Williamson (3), Pfeffer (2). Balls called – on Whitney 43, on Corcoran 74. Strikes called – Of Whitney 26; off Corcoran, 39. Double plays – Burns, Pfeffer and Anson; Burdock and Wise. Passed balls – Hines 1, Flint 2. Wild pitch – Corcoran. Left on bases – Boston 3, Chicago 6. Time -- 1:53. Umpire – Bradley. Attendance, 1,897.

Notes:

1. Lewis, Jeff. "Nicknames Colorful in Sports Arena, " *Rockmart Journal* (Georgia), September 10, 1986, p. 2B; entry for "Whitney, James Evans" in *Major League Baseball Profiles, 1871-1900, Vol. 1*, ed. David Nemec (Lincoln, NE: University of Nebraska Press, 2011), p.198.

2. Ivor-Campbell, Fred. Entry for "Whitney, James Evans" in *Biographical Dictionary of American Sports: 1992-1995 Supplement* (Westport, CT: Greenwood Press, 1995), p. 226.

3. *Boston Daily Advertiser*, September 11, 1883, p. 8.

4. Ibid.

5. *Chicago Daily Tribune*, Sept. 14, 1883, p. 2.

6. *Boston Daily Advertiser*, Sept. 14, 1883, p. 9.

7. Ibid.

One Hand, No Hits

Cleveland Blues vs. Philadelphia Phillies

Recreation Park, Philadelphia, Pa.
September 13, 1883

By Jon Barnes

Cleveland fans had good reason for optimism heading into the start of the 1883 baseball season. In its first four years of National League competition, the Cleveland club had finished sixth, third, seventh, and fifth in the standings, with the 1882 squad sporting a distinctly mediocre record of 42–40. But management was determined to build a contending team for the following year, and one of the priorities had been to sign another top pitcher to take some of the load off the team's ace, Jim McCormick, especially since the schedule was being expanded to 98 games.

Tall and mutton-chopped, at 6-feet-2 and 180 pounds, Hugh "One Arm" Daily turned out to be that man. As a 34-year-old rookie the season before, he had finished 15–14 with a 2.99 ERA as Pud Galvin's backup for third-place Buffalo. Then in December 1882 Daily signed with Cleveland for a salary of $2,000.

The *Cleveland Herald* described Daily as "a strong man in many respects … a remarkable batter for a one-handed man, hitting hard and often … a careful base watcher" with a quick, puzzling delivery, and good pace and command. His weak points, the newspaper contended, "are wildness of delivery at times and a bad disposition."[1] Indeed, part of the Daily legend is that he once punched out his catcher for throwing the ball back to him too hard and making his stump sore.

Accounts differ on the circumstances of the boyhood accident that caused Daily to lose his left hand, and his age at the time of the injury. He may have been shot accidentally by a friend playing with a loaded musket, or he may have been burned while simulating fire on a theater set in Baltimore.

Before signing with Buffalo, Daily spent many years playing in the sandlot and semipro leagues of Baltimore. He wore a leather glove on his left arm with a square pad to protect his stump, and was able to trap groundballs against it with his right hand. He usually attempted to catch popups and line drives with his pitching hand. He used a shortened bat at the plate that he could swing more easily with only one arm.

Led by the McCormick-Daily pitching duo, Cleveland moved into sole possession of the league lead for the first time in the franchise's history on June 11, 1883.[2] Although the offense was erratic (Providence's Hoss Radbourn no-hit the team on July 25), Cleveland was still in the thick of a tight four-team race before the September 13 game at Philadelphia.

Daily was now pitching almost every game because McCormick had been injured, and he was showing signs of wear. He had lost three of his last

Hugh Daily: The Cleveland pitcher was working virtually every game when he no-hit Philadelphia in 1883.

four starts, including a 21–7 rout by Chicago. Maybe the weak bats of the last-place Philadelphia club, the sloppy conditions of the field,[3] or the week's rest because of rainouts allowed Daily to find new life in his curveball. Whatever the reason, the one-handed man was unhittable that day and walked only three in a 1–0 victory.

There were no telegraph wires running to the Philadelphia ballpark, and carrier pigeons were used to dispatch reports of the game. Perhaps that is why the Cleveland papers ran only sketchy recaps of the contest, though they duly noted the significance of Daily's feat.

"Daily's work of yesterday was wonderful and only equaled four times since the League has been organized," wrote the *Cleveland Herald*.[4] It was actually the eighth no-hitter in National League history.

"Daily did great work in the box yesterday," said the *Cleveland Leader*.[5]

The *Cleveland Plain Dealer* was the most descriptive: "The Clevelands 'scratched' a game at Philadelphia yesterday—and a stunning 'fluke' it was too. The tail-enders of the League failed to make a base hit and consequently made no run. Cleveland worried in a lonesome run but it proved of sufficient size to make a game out of. Either Daly (sic) pitched a wonderful game or the Philadelphias have been taking batting lessons of the Clevelands."[6]

The lone run came in the seventh inning when left fielder Tom York singled, stole second, and scored as right fielder Bill Crowley hit one through Blondie Purcell's legs in left field.

With an earlier game still under dispute (the league eventually ruled that Cleveland had forfeited its August 1 game to Boston when Daily was replaced in the box; substitutions at the time could be made only for injury), the September 14 papers showed Cleveland at the top of the standings after Daily's no-hitter. The club had a 52–34 record, creating a virtual three-way tie with Providence and Boston, both 53–35. Chicago was a game and a half back at 52–37.

A doubleheader sweep the next day over Philadelphia, including another gem by Daily—a 5–1 victory in the second game—put Cleveland on top by itself at 54–34. But the team, which was in the middle of a 25-game road trip to end the season, faded and managed only two wins the rest of the way. Adjusted for the forfeited game, the Clevelands finished with an official record of 55–42, in fourth place, 7½ games out. Its 2.22 team ERA led the league. McCormick won the individual title with a 1.84 ERA. Daily was fifth at 2.42. He also led the league in walks with 99, and was seventh in strikeouts with 171.

Daily jumped to the Union Association—a league that coincidentally had been organized by delegates in Pittsburgh just a day before his no-hitter—in 1884.[7] That season he struck out an incredible 483 batters—more than half his career total—walked only 72 in 500 innings, and batted .214 in 201 at-bats.

It was the last hurrah for Daily. Initially blacklisted by the other major-league teams after the Union Association folded, he eventually signed with the St. Louis National League team in 1885, and posted a 3–8 record and a 3.94 ERA. He last pitched in the major leagues in 1887, when he returned to Cleveland, now a last-place team in the American Association. His record that year was 4–12, with a 3.67 earned-run average, 30 strikeouts, and 44 walks. By that time his 1883 pennant-race and no-hit heroics were just a distant memory.

Cleveland	AB	R	H	Philadelphia	AB	R	H
Dunlap, 2b	4	0	1	Manning, rf	3	0	0
Hotaling, cf	3	0	0	Harbridge, cf	4	0	0
Glasscock, ss	3	0	0	Gross, c	3	0	0
York, lf	3	1	1	McClellan, ss	3	0	0
Phillips, 1b	3	0	1	Purcell, lf	2	0	0
Crowley, rf	3	0	1	Farrar, 1b	3	0	0
Muldoon, 3b	3	0	1	Coleman, p	3	0	0
Bushong, c	3	0	0	Ferguson, 2b	3	0	0
Daily, p	3	0	1	Warner, 3b	3	0	0
	28	1	6		27	0	0

Philadelphia   000 000 000 – 0
Cleveland   000 000 10* – 1

*- The coin toss was won by Cleveland, and the home team batted first.
Earned Runs – none. First Base on Called Balls – Philadelphia 3. Left on Bases – Philadelphia 1, Cleveland 2. Struck Out – Philadelphia 2, Cleveland 3. Passed Balls – Gross 1. Time of Game – 1:30. Umpire – Mr. W. McLean.

Notes:

1. *Cleveland Herald*, December 20, 1882.

2. *Cleveland Herald*, June 13, 1883.

3. "At Recreation Park, 13th, the Philadelphia and Cleveland clubs contested. The ground was in a wretchedly soggy condition, and this soon made the ball so mushy that it was almost impossible to hit it effectively, consequently the batting was extremely weak." –*Sporting Life*, September 17, 1883.

4. *Cleveland Herald*, September 14, 1883.

5. *Cleveland Leader*, Sept. 14, 1883.

6. *Cleveland Plain Dealer*, September 14, 1883.

7. *Cleveland Herald*, September 13, 1883.

Nipped at the Wire

Philadelphia Athletics vs. St. Louis Browns

Sportsman's Park, St. Louis, Mo.
September 21-23, 1883

By Jim Rygelski

The 1883 American Association season had the closest major-league pennant race then on record, as the Philadelphia Athletics finished first by a single game over the St. Louis Browns. The two teams virtually decided things in St. Louis the next to last weekend of the season.

Such a late-season showdown seemed unlikely in the campaign's early days. The Athletics led the league with an 18–3 mark at the end of May. St. Louis stumbled in the beginning and had climbed to 11–10 by month's end, in fifth place and 6½ games back.

From mid-June until the end of July, the A's and Browns were never separated by more than three games, the Browns taking the lead in late July before giving it back.

The teams were 2½ games apart as the first-place Athletics (63–28) came to St. Louis's Sportsman's Park for three games against the 61–31 Browns beginning Friday, September 21.

The opener featured veteran right-hander Bobby Mathews, a newcomer to the A's that year and in the box for 30 of their wins, against the Browns' Tony Mullane, pitching for his third team in three years. More than 10,000 people squeezed into the wooden ballyard, a high turnout for the time.

The first game was often a comedy of errors—literally. The 28 fielding miscues by both clubs exceeded the teams' 24 total hits. The Browns pulled off an inning-ending double play in the first after three errors; second baseman Joe Quest twice dropped throws attempting to nail a runner at second, only to recover to throw out a runner trying to score.

The Philadelphia club built up 6–0 and 9–3 leads but saw the Browns pull to 9–8 entering the eighth. Three Athletics hits and three passed balls by the Browns' Pat Deasley gave the A's four runs in their

On the cusp of dominance in the American Association, the 1883 St. Louis Browns.
Standing: Charlie Comiskey, three unidentified men, Pat Deasley.
Sitting: Bill Gleason, Jumbo McGinnis, unidentified player, Tony Mullane, unidentified player.
On ground: Hugh Nicol, Tom Dolan, Arlie Latham, Charlie Hodnett.

eighth. But St. Louis rallied for three runs, helped by two errors charged to first baseman George Washington Bradley, who was filling in for injured slugger Harry Stovey.

Down 13–11, the Browns appeared to have tied the game when with one out and one on in the home ninth, shortstop Billy Gleason blistered a ball to deep center field. But Bradley, who'd been moved to center after his disastrous innings at first base, made a spectacular over-the-shoulder catch. The next man grounded out to end the game.

With that victory, the Athletics looked toward clinching the pennant before leaving town. George McGinnis started the second game for the Browns, who batted first after having lost the coin toss to determine the matter. He was opposed by right-hander Jack Jones, who pitched only seven games for Philadelphia that year, winning five.

Each team's scoring mirrored the other's in the first three innings, both clubs scoring once in the first, three times in the second, and twice in the third. The Browns took the lead in the fifth when right fielder Hugh Nicol led off with a double to left. He moved to third on a passed ball by Jack O'Brien. Second baseman George Strief's single brought Nicol home.

From there McGinnis, aided by a solid defense that committed only two errors, stopped the Athletics. The Browns put the game away in the eighth with a pair of runs on a single by Gleason, a double by Charlie Comiskey, and two passed balls that allowed the Browns first baseman to score. The Athletics went down in order in their ninth. The Browns' 9–6 win set the stage for the rubber game on Sunday.

St. Louis fans could be forgiven for feeling overconfident going into the finale. Their nine would be led by Mullane, certainly due to pitch a better game than on Friday. The A's would depend on someone the local fans once lionized but now considered a has-been: George Washington Bradley.

Bradley had been the ace of the St. Louis Browns, first of the National Association in 1875, then of the National League in 1876. Bradley had pitched the

George Bradley, winning pitcher of the rubber game.

first NL no-hitter in its initial season. After several stops, he played third when not occasionally pitching for the 1883 Athletics.

Six years after this crucial game, Bradley re-created its atmosphere for a *Sporting News* reporter. "I remember how the Browns smiled when they heard I was going to pitch. Oh what pie and oh what pudding. When I got in the square, however, it was as though I was born again. 'Go in, old Brad,' I heard someone say, 'and let the folks know you have come to life again.' Well, I went in and you know the rest."

Bradley limited the Browns to three hits. En route to a 9–2 victory, his teammates scored two for him right away in the first as Jud Birchall lined one just inside the right-field line, and Stovey, banged up in both previous games, got the first of his three hits, a ground-rule double to right-center. Birchall scored on a groundout and Stovey tallied on a wild pitch.

The Athletics plated three in the fifth to put the game out of reach. With one out, Cub Stricker singled to center, stole second, went to third on a passed ball, and scored when Birchall grounded to Comiskey and Stricker beat the throw to the plate. Comiskey left the bag, but Tom Dolan, catching this game, threw to it anyway, and the ball went into right field. Stovey's second hit drove home Birchall, and Stovey took second on the throw home. He scored when Fred Lewis dropped Lon Knight's fly ball.

The score was 6–0 when the Browns finally plated a run in the eighth; but the Philadelphia team came back with a pair in their eighth before the Browns marked once in the ninth.

The victory allowed the Athletics to leave for their final trip of the season, to Louisville, ahead by 3½ games and having clinched no worse than a tie for the league championship. They lost three of four in Louisville, but the one victory allowed them to finish 66–32. The Browns stayed home and swept three from the Alleghenies of Pittsburgh, but still came up one game short at 65–33.

	AB	R	H	PO	A	E
ST. LOUIS						
Gleason, ss	4	0	0	1	2	0
Comiskey, 1b	4	0	0	8	0	0
Lewis, cf	4	0	0	3	0	1
Nicol, rf	4	0	1	2	0	1
Quest, 2b	4	1	2	1	1	0
Latham, 3b	4	0	0	1	3	0
Strief, lf	4	0	0	0	0	0
Mullane, p	3	1	0	1	0	0
Dolan, c	3	0	0	7	2	2
Totals	34	2	3	24	8	4
ATHLETIC						
Birchall, lf	5	2	3	0	0	0
Stovey, 1b	5	3	3	14	1	1
Knight, rf	4	0	0	2	0	0
Moynahan, ss	4	0	0	0	3	1
O'Brien, c	4	0	0	6	0	0
Corey, 3b	2	2	2	1	5	1
Blakiston, cf	4	1	1	2	0	0
Bradley, p	4	0	0	1	2	0
Stricker, 2b	4	1	2	1	4	1
Totals	36	9	11	27	15	4

```
St. Louis      0 0 0   0 0 0   1 1 0 – 2
Philadelphia   2 0 0   0 3 1   1 2 x – 9
```

2b – Stovey 2, Stricker, Birchall. SB – Corey, Stricker, Mullane. Earned runs – off Mullane 7, off Bradley 0. Bases on balls – off Mullane 2 (Corey 2). Struck out – by Mullane 8 (Knight 2, Moynahan 3, Bradley 2, Stricker), by Bradley 3 (Lewis, Quest, Dolan). Wild pitches – Mullane 5. Passed balls – Dolan, O'Brien. Time – 1:40. Attendance – 16,800. Umpire – Charles Daniels.

Fleet Walker's Major League Debut

Toledo Blue Stockings vs. Louisville Eclipse

Eclipse Park, Louisville, Ky.
May 1, 1884

By John R. Husman

Although the misconception has long been debunked by baseball historians, many still believe that Jackie Robinson in 1947 became the first black man to play major-league baseball. Others contend that the recent discovery that former slave and mulatto William Edward White had a one-game major-league career in 1879 means he should be acclaimed as the first.

But White played baseball and lived his life as a white man. He said that he was white and so he was in his time. The distinction of being the first black man to play major-league baseball actually belongs to Moses Fleetwood Walker, who played the game openly as a black man in the 1880s and endured the consequences that resulted.

Walker first played professionally for the Toledos of the Northwestern League in 1883. That team won the pennant, and its success propelled the city into the major American Association the following year. Moses Fleetwood Walker went, too. Toledo and Walker made their major-league debut in Louisville on May 1, 1884.

Walker's reputation preceded him to Louisville that day. In August of 1881, he had been in the city as a catcher for Cleveland's semiprofessional White Sewing Machine club. His club was matched against the Eclipse, a team destined to become a charter member of the American Association the following season. Because some Eclipse players and management objected, Walker did not play.[1] The *Louisville Courier-Journal* speculated as to the reasons: "The prejudice of the Eclipse was either too strong, or they feared Walker, who has earned the reputation of being the best amateur catcher in the Union."[2]

Prejudice remained in the Kentucky city when Walker returned for his major-league debut on May 1, 1884. The nation's press paid him considerable attention. Walker's biographer, David Zang, opined, "The *Blade* [Toledo, Ohio] remained loyally sympathetic throughout the season, and while the national *Sporting Life* decried overt racial incidents, other papers, particularly in the South, engaged in a constant—sometimes savage—campaign to denigrate Walker."[3]

Despite the many distractions presented to Walker, which included a refusal to serve him breakfast at the St. Cloud Hotel,[4] the catcher presented himself before the crowd of 3,500 at Eclipse Park and did play as scheduled. The *Courier-Journal* reported the game at length and in detail, calling it "a remarkably fine game, in which good pitching and fielding are the features."[5] The paper did mention Walker's color in its commentary but reported no

Fleet Walker had a tough day behind the bat.

racial incidents. The final score of 5–1 in Louisville's favor featured pitching and fielding. The pitchers were two of the 19th century's best, Toledo's Tony Mullane and Guy Hecker of Louisville. The pair would record 88 wins between them (52 for Hecker) in 1884. Both teams' defenses played errorless ball—except for Walker.

The Toledo catcher had his troubles on defense, especially throwing, with—depending on the source—four or five errors and a passed ball. *Sporting Life* reported that "Toledo suffered greatly through the errors of Walker, who made three terrible throws."[6]

The local press judged that "Mullane did good work in the square, but was poorly supported. Walker, the colored catcher, who has been spoken of as something of a wonder, appeared to be badly rattled, and made all the errors himself."[7] It also detailed each of the errors. In the fourth inning Chicken Wolf, who had drawn a walk, attempted a steal of second base. "Walker attempted to throw him out, but the ball went wide of its mark, [first error] and Wolf galloped on to third. [Monk] Cline hit an easy grounder to short, and Wolf made a dash for the home plate. [Joe] Miller fielded the ball to Walker, who failed to hold it [second error]. …"[8] Later, in the sixth, "Cline struck out, but Walker dropped the ball [third error], and then threw badly to first [fourth error], letting Wolf score and Cline go to second."[9] Cline later scored.

The *Toledo Evening Bee* devoted much less space to the game account under the ambiguous headline "Walker Did It."[10]

From 4 o'clock until 7 the pool rooms were filled with the friends of the Toledos, and the result of each inning was watched with

Guy Hecker pitched a five-hitter for Louisville.

The Colonel's Chicken Wolf scored twice.

much interest. … The fielding of both clubs was fine, Walker, of the Toledos, proving the only exception, he making five [sic] errors and throwing low to the bases. …[11]

Fleet Walker's debut performance was a very poor one and, ironically, in his area of greatest perceived strength his defense. He fared poorly at the plate as well, but had plenty of company in that regard as his teammates managed only five hits off Hecker in a 5–1 loss. Walker sat out the next day but returned for the season's third game, getting a hit from his cleanup spot and allowing three passed balls but otherwise playing errorless ball.

	AB	R	H	TB	PO	A	E
Louisville							
Browning, 3b	4	0	1	1	2	1	0
Hecker, p	3	1	1	2	0	3	0
Wolf, rf	3	2	1	1	2	1	0
Cline, cf	3	2	0	0	0	1	0
Latham, 1b	4	0	0	0	11	0	0
Maskrey, lf	4	0	2	3	2	0	0
Sullivan, c	4	0	0	0	9	2	0
Gerhardt, 2b	4	0	0	0	1	3	0
McLaughlin, ss	3	0	1	1	0	4	0
	32	5	6	9	27	15	0

	AB	R	H	TB	PO	A	E
Toledo							
Barkley, 2b	4	1	3	6	1	5	0
Poorman, rf	4	0	2	2	2	0	0
Miller, ss	3	0	0	0	1	2	0
Walker, c	3	0	0	0	8	0	4
Welch, cf	3	0	0	0	1	0	0
Mullane, p	3	0	1	0	0	3	0
Lane, 1b	3	0	0	0	11	0	0
Brown, 3b	3	0	0	0	0	0	0
Tilley, lf	3	0	0	0	0	0	0
	29	1	5	8	24	10	4
Toledo	000	001	000 – 1				
Louisville	000	203	00x – 5				

Runs earned – Louisville 1. Two base hits – Hecker, Wolf, Maskrey, Barkley. Three-base hits – Barkley. Left on bases – Louisville 6, Toledo 2. Struck out – By Hecker 7, by Mullane 7. Bases on balls – By Hecker 1, by Mullane 1. Bases for hitting batter – By Mullane 2. Passed balls – Sullivan 1, Walter 2. Time – 1:15. Umpire – Valentine.[12]

Notes:

1. Thorn, John. *Baseball in the Garden of Eden* (New York: Simon & Schuster, 2011), p. 185.

2. "A Disabled Club," *Louisville Courier-Journal*, August 22, 1881, quoted in Dean Sullivan, ed., *Early Innings: A Documentary History of Baseball 1825-1908* (Lincoln: University of Nebraska Press, 1995), p. 117.

3. Zang, David W. *Fleet Walker's Divided Heart* (Lincoln: University of Nebraska Press, 1995), p. 41

4. "A Disabled Club."

5. *Louisville Courier Journal*, May 2, 1884, p. 8.

6. *Sporting Life*, May 7, 1884, p. 6.

7. *Louisville Courier-Journal*, May 2, 1884, p. 8.

8. Ibid.

9. Ibid.

10. *Toledo Evening Bee*, May 2, 1884.

11. Ibid.

12. *Louisville Courier-Journal*, May 2, 1884.

Sweeney Strikes Out Nineteen

Boston Beaneaters vs. Providence Grays

South End Grounds, Boston, MA
June 7, 1884

By Edward Achorn

Providence, Rhode Island, was an awfully small city for two egos as big as those of Charles "Old Hoss" Radbourn and Charlie Sweeney, the starting pitchers for the hometown Grays in 1884. As early as spring training the surly veteran Radbourn, a wily strategist from Bloomington, Illinois, and the boastful young Sweeney, a blunt power pitcher from San Francisco, had become "jealous of each other," the *New York Times* observed, and a month of harsh regular-season play had failed to burn away their hostility.[1]

So when Radbourn pitched all 16 innings of a brilliant 1–1 tie on June 6 in Providence against the defending National Leagues champion Boston Beaneaters—a "phenomenal game, the like of which will probably never be seen again," the *Providence Journal* raved—Sweeney knew he had to do something special to win back the city's attention and applause.[2]

June 7 was the kind of late-spring day that made New England hearts soar—sunny, warm, and breezy—and a fine Saturday crowd of 7,387 thronged Boston's South End Grounds, the rotting wooden ballpark crammed in between Columbus Avenue and several sets of railroad tracks. In a feat of bravado, even for 1880s pitchers, Boston Beaneaters ace Jim "Grasshopper" Whitney worked again after pitching 16 innings the day before, and he was superb, allowing only two runs and six hits while striking out 10. But Sweeney, a 21-year-old right-hander with a square jaw and burning, wide-set eyes, was stoked to pitch one of the greatest games in major-league history. That was clear from the moment the 5-foot-10, 181-pound Californian stepped into the 6-by-4-foot pitcher's box.

"Outs and ins, drops and rises seemed to be all the same to Sweeney," the *Boston Globe* reported. "He could give them all, and pitched some of the most deceptive curves imaginable."[3] The son of Irish immigrants was "in magnificent form, and he pitched with such remarkable strategy and speed that Boston's heavy hitters were forced to go down before him one after another," the *Providence Journal* wrote.[4]

He struck out five of the first six batters who faced him—all without the modern advantage of foul balls being strikes. Eight of Sweeney's first nine outs were strikeouts. After six innings, he had mowed down 14 men.

Providence broke a 0–0 tie in the fifth, when Boston center fielder Jack Manning juggled a fly, permitting the Grays' Arthur Irwin to scoot in from third. But Manning more than made up for it moments later, catching a line drive at full sprint and firing the ball to

Charlie Sweeney's 19-strikeout performance for Providence made headlines.

Providence's #1 pitcher, Hoss Radbourn, was consumed by jealousy.

first to double up the runner there. When Boston captain and first baseman John Morrill whipped the pill across to third to catch the Grays' Jerry Denny sliding in there, the Beaneaters had pulled off a stunning triple play. "Immediately there was the wildest excitement and confusion," the *Globe* reported. Men threw their hats in the air, women flashed smiles and waved handkerchiefs, and everyone carried on joyfully.

In the seventh inning, after the Grays had taken a 2–0 lead, Sweeney surrendered a walk to Whitney—though the *Journal* was certain it should have been another strikeout, since in the reporter's eyes Charlie split the plate five times. The Grasshopper later scored on an error, to cut the lead to 2–1.

As the ninth inning opened, the crowd exhorted the Beaneaters to close the gap. But the real story was Sweeney's astounding performance. With his zipping fastball and biting curve, he was smashing the major-league strikeout record. Sweeney whiffed Morrill, a very tough out, for strikeout number 17. Manning, next up, swung "at the sphere as if he would lift it over the centre-field fence, but only empty air met the willow, and he, too, retired on strikes." Bill Crowley, a 27-year-old from Philadelphia who would hit .270 that year, stepped into the right-handed batter's box, and stared down Sweeney. But it was no match, as Crowley whiffed to end it. The mighty crowd, silent for most of the day, erupted in cheers for the visiting pitcher's astonishing feat. "NINETEEN STRUCK OUT; Sweeney's Mysterious Curves Baffle Boston's Batters," read the *Globe*'s headline the next day. "It was "a record," the *Journal* predicted, "which will not be broken in many a day." Hugh "One Arm" Daily officially tied it, on July 7, but that was against vastly weaker competition, the Boston Reds of the hapless Union Association, whose very status as a major league has been sharply questioned by such savants as Bill James.[5] But it wasn't officially broken until more than a century later, on April 29, 1986, when another bigheaded young man posted a 20-strikeout masterpiece in Boston. His name was Roger Clemens.

Alerted by telegraph, Providence leaders rushed to provide a grand welcome home. When the Grays arrived at Union Depot at 7:45 P.M., horse-drawn carriages and Herrick's Providence Brigade Band were waiting. Men plucked up Sweeney and carried him on their shoulders to his carriage, the band struck up "Hail to the Chief,"

Boston pitcher Jim Whitney's 10 strikeouts weren't enough.

the lesser players piled in, and the triumphal parade set off from the station. Colored flares lit up a dusky sky thick with coal smoke. The "streets were one vast blaze of red fire and the crowd packed the sidewalks thicker than sardines," *Sporting Life* reported.[6]

One observer who clearly did not share in the delight was Radbourn. His incessant brooding about the man of the hour, the focus of the accolades, the arrogant Sweeney, led to a rupture in the club later in the season—and to the most brilliant sustained pitching performance in history, as Old Hoss, working virtually alone, day after day, went on to win 59 games.

But that was ahead. For weeks after the June 7 masterpiece, the crowd at the Messer Street Grounds taunted Radbourn, "nagging him to 'break the record' " that Sweeney had set. Not surprisingly, this was said to bother the proud veteran "exceedingly."[7]

	AB	R	H	TB	PO	A	E
Providences							
Hines, cf	4	0	1	1	1	0	0
Farrell, 2b	4	1	1	1	0	0	1
Radbourn, 1b	4	0	1	1	5	0	1
Sweeney, p	4	0	1	1	1	19	1
Irwin, ss	3	1	1	1	0	1	0
Denny, 3b	3	0	1	1	0	1	0
Carroll, lf	3	0	0	0	1	0	1
Nava, c	3	0	0	0	19	3	0
Radford, rf	3	0	0	0	0	0	0
	31	2	6	6	27	24	4

	AB	R	H	TB	PO	A	E
Bostons							
Hornung, lf	4	0	0	0	2	0	0
Sutton, 3b	4	0	1	2	1	2	0
Burdock, 2b	4	0	0	0	2	1	0
Whitney, p	3	1	1	1	0	11	0
Morrill, 1b	4	0	1	1	11	1	0
Manning, cf	4	0	0	0	1	1	1
Crowley, rf	4	0	1	2	2	0	0
Hines, c	3	0	0	0	7	6	2
Wise, ss	3	0	0	0	1	1	1
	33	1	4	6	27	23	4
Providences	000	011	000 – 2				
Bostons	000	000	100 – 1				

Two-base hits—Sutton, Crowley. First base on balls – Bostons, 1. First base on errors – Bostons, 3; Providences, 2. Struck out – Farrell, Radbourn, Sweeney, Irwin, Denny, Carroll, Nava (2), Radford (2), Hornung (3), Burdock (4), Whitney, Morrill (2), Manning (2), Crowley (2), Hines (2), Wise (3). Triple plays – Manning, Morrill and Sutton. Passed balls – Hines, 1. Fumbles – Wise, Farrell, Radbourn, Carroll. Muffed fly – Manning. Wild throw – Hines. Attendance – 7387. Time – 1:35. Umpire – Burns.

Notes:

1. "Ball Players Who Won't Play," *New York Times*, July 23, 1884.

2. *Providence Journal*, June 7, 1884.

3. *Boston Globe*, June 8, 1884.

4. *Providence Journal*, June 9, 1884.

5. James, Bill. "State of the Union," *The New Bill James Historical Abstract* (Free Press, New York, 2001), p. 21-22.

6. *Sporting Life*, June 18, 1884.

7. *Fall River Daily Evening News*, September 5, 1884.

One-Arm Daily Strikes Out 19 (or 20)

Chicago Browns vs. Boston Reds

Dartmouth Street Ballpark, Boston, Mass.
July 7, 1884

By Mark Pestana

Like Three-Fingered Brown after him, One-Arm Daily was saddled with a sobriquet more fanciful than factual. For, as sure as Mordecai Peter Brown had digits enough to count to four on his right hand, so Hugh Ignatius Daily was possessed of a full complement of brachial appendages: the left one, owing to an accident in youth, merely lacked a hand at the end. In a fleeting and far-flung career—six seasons, seven teams, three leagues—and with the hindrance of his handicap, he achieved some remarkable feats.

Coming off a 23-win 1883 season for Cleveland in which he threw a no-hitter, Daily could not have been blamed for succumbing to a bit of hubris when it came to signing a contract for '84. Unsatisfied with his Cleveland salary, he grabbed a better offer from the new Chicago Browns entry in the Union Association.

Daily was uneven in the season's early going, but found his groove with consecutive one-hitters against Washington in May, and by mid-June the Browns were wrestling Baltimore for second place and Hugh was 14–8. But things went rapidly downhill from there. Chicago tumbled into an 11-game losing streak, Daily taking the loss in seven of them and suffering the further indignity of being pulled from the box in two of his starts.

Having fallen to fifth place, the Browns traveled to Boston to meet the third-place Reds, who were enjoying a cozy 23-game homestand at their Dartmouth Street ballpark. The "one-armed" ace would hurl in the July 7 series opener.

Though a somewhat ragtag bunch (like most UA squads) the Reds were not pushovers by any means: They would finish third in wins, third in total bases, and fourth in runs scored. At their helm was first baseman-manager Tim Murnane. A veteran of the National Association era, he brought much-needed experience to a team on which most of his starters were 10 or more years younger than he.

It's possible that some of the 1,000 patrons present at Dartmouth Street on July 7 had been in attendance at the other Beantown park, the South End Grounds, exactly a month earlier, when Providence's Charlie Sweeney fanned 19 Boston batters in a National League contest. If so, they would have the privilege of seeing another pitching masterpiece on this day.

Third baseman John Irwin led the game off for Boston. His brother Arthur, shortstop for the pennant-bound Grays of the National League, had a more accomplished career, but John did manage to loiter in the big leagues through 1891. He quickly became Daily's first strikeout victim. Catcher Ed Crane was up next. Crane would earn the nickname "Cannonball" while carving out a decent pitching career, twirling in more than 200 games, but as a rookie in 1884 he split his time mostly between outfield and backstop and was the heaviest hitter in the lineup. He too went down on strikes. To the plate now came shortstop Walter Hackett—a local boy, born in Cambridge, like brother Mert of the NL Bostons. He made the third notch on Daily's belt.

Cannonball Crane: His triple was the only hit off Daily, but he also fanned twice.

Hugh registered one strikeout in the second in-

– 167 –

ning, and fanned the side again in the third. Meanwhile, the Browns got a run in the first, then took a 2–0 lead when Daily himself singled and scored in the third.

Irwin and Crane brought the top of the Boston order around in the fourth and both whiffed again. Hackett became the first Reds runner, awarded first base when umpire Pat Dutton called a foul pitch on Daily. Apparently, his delivery was an issue all day; the *Boston Globe* claimed he "used the drop continuously, and every time he did so he delivered the ball from above the shoulder and violated the rule."[1] Murnane then reached safely on an error by Charlie Briggs at second. With a rally in the making, center fielder Mike Slattery stepped to the plate. Only 17, he would go back to the minors for seasoning for the next three years before returning to big-league play with the National League Giants in 1888. Here, facing the "wonderful one-armed pitcher,"[2] the 6-foot-2 lad made the third strikeout of the frame.

The Browns went up 4–0 as Charlie Fisher, playing in the last game of his short (11-game) career, singled, and Briggs tripled him home and scored on a putout. Showing no signs of letting up, Daily proceeded to erase opposing pitcher James Burke, left fielder Pat Scanlon, and second baseman Frank Butler—all on strikeouts, giving him 13 in five innings.

In Chicago's half of the fifth, Jumbo Schoeneck doubled and scored on another single by Fisher. The Browns now led 5–0, and thus ended the day's scoring. Burke settled down and retired nine of the final ten batters.

Meanwhile, Daily continued to blank the Reds. The *Boston Globe* remarked: "A pitcher never had nine base ball players as completely at his mercy as did the one-armed Daily. ... He was so skillful, and employed so many ins and outs and drops, that when the ball did come over the base the home players would stand and look at it as if dazed."[3] The *Boston Daily Advertiser* referred to his "mystic curves and peculiar drop."[4]

With two outs in the sixth, Crane cracked a three-bagger for the sole Boston hit. Daily issued no walks. When Slattery made the last out in the ninth, Daily's strikeout tally was 19, equaling Sweeney's month-old record.

Or did Daily actually fan 20? At one point in the game, catcher Bill Krieg dropped a third strike and then threw wide of first trying to peg the batter out. What should have been credited as a strikeout was instead deemed a "base on error."[5]

By season's end Daily had amassed a record 483 strikeouts. Two years later, Matt Kilroy (513) and Toad Ramsey (499) surpassed that total, but no one else ever has. Perhaps most amazing of Daily's 1884 achievements is his strikeouts-per-nine-innings mark of 8.7. It was the highest recorded by any 19th-century pitcher, and would not be bet-

T. H. MURNAN.

Tim Murnane: Player-manager of the 1884 Boston Reds of the Union Association.

tered for 71 years.[6]

	AB	R	H	TB	PO	A	E
Chicago Unions							
Ellick, rf	4	0	0	0	0	0	0
Schoeneck, 1b	1	2	2	3	5	0	0
Horan, cf	4	0	0	0	1	0	0
Krieg, c	4	0	2	2	18	1	4
Fisher, 3b	3	1	2	2	1	0	1
Briggs, 2b	4	1	1	3	1	1	1
Suck, ss	4	0	0	0	0	1	0
Householder, lf	3	0	0	0	1	0	0
Daily, p	3	1	1	1	0	22	1
	33	5	8	11	27	25	7
Boston Unions							
Irwin, 3b	4	0	0	0	1	3	0
Crane, c	4	0	1	3	9	2	5
Hackett, ss	3	0	0	0	1	1	1
Murnane, 1b	4	0	0	0	9	0	0
Slattery, cf	4	0	0	0	1	0	0
Burke, p	3	0	0	0	0	12	3
Scannell, lf	3	0	0	0	2	0	0
Butler, 2b	3	0	0	0	1	2	0
McKeever, rf	3	0	0	0	0	0	0
	31	0	1	3	24	20	9

Bostons   000 000 000 – 0
Chicagos   101 210 000 – 5

Earned runs – Chicagos 4. Two-base hits – Schoeneck. Three-base hits – Briggs, Crane. First base on balls – Chicagos 1, First base on errors – Chicagos 2, Bostons 3. Struck out – Chicagos 10, Bostons 19. Passed balls – Krieg 1, Crane 3. Wild pitches – Burke 2. Time – 1:55. Umpire – Dutton.

Notes:

1. *Boston Globe,* July 8, 1884, p. 5.

2. *Boston Daily Advertiser,* July 8, 1884, p. 8.

3. *Boston Globe,* July 8, 1884, p. 5.

4. *Boston Daily Advertiser,* July 8, 1884, p. 8.

5. *Boston Globe,* July 8, 1884, p. 5; Vaccaro, Frank. "Hugh Daily," in SABR Bio Project, http://bioproj.sabr.org/bioproj.cfm?a=v&v=l&bid=167&pid=3200.

6. Baseball-Reference.com, http://www.baseball-reference.com/leaders/strikeouts_per_nine_season.shtml.

Hoss Radbourn: 59 or 60?

Providence Grays vs. Philadelphia Phillies

*Recreation Park, Philadelphia, Pa.
July 28, 1884*

By Edward Achorn

Two remarkable pitchers powered Providence's drive toward the 1884 National League pennant. In late June the Grays stood first at 33–10, thanks in large measure to the work of 21-year-old Charles Sweeney and veteran Charles "Old Hoss" Radbourn, who was eight tough years older. Sweeney won 15 of his 21 starts, including his sensational 19-strikeout performance on June 7 against Boston (see earlier essay), while Radbourn won 18 of his 22 games.

Trouble, however, lay ahead. Sweeney's brilliant performance against Boston fueled his alcohol-laced ego, while Radbourn grew sulky about losing his role as the Grays' dominant starter. In mid-July the Grays felt compelled to suspend the Hoss for all-around cussedness, including open contempt for his teammates (he had begun dressing in the visitors' locker room) and ostentatiously blowing his stack during one game, endangering catcher Barney Gilligan.[1]

After Radbourn had fumed on the sidelines for a week, a new crisis erupted. On July 22 Sweeney, incensed at the orders of Grays manager Frank Bancroft to leave the pitcher's box during the game he had started and trade places with the right fielder, instead stormed off the field and declared his intent to quit the team. The Grays directors expelled him and then came exceedingly close to folding the club, having no real pitchers left. Old Hoss, after all, wanted to leave Providence, and had little interest in pitching any more for the Grays. But National League President A.G. Mills begged Providence to stay afloat, and the Grays decided to go forward, as manager Bancroft coaxed, or perhaps bribed, the moody Radbourn to rise above his bitterness and return.[2] The reinstated Radbourn won his 25th game on July 23, and his 26th on July 26, and Providence was back, breathing down Boston's neck.

On Monday the 28th, at Philadelphia's Recreation Park, located along Ridge and Columbia (now Cecil B. Moore) avenues, Radbourn got a well-deserved break from pitching. Cyclone Miller, whom the Grays had stolen from the outlaw Union Association, got the start, and "showed up strong," surrendering only one hit in the first four innings. But in the fifth Miller lost his edge, as he tended to do in later innings. The mediocre Phillies bunched three singles, along with a base on balls, and by the time the carnage was over, Providence trailed 4–3.[3]

After Providence stormed back with four runs in the sixth to go ahead 7–4, manager Bancroft decided to play it safe by ordering the erratic Miller to trade places with Radbourn, who to that point had been stationed out in right field. Radbourn proved untouchable for the next four innings, allowing no hits as the Grays coasted to an 11–4 win, taking over first place in the National League.[4] The Grays would go

Hoss Radbourn: 59 wins or 60; either way 1884 was a very good year.

on to win the pennant easily with Radbourn pitching almost every game.

The July 28 game was hardly a great one, and no one would pay the slightest attention to it all these years later, if not for one thing: It set off a fiery debate among baseball aficionados about whether Radbourn really won 60 games during his immortal 1884 season, or only 59, the accepted figure today. We have the late Frederick Ivor-Campbell, a brilliant baseball scholar and Radbourn expert, to thank for the controversy.

The editors who compiled the epochal first edition of Macmillan's *Baseball Encyclopedia* (1969) knew that creating a standardized and official collection of baseball numbers would be a difficult task because rules for statistics had changed dramatically over the years. The concept of pitching wins, for instance, did not even exist during Radbourn's immortal season of 1884; fans just looked at the records of the teams themselves, forming a general impression of which pitcher was doing the best work. To draw early baseball into the grand sweep of the record book, a Special Baseball Records Committee had to be created. "Most of the important issues concerned the period before 1920, a time that was somewhat chaotic in baseball for record-keeping procedures," the *Encyclopedia* editors noted, in a grand understatement.[5] The committee resolved to count pitching wins and losses prior to 1920 by using the 1950 rule, which had established inflexible guidelines for defining wins and losses, sparing scorers the judgment calls they had been making.[6]

Using the 1950 rule, the *Encyclopedia* gave Radbourn the grand total of 60 wins, the all-time record for a single season, and one of baseball's golden numbers. Since Radbourn finished all 73 of the games he started that year, most wins and losses are beyond dispute. But Ivor-Campbell, delving into the July 28 game, discovered that the *Encyclopedia* had erred in assigning Radbourn a victory that day, meaning he should have been given only 59 wins.[7] According to the 1950 rule, if a starter pitches five full innings (as Miller did), and if a reliever comes in with his team ahead and preserves the victory, the starter gets the win, not the reliever.[8] It did not matter that Radbourn pitched nearly half the game—and pitched markedly better than Miller.

Though the *Encyclopedia* kept claiming Old Hoss had won 60, other sources, such as *Total Baseball* (1989), came to accept the less exalted 59 as the official total. But, as Ivor-Campbell well knew, some of this was like the efforts of medieval clerics to estimate how many angels could dance on the head of a pin. Any number is inclined to be a modern extrapolation and interpretation, since the statistic of pitching wins simply did not exist in Radbourn's day.

Whichever win total we use (I go with 59, as much as I wish it were 60), it is undeniable that Radbourn's performance in 1884 was one of the greatest, grittiest performances in baseball's long history—something recognized in his time and well over a century later.

Cyclone Miller is recognized as the winning pitcher in that game of July 28, 1884.

Notes:

1. Radbourn blew up in the July 16 game against Boston. See *Providence Journal*, July 17, 1884. Dressing-room detail from *Providence Evening Telegram*, July 17, 1884.

2. Recounted in my book *Fifty-nine in '84: Old Hoss Radbourn, Barehanded Baseball and the Greatest Season a Pitcher Ever Had* (New York: HarperCollins, 2010), p. 204-7.

3. *Sporting Life*, Aug. 6, 1884.

4. Ibid.

5. *The Baseball Encyclopedia* (Toronto: Maxwell Macmillan Canada, 1969), p. 2,327.

6. Ibid, p. 2328, decision No. 12

7. Ivor-Campbell describes his discovery in an April 20, 1991, article, "How Many Wins for Radbourne in 1884 – 59, 60 or 61?" which he provided to me in manuscript form.

8. *The Baseball Encyclopedia*, Appendix C, p. 2,335.

The First "World Series"

Metropolitans (AA) vs. Providence Grays (NL)

Polo Grounds, New York, N.Y.
October 23-25, 1884

By Peter Mancuso

This chapter is not about a single game. Instead, it is about three games, the first post-season interleague series intended to create a baseball "Championship of America" or a "World's Championship." Although nearly all baseball fans rattle off 1903 as the first World Series, this 19th-century match-up is recognized among baseball historians as the real first "World Series."

There was no model for post-season interleague championship play before 1884. No such series had even been possible until 1883 when the National League, the American Association, and a minor league (the Northwestern League) reached a peace settlement that became known as the Tripartite Agreement or National Agreement.

The 1884 season started with unprecedented excitement for fans (then called cranks) and great anxiety for team owners. The cranks had much to be excited about with more teams and players to follow after the addition of a new upstart league, the Union Association, and the expansion of the American Association. Meanwhile, owners fretted over players jumping their contracts to join the new league and over greater competition for attendance from it.

The established circuits moved through their schedules pretending the UA didn't exist. In the NL, the Providence Grays were highly regarded. The Grays had won the pennant in 1879, finished second in '80, '81, and '82, and third in '83. In the AA, the Metropolitans of New York showed hope when they landed in second a few weeks into the season.

The Grays were managed by Frank Bancroft, in his first season with Providence and his fifth as a major-league manager. The Mets were led by Jim "Truthful Jeems" Mutrie, who had organized and managed the team as a Manhattan-based independent club in 1880 with financial backing from John B. Day, and placed the team in the AA in 1883. Mutrie continued as manager through this 1884 championship season.

Both teams believed that "good pitching beats good hitting." The Grays had Charlie Sweeney and Charles "Old Hoss" Radbourn, while the Mets relied on Tim Keefe and Jack Lynch. In July, while the Grays were battling for the NL lead, Radbourn was suspended for indifferent play.[1] A week later, Sweeney, an incurable alcoholic, was released.[2] Radbourn returned and was nearly untouchable, winning 35 of his next 40 games, giving him a record 59 wins, the all-time major-league season high. Keefe and Lynch finished with 37 wins each.

Although the Mets didn't wrap up their pennant until the last week of the season, Mutrie began an

Mets manager Jim Mutrie.

early campaign to play Providence, the likely National League winners. Mutrie and Bancroft were old associates. Mutrie had played shortstop on Bancroft's New Bedford team in 1878 and the two had managed or played contemporaneously from 1876 through '79.

There were, however, issues to be worked out: number of games, rules, where to play, and finances. As challenges started in the form of wagers, with the winning team's players taking all, the National League was not enthusiastic and was relieved when the managers worked out a split of the proceeds. Although Mutrie offered a five-game series of two games in each team's city and a fifth game, if necessary, in a neutral location, Bancroft did not want to risk the travel expenses. Because Manhattan's population was 1.2 million, Bancroft proposed a three-game series at the Polo Grounds in Manhattan, then located at 110th Street and Fifth Avenue.[3]

It was decided that the American Association's rules would be used. Bancroft had sought an exception permitting use of the NL pitching rule—which allowed the ball to be thrown overhand. That would have been an advantage to Radbourn. Instead the AA rule, which prohibited the pitcher from raising his arm above the belt, was used.[4]

The games were scheduled to take place on Thursday through Saturday, October 23–25. Two victories would crown the champion. Radbourn was to pitch all three games, which was no surprise, given that he pitched nearly every game after Sweeney jumped the team. This was not good news for the Mets and their cranks. Nor was it good news that the injured Jack Lynch was unable to pitch, requiring that Keefe might have to pitch all the games.

Bad news or not, a championship series in the nation's largest and wealthiest city had everyone convinced that these would be the greatest games ever played. On Wednesday the 22nd a huge throng began assembling in the afternoon for a torch-lit parade. It was 76 degrees. Just as the evening parade got underway, rain began and the temperature fell. The rain and wind increased, and the cranks dispersed.

The next day was horrible. The rain stopped, but the temperature never got above 51 and a whipping wind made it feel colder. Only 2,500 cranks turned out, one-tenth of the expected crowd. Keefe was decidedly off his game, and Radbourn surprised no one, winning 6–0.

The 1884 National League-champion Providence Grays. Top row: Hoss Radbourn, Frank Bancroft, Barney Gilligan. Second row: Cliff Carroll, Jack Farrell, Sandy Nava. Third row: Paul Radford, Jerry Denny, Ed Conley. Bottom row: Joe Start, Arthur Irwin, Paul Hines.

That outcome put the onus on Keefe to attempt to prevent a Providence championship in Game Two (although all three games were scheduled to be played, regardless of the outcome of the first two). With temperatures in the 40s and because of the Mets' poor play the day before, the turnout was only about 1,000. Keefe was sore from the previous day and although he made it closer, holding the Grays to three runs, Radbourn allowed the Mets only one, in a game shortened to seven innings by darkness. The Grays were now the "World's Champions."

Game Three was punishing. The game was nearly canceled as the Grays balked at playing a meaningless game before 500 freezing cranks. Much to their credit, they gave in to the Mets, who reminded them how often the New York National League team (also owned by Day) had to play before small crowds in Providence.[5] The Mets' Buck Becannon pitched only his second game of 1884, a 12–2 loss in a contest called after six innings because of the cold.

Providence was able to celebrate only briefly—the following season was its last as a major-league city. More importantly, post-season interleague championship play had been introduced at the major-league level. Although there would never be as short a series, the World Series tradition had begun. It would continue, with only a few lapsed seasons, right up until today.

Oct. 23, 1884

Metropolitans	AB	R	H	PO	A	Providence	AB	R	H	PO	A
Nelson, ss	4	0	0	2	2	Hines, cf	3	2	1	1	0
Brady, rf	4	0	0	1	0	Carroll, lf	3	1	0	1	0
Esterbrook, 3b	4	0	0	1	3	Radbourn, p	4	0	0	0	1
Roseman, cf	3	0	0	0	0	Start, 1b	3	0	0	13	0
Orr, 1b	3	0	0	14	0	Farrell, 2b	4	1	1	2	2
Troy, 2b	3	0	1	0	5	Irwin, ss	3	1	1	0	6
Reipschlager, c	3	0	0	6	3	Gilligan, c	4	1	1	8	2
Kennedy, lf	3	0	0	0	0	Denny, 3b	3	0	1	0	2
Keefe, p	3	0	1	0	1	Radford, lf	3	0	0	2	0
	30	0	2	24	14		30	6	5	27	13

Metropolitans	000	000	000 – 0
Providence	201	000	03x – 6

Errors—Farrell, Irwin. Left on base – Metropolitans 3, Providence 1. Double play – Irwin, Farrell and Start. Bases on balls – None. Struck out – By Keefe 8, Radbourne 9. Wild pitch – Keefe 4, Radbourn 3. Passed ball – Reipschlager 2, Gilligan 1. Umpire – Kelly. Time – 2:00.

Notes:

1. Achorn, Edward. *Fifty-nine in '84: Barehanded Baseball & The Greatest Season a Pitcher Ever Had* (New York: Smithsonian Books, Harper Collins, 2010), p. 191-192.

2. Ibid., p. 202.

3. Bowman, Larry G. *Before the World Series: Pride, Profits and Baseball's First Championship* (DeKalb: Northern Illinois University Press, 2003), p. 47.

4. Achorn, p. 202.

5. Bowman, p. 52.

Tim Keefe, unsuccessful in two starts for the Mets.

Capping A Pennant Chase

New York Giants vs. Chicago White Stockings

West Side Park, Chicago, Ill.
September 29-October 3, 1885

By Bob Tiemann

The 1885 National League pennant race was a battle between two dominating teams, the Chicago White Stockings and the New York Giants. Neither team ever lost more than two games in a row from Opening Day all the way through September. When these juggernauts met with two weeks left in the season, they both had astounding winning percentages, Chicago at .798 (83–21) and New York at .779 (81–23). All four games of the eagerly anticipated final series were sold out in advance, an unprecedented occurrence.

Although the games were played in Chicago, the Giants had every reason to be confident of gaining ground and at least tying the race. After all, they had won nine of the 12 previous head-to-head match-ups. Moreover, they had won seven of the eight games that White Stockings ace John Clarkson had pitched against them, while their own ace, Mickey Welch, was a perfect 7–0 against Chicago.

The series took place at the White Stockings' new West Side Park, a narrow horseshoe of a field with short foul lines and high fences. At least the lines were not as short as at the team's previous yard, which had yielded an inordinate number of home runs in 1884. The sellout crowds were variously reported in the papers as between 8,000 and 11,000 each, but team attendance ledgers put the actual crowds between 6,657 and 6,908.

For the opening game, Tuesday, September 29, White Stockings captain Adrian Anson chose Jim McCormick to pitch for Chicago, while New York sent Welch to the pitcher's box. With fans sitting in foul territory and standees stringing out down the outfield fences, Giants captain John M. Ward insist-

The 1885 National League champion Chicago White Stockings: 1 - George Gore, 2 - Silver Flint, 3 - Cap Anson, 4 - Sy Sutcliffe, 5 - Mike Kelly, 6 - Fred Pfeffer, 7 - Larry Corcoran, 8 - Ned Williamson, 9 - Abner Dalrymple, 10 - Tom Burns, 11 - John Clarkson, 12 - Billy Sunday.

ed on ground rules giving three bases on hits into the overflow. He quickly regretted this as Chicago used two-out triples into the crowd by Fred Pfeffer and Ned Williamson to build a four-run first inning. Chicago catcher Mike Kelly added three ground-rule triples and finished with a 5-for-5 day, while pitcher McCormick hit a triple of his own and held the Giants to just six singles. The White Stockings won, 7–4, finally beating Welch, and increasing their lead to three games with seven to play.

The next day the Giants insisted on a cleared outfield. The crowd was shoehorned into every nook and cranny of the grandstand, and there were fanatics sitting in foul territory. They witnessed the tensest battle of the year. Chicago's battery was Clarkson and Silver Flint, New York's was Tim Keefe and Buck Ewing. Clarkson walked two in the first inning, but he picked Jim O'Rourke off first base, and Roger Connor was doubled off after a line drive was caught. In the Chicago first, Abner Dalrymple and George Gore were both caught trying to steal second base.

The home team finally broke the scoreless tie in the last half of the fourth inning. Dalrymple sent a hot grounder to left and sprinted around to second just ahead of Pete Gillespie's throw. Gore followed with a hot grounder of his own that shot through shortstop John Ward and allowed Dalrymple to score an earned run. Gore moved to second on a passed ball, but the next three men flied out. Keefe then ran this string of men retired to 11 before Pfeffer stepped into one and sent a beauty over the cozy right-field fence with two out in the seventh inning.

The score remained 2–0 until the ninth. Connor opened with a walk. Ewing struck out. Gillespie reached base when first baseman Anson muffed a throw. With two on, Mike Dorgan bounced to shortstop Tommy Burns, who tossed to Pfeffer to force the runner. Pfeffer's desperate attempt to complete a game-ending double play went wild, and before the dust cleared, Connor had scored and Dorgan was perched on second with the potential tying run. But Clarkson snagged Danny Richardson's come-backer, tossing it to Anson for the final out. Clarkson had won, 2–1, on a three-hitter despite six fielding errors by his teammates. It was his 53rd and final win of the season.

The third game was played on Thursday, October 1. New York's 42-game winner, Welch, lost to McCormick again, this time 8–3. A two-out error by Ward prolonged the Chicago second inning, then second baseman Gerhardt let another grounder go through him and two men scored. With Chicago runners on second and third and two out in the fourth, Ewing let a passed ball get by for one run

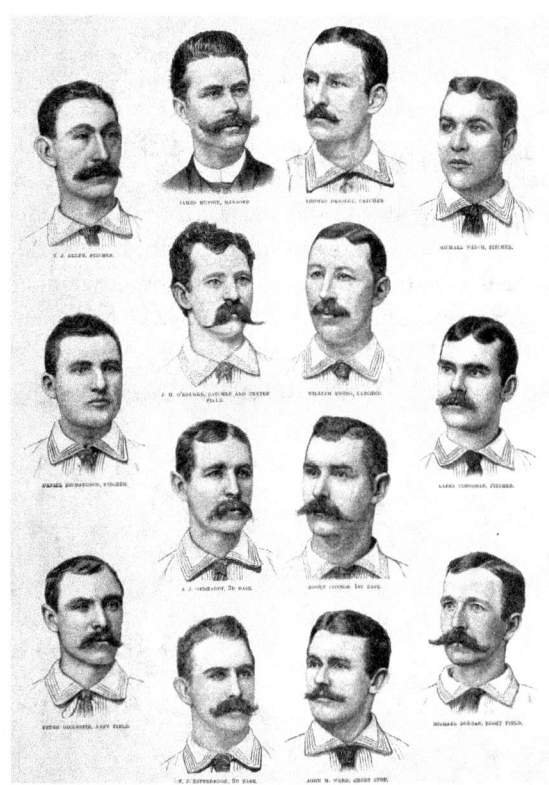

The 1885 New York Giants. Outside clockwise from top left: Tim Keefe, Jim Mutrie, Pat Deasley, Mickey Welch, Larry Corcoran, Mike Dorgan, John Ward, Dude Esterbrook, Pete Gillespie, Danny Richardson. Inside clockwise from top left: Jim O'Rourke, Buck Ewing, Roger Connor, Joe Gerhardt. Corcoran pitched occasionally for the White Stockings that season before making three appearances for the Giants.

and then threw wildly past third to give the White Stockings two more gift tallies. New York counted one in the third and two in the sixth, all thanks to errors and passed balls, and the score stood at 4–3 before Chicago put the game away with four clean hits in a four-run top of the ninth. Dalrymple finished with three hits, Burns scored three runs, and McCormick tossed a three-hitter.

Leading the race by five games with five to play, the White Stockings aimed to mathematically clinch the championship in the series finale on Saturday, October 3, with Clarkson pitching against Keefe. Paced by a three-run poke over the left-field fence by Kelly, they roared out to an 8–2 lead after three innings. But the Giants showed their mettle by tallying one in the fourth, two in the fifth, and (aided by a controversial call at second base) five in the sixth to take a 10–8 lead. When they added two runs in the approaching darkness in the bottom of the eighth, the game was called.

The pennant was officially decided on Tuesday, when the White Stockings beat the Phillies and the Giants lost to the St. Louis Maroons. After clinching the race, the White Stockings relaxed and finished the season with their only three-game losing streak of the year and an 87–25 record, two games ahead of New York. Chicago's final .777 winning percentage has not been matched in all the years since.

Game 2, September 30, 1885

	AB	R	H	TB	PO	A	E
New York							
O'Rourke, cf	3	0	0	0	0	0	0
Connor, 1b	2	1	1	1	7	1	0
Ewing, c	4	0	0	0	10	1	1
Gillespie, lf	4	0	0	0	2	0	0
Dorgan, rf	4	0	0	0	1	0	0
Richardson, 3b	4	0	0	0	1	1	0
Keefe, p	3	0	1	1	0	8	0
Gerhardt, 2b	3	0	1	1	2	3	0
Ward, ss	3	0	0	0	1	1	0
	30	1	3	3	24	15	1
Chicago							
Dalrymple, lf	3	1	2	3	2	0	0
Gore, cf	3	0	2	2	1	0	0
Kelly, rf	3	0	0	0	1	0	0
Anson, 1b	3	0	0	0	11	2	3
Pfeffer, 2b	3	1	1	4	3	5	2
Williamson, 3b	3	0	0	0	1	0	0
Burns, ss	3	0	0	0	2	4	0
Clarkson, p	3	0	0	0	2	10	3
Flint, c	3	0	0	0	4	3	2
	27	2	5	9	27	24	10

New York   000 000 000 - 1
Chicago   000 100 10x - 2

Earned runs – Chicago 2. Left on base – Chicago 1, New York 5, Reached Base of Fielding Errors – NY 5, Bases on Balls – off Clarkson 3, Runs Batted In – Gore, Pfeffer, Struck Out – by Clarkson 7, by Keefe 7, 2B – Dalrymple, Passed Balls – Flint 1, Ewing 1, HR – Pfeffer,
Umpire – W. Curry, DP – Anson to Pfeffer to Burns, Pfeffer to Anson. Time – 2:10, Attendance 6,661.

"A Glorious Victory"

Cincinnati Red Stockings (AA) vs. Cuban Giants (Ind.)

Trenton, N.J.
July 21, 1886

By Paul Browne

Formed by Frank P. Thompson, headwaiter of the Argyle Hotel in Babylon, Long Island, New York, and Stanislaus Kostka "Cos" Govern, who acted as manager, the Cuban Giants were the first salaried black baseball team. They began play in August of 1885 and took on their first major-league opponent, the American Association Metropolitans, on October 5 of that year. The Cubans weren't ready for such fast company yet and the Metropolitans jumped off to a nine-run lead in the top of the first on their way to an 11-3 victory in a game called after six innings on account of darkness.

At first, such opportunities to prove their worth against big-league teams were rare. The Cuban Giants were an independent club, a status that meant filling its schedule with games against college, minor-league, and local town teams. The latter could be professional, semipro, amateur, or even thrown together for the occasion. Fortunately for the Cuban Giants, the black team proved to be a great draw, so after a time major-league teams were happy to include them on their schedule.[1]

One such game took place at Trenton, New Jersey, on July 21, 1886, against the American Association's Cincinnati team, and it gave the Cuban Giants a chance to prove that a black baseball club could compete on an even basis with a big-league team. Although not an Association powerhouse, the Reds were a competent Association club, carrying a 38-40 record into the game, which was fitted between the end of a three-game series in Philadelphia and the start of one in Baltimore. The Reds lineup included several familiar names, among them Bid McPhee, Pop Corkhill, Charley Jones, and Hick Carpenter. Famed pitcher Tony Mullane took part, although he played outfield.

A standing-room-only crowd filled the stadium in Trenton as the home-team Cubans took the field. Clarence Williams put the Cubans ahead in the first inning, scoring on a single and two stolen bases.

The score remained 1–0 when Cubans pitcher Shepard "Shep" Trusty led off the third with a walk. That touched off a five-run inning that included doubles by Jack Fry and Abe Harrison.

In the bottom of the third, Charley Jones of the Reds reached base on an error, moved to second on a single and scored on another single. The Reds added three more runs in the fourth when Jim Keenan doubled to drive home Frank Fennelly and Tony Mullane, who had both reached on errors by third baseman Ben Holmes. Keenan reached home on a passed ball.

But that was as close as the Reds got. Fry walked in the top of the fifth inning and was brought home on Parago's single. The Cuban Giants added a final two runs in the ninth to wrap up their first victory over a major-league team, 9–4.[2]

The Reds were not too happy about their loss. The July 22, 1886, *Cincinnati Commercial Tribune* lamented that there had been no report sent of the game and they were not even sure it had been played.

How did the Cuban Giants beat a big-league team? The Cuban Giants were not just any independent team. Jerry Malloy, in his edition of Sol White's *History of Colored Base Ball*, compiled a list of some of the best black players in the 19th century. The Cuban Giants team that took the field that day included five of the 13 position players on the Malloy-White list. Sol White noted that "With the exception of F(rank) Grant, (Moses Fleetwood "Fleet") Walker and (John "Bud") Fowler, they (the 1886 Cuban Giants) had the best the colored base ball world could produce."[3]

The five players listed by Malloy were Clarence

Williams, Boyd, Fry, Harrison, and Thomas. Abraham "Abe" Harrison played with the Orions at the time of the creation of the Cuban Giants, and Benjamin "Ben" Boyd was with the Keystone Athletics. The other players came later. Arthur Thomas had played with the semipro Manhattan of Washington in 1880 and the West End of Long Branch in 1881 and 1882 before joining the Cubans in 1885. Clarence Williams played with a team in Harrisburg in 1882 and neighboring Middleton in 1883. He started 1885 with the professional Williamsport team before joining the Cuban Giants later that season. Fry came partway through the 1886 season from Lewistown of the mostly white Pennsylvania State Association.

The Cuban Giants were year-round professionals, committed to doing whatever it took to compete on the ballfield. Sometimes that meant going to unusual lengths. In 1885 they established the pattern of playing their way through the South on their way to Florida in the fall. They then played ball and waited tables at the Hotel Ponce de Leon, in St. Augustine. As the weather began to improve, the team would play its way back north in preparation for the coming year's season. While in Florida, there are reports that they played in Cuba.

Cuban Giants	R	BH	PO	A	E	Cincinnati	R	BH	PO	A	E
C. Williams, c	2	2	9	2	0	Jones, lf	1	0	2	6	0
Boyd, cf	1	2	2	0	1	Corkhill, 1b	0	3	17	0	0
Fry, 2b	2	1	4	2	0	Carpenter, 3b	0	1	0	2	1
Harrison, ss	2	2	3	1	1	McKeon, cf	0	1	4	2	0
Thomas, 1b	1	2	5	1	0	McPhee, 2b	0	0	3	1	0
Parago, rf	0	3	0	1	0	Fennelly, ss	1	2	1	2	0
Holmes, 3b	0	1	2	2	2	Mullane, rf	1	1	1	0	0
Whyte, lf	0	0	2	0	0	Keenan, c	1	1	1	1	1
Trusty, p	1	1	0	?	0	Morton, p	0	0	0	4	0
	9	14	27	?	4		4	9	27	20	2

Trenton   105 010 002 - 9
Cincinnati 001 300 000 - 4

Notes:

1. Most of the information on the early development of the Cuban Giants is drawn from Sol White's *History of Colored Baseball* and Michael E. Lomax's *Black Baseball Entrepreneurs, 1860-1901*.

2. The game account paraphrases a report in "A Glorious Victory," *Trenton Times*, July 22, 1886, copy provided by SABR member Gary Fink.

3 White, Sol, introduction by Jerry Malloy. *Sol White's History of Colored Base Ball* with other documents of the early Black game, 1886-1936. (Lincoln and London: University of Nebraska Press, 1995.) p.10.

The famed Cuban Giants circa 1886. Back: possibly Andrew Randolph, Harry Johnson, Ben Holmes, Shep Trusty, Art Thomas, possibly G. Day. Middle: Billy Whyte, Ben Boyd, George Parago, Clarence Williams. Front: possibly G. Shadney, possibly Milton Dabney, possibly S. Epps.

Guy Hecker: Hitting Pitcher

Baltimore Orioles vs. Louisville Colonels

Eclipse Park, Louisville, Ky.
August 15, 1886

By Bob Bailey

At a game on a pleasant afternoon at Eclipse Park in Louisville, the home fans saw *five* batting records set or tied. Remarkably, they were all set or tied by the same player. Even more remarkably, the record-setting player was a pitcher, Louisville's Guy Hecker.

The trail of statistics was not as well marked in 1886 as it is today, so some of the details of Hecker's record run have been lost. But we do know he set single-game records for runs scored (7), total bases (15), and home runs by a pitcher (3). Those three homers also tied the single-game record by a player at any position, and Hecker's six hits equaled the existing single-game record in that category as well.

The game was the second that Sunday between the hometown Louisville Colonels and Baltimore of the American Association. The Colonels had easily won the morning game (played to make up an earlier tie), 13–6, behind the pitching of Tom Ramsey.

In his fifth American Association season, Hecker had always been known as a competent hitter, usually batting in the .270s. To that point in 1886, it was his pitching that had been subpar. A sore arm early in the year had prevented him from taking his turn in the box for several weeks, during which time Ramsey had become one of the Association's top pitchers. In 1886 he sported a 38–27 record with 66 complete games. Hecker was on his way to a 26–23 record, down somewhat from his record of 110–66 over the previous three seasons. Ramsey felt unappreciated and made several less-than-kind public statements about Hecker's poor performance. But Ramsey's remarks did not appreciably cut into Hecker's popularity; he was a fan favorite on a level with Louisville native Pete Browning.

The afternoon game began at 3:30, Louisville batting first and quickly putting a run across. The reporting in the local papers and the sporting weeklies of the time do not provide a full play-by-play, but we do know that Hecker singled and scored that first Louisville run. He reached on an error in the second on another drive to left field that Joe Sommer could not hold. In the fourth inning Hecker sent a drive to the wall in deep left field and slid safely into home ahead of Sommer's peg.

Louisville led 7–5 after scoring four times in the sixth off Baltimore right-hander Dick Conway. Although the papers do not tell us what Hecker did in that inning, we surmise he contributed his second single of the day. In the seventh Hecker sent another drive to the left-field wall and easily completed his second inside-the-park home run, this time with a man on base.

Louisville scored four more times in the eighth as Hecker probably garnered his third single of the afternoon, coming around to score his sixth run. The pitcher closed out his day at bat with a three-run homer in the ninth on another long drive to left. The final score was 22–5. Hecker also collected a win on his complete-game, four-hit performance.

Hecker's showing notwithstanding, the game was not an artistic success. Baltimore committed eight errors, which led to eight unearned runs. Louisville's defense was only a little better, making five errors good for a single unearned run. Conway probably did not blame his catcher for his poor performance. That could have caused some familial strife as the receiver was his brother, Bill.

One Louisville paper noted that Hecker had set a record for runs scored in a game and for single-game total bases, and also tied the record for home runs in a game. But most game stories focused on the total-base count. Hecker's 15 topped the American Association record of 13, held by Dave Orr of the

Metropolitans.

Two days after Hecker's showing, Bob Caruthers of St. Louis hit two home runs, a triple, and a double against Brooklyn. His 13 total bases would have tied the record but for Hecker's performance. Caruthers also missed out on a three-home run game when he was out at the plate trying to stretch a triple.

The three-homer game was the fourth time the feat had been accomplished and the only time an American Association player did it. In 1884 Chicago's Ned Williamson and Cap Anson collected three home runs in a game, as did Jack Manning of Philadelphia. The record stood until 1894, when Bobby Lowe of the Boston Beaneaters hit four. Lowe's performance also wiped out Hecker's record of 15 total bases. Hecker still holds the record for home runs by a pitcher in a game, although he shares it with Jim Tobin of the Boston Braves, who matched the feat in 1942.

The most enduring record of the August 15, 1886, game turned out to be Hecker's seven runs scored, which broke a record set by Jim Whitney for the National League's Boston club against Detroit on June 9, 1883. It has not been matched in the century and a quarter since.

Hecker's best game as a hitter occurred in his best season at the bat. Throughout the year, even when his arm did not allow him to pitch, he was in the thick of the race for the batting title of the American Association. When the Association released final statistics, Hecker was listed with a .342 average, second to Dave Orr's .346. When efforts were made in the 1960s and 1970s to verify all baseball records for inclusion in various encyclopedias, one of the discoveries dropped Hecker's final average by a point, to .341. Oddly, while Hecker lost a point, Orr lost more in that recheck process, his average dropping to .338.

That left Hecker three points ahead of Orr and one point ahead of his teammate Browning. It also gave him one more enduring claim; he remains the only pitcher ever to win a big-league batting title.

Any modern pitcher would love to have a day like Guy Hecker had in 1886: three home runs, six hits, seven runs scored, and an easy victory.

Louisville	R	H	PO	A	E	Baltimore	R	H	PO	A	E
Kerins, 1b	4	2	9	0	0	O'Connell, cf	1	0	6	0	0
Hecker, p	7	5	0	0	0	Manning, rf	0	0	1	0	1
Browning, lf	2	3	4	0	0	Muldoon, 2b	0	1	2	2	1
Cross, c	0	2	4	1	0	Summer, ss	0	0	4	0	1
Warrick, 3b	1	0	1	2	0	Davis, 3b	0	0	0	0	3
Wolf, rf	1	1	0	0	1	Conway, p	1	0	0	2	0
White, ss	3	3	3	2	1	Scott, 1b	1	2	9	0	0
Mack, 2b	2	2	3	7	0	Macullar, ss	1	1	3	1	1
Sylvester, cf	2	3	3	0	0	W. Conway, c	1	0	4	1	1
	22	21	27	12	2		5	4	27	8	8

Louisville 150 104 245 - 22
Baltimore   020 030 000 - 5

Earned runs – Louisville 14, Baltimore 1. Two-base hits –Cross, White and Macullar. Home runs – Hecker 3. Left on base – Louisville 2, Baltimore 2. Double play – White, Mack and Kerins. Struck out – 4 each. Bases on balls – By Conway 6. Passed balls – Cross 1, Conway 3. Wild pitches – Conway. Time – 2:45. Umpire -- Walsh

Matt Kilroy, Strikeout King

Baltimore Orioles vs. Louisville Colonels

Eclipse Park, Louisville, Ky.
Oct. 3, 1886

By Jimmy Keenan

In 1886 the pitcher's box was made a foot deeper and the rule requiring the pitcher to keep both feet on the ground when delivering a pitch was lifted, prompting an increase in strikeouts in both the American Association and the National League.

Nowhere did this change have more impact than in Baltimore, where Matt "Matches" Kilroy, a rookie pitcher for the American Association Orioles, set a record for strikeouts in a season with 513. On October 3, in a game against Louisville, Kilroy surpassed the previous strikeout record of 483, set in 1884 by Hugh "One Arm" Daily.

Kilroy was a Philadelphia native who began his professional baseball career with the Augusta Browns in 1884. The following year he led the Browns into contention in the Southern League. That fall he signed with the Orioles. The left-hander's signature pitch was a knee-buckling curve that was practically unhittable for left-handed batters.

The hard-throwing 19-year-old made his debut in Baltimore on April 7, 1886, in an exhibition game against Washington, and struck out 15 while earning the win. "He pitched a speedy and curved ball, and gave promise of good work," the *Washington Post* wrote. The *Baltimore American* noted, "His curves are peculiar and deceptive, especially the in and out shoots."

Kilroy put together a great rookie season. He had won 28 games and struck out 472 batters by the time the Orioles reached Louisville in late September. Both the Colonels and Orioles had played themselves out of contention for the American Association pennant. Baltimore had performed poorly all year and finished 35 games under .500. Louisville ended the season 25½ games out of first place.

The Orioles won the first game of the series at Eclipse Park. In the second game Kilroy squared off against Louisville ace Toad Ramsey. The Colonels got to Kilroy early and ended up beating Baltimore 7–3. Ramsey, who finished second to Kilroy in strikeouts that season with 499, fanned 11 Orioles, including nine in a row. Kilroy struck out nine Louisville batters in the loss, putting his total for the season at 481.

On the next day, a Sunday, the teams played in front of 1,000 wind-chilled fans. In an era where pitching on consecutive days was commonplace, Kilroy was back in the box for Baltimore. From the outset, the Louisville players and spectators complained to umpire Tom York that Kilroy was not releasing the ball from the designated pitching area. Frustrated over York's failure to censure Kilroy,

Matt Kilroy: His 513 strikeouts remain the all-time single-season record.

Colonels manager Jim Hart instructed his rookie hurler, Elton Chamberlain, to retaliate by running out of the box while delivering his pitches. According to the *Louisville Courier Journal*, "This scared the Baltimore batters out of their wits" and Kilroy refrained from any more questionable pitching tactics for the remainder of the game. Louisville's starting catcher, Amos Cross, split his finger severely in the fourth inning and had to be removed from the game. His replacement, Jimmy Wolf, had a tough day, allowing seven passed balls while committing two costly throwing errors.

Baltimore scored first, a run in the third inning. The Colonels, who chose to bat first that day, scored three runs in the fifth with hits from Pete Browning, Guy Hecker, Jimmy Wolf, and Joe Werrick. In the Baltimore half of the fifth, with a man on base, Kilroy hit a fly into shallow center field that dropped in for a hit. A throwing error on the play allowed both men to come home. In the next two innings, each team scored twice more. With darkness approaching, the game was called at the end of the seventh inning with the scored tied, 5-5. Throughout the contest, Louisville had had a number of chances to take the lead, but failed to do so for lack of timely hitting. (Also, Hecker and Wolf were picked off base by Kilroy.) Defensively, Louisville left fielder Hub Collins made the best catch of the afternoon, robbing Orioles right fielder Jack Manning of extra bases in the third inning. Bill White and Reddy Mack also contributed good plays in the field for the Colonels. Jimmy Macullar, Joe Sommer, and Jumbo Davis did the best glove work for Baltimore.

Starting the game with 481 strikeouts, Kilroy passed Daily's mark of 483 with the third of four batters he fanned that day. The durable southpaw pitched four more regular-season games for Baltimore that year, including a no-hitter against Pittsburgh three days later. He finished the 1886 season with 29 wins, 66 complete games, and five shutouts.

The next season Kilroy won 46 games, the record for wins by a left-handed pitcher. But his meteoric rise was followed by an equally rapid fall. In an age where managers gave little thought to overworking their pitchers, Kilroy was a prime example of the negative effects of this practice. During his first four major-league campaigns, he pitched 1,974 innings, with 222 complete games. These figures do not take into account the numerous exhibition games he pitched before, during, and after the season. In the years that followed, Matches' arm was worn down from overwork and he was never the same pitcher. The level of greatness Kilroy achieved early in his career eluded him for the rest of his days on the diamond.

Elton "Icebox" Chamberlain: The Colonels rookie fought Kilroy to a draw on the hill.

Louisville	R	H	O	A	E	Baltimore	R	H	O	A	E
Cross, c	0	1	1	2	0	Manning, rf	0	0	1	0	1
Kerrins, rf	1	0	0	0	0	Purcell, lf	1	0	0	0	0
Browning, cf	1	1	0	1	0	Sommers, 2b	0	1	3	3	0
Hecker, rf & 1b	1	3	5	1	0	Sowders, cf	0	1	1	0	0
Wolf, 1b & c	1	1	6	2	2	Davis, 3b	0	1	1	2	0
Werrick, 3b	0	1	2	0	1	Macullar, ss	1	1	1	5	0
White, ss	1	2	2	3	0	Scott, 1b	1	1	7	0	0
Mack, 2b	0	3	2	2	1	Fulmer, c	1	0	5	2	0
Collins, lf	0	0	2	0	0	Kilroy, p	1	1	2	1	0
Chamberlain, p	0	0	1	0	0						
	5	12	21	11	3		5	6	21	13	1

Louisville 000 031 1 - 5
Baltimore 001 021 1 - 5

Earned runs – Louisville 4. Passed balls – Wolf 7, Cross 1, Fulmer 3. Wild pitches – Kilroy 2. - First base on balls – by Chamberlain 5. by Kilroy 3. Struck out - by Chamberlain, 4. Kilroy, 4. Double plays, White 1. Hecker and Wolf 1. Umpire York.

Curt Welch's Winning Slide

St. Louis Browns vs. Chicago White Stockings

West Side Park, Chicago, Ill.
October 23, 1886

By Bob Tiemann

After the 1885 season the two major-league pennant winners, the Chicago White Stockings of the National League and the St. Louis Browns of the American Association, had played a postseason series to showcase their champions. As incentive for the players, the club owners, Albert Spalding of Chicago and Chris Von der Ahe of St. Louis, put up $500 each, with the winning players to divide the prize.

One game was played in Chicago and three in St. Louis (one a rancorous forfeit win for the visitors). The teams then headed to Cincinnati, Pittsburgh, and points east. The traveling games were not a pecuniary success (only around 500 fans showed up for the Pittsburgh game), and before the seventh game was played in Cincinnati, on October 24, 1885, the two teams announced an abrupt end to the series. Each team had won two completed games, one had ended in a tie, and there had been that five-inning forfeit.

A wire-service report said the teams mutually agreed to throw out the forfeit and make one final contest decisive. The Browns won easily, 13–4, and were headlined (in *Sporting Life*, at least) as "The World Champions."[1] Spalding, however, quickly disavowed the Cincinnati agreement, the prize money was divided evenly by the teams,[2] and the series has ever after been listed as a tie.

In late September 1886, with the pennant races winding down and both teams headed for repeat pennants, Von der Ahe issued a formal challenge to Spalding and his club to a "World Championship series." Spalding quickly accepted and added the proviso that the winning club would "receive the total gross gate receipts, including the grandstand receipts."[3] Von der Ahe agreed to this, and a seven-game "Winner Take All" series was arranged, starting with three games in Chicago, followed by three in St. Louis. If a seventh game was necessary to decide the outcome, it was to be held in a neutral city.

The White Stockings won at home on Monday and Wednesday, the Browns taking the Tuesday game. When the series shifted to St. Louis, the home team won on Thursday and Friday, position-

Curt Welch scored the winning run, but did he slide?

ing the Browns to win the series with a victory in Game Six.

The skies were cloudy, but the game time had been moved up to avoid the early-autumn darkness, and a full house of rabid rooters was on hand at Sportsman's Park. The starting pitchers were John Clarkson for Chicago, pitching his fourth game in six days, and Bob Caruthers for St. Louis, pitching for the third time in five days.

The game started out well enough for Chicago, as Clarkson held St. Louis hitless through the first six innings, while teammate Fred Pfeffer scored three runs. In the second inning Pfeffer started with a single, stole second, moved up on a passed ball, and scored on a two-out hit by Tommy Burns. In the fourth inning Pfeffer blasted a home run into the right-field seats. And in the sixth he raced all the way to third on a groundball that went through the second baseman's legs and then rolled past the right fielder, then scored on a long fly out by Ned Williamson.

Tip O'Neill got the Browns' first hit, a rousing triple in the seventh inning, but spoiled it by overrunning third base and getting tagged out. But in the eighth, St. Louis finally broke through. Captain Charlie Comiskey opened with a clean hit and Curt Welch followed with a bunt that third baseman Burns threw wildly past first. Comiskey sprinted all the way home while Welch made second as the crowd erupted. The next two hitters flied out, but Welch took third on a short passed ball and Doc Bushong walked. Vociferous Arlie Latham was the next batter, and as Bushong edged off first Latham yelled, "Stay there, Doc, and I'll bring you both in." With two strikes against him, Latham whaled away at a low pitch from the tiring Clarkson, sending it soaring to deep left. Outfielder Abner Dalrymple started in on the ball, then watched it sail over his head for a triple, tying the score, 3–3.

Dalrymple had a chance to redeem himself when he batted in the ninth with Burns on third and two out, but he struck out. O'Neill nearly won the game in the St. Louis ninth, but a leaping catch by Jimmy

Abner Dalrymple committed a critical error in the eighth inning.

Ryan robbed him of a potential home run. Chicago was retired in order in its tenth.

Welch led off the bottom of the tenth and was hit by a pitch. But Anson protested that he had made no effort to avoid the pitch, and the umpire made him bat again. On the next pitch Welch lined a single to center. A fumble by shortstop Williamson put two men on. Yank Robinson calmly bunted the men to second and third, bringing up Bushong. On the second ball pitched, catcher King Kelly signaled for a low ball outside. But Clarkson's pitch sailed in high and inside, bouncing to the backstop. Welch ran home with the championship-winning run as Sportsman's Park turned into a madhouse.

Fans poured out of the stands and carried several of the Browns players off on their shoulders. Many then waited nearly an hour for their heroes to emerge from the clubhouse so they could cheer them again. The *Chicago Daily News* extra edition headlined its story simply, "ST. LOUIS CRAZY."[4]

Although the winning run has come down in history with the label "Curt Welch's $15,000 Slide," there is no contemporary evidence that he actually slid. In fact, the *Missouri Republican* said he "trotted home,"[5] and the *Globe-Democrat* said that "Kelly made no effort to get (the ball), and … in a dazed manner stood and watched Welch come in."[6] As for the money, the *Chicago News* put the winnings at "exactly $13,781.95."[7] These discrepancies notwithstanding, the 1886 St. Louis Browns were world champions, the only American Association team with an undisputed claim to that title.

Von der Ahe gave half the winnings to the 12 players, around $575 per man. At the betting parlors, it was estimated that more than $100,000 changed hands on the results.[8]

St. Louis owner Chris Von der Ahe challenged Chicago to a "World's Champioship Series."

	AB	R	H	BI	PO	A	E
Chicago							
Gore, cf	5	0	0	0	2	0	0
Kelly, c	5	0	0	0	9	2	0
Anson, 1b	4	0	0	0	13	0	0
Pfeffer, 2b	4	3	2	1	0	1	0
Williamson, ss	4	0	0	1	0	2	1
Burns, 3b	4	0	2	0	1	5	1
Ryan, rf	4	0	1	1	3	1	0
Dalrymple, lf	4	0	1	0	0	0	0
Clarkson, p	4	0	0	0	0	2	0
	38	3	6	3	28	13	2
St. Louis							
Latham, 3b	4	0	1	2	1	1	1
Caruthers, p	1	0	0	0	2	0	0
O'Neill, lf	3	0	1	0	5	0	0
Gleason, ss	4	0	0	0	0	3	0
Comiskey, 1b	4	1	1	0	7	0	1
Welch, cf	4	2	2	0	5	0	0
Foutz, rf	4	0	0	0	3	0	1
Robinson, 2b	4	0	0	0	1	3	1
Bushong, c	2	1	0	0	6	0	0
	33	4	5	2	30	7	4

Chicago   010 101 000 0 - 3
St. Louis 000 000 030 1 - 4

	IP	H	R-ER	BB	SO	WP
Clarkson (L 2-2)	9 1/3	5	4-3	2	10	1
Caruthers (W 2-1)	10	6	3-2	0	5	1

LOB – Chicago 5, St. Louis 3
Reached Base on Error – Chicago 2, St. Louis 1
One out when winning run scored
2B – Burns. 3B – O'Neill, Latham
HR – Pfeffer
SB – Pfeffer
Time – 2:20
Attendance – 8,000
PB – Bushong, Kelly
Umpire – G. Pearce

Notes:

1. *Sporting Life,* November 4, 1885

2. Anson, Adrian C. *A Ball Player's Career* (Chicago: Era Publishing Co.), 1900.

3. *The Sporting News,* October 4, 1886.

4. *Chicago Daily News,* October 23, 1886.

5. *Missouri Republican,* October 24, 1886.

6. *St. Louis Daily Globe-Democrat,* October 24, 1886.

7. Article reprinted in *St. Louis Globe-Democrat,* October 26, 1886.

8. *Missouri Republican,* October 24, 1886.

The First African American Battery

Buffalo (IL) vs. Newark Little Giants

Newark Base Ball Grounds, Newark, N.J.
May 2, 1887

By Peter Mancuso

Catchers have been prized from baseball's beginning, as evidenced by the Knickerbocker rule requiring that a third strike be caught for the batter to be out.[1] Casey Stengel had that in mind when he explained the Mets' selection of a catcher with the first pick in the 1961 expansion draft. "You have to have a catcher or you'll have a lot of passed balls," Stengel remarked.[2]

In the early 1860s Jim Creighton effectively demonstrated, with his delivery of controlled fastballs, the value of good pitching. From that time forward the battery (pitcher and catcher) took on increasing significance.

Professional baseball's beginnings in the early 1870s soon evolved into the "scientific" game, so the relationship between pitchers and catchers became more significant. It was not just the ability of one player to throw and the other to catch, it was also their ability to play the head game—conspiring with each other to outthink the batter. In the nearly all-white organized baseball of the 19th century, the idea of an African American battery trying to outwit their white opponents resulted in cultural implications that went beyond the outcome of an at-bat.

Given the prevailing attitudes, it is no wonder that professional baseball was almost two decades old before a pair of African American players constituted the battery of a team in organized baseball beyond the all-black teams of the day. Yet African American pitcher George Stovey and catcher Moses Fleetwood "Fleet" Walker stepped into this environment in the spring of 1887 as members of the otherwise all-white Newark Little Giants of the International Association.

Walker, 30, was an experienced and well-regarded catcher who was entering his fifth professional season, all on predominantly white teams, including the 1884 Toledo Blue Stockings of the major-league American Association. Walker was also a college man, having attended the University of Michigan and Oberlin College in Ohio. In addition, he had played in the Eastern League, a forerunner of the International League, in the two preceding seasons and was generally tolerated, if not liked, by his teammates.

Stovey, 20, was a pitching phenomenon in only his second season of organized baseball. He had the year before been lured away from the Cuban Giants by Jersey City, a league rival of Newark. He was signed by Newark for the '87 season, precipitating a bitter contract dispute with the owners of the Jersey City club that Newark won.[3]

As the opening day of the season approached, Newark fans had high hopes for a league championship (they had won the Eastern League pennant the year before) and viewed the acquisition of Walker and Stovey as making an already strong team even stronger.

Although Walker would be placed in the lineup to catch white pitchers, Stovey was never matched up with any catcher other than Walker. On April 20, before the league season began, for example, Mickey Hughes, a white pitcher, was matched with Walker for a game against Waterbury,[4] a team Walker had played for in 1885 and which was in the Eastern League in 1886. The next day, April 21, Stovey went into the box with Walker catching in a loss against the Brooklyn team of the American Association.[5] On the 22nd Stovey rested while Walker caught against Bridgeport.

On April 26, the next time Newark played, Stovey was beaten by Jim Mutrie's New York Giants, who played their regular starting lineup, which included five future Hall of Famers. Stovey was characterized as wild (with 11 runs and 14 hits allowed) while the work of Walker "behind the bat" was described as "absolutely perfect." Walker also scored one of the three runs that pitcher Mickey Welch (one of the future Hall of Famers) gave up.[6] It is reasonable to assume that Stovey needed a rest the following day, April 27; Walker was also held out of that exhibition game against Boston of the National League. Whether this was the result of any racial overtones is not recorded.

Walker caught Hughes in Newark's 12–3 Opening Day victory over Buffalo.[7] With no baseball on Sunday, it was an obvious choice to place the two players at the points of the battery for the teams' second meeting on Monday, May 2. Stovey faced Michael Walsh, considered one of the International League's best pitchers.

The game was described as a "splendid contest," except that Walsh surrendered five walks and threw one wild pitch while battery mate Thomas Calihan allowed four passed balls. Newark scored three runs in the top of the first inning. Stovey kept the Buffalo club scoreless through its first three innings, but in the bottom of the fourth he allowed three hits, which produced three Buffalo runs.

With the score tied, Newark center fielder John Henry hit a solo home run over the left-field fence in the top of the fifth inning to give the home team a one-run lead. Stovey did the rest, not allowing Buffalo another run for the next five innings and securing a 4–3 victory for the Little Giants. Stovey also provided one of Newark's 15 hits while allowing the opposition eight. Walker had no hits in four attempts but was his usual reliable self behind the plate.[8]

The next day Walker caught Hughes, and the day after that he again caught Stovey, who won his second game. In fact, Walker and Stovey combined for Stovey's first ten games pitched that season, all of which were wins.[9]

	AB	R	H	SB	PO	A	E
Newark							
Irwin, 3b	5	1	2	1	0	1	0
Fields, 1b	5	1	1	0	10	0	0
Henry, cf	5	2	4	3	0	0	0
Coogan, rf	5	0	1	0	1	0	0
Annis, lf	5	0	3	1	1	0	0
Walker, c	4	0	0	0	9	1	0
Smith, ss	4	0	2	1	0	2	0
McLaughlin, 2b	4	0	1	0	4	3	0
Stovey, p	4	0	1	0	2	7	0
	41	4	15	6	27	14	0
Buffalo							
Gilligan, rf	4	0	0	0	1	0	0
Reidy, 3b	4	0	2	0	0	2	0
Grant, 2b	4	1	2	0	4	2	1
Lehane, 1b	4	1	3	0	13	2	0
Remsen, cf	4	1	1	1	2	0	0
Hamburg, lf	4	0	0	0	1	0	0
Callaghan, c	4	0	0	0	3	1	0
Esterday, ss	4	0	2	0	3	5	0
Walsh, p	4	0	0	0	0	7	1
	36	3	10	1	27	19	2

Newark   300 110 000 - 4
Buffalo 000 300 000 - 3

Earned runs – Newark 3, Buffalo 3. Left on bases – Newark 10, Buffalo 6. Struck out – Newark 2, Buffalo 5. Wild pitches – Walsh 1. Passed balls – Callaghan 4. Double plays – Esterday, Grant and Lehane. Base on balls – Irwin 1, Fields 1, Henry 1, Smith 2, Stovey 1, Grant 1. Two-base hits --- Esterday. Home runs – Henry. Time – 1:40. Umpire – Richard Pearce.

Notes:

1. Chadwick, Henry. *Beadle's Dime Base-Ball Player: A Compendium of the Game*; First Rules of Baseball, Section 5 (New York: Irwin P. Beadle & Co. 1860), p. 7.

2. Morris, Peter. *Catcher, How the Man Behind the Plate Became an American Folk Hero* (Chicago: Ivan R. Dee, 2009), p. 39.

3. McKenna, Brian. "George Stovey"; in Bioproject, Society for American Baseball Research: www.sabr.org/bioproject/stovey.

4. *Newark Evening News*, April 21, 1887, p. 4.

5. Loc. cit., April 22, 1887, p.1.

6. Loc. cit., April 27, 1887, p. 4.

7. Loc. cit., May 3, 1887, p. 1.

8. McKenna, op. cit.

The Color Line is Drawn

Chicago White Stockings vs. Newark Little Giants

*Newark Base Ball Grounds, Newark, N.J.
July 14, 1887*

By Peter Mancuso

On the morning of July 15, 1887, the *New York Herald* boldly titled one of its front-page stories, "THE COLOR LINE." The story under the headline, from New Orleans, involved a claim by former Union Army "negro soldiers" that they were being denied admission into the local post of the Grand Army of the Republic, a veterans organization, solely on account of color. The "negro Union veterans" complained that "the local posts of the G.A.R. prefer to fraternize with the ex-Confederate organizations ... rather than with their colored ex-comrades."[1] Higher-ups in the G.A.R. offered not the slightest apology.

Meanwhile, on the sports page, the *Herald* reported that Newark of the International League had defeated the Chicago White Stockings, the reigning National League champion, 9–4. The brief report said, in part, "The home club hit (Mark) Baldwin very hard, but the visitors were not so fortunate with (Mickey) Hughes." Newark had 18 hits and two errors while Chicago had 12 hits and five errors. The account noted that the batteries consisted of Hughes and Bart Cantz for Newark and Baldwin and Dell Darling for Chicago.[2]

The real story of this day, however, was what was not reported—events that would change the face of baseball for the next 60 years.

Chicago and Newark played because the White Stockings had an off day after completing a series in Washington. The White Stockings were to start a series with the Giants in New York on the 15th. This gave Chicago a lucrative opportunity for an exhibition game on the 14th at the Newark ballpark.

Newark had a powerful team that had won the Eastern League championship the preceding season and had jumped out to a strong start in its first year in the International League. The team's ownership correctly anticipated that fans would come to the ballpark in droves to see the White Stockings. The Newark fans were confident; after all, they had one of the best batteries in minor-league baseball. Twenty-one-year-old left-handed pitcher George Stovey began the season by capturing his first 10 decisions, and Moses Fleetwood Walker was one of the better defensive catchers in the International League. Both were men of color.

A story in the *Newark Evening News* provided some information that the *Herald*'s story lacked. In a front-page article headlined "DRAWING THE COLOR LINE; Chicago Unwilling to Play With Stovey, No More Colored Players," the *Evening News* reported fully on what happened in Newark as well as at an International League meeting in Buffalo that day.

"Before the game with the Chicago Club yesterday, Manager (Charles) Hackett (of Newark) received a telegram from Captain Anson (of Chicago) saying that the Chicago Club would not play if Stovey and Walker, the colored men, were put at the points," the newspaper reported. It said Hackett "would probably have had Stovey pitch, however, but for the fact that that player was not feeling well, so Hughes was substituted at the last moment." No explanation was offered for why Walker was also not played.

The report then shifted to the upstate New York meeting: "The International League representatives held a meeting at the Genesee House, in Buffalo, yesterday and passed a resolution instructing Secretary (C.D.) White not to approve the contract of any more colored players. Jersey City and some of the other clubs insisted the African players drove white men from the league."[3]

A biography of Stovey by Brian McKenna of the Society for American Baseball Research sheds addi-

The 1887 Chicago White Stockings:
1 - Billy Sunday, 2 - Ned Williamson, 3 - John Clarkson, 4 - Marty Sullivan, 5 - Shadow Pyle,
6 - Mark Baldwin, 7 - Tom Burns, 8 - Cap Anson, 9 - Fred Pfeffer, 10 - Jimmy Ryan, 11 - Jocko Flynn,
12 - Dell Darling, 13 - Lew Hardie, 14 - Sliver Flint, 15 - Tom Daly.

tional insight on the matter. According to the biography, the *Newark Sunday Call* effectively dismissed the Stovey "not feeling well" report and offered this version: "It was announced on the (grounds) that he was sulking, but it has since been given out that Anson objected to a colored man playing."[4]

McKenna's research on Stovey's life amplified what else may have driven the banning of further contracts with "colored players" at the International League meeting in Buffalo. The vote, he says, "was sparked by a revolt in the Binghamton club" against two black Binghamton players, Bud Fowler and William Renfro. He added: "After the contest on June 27, one of Binghamton's white players, Buck West, rallied the rest of the team around his cause. A petition was signed by nine players and a telegram was sent to the club directors demanding that Fowler and Renfro be released or the protesters would strike.[5]

With the Binghamton players' petition looming and Anson's chilling financial threat to withdraw his popular White Stockings from play with clubs fielding "colored players," it was probably a relatively easy step for the International League team representatives to pass the ban. McKenna's research, however, adds another layer to the story.

The Newark and Jersey City teams had joined the International League in 1887 after playing in the Eastern League the season before. In 1886 Pat Powers, owner of the Jersey City team, had signed Stovey from the all African American Cuban Giants, "and Stovey had pitched exceedingly well in '86 for Jersey City; 270 IP, 1.13 ERA and 203/43 SO/BB ratio." But after the season Powers lost a contract dispute that involved Stovey jumping to Newark. "Powers had little motive to save Stovey from being banned and perhaps all the motive in the world to see him excluded from IL play," McKenna wrote.

Stovey and Walker remained with Newark until season's end, Stovey's 2.42 ERA ranking sixth among 32 International League pitchers for the year. Stovey remained active in minor league and semiprofessional baseball as a player and umpire for a good number of years. Walker remained in the International League through 1889 despite the ban.

At the same time, on the day that Stovey was withdrawn, Organized Baseball effectively committed to a policy to exclude "colored players." The prohibition remained in effect for six decades until it was breeched by Jackie Robinson and Branch Rickey.

Earned runs, Newark, 5 Chicago, 1; base on errors, Newark 4, Chicago, 1; left on base, Newark 8, Chicago, 6; struck out, Newark 4, Chicago, 4; wild pitches, Hughes 2, Baldwin 1; passed balls, Cantz 2, Darling 2; double plays, Ryan, Pfeffer and Anson; base on balls, McLaughlin 2, Van Haltren, Anson, Burns; two-base hits, Coogan, Annis, Irwin, McLaughlin, Ryan, Anson, Darling. Umpire, Robert Neil.

Notes:

1. *New York Herald,* July 15, 1887, p. 1.

2. Ibid. p 9.

3. *Newark Evening Journal,* July 15, 1887, p.1.

4. *Newark Sunday Call,* July 17, 1887, cited by Brian McKenna, in "George Stovey", biographical research paper, Society for American Baseball Research (SABR), Bioproject, www.sabr.org/bioproject.

5. McKenna, Ibid.

6. McKenna, Ibid.

	AB	R	H	SB	PO	A	E
Newark							
Coogan, rf	5	2	1	0	5	1	0
Annis, lf	5	1	3	2	1	0	0
Stuart, cf	5	0	2	0	2	2	0
Irwin, 3b	5	0	3	2	3	0	0
Fields, 1b	5	1	2	1	6	0	0
Cantz, c	5	1	1	0	6	1	2
Smith, ss	5	1	2	1	4	2	0
McLaughlin, 2b	5	2	3	0	0	0	0
Hughes, p	4	1	1	1	0	5	0
	41	9	18	7	27	11	2
Chicago							
Daly, rf	5	0	2	1	0	1	0
Ryan, ss	4	1	1	1	1	3	2
Sullivan, lf	4	0	0	0	0	0	0
Anson, 1b	4	2	4	0	5	1	1
Pfeffer, 2b	4	0	0	0	2	3	0
Van Haltren, cf	4	1	3	1	7	1	0
Burns, 3b	4	0	1	0	6	1	1
Darling, c	4	0	1	0	6	1	1
Baldwin, p	4	0	0	0	0	4	0
	37	4	12	3	27	15	5

```
Newark    100 305 000 - 9
Chicago   100 101 001 - 4
```

Sam's Triple Trouble

Detroit Wolverines vs. St. Louis Browns

October 21, 1887

By Mike Harrington

Sam Thompson may have been the best hitter in baseball in 1887. But at what might have been the season's climactic moment, a single swing of his bat nearly turned the powerful Indianan known as Big Sam from hero to goat.

The setting was the 10th game of a 15-game World Championship Series between Thompson's National League champion Detroits (widely known as the Wolverines) and Chris Von der Ahe's American Association champion St. Louis Browns. The Browns were reigning world champions, having beaten the Chicago White Stockings in a dramatic postseason series in 1886. They had compiled a .704 winning percentage against Association teams in 1887. But the Wolverines were also formidable, even without their other star slugger, Dan Brouthers, who was injured. Detroit's .637 winning percentage had been good for a 3½-game advantage over second-place Philadelphia.

Detroit held a commanding seven games to two lead in the scheduled 15-game World Championship Series and needed just one more victory as the teams prepared for the 10th game on Thursday, October 20, in Washington. But a steady rain postponed the game, and created a dilemma. Since the next game in the series was already on the schedule for the following day in Baltimore, the teams agreed to play two games on Friday, the first in Washington at 10:30 A.M. and a second 40 miles away in Baltimore that afternoon.

Umpire John Gaffney called the game to start at 10:30. Despite the early start, between 3,000 and 4,000 spectators were in attendance.

The first batter was Hardy Richardson, second baseman of the Detroits, and he put the fourth pitch from Bob Caruthers over the left-field fence for a home run. It was a great start for Detroit, but even so, at the end of the first inning the score stood 2–2.

That remained the situation as Detroit came to bat in the top of the third inning. Richardson singled to left, and Charlie Ganzel followed with a line single to right. Jack Rowe then dropped one between first baseman Charlie Comiskey and right fielder Dave Foutz that loaded the bases with no one out. The Wolverines appeared poised to take command of the game that would bring the team the world championship, even more so since the next batter was Thompson. Big Sam had 203 hits and 166 runs batted in during the 1877 season. Except for the rule put in place that season counting walks as hits (in fact, *Total Baseball*,

Yank Robinson: The Browns second baseman closed out a rally-killing triple play.

The 1887 National League champion Detroit Wolverines. Standing: Charlie Bennett, Dan Brouthers, Sam Thompson, Charlie Ganzel, Larry Twitchell, Lady Baldwin. Sitting: Jack Rowe, Fatty Briody, Fred Dunlap, Bill Watkins, Deacon White, Ned Hanlon, Billy Shindle, Pretzels Getzien. On ground: Stump Wiedman, Hardy Richardson.

eighth edition listed Thompson with 235 hits), Thompson's .372 batting average would have been good for the league leadership in that category as well. So remarkable were Thompson's accomplishments that in 1974 he would be voted into the Hall of Fame. Detroit fans in Washington that day could not have hoped for a better hitter to come to the plate in that spot.

Thompson picked out a Caruthers pitch and hit a crisp line drive. But the ball flew right to Browns shortstop Bill Gleason, who caught it to retire Thompson and fired to third baseman Arlie Latham. He touched third base for the second out, retiring Richardson, who was headed down the third-base line toward home plate with what he presumed would be the go-ahead run. Latham then threw to second baseman Yank Robinson, who touched that base before Ganzel could return to it. In a matter of a couple of seconds, a rally that could have led to a world championship turned into a 6-5-4 triple play, the first in World Series history.

It was the last rally for Detroit that morning. The Wolverines scored single runs in the fifth and ninth innings, but lost 11–4. Curt Welch led the Browns with a three-run home run, while Latham, Gleason, Comiskey, and Foutz each contributed three hits, one of Latham's also being a home run. The series stood at seven games to three.

Immediately after the game, the players of both teams boarded a train to Baltimore to play the afternoon game. Detroit won 13–3 and clinched the city's first world championship. It was a title delayed by a few hours thanks in part to the first triple play in post-season history, one that came off the bat of a future Hall of Famer.

Detroit	AB	R	BH	PO	A	E	Browns	Ab	R	BH	PO	A	E
Richardson lf, 2b	4	1	3	1	4	1	Latham 2b	5	1	3	1	3	1
Ganzel 1b, C	4	0	2	5	1	0	Gleason ss	5	0	3	1	5	1
Rowe ss	4	1	1	3	0	0	O'Neil lf	5	2	2	3	0	1
Thompson rf	4	0	0	0	1	0	Comiskey 1b	5	3	3	11	0	0
White 3b	4	0	1	3	1	2	Caruthers p	5	1	2	0	3	0
Dunlap 2b	2	0	0	2	1	0	Foutz rf	5	1	3	0	0	0
Bennett C, 1b	4	0	1	8	2	1	Welch cf	5	2	2	2	0	0
Hanlon cf	4	1	2	2	0	0	Robinson 2b	4	0	1	4	3	0
Getzien p	4	0	0	0	3	0	Boyle C	4	1	1	5	2	1
Twitchell lf	2	1	0	0	0	0							
Totals	36	4	10	24	13	4	Totals	43	11	20	27	16	4

Innings	1	2	3	4	5	6	7	8	9	Total
Detroit	2	0	0	0	1	0	0	0	1	4
Browns	2	0	0	0	3	1	4	1	x	11

Attendance: 3,000-4,000
Earned Runs: Detroit 2; Browns 10. Three-base hit – Foutz. Home Runs – Richardson, Latham, Welch. Left on bases – Detroit 5, Browns 8. Triple Play – Gleason, Latham, and Robinson. Struck out – Getzien 2, Boyle 2. Bases on balls – Hanlon, Gleason, Robinson, Caruthers. Stolen Bases – Rowe, Hanlon, Welch, Robinson. Wild Pitch – Caruthers. Time: 1:45. Umpires: Kelly and Gaffney

Tim Keefe Finally Loses

Chicago White Stockings vs. New York Giants

Polo Grounds, New York, N.Y.
August 14, 1888

By Peter Mancuso

The record for consecutive games won by a pitcher in a single season has stood for more than a century. It is 19 games, first set by New York Giants ace Tim Keefe between June 23 and August 10, 1888. The streak ended on August 14 at the Polo Grounds in New York when the Chicago White Stockings defeated him, 4–2.

Remarkably, from the standpoint of baseball's role in American culture, the breaking of Keefe's streak represented just the second-biggest development involving the Giants and White Stockings that day.

Keefe began his streak by defeating Philadelphia. Two days earlier, John Clarkson of the Boston Beaneaters had beaten the Giants ace, 4–2, in Boston. The defeat dropped Keefe's record for the season to 8-6, and the fourth-place team's record to 25-21.

But over the next two months both the pitcher and team got hot. The Giants won 32 of 39 games between then and August 10, seized first place at the end of July, and opened up a 7½-game advantage by August 10. During his stretch of 19 straight wins, Keefe allowed just 50 runs; the Giants scored 111.

Before breaking the record, Keefe tied it on Au-

The 1888 National League champion New York Giants: 1 - Stump Wiedman, 2 - Tim Keefe, 3 - Bill George, 4 - Ed Crane, 5 - Pat Murphy, 6 - Cannonball Titcomb, 7 - Roger Connor, 8 - John Ward, 9 - Elmer Foster, 10 - Jim Mutrie, 11 - Buck Ewing, 12 - Danny Richardson, 13 - William Brown, 14 - Mike Tiernan, 15 - Jim O'Rourke, 16 - Mickey Welch, 17 - Gil Hatfield, 18 - George Gore, 19 - Elmer Cleveland, 20 - Mike Slattery.

gust 8, with a 4–1 victory over Indianapolis. Curiously, both his achievement in tying the record, then breaking it by defeating Pittsburgh, 2–1, on the 10th went unreported.[1] It wasn't as if the old record was buried decades in the past; the National League was in only its 13th season of play. The previous record had been achieved only four seasons before, when "Old Hoss" Radbourn of the 1884 Providence Grays went undefeated from August 7 through September 6 on his way to the still unequaled record of 59 wins in a season.[2] Nor was Radbourn unknown to New Yorkers or their baseball press. He had defeated their own Metropolitans of the American Association, three straight games, during baseball's first "World Series" in the fall of 1884, and was pitching for Boston at the time of Keefe's feat.

For New York's baseball cranks, the important story of the August 14 game was that the first-place Giants led Chicago, their archrival, by 6½ games as play began. The fact that Keefe had not lost in his last 19 decisions only added to the pre-game interest, with more than 10,000 New Yorkers making their way to the Polo Grounds.

The crowd on hand to watch Keefe try for 20 straight included some of the city's rich and famous. Among them were the cast of McCaull's Light Opera Company, including Colonel McCaull and such headliners as DeWolf Hopper, Mathilde Cottrelly, and Marion Manola. The next morning the *New York Times* reported that about 80 members of the opera company "came up to the game in large horse drawn tally-ho coaches, and kept cheering the New-Yorks from start to finish"[3] despite the Chicago victory.

Keefe's defeat did not dent his reputation. "In justice to Keefe ... it is only fair to state that the defeat was not due to any poor work on his part," the *Times* correspondent wrote. "He pitched the ball with his accustomed skill, but the contest was lost by poor work in the field."[4] Keefe allowed only two earned runs as did Chicago's pitcher, August "Gus" Krock.

Keefe's 19-game winning streak was equaled in 1912 by another Giant, Rube Marquard, who ironically also lost to Chicago in his bid for 20 straight. In the 1930s a third Giant, Carl Hubbell, won 24 straight games, but that string extended over two seasons, the final 16 of 1936 and the first eight of 1937.

After Keefe's defeat the *Times* correspondent interviewed the McCaull's Light Opera Company cast, reporting that they were distraught. "DeWolf Hopper was exasperated. ... Miss Cottrelly thought it was too real mean, and Miss Manola regarded it as the height of impoliteness on the part of Mr. Anson and his men to take the game from the Giants," the correspondent recounted.[5] Despite the defeat, the Light Opera Company honored an invitation it had extended the day before to host both teams to their performance of Prince Methusalem that evening at Wallack's Theater, at Broadway and 30th Street.[6] Besides, their Giants were still in first place by a respectable margin, and would remain there until the end of the season.

In formal attire, the members of both teams arrived at Wallack's Theatre to the cheers of those outside and inside. But the evening's highlight was still yet to come. During the intermission of *Prince Methusalem* Hopper strode to the center of the stage. After much applause for his performance up to that point, he began a recitation of a poem that had never been heard publicly before. The audience was in a state of rapture. When Hopper finished,

DeWolf Hopper: A stage personality and Giants fan who debuted "Casey At the Bat" during team's victory celebration.

Chicago pitcher Gus Krock.

the place went wild with cheering.[7] Tim Keefe's incredible streak of 19 straight victories ended on the afternoon of August 14, 1888, but DeWolf Hopper's streak—reciting "Casey at The Bat" well into the next century (10,000-15,000 times by his estimate)—had just begun.

	AB	R	H	PO	A	E
New York						
Ewing, c	4	0	2	8	4	0
Ric'son, 2b	4	0	1	0	3	0
Hatf'ld, ss	4	0	0	0	3	1
Tiernan, rf	4	1	1	2	0	0
Connor, 1b	3	0	0	11	0	0
O'R'ke, lf	4	0	1	1	0	0
Sl'ery, cf	4	0	0	1	0	0
Whitney, 3b	4	0	0	0	1	1
Keefe, p	3	1	2	1	9	2
	34	2	7	24	20	4
Chicago						
Ryan, cf	4	1	2	3	0	0
VanH'n, lf	3	1	2	2	0	0
Duffy, rf	4	0	0	1	2	0
Anson, 1b	4	1	1	15	1	0
Pfeffer, 2b	4	1	1	0	2	3
Will'on, ss	4	0	0	0	1	0
Burns, 3b	4	0	1	2	4	0
Flint, c	4	0	0	4	1	1
Krock, p	3	0	1	0	4	0
	34	4	8	27	15	4

New York   000 011 000 - 2
Chicago   000 220 00x - 4
Time – 2:05.
Umpire – Mr. Lynch.
Attendance – 10,240

Notes:

1. *New York Herald*, August 11, 1888, p. 8.

2. Achorn, Edward. *Fifty-nine in '84: Old Hoss Radbourn, Barehanded Baseball & The Greatest Season a Pitcher Ever Pitched* (New York: Smithsonian Books, Harper Collins Publishers, 2010), p. 308-310.

3. *New York Times*, August 15, 1888, p. 3.

4. Ibid.

5. Ibid.

6. *New York Herald*, August 14, 1888, p. 8.

7. Walsh, John Evangelist. *The Night Casey Was Born* (New York: The Overlook Press, 2007), p. 113-137.

The Little Steam Engine That Could

Pittsburgh Alleghenies vs. Indianapolis Hoosiers

Seventh Street Park, Indianapolis, Ind.
September 4, 1888

By Mark Pestana

The 21st-century baseball devotee has at his fingertips an abundance of statistical trivia the likes of which were undreamed of by his 19th-century counterpart. He is duly advised by the media when So-and-so has collected his 700th hit or Whatzizname has notched his fifth straight season of 20 stolen bases.

In the first decades of the National League, with Organized Baseball still relatively young, the concepts of "milestones" and "all-time records" had yet to coalesce in the minds of fans, media, and, no doubt, the players themselves.[1] Perhaps, too, there was a healthy disregard for becoming too obsessed with "the numbers." The author of a May 12, 1878, Special Dispatch to the *Chicago Daily Tribune*, lamenting the intricacies of scoring fielder's choices and players hit by batted balls, concluded that "It would be a splendid thing for the game if no record except that of runs were kept."

There was a maddening inexactness in contemporary record-keeping anyway: three newspapers could offer three different strikeout or error totals—with no video evidence to certify accuracy. So diamond warriors of that bygone age went merrily along without knowing what fodder they had strewn for the stat-gorging generations to come.

James Galvin, known to posterity as Pud (because he "made pudding of opposing batters"),[2] hit the National Association in 1875, but kicked around for a few years before making his National League debut in 1879. Packing 190 pounds into a 5-foot-8 frame, he was sometimes called the Little Steam Engine, and he carved his Hall of Fame niche with consistency and endurance. The 1888 season was his 10th, excluding the one year in the National Association, and though still a valued hurler, he floundered through much of the season, thanks in considerable part to minimal run support. In mid-July his record stood at a miserable 5–17, but a couple of good streaks lifted him to 17–18 by the time his Pittsburgh club traveled to Indianapolis in the first week of September.

The five-game series promised little in the way of fireworks. Pittsburgh held a formidable 11-to-3 advantage in the season series against the Hoosiers. But the Alleghenies were long since out of pennant contention, struggling to pull themselves up to .500, and at best perhaps hoping for a fifth-place finish. Their hosts inhabited last place, having won only 37 of 103 games entering the series. Not exactly a marquee match-up.

Jim Galvin was called "Pud" because he made pudding of opposing batters.

The 1888 Indianapolis Hoosiers became the 300th team to fall victim to Jim Galvin when he beat them 5–4 on September 4. Back row: Unidentified player, Charley Bassett, unidentified player, Harry Spence, Jerry Denny, Jack Glasscock, Paul Hines. Front row: Unidentified player, Emmett Seery, Lev Shreve, Henry Boyle, Dick Buckley, Jack McGeachey.

On Monday, September 3, Galvin pitched ineffectively in the first game of a morning-afternoon twin-bill and went down to a 5-1 defeat. Pittsburgh rebounded to win the afternoon game, and The Little Steam Engine was due back in the box for game three the next day.

Seventh Street Park in Indianapolis seated a paltry crowd of 1,400 fans on Tuesday, September 4. For the second time in two days Galvin turned in a less-than-masterful effort, yielding nine hits and four earned runs, and winning only by the grace of three unearned runs scored by his team. In the seventh inning, rookie Indianapolis pitcher Bill Burdick, pressed into center-field duty when Paul Hines was injured, mishandled the only outfield chance of his major-league career, allowing the fifth and deciding Pittsburgh run to score. *Sporting Life* wrote that the home team was "demoralized in its field work, although it batted Galvin very hard."[3] Pud managed but a solitary strikeout—the opposing pitcher, Handsome Henry Boyle. Rookie first baseman Jake Beckley, with 19 more seasons and an eventual place in the Hall of Fame ahead of him, went 4-for-4 in support of Galvin.

Seen merely in the context of the day, Galvin's utterly unprepossessing pitching performance and, indeed, the game itself merit little attention. Yet on that date what would become the ultimate standard of pitching immortality was first reached—for the victory was the 300th of Pud Galvin's career, a total no previous pitcher had achieved.

Since the National Association—in which Galvin won his first four victories—is not recognized by most authorities as a genuine major league, it should be mentioned that Galvin's 300th victory in a league today recognized as "major" came about a month later, on October 5, when he triumphed on the road against Washington, 5–1. This time he let just one unearned run slip by, but again his teammates faltered at the bat and needed eight Washington errors and four unearned runs to post the victory.[4]

Galvin lasted four more seasons, retiring after the 1892 campaign with 365 victories to his credit,

361 of them in recognized major leagues. By that time Tim Keefe, Mickey Welch, Hoss Radbourn, and John Clarkson had also reached 300. But not until 1903 was Pud's victory total surpassed, by Denton True Young, and only a handful have passed it since.

There was no mention of the milestone in the newspapers of the day. Reporters noted Pittsburgh's brilliant fielding,[5] a good throw from right field by McGeachey,[6] and Beckley's four hits[7]—but nothing about 300 wins. Who knows how long it took for someone—*anyone*—to take note? In 1906 a retrospective titled "Pitchers of the Past: Crack Twirlers of a Quarter Century Ago," lauded Galvin as "a magician in the points" but made no mention of his 300 wins.[8] The *New York Times*, proclaiming Lefty Grove "Twelfth To Gain No. 300" in 1941, appended a list of the elite dozen, which erroneously included non-300-game winner Tony Mullane and omitted Galvin.[9] The Hall of Fame plaque etched for his 1965 induction makes note of his two no-hitters and 649 complete games … but not that he was the first to break the 300 barrier.

Pud was not done with record-setting. Four seasons later, in his final major-league tour, he founded an even more exclusive club – only Cy Young has joined since then - when he became the first pitcher to *lose* 300 games.

Indianapolis	R	H	PO	A	E	Pittsburgh	R	H	PO	A	E
Hines, cf	2	2	0	0	0	Miller, c	1	2	3	1	0
Burdick, cf	0	0	0	0	1	Coleman, rf	1	1	2	2	0
Denny, 2b	1	1	4	3	1	Smith, 2b	1	1	4	4	1
Seery, lf	0	1	1	0	0	Beckley, 1b	1	4	9	1	0
Buckley, 3b	0	1	1	0	0	Dalrymple, lf	0	0	1	0	0
Glasscock, ss	0	0	1	4	2	Kuehne, ss	0	0	1	0	0
McGeachy, rf	0	1	0	1	0	Maul, cf	1	1	5	0	0
Schoeneck, 1b	0	0	12	0	0	Cleveland, 3b	0	1	2	1	1
Myers, c	0	2	5	3	1	Galvin, p	0	2	0	3	0
Boyle, p	1	1	0	11	0						
	4	9	24	22	5		5	12	27	12	2

Indianapolis   200 020 000 - 4
Pittsburgh   110 020 10x - 5

Runs earned – Indianapolis 4, Pittsburgh 2. Two-base hits – Seery, Myers, Hines. Three-base hit – Beckley. Stolen bases – Pittsburgh 2. Double plays – Smith to Beckley (2). Hit by pitched ball – Schoeneck. First base on errors – Indianapolis 2, Pittsburgh 2. Struck out – Boyle, Cleveland (2), Smith, Miller, Dalrymple, Kuehne. Passed ball – Myers. Wild pitch – Boyle. Time – 1:30. Umpire – Daniels.

Notes:

1. Bill Felber, correspondence with author, April 7, 2010.

2. Overfield, Joseph. "Jim Galvin," *Baseball's First Stars* (Cleveland, Ohio: SABR Publications, 1996), p. 65.

3. *Sporting Life*, September 12, 1888, p. 3.

4. *Sporting Life*, October 10, 1888, p. 2.

5. *Boston Daily Globe*, September 5, 1888, p. 5.

6. *Chicago Daily Inter Ocean*, September 5, 1888, p. 2.

7. *New York Clipper*, September 15, 1888, p. 432.

8. *Washington Post*, February 11, 1906, p. S3.

9. *New York Times*, July 26, 1941, p. 10.

A Wondrous Ball Park

All-Americas vs. Chicago White Stockings

Giza, Egypt
February 9, 1889

By Bill Felber

Baseball fans can debate incessantly over what is the greatest game ever played. But there's no debate concerning the greatest site to host a game. Only one "ballpark" in history can trace its lineage across three millennia, or boast the status of one of the Seven Wonders of the World.

On February 9, 1889, about 20 stars of the National League played ball on the desert sand of the Great Pyramids at Giza, Egypt. The event was the centerpiece of a world tour organized by Chicago White Stockings executive and sporting goods manufacturer Albert G. Spalding in an effort to promote America's national pastime in foreign locales.

As a business proposition, the event was a bust. In addition to Egypt, the tour visited Hawaii, Australia, New Zealand, India, Italy, France, Scotland, and England, generally attracting small crowds that consisted largely of American tourists. "I consider base ball an excellent game, but cricket a better one," Britain's Prince of Wales famously observed after the players' March exhibition at London's Kensington Oval.[1] Spalding was said to have lost between $30,000 and $40,000 on the venture.[2]

The tour did succeed, however, as a statement that baseball had come of age as America's national pastime. Firmly in that belief, the 20 players—10 representing the White Stockings, the rest drawn from other National League teams—had set off the previous October for a trip designed to keep them abroad through March.

Three future Hall of Famers were among the tourists. Adrian C. "Cap" Anson was the first baseman and captain of the White Stockings, John Montgomery Ward played shortstop and Ned Hanlon center field for the All-Americas, as the opponents were called. Two other future Hall of Famers accompanied the group: George Wright as umpire and Henry Chadwick, the era's best-known baseball writer. Yet another, King Kelly, played on the U.S. portion of the tour, but did not go overseas.

Here are the rosters:

White Stockings: Mark Baldwin and John Tener, pitchers; Tom Daly, catcher; Cap Anson, first base; Fred Pfeffer, second base; Tommy Burns, third base;

A scene from the Pyramid Game of February 9, 1889, with a pyramid in the background.

Ned Williamson, shortstop; Martin Sullivan, Jimmy Ryan, and Robert Pettit, outfielders.

All-Americas: John Healy, Indianapolis, and Cannonball Ed Crane, New York, pitchers; Billy Earl, Cincinnati, catcher; G.A. Wood, Philadelphia, first base; Fred Carroll, Pittsburgh, second base; Jimmy Manning, Kansas City, third base; John Montgomery Ward, New York, shortstop; James Fogarty, Philadelphia, Ned Hanlon, Pittsburgh, and Tom Brown, Boston, outfielders.

In the absence of daily communication from overseas, knowledge of the actual play is limited to the accounts furnished by Francis Richter, editor of *Sporting Life*, one of the two popular baseball weeklies of the era, and Harry Clay Palmer, an author who wrote a book about the trip. If any box score was kept, it no longer exists. *The Sporting News*, Richter's archrival in the coverage of baseball-related happenings, scorned the enterprise and ignored the Pyramid Game.

The teams arrived in Cairo after a sea passage from Ceylon with the All-Americas holding a 15–13–1 edge in the series. They took up lodgings in the Orient Hotel, and, after an evening to regain their land legs, set out the next morning for the playing site. The transportation was unusual to say the least: The White Stockings were provided donkeys, the All-Americas took camels. The teams switched mounts halfway along. They arrived at 2 P.M., had lunch, posed for photographs, and toured the historic sites before proceeding to what Anson described as "the hard sands of the desert, where a diamond had been laid out."[6]

Their audience for the game consisted largely of what Anson referred to as "Arabs"—presumably local Egyptians—with a few tourists thrown in. The Chicagos got away quickly, scoring twice in the first

The All-Americas team that took part in the 1888–89 world tour, including the Pyramid Game. Back: Tom Brown, Fred Carroll, Egyptian Healy, George Wood, Jim Manning. Front: Jim Fogarty, John Ward, Ned Hanlon, Ed Crane, Billy Earle.

The world tour teams pose at the Sphinx prior to the start of their ballgame.

inning off Healy, whose nickname, ironically, was Egyptian. The All-Americas heartily returned fire in the second, swatting Tener around for seven runs and effectively deciding the outcome. From that point on, Daly provided the on-field excitement with a home run in the fourth.[7] Spalding, who umpired in Chadwick's absence, called the game after five innings and declared the All Americas the winner by a score of 10–6. "I apologized to the Sphinx on behalf of my team … to this she turned a deaf ear,"[8] Anson reported.

The spectators were generally respectful, but puzzled by what was happening before them. In an age when games began and ended with the same ball, fouls hit into the crowd presented a particular difficulty. "When the ball was thrown or batted into the crowd, the Arabs would pounce upon it and examine it as though it were one of the greatest of curiosities, and it was only after a row that we could get it in our possession,"[9] Anson wrote.

After the game, both teams dallied a while at the site. Observers reported that they amused themselves by throwing baseball's at the Sphinx's right eye, and that Fogarty, the Philadelphia outfielder, actually hit it.[10]

The All-Americas also prevailed during the overall tour, winning 14 of the 28 games contested on foreign soil. The White Stockings won 11 and three ended in a tie.

Although the tour did little to promote baseball around the world, it still had plenty of impact. Since 1885, Ward had been a leader of the Brotherhood Movement, the game's first players union. While he cavorted with Spalding on the other side of the world, the other National league club owners drew up revised rules that had the effect of reducing the Brotherhood's impact. Learning of this in Europe, Ward deduced—probably correctly—that he and the players he represented had been taken advantage of. He quit the tour, rushed home, and began to draw plans for what would become the Brotherhood War of 1890.

Notes:

1. Spalding, Albert G. *America's National Game* (New York: American Sports Publishing Company, 1911).

2. "Just Like Emigrants," *The Sporting News*, March 9, 1889, p. 1.

3. Spalding.

4. "Just Like Emigrants," *The Sporting News*, March 9, 1889, p. 1.

5. *The Sporting News*, March 3, 1889, p. 4.

6. Anson, Adrian C. *A Ball Player's Career* (Mattituck, N.Y., Amereon House, 1900).

7. Lamster, Mark. *Spalding's World Tour* (New York: Perseus Books, 2006).

8. Anson.

9. Ibid.

10. Ibid.

Sad-sack Colonels

St. Louis Browns vs. Louisville Colonels

Eclipse Park, Louisville, Ky.
June 22, 1889

By Bob Bailey

There are days when nothing goes right. In 1889 the Louisville Colonels of the American Association had a month like that. The hapless Colonels, on their way to a dismal 27–111 season record, set the major-league team record for consecutive losses at 26.

The final loss of the streak came in the second game of a doubleheader against the St. Louis Browns on June 22. The Colonels were just back from a four-week Eastern road trip, having lost 21 games in Cincinnati, Columbus, Philadelphia, Brooklyn (one of them played in Newtown, the Brooklyn club's Sunday home), and Baltimore. The losses were hardly the only unusual aspect of the trip.

After a pair of home losses to Baltimore, Louisville had been swept in four-game series at Cincinnati and Columbus. The Colonels were scheduled to play in Philadelphia on June 4, but the squad did not show up. The players turned up two days later in Philadelphia, reporting that their train had been stuck for two days in northern Pennsylvania because of flooding along the Conemaugh River that had washed over the track. It turned out to be backwater from the deadly Johnstown Flood.

The delay did nothing to improve Louisville's performance. The Colonels dropped four to Philadelphia and then went to Brooklyn and did the same. The road trip moved on to Baltimore, where things really got interesting. The Colonels were owned by Louisville businessman Mordecai Davidson, a man who brooked no opposition to his management

Identifiable players in this team image include Scott Stratton at far left, and Farmer Vaughn, next to Stratton, as well as the four figures seated farthest right: Phil Tomney, Dan Shannon, Red Ehret, and Jim Galligan.

The four-time defending American Association champion St. Louis Browns were beaten out by Brooklyn in 1889. Back: Silver King, Tommy McCarthy, Charlie Comiskey, Yank Robinson, Jocko Milligan. Front: Jack Boyle, Charlie Duffee, Arlie Latham, Shorty Fuller, Jack Stivetts, Tip O'Neill.

actions. A hard contract negotiator, Davidson was deeply unpopular with the players.

In the midst of the losing streak, Davidson decided to motivate the players by instituting fines for poor play. He doled out such punishments as a $25 levy on Paul Cook for "stupid base running," and $25 on Dan Shannon for "a fumble and a disastrous wild throw."

After losing the opening game at Baltimore and experiencing several more Davidson fines, members of the club went on strike. All but one unknown player signed a letter to Davidson stating that they wouldn't play unless the fines were dropped. Davidson, not surprisingly, refused.

The player uprising was not Davidson's only concern. A week earlier he had attempted to sell off most of his players to recoup his investment in the team, only to be blocked by the league since it meant the dissolution of the franchise. While the player strike was in progress, Davidson was also defending himself at an American Association meeting in New York. Davidson met with the players in Baltimore, but it was hardly a conciliatory session. He increased the fines for errors on the field to $50.

The result was that six players—Guy Hecker, Pete Browning, Dan Shannon, Harry Raymond, Red Ehret, and Paul Cook—refused to take the field for the game on June 15. Filling out their lineup with local amateurs, Louisville lost a 20th straight game, 4–2. Baltimore manager Bill Barnie intervened and persuaded the six strikers to return to the field, telling them that the league would determine the outcome of the fines.

After three more losses, the ragtag Colonels headed back to the Bluegrass with a season's record of 8–43.

When the club arrived in Louisville on June 21, it was payday. Since the Association had not considered the players' complaint and since Davidson was holding firm on the fines, the players received meager pay envelopes. Guy Hecker, a winner of 52 games in 1884, was reported to have received a total of $1.95. Browning, the team's batting star since 1882, was in the hole by $325. These events did not inspire the players to new heights of vigor, and they dropped the first game of the home series with St. Louis, 7–3.

The first game of a June 22 doubleheader saw Louisville jump out to a 3–0 lead after three innings. But they trailed 6–3 after four and ultimately lost 7–6, with St. Louis pushing over the winning run in the ninth.

Game two matched Louisville's John Ewing against Nat Hudson for St. Louis. Louisville elected to bat first and the Colonels were retired in order. Ewing, brother of future Hall of Famer Buck Ewing, retired lead-off hitter Arlie Latham before surrendering a scratch single to Tommy McCarthy. A passed ball and a double by Tip O'Neill put the Browns up 1–0. With two outs in the Colonels' second, Browning and Farmer Vaughn delivered infield singles. Browning stole third and scored the tying run. Louisville threatened again in the fourth when a two-out error by second baseman Yank Robinson put Harry Raymond on first. Raymond stole second and took third on catcher Jocko Milligan's wild throw. Browning then sent a scorcher down the third-base line. Latham corralled it and threw out Browning at first to end the inning.

Latham opened the St. Louis sixth with a single, but was thrown out by Vaughn attempting to steal second. McCarthy was issued a four-ball walk. (1889 was the first season in which the walk rule was reduced to four balls.) O'Neill singled, sending McCarthy to third, and he scored on Charlie Comiskey's sacrifice fly to center.

Louisville was retired routinely in the sixth and seventh. In the eighth, the Colonels' Chicken Wolf singled with two outs and took second on an error at first base. Farmer Weaver singled him home with a hit to center. The score remained 2–2 into the 11th. After Louisville was blanked in the top half, Comiskey led off the bottom of the inning with a line drive to left field. Browning made a long run and briefly had the ball in his grasp, but it fell to the ground for an error. Jack Boyle, who had replaced the injured Robinson in the ninth, singled, putting men at first and second with no outs. Charlie Duffee hit a long single to center, scoring Comiskey and giving St. Louis a 3–2 win, and the Colonels a 26th consecutive loss, a major-league record that still stood in 2012.

The losing streak came to an end the next afternoon. Louisville built a 5–0 lead off Icebox Chamberlain after three innings, two of the runs courtesy of Comiskey, Yank Robinson's fill-in at second, who made four errors in the third inning alone. Tom Ramsey got the 7–3 win, Louisville's first since May 21.

In early July Davidson surrendered the franchise to the American Association. A new group of Lou-

Nat Hudson: St. Louis pitcher edged out the Colonels 3-2, handing them defeat number 26 in succession.

isville businessmen bought the team and paid the players the fines Davidson had refused to return.

	AB	R	H	PO	A	E
Louisville						
Shannon, 2b	5	0	0	0	3	1
Wolf, rf	5	1	1	3	0	0
Weaver, cf	5	0	2	4	1	0
Hecker, 1b	5	0	1	11	0	0
Raymond, 3b	4	0	1	7	1	0
Browning, lf	4	1	1	1	0	1
Vaughn, c	4	0	1	0	4	0
Ewing, p	4	0	0	1	1	0
Tomney, ss	3	0	0	3	1	0
	39	2	7	30	11	2
St. Louis						
Latham, 3b	5	0	1	2	3	0
McCarthy, cf	4	2	1	3	0	0
O'Neill, lf	5	0	3	3	0	0
Comiskey, 1b	5	1	0	17	0	0
Robinson, 2b	4	0	1	3	5	2
Duffee, cf	5	0	1	2	0	0
Fuller, ss	4	0	1	2	3	0
Milligan, c	3	0	1	1	4	1
Hudson, p	4	0	1	0	1	0
Boyle, 1b	1	0	1	0	1	1
	40	2	11	33	17	4

Louisville 010 000 010 00 - 2
St. Louis   100 010 000 01 - 3

Earned run – Louisville. Two-base hits – O'Neill and Milligan. Stolen bases – Wolf, Hecker, Raymond, Browning 2, Vaughn and Tomney 2. First on balls – Off Ewing 2, Hudson 2. Struck out – By Ewing 4, Hudson 1. Time – 1:55. Umpire – Ferguson.

The Candlelight Game

St. Louis Browns vs. Brooklyn Bridegrooms

Washington Park, Brooklyn, N.Y.
September 7, 1889

By Bob Tiemann

The September 7, 1889, game between the St. Louis Browns and the Brooklyn Bridegrooms is now remembered for the humorous episode when the Browns had lighted candles put up in front of their bench to emphasize to the umpire that it was too dark to play. But the game's riotous ending and rancorous denouement fractured the American Association, and went a long way toward putting the organization on the road to extinction.

The Browns, led by Captain Charlie Comiskey and owner Chris Von der Ahe, were looking for their fifth consecutive pennant in 1889, and they led the race for most of the summer. Under the ownership of Charles Byrne, the Bridegrooms had gone to considerable expense to unseat the champs. Now finally in September of 1889, the Bridegrooms had moved into first place and led the Browns by 2½ games when the champs came to Brooklyn for a three-game series. But the future looked far from rosy for Byrne. On September 1, the Queens County sheriff had stopped the Bridegrooms game at Ridgewood Park, the venue the team had used since 1886 for lucrative Sunday games just beyond the city limits. State law prohibited Sunday amusements, but the authorities in Queens had allowed them to go on unmolested until now. Other Sunday games could be played while the case went through the courts, but there would be no law enforcement at the site in the meantime.

The big series opened on Saturday, September 7, with an immense crowd of more than 15,000 packed into Washington Park in downtown Brooklyn. The game they saw was quintessential American Association baseball, replete with brilliant fielding, desperate baserunning, and constant wrangling with the umpire. In the first five innings four men were caught stealing, three were tagged out at home, and two others were retired in rundowns between third and home.

Fred Goldsmith, the old Chicago pitcher, was the arbiter, and he called "Play" at the usual 4 P.M. starting time under overcast skies. Brooklyn chose first bats and drew first blood, scoring two runs and giving Browns third baseman Arlie Latham a nasty spike wound in the process. St. Louis finally scored a run in the fifth. Charlie Duffee led off with a single to left and advanced to second when the return throw got away. Brooklyn put up a kick, claiming that Duffee had interfered with the throw. He then came around on an infield out and a scratch hit.

With the lead cut to 2–1 and the skies ominous, Brooklyn Captain Darby O'Brien urged Goldsmith

Charlie Duffee scored the first run for St. Louis.

The 1889 American Association-champion Brooklyn Bridegrooms. Back: Germany Smith, Pop Corkhill, Adonis Terry, Dave Foutz, Darby O'Brien, Doc Bushong, Joe Visner. Middle: George Pinkney, Bob Caruthers, Hub Collins, Bill McGunnigle, Oyster Burns, Bob Clark, Tom Lovett. Front: Mickey Hughes.

to call the game, but the ump would have none of it. In the last of the sixth, the Browns grabbed the lead with a pair of runs, thanks to singles by Tip O'Neill and Yank Robinson and a double by Shorty Fuller, with a sacrifice and a wild throw added in. St. Louis comic Latham "turned flipflaps, stood on his hands and rolled over the ground in a perfect paroxysm of delight,"[1] much to the amusement of the crowd.

Now it was Captain Comiskey's turn to harangue for an end due to darkness. As the seventh inning began at around 5:40 P.M., there was some light left.[2] But it seemed that every play caused an argument, and St. Louis delayed at every opportunity. Goldsmith assessed fines and threatened a forfeit to get the Browns back to their positions. St. Louis tallied another run in the seventh when O'Neill's single brought in Latham. Before the start of the eighth inning, St. Louis right fielder Tommy McCarthy dunked the game ball in the water bucket to make it hard to hit. An enraged Goldsmith saw the trick and put a new ball into play. Meanwhile, Von der Ahe had sent an errand boy to a local grocery store for candles, and in the eighth inning he had them lighted and placed them by the visitors' bench.

The Browns' "impudent exhibition of bulldozing" had made the crowd "like an excited mob," and the fans "hooted and yelled and shouted like maniacs."[3] But despite Goldsmith's indignation and injured sense of authority, by the time the ninth inning began it really was too dark to see. The first Brooklyn batter struck out but reached base when the catcher missed the ball. After another passed ball, the Browns refused to continue, leaving the field and heading for the clubhouse. A few of the players were hit by objects thrown by a frenzied portion of the crowd that followed them. Goldsmith, after waiting the required five minutes, declared the game a forfeit victory for Brooklyn.

Fearing further violence and knowing there would be no police presence on Sunday, Von der Ahe refused to have his team appear at Ridgewood the following day, again forfeiting. Rain prevented the final game of the series. The fine for forfeiting a game was $1,500, and the penalty for purposely failing to appear was expulsion from the Association. After a tortuous 10-hour meeting on September 23, the Association board of directors handed down a compromise verdict: The Saturday forfeit was overturned, the Sunday forfeit upheld, and no expulsion mentioned. There was a certain logic to the ruling, since the game played 10 miles away in New York on the same date had been called due to darkness about 45 minutes before the game in Brooklyn was ended. But owner Byrne was apoplectic with the ruling, and *Sporting Life*'s local correspondent reported "disgust and contempt" in Brooklyn over it, adding that the decision had "put a keen edge on the desire for jumping out of the American Association and given new zest to the … possibility of Brooklyn joining the (National) League."[4] That is exactly what happened. At the Association's December meeting, both Brooklyn and Cincinnati (which had also had its Sunday games interfered with by authorities) quit the AA and joined the NL, while Baltimore and Kansas City left for the minor leagues. The emasculated American Association limped through two more seasons before finally succumbing to the buyout that brought four of its members into the National League in 1892.

(Modern box score derived from Henry Chadwick's scorebook)

	AB	R	H	BI	PO	A	E
Brooklyn							
D. O'Brien, lf	4	1	1	0	2	0	1
H. Collins, 2b	4	1	2	1	4	4	2
D. Foutz, 1b	4	0	2	1	11	0	0
T. Burns, rf	4	0	0	0	1	0	0
G. Pinkney, 3b	4	0	1	0	1	1	1
J. Corkhill, cf	3	0	0	0	0	0	1
B. Clark, c	4	0	1	0	4	4	1
B. Caruthers, p	2	0	0	0	0	5	0
G. Smith, ss	2	0	0	0	1	4	0
Total	31	2	7	2	24	18	6

	AB	R	H	BI	PO	A	E
St. Louis							
A. Latham, 3b	4	1	1	0	2	3	0
T. McCarthy, rf	4	0	0	0	3	1	1
T. O'Neill, lf	4	1	3	1	1	0	0
C. Comiskey, 1b	4	0	0	0	3	2	0
Y. Robinson, 3b	4	1	1	0	0	3	1
C. Duffee, cf	4	1	1	0	4	0	1
S. Fuller, ss	4	0	1	1	3	1	1
J. Milligan, c	3	0	2	1	7	2	1
E. Chamberlain, p	3	0	1	1	1	1	0
Total	34	4	10	3	24	13	5

BROOKLYN	R	1B	PO	A	E	ST. LOUIS	R	1B	PO	A	E
O'Brien, l.f.	1	1	1	0	1	Latham, 3b.	1	2	3	2	0
Collins, 2b.	1	1	4	2	2	McCarthy, r.f.	0	0	3	1	1
Foutz, 1b	0	2	12	1	0	O'Neill, l.f.	1	2	1	0	0
Burns, r.f.	0	0	1	0	0	Comiskey, 1b.	0	0	4	0	0
Pinkney, 3b.	0	1	1	2	0	Robinson, 2b.	1	1	0	2	1
Corkhill, c.f.	0	0	0	0	0	Duffee, c.f.	1	1	3	0	1
Clark, c.	0	1	4	3	0	Fuller, s.s.	0	1	3	1	1
Caruthers, p.	0	0	0	4	0	Milligan, c.	0	2	7	1	0
Smith, s.s.	0	0	1	2	0	Chamb'l'in, p.	0	1	0	1	0
Total	2	6	24	15	3	**Total**	4	10	24	8	4

Brooklyn   200 000 00* - 9
St. Louis 000 012 10 - 0

*Forfeited to Brooklyn with no outs in the top of the ninth inning.

LOB – Bkn 8, StL 6; Reached base on Error – Bkn 3, StL 3; DP – McCarthy-Latham; 2B – Collins, Pinkney, O'Neill, Fuller; SB – O'Brien, Corkhill, Latham, Clark; CS – Latham, O'Neill, O'Brien, Chamberlain.

	IP	H	R-ER	BB	SO
Caruthers	8	10	4-1	0	3
Chamberlain	8+	7	2-1	3	4

+pitched to two batters in the ninth
WP – Chamberlain.
PB – Clark, Milligan.
Umpire – F. Goldsmith
Time – 2:25
Attendance – 15,143

Notes:

1. *Brooklyn Daily Eagle*, September 8, 1889.

2. Ibid.

3. *The Republic*, St. Louis, September 8, 1889.

4. Donnelly, J.J. *Sporting Life*, October 2, 1889.

A King's Downfall

Boston Beaneaters vs. Cleveland Spiders

League Park, Cleveland Ohio
October 2, 1889

By J.P. Caillault

From mid-July until the final days of the 1889 season, the National League pennant race was a fierce, two-team battle, with the Boston Beaneaters, led by workhorse pitcher John Clarkson and team captain Mike "King" Kelly, trying to unseat the defending champion New York Giants from their throne.

At the end of play on September 26, with little more than a week left in the season, the two teams were deadlocked with identical 78–42 records. Over the next three days, Boston won two of three, while New York won one and tied two. The two teams were both 37 games over .500, but the Giants held first place with a winning percentage of .653 (79–42), barely ahead of the Beaneaters' .650 (80–43).

As the teams headed into the October home stretch, the final five days of the season would be decisive. And New York stumbled right out of the gate, losing to Pittsburgh, while Boston beat Cleveland. The Beaneaters were back in command, 81–43 versus 79–43. The 1889 National League pennant was theirs for the taking.

But then came October 2, 1889, the decisive day of the race. New York was playing Pittsburgh for the last time, while Boston was wrapping up its series in Cleveland. The Giants won their game, beating the Allegheny team, 6–3. For Boston, though, a huge drama was about to unfold, one that would ultimately cost it the pennant of 1889.

Pitching for Cleveland was Ed Beatin, a 23-year-old who had shut out the Beaneaters on consecutive days back in mid-September. He would be going up against the fantastic but overworked Clarkson, making his 70th start of the season for Boston. Clarkson, who had already logged nearly 600 innings pitched en route to an incredible 49–19 record, had started the Beaneaters' previous six games and 11 of their previous 12.

The biggest news of the day, though, was that the Beaneaters' captain—right fielder Kelly—claimed to have injured a finger in pre-game catching practice and would be relegated to a seat on the bench.[1] However, it was clear to all of the onlookers that Kelly was "considerably under the influence of liquor." Although dressed in his Boston uniform, Kelly sat on the Cleveland bench next to the Spiders team manager.[2]

Through the first three innings of the tense match, neither team could manage a single hit, let alone a run. Clarkson retired the first nine batters he faced, while Beatin allowed only one walk. In the top of the fourth inning, though, the Spiders hit Clarkson hard, scoring three runs on a double and three singles. At this point, Kelly began shouting at his own teammates. "You never win," he said with characteristic modesty, "when I don't play. Kelly is king. I am a king." No attention was paid to his little pleasantries, which were muttered at times and shouted at others.[3]

Cleveland scored two more in the top of the sixth so that when Boston came to bat in the bottom of the sixth,

"King" Kelly: His shenanigans contributed to the Beaneaters' demise in 1889.

John Clarkson: Pounded by Cleveland in his crucial 70th start.

they were in a desperate situation. With one out, Clarkson was walked by Beatin. Hardy Richardson followed with a hard hit to right field. On his way to scoring Boston's first run of the game, Clarkson fell rounding third base, making it appear that he would have to go back to third, so Richardson returned to secnd. After another walk issued by Beatin, Billy Nash singled to right field. Richardson had plenty of time to score, and "did so as clearly as ever a man did." But when umpire John McQuaid declared Richardson out on the throw home, it seemed to paralyze the visitors. The Cleveland spectators themselves did not believe Richardson was out "till he informed them himself."[4]

When the inning ended (with no more scoring for Boston), Kelly sprang from his seat on the bench and "strode toward McQuaid with blazing eye and inflamed face."[5] He accused McQuaid of being a robber, charged him with having said he would give the Bostons a "roasting," and finally made a motion as if to hit him. McQuaid called a police officer and told him to remove Kelly from the grounds. The officer at first tried to reason with Kelly, but this only added to Kelly's anger. Breaking away from the officer, he again approached McQuaid in a threatening manner, but he was prevented from doing so by several additional officers, who, "with drawn clubs, made a ridiculous display of their power over one man." Kelly struggled, but he was ejected from the grounds.[6]

"Lighting a cigarette, he strode into the street with the dejected air of Napoleon in exile." Kelly attempted to enter the Payne Avenue grounds again, but the gate was locked, and the fence was too high to vault. Small boys harassed him, and the fans in the bleachers suggested that he buy a ticket and return to the grounds through the turnstiles.[7]

Boston team manager James Hart stated after the game that certain men in Cleveland induced Kelly to get drunk, so that he would make a scene at the grounds and thus give the policemen an excuse for ejecting him. The Cleveland club vehemently denied Hart's story; Kelly, they said, became intoxicated on his own, and he alone was to blame for his actions.[8]

As for the game itself, Cleveland added a couple more runs in the top of the eighth to put the game away for good. With the loss, Boston again fell behind New York by mere percentage points, .650 (80–43) to .648 (81–44). But it was a deficit from which the Beaneaters would never recover, as the Giants won their final three games to clinch their second consecutive National League pennant.

Ed Beatin: The Spiders pitcher easily bested Boston's Kelly-less lineup.

Cleveland	AB	R	H	PO	A	E
Radford, rf	4	1	1	0	1	0
Stricker, 2b	4	3	1	1	1	1
McKean, ss	3	2	1	2	3	0
Twitchell, lf	4	0	0	0	0	0
Tebeau, 3b	4	1	1	3	3	0
Gilks, cf	4	0	3	4	0	0
Fantz, 1b	4	0	0	12	1	0
Sutcliffe, c	4	0	0	4	1	0
Beatin, p	4	0	0	1	2	0
TOTALS	35	7	7	27	12	1
Boston	**AB**	**R**	**H**	**PO**	**A**	**E**
Richardson, lf	3	0	1	2	0	1
Ganzel, rf	3	0	1	0	0	1
Nash, 3b	4	0	0	1	5	0
Brouthers, 1b-p	3	0	0	17	0	0
Johnston, cf	4	0	0	2	0	0
Quinn, 2b	4	0	0	1	2	0
Smith, ss	3	0	1	2	6	0
Bennett, c	3	0	0	2	0	0
Clarkson, p-3b	2	1	0	0	1	0
TOTALS	29	1	3	27	14	2

Cleveland 000 302 020 – 7
Boston 000 001 000 – 1

Earned runs – Cleveland 4. Two-base hits – Stricker, Gilks, Richardson, Smith. Three-base hits – Tebeau, Ganzel. Total bases on clean hits – Cleveland 11, Boston 7. Reached first base – Cleveland 11 (Radford 2, Stricker 3, McKean 2, Tebeau, Gilks 3), Boston 9 (Richardson 2, Ganzel 2, Nash, Brouthers 2, Smith, Clarkson). Sacrifice hits – Cleveland 2 (McKean, Tebeau), Boston 1 (Ganzel). Bases on balls – By Beatin 4 (Richardson, Brouthers, Clarkson, Ganzel), By Clarkson 2 (Stricker, McKean), By Nash 1 (Radford). Base on error – Cleveland 1 (Stricker). Struck out – By Beatin 3 (Nash, Quinn, Richardson), By Clarkson 1 (Twitchell). Left on bases – Cleveland 4 (Radford, Gilks 3), Boston 5 (Richardson, Nash, Brouthers, Ganzel, Smith). Passed balls – Sutcliffe 1. Wild throws – Boston 1 (Ganzel). Muffed flies – Boston 1 (Richardson). Muffed thrown ball – Cleveland 1 (Stricker). Time – 1:32. Umpire – John McQuaid.

Notes:

1. *Boston Herald*, October 3, 1889.

2. *Boston Journal*, October 3, 1889.

3. *New York Times*, October 3, 1889.

4. *Boston Herald*, October 3, 1889.

5. *Worcester Daily Spy*, October 3, 1889.

6. *Boston Herald*, October 3, 1889.

7. *New York Times*, October 3, 1889.

8. *Worcester Daily Spy*, October 3, 1889.

References:

Some of the information used here was obtained free of charge from, and is copyrighted by, Retrosheet. Interested parties may contact Retrosheet at www.retrosheet.org.

The Giants Win the Pennant on the Last Day

New York Giants vs. Cleveland Spiders

League Park, Cleveland, Ohio
October 5, 1889

By Don Jensen

The 1889 New York Giants were loaded with talent and charisma, but they still needed to overcome formidable challenges off and on the diamond if they were to repeat as world champions. Prompted by private real-estate interests, city fathers in February evicted the team from the Polo Grounds, their home park at 110th Street and Fifth Avenue, so that 111th Street could be extended through the field. Giants owner John B. Day moved the team to swampy Oakdale Park in Jersey City for two games to begin the season and then to the St. George Grounds in Staten Island for an extended stay as he sought a new venue in Manhattan.[1]

The team was also wracked by internal divisions. Since the end of the 1888 season the press had been full of speculation that star shortstop John Montgomery Ward would seek to leave the Giants—Boston and Washington were often mentioned as destinations. Nor was Ward popular with some teammates. On the eve of the 1889 season, one player, speaking anonymously, described Ward as "a very jealous man," who "could not bear to see the club win with [Buck] Ewing as captain. ... I voice the sentiment of nearly all the players when I say that the Giants can play good ball and win the championship without the services of Ward."[2]

Even more ominously, Giants players—led by Ward and pitcher Tim Keefe—formed the backbone of the Brotherhood of Professional Base Ball

The 1889 Boston Beaneaters, caught by the Giants. Back: Joe Quinn, Tom Brown, Pop Smith, Dan Brouthers, Charlie Ganzel, Charlie Bennett. Middle: Hardy Richardson, Hoss Radbourn, John Clarkson, James Hart, Mike Kelly, Dick Johnston, Billy Nash. Front: Bill Daley, Kid Madden.

The 1889 National Legaue champion New York Giants: 1 - George Gore, 2 - Elmer Foster, 3 - Mike Slattery, 4 - Buck Ewing, 5 - William Brown, 6 - Bill George, 7 - Gil Hatfield, 8 - Jim O'Rourke, 9 - Mike Tiernan, 10 - Ed Crane, 11 - Danny Richardson, 12 - Cannonball Titcomb, 13 - Roger Connor, 14 - Mickey Welch, 15 - Jim Mutrie, 16 - Art Whitney, 17 - Tim Keefe, 18 - Pat Murphy, 19 - John Ward.

Players, which claimed the allegiance of a majority of National League players. The team owners' decision in the offseason to impose the Brush Classification Plan, a salary cap that would take into account a player's "habits, earnestness, and special qualities," outraged Brotherhood members, who sought more bargaining power in contract negotiations.[3]

The ongoing labor tension almost overshadowed the thrilling final stages of the pennant race. The Giants fell a game behind the Beaneaters after losing to Pittsburgh on October 1. They regained the top spot the next day with a 6–3 win over the Alleghenies while Boston lost to Cleveland. Both teams won their next two games, leaving the New York at 82–43 and Boston at 83–44. The pennant race would thus be decided on the last game of the season. To make sure that Boston did not resort to any "underhand work" to steal the pennant, New York manager Jim Mutrie left his team in Cleveland before its final contest and departed for Pittsburgh, where the Beaneaters and Alleghenies were playing, so he could monitor any shenanigans firsthand.[4] (Before the crucial games of Saturday, October 5, Boston manager Jim Hart and star pitcher John Clarkson sent a telegram to Cleveland manager Tom Loftus offering the Spiders starting battery $500 and an equal sum to the rest of the team if Boston won the pennant.) Mutrie announced before his trip to Pittsburgh that Tim Keefe would start the deciding game for the Giants. Keefe, who had thrown a two-hitter against Cleveland on October 3, declared that he would pitch the best game of his life.[5]

New York's contest against Cleveland, played before a crowd peppered with a surprisingly large number of Giants fans, was a "grand one."[6] Giant center fielder George Gore led off the first inning with a four-pitch walk and Mike Tiernan followed immediately with a home run. The Giants scored again in the fourth when Art Whitney's sacrifice brought in big Roger Connor from third. Cleveland narrowed the score to 3–2 in the fifth inning, when Paul Radford doubled home Jay Faatz and Sy Sutcliffe, but New York responded with a run in the bottom of the inning and another in the sixth. Sutcliffe drove in the

Spiders' Bob Gilks with a sacrifice fly in the ninth inning, but a fly ball by Cleveland pitcher Henry Gruber to Gore ended the game with New York a 5–3 victor. Keefe was almost as good as his promise, striking out five and yielding only six hits.

In Pittsburgh, meanwhile, the Alleghenies took a 3–0 lead over a weary and wild John Clarkson in the first inning. The *Boston Herald* wrote that the Beaneaters appeared "anxious" and "overconfident" at the same time—in part, no doubt, because the progress of the Giants-Spiders game was posted on the left-field fence.[7] When the Giants' win was announced, many people in the stands felt the life go out of the Beaneaters, who managed but five hits and committed five errors in a 6–1 loss. New York was again champion. "There are [G]iants in our day," lamented the *Boston Gazette*, "but they live in New-York, not in Boston"—and only after the closest race in the National League's 14-year history.[8]

The Giants spent the evening in "jollification" at Cleveland's Hollenden Hotel as congratulatory telegrams rolled in, including one from the Boston team. So large was the celebrating mob upon the club's arrival in Jersey City the next day that team members had trouble boarding the ferryboat to take them across the Hudson River. When the craft reached Manhattan, the Giants were met by another enthusiastic crowd, which cheered them at every street corner until the players disappeared into their homes.[9]

Within weeks, the mood had soured: Ward's Brotherhood issued a manifesto declaring that "players have been bought, sold, and exchanged as though they were sheep instead of American citizens." Within months the new Players League began play. Although it lasted only one season, the league ripped away the core of the Giants and pushed John Day toward financial ruin. New York would not be National League champion again for 15 years.

Cleveland	R	1b	PO	A	E	New York	R	1b	PO	A	E
Radford, rf	0	1	1	0	0	Gore, cf	1	1	3	0	0
Stricker, 2b	0	1	2	3	0	Tiernan, rf2	1	2	0	0	0
McKean, ss	0	0	1	2	1	Ward, ss	0	0	1	3	0
Twitchell, lf	0	2	2	0	0	Ewing, c	0	0	5	1	0
Tebeau, 3b	0	1	3	2	1	Ri'son, 2b1	1	2	3	1	0
Gilks, cf	1	0	2	0	0	Connor, 1b1	2	11	1	0	0
Faatz, 1b	1	1	10	0	0	O'R'ke, lf 0	1	2	0	0	0
Sutcliffe, c	1	0	3	4	1	Whitney, 3b0	1	1	1	0	0
Gruber, p	0	0	0	2	1	Keefe, p	0	0	0	3	0
	3	6	24	13	4		5	7	27	12	1

Cleveland 000 020 001 – 3
New York 200 111 00x – 5

Earned runs -- Cleveland 1, New York 2. Two base hits – Radford, Twitchell. Home run – Tiernan. Stolen base – Tiernan. Double play – Richardson, Ward and Connor. First base on balls – Cleveland 3, New York 4. Hit by pitched ball – Faatz, Whitney. Struck out – Cleveland 5, New York 3. Umpire – Mr. Lynch.

Notes:

1. Chadwick, H. "Editor's Open Window," *Outing: an Illustrated Monthly Magazine of Recreation*, April 1889, p. 14, 1; Kieran J., *New York Times*: January 7, 1931; *New York Times*, April 24, 1889.

2. *New York Times*, April 24, 1889.

3. Koppett, Leonard. *Koppett's Concise History of Major League Baseball*, p.58.

4. Pearson, D.M. *Baseball in 1889* (1993), p. 152.

5. Seamheads.com, http://www.seamheads.com/2010/08/06/part-two-the-story-of -the-1888-1889 Giants. *New York Times*, October 5, 1889.

6. *New York Times*, October 6, 1889.

7. *Boston Herald*, October 6, 1889.

8. *New York Times*, October 17, 1889.

9. *Sporting Life*, October 16, 1889.

Genesis of a Rivalry

Brooklyn Bridegrooms at New York Giants

Polo Grounds, New York, N.Y.
October 18, 1889

By Clifford Blau

In 1889, for the first time, both the National League and the American Association had tight pennant races that weren't decided until the last day of the season. In the NL, the defending champion New York Giants just nipped Boston. When Brooklyn, known informally as the Bridegrooms, clinched the AA pennant on October 15, the two clubs arranged for a post-season championship, which the two leagues had been carrying on since 1884. They agreed upon a best-of-11 series, with the first game in New York at the newly opened Polo Grounds.

There were some hills to the west of the Upper Manhattan park, causing an early sunset there, which would prove to be a factor in the series.[1] While the two clubs had faced each other in exhibition games previously, this was the first time they had met in a championship game. After Brooklyn joined the National League the following year, they would play each other more than 2,000 times in the regular season,[2] including two tie-breaking playoffs. New York and Brooklyn, eight years away from merging, had long been rivals, and the teams would develop the fiercest rivalry in baseball history. This is where it began.

The teams arranged for one umpire from each league to work the series, but National Leaguer Tom Lynch didn't show up as expected, apparently deciding that the pay offered was not enough. Brooklyn native Bob Ferguson was on hand, so he was chosen to work with fellow American Association umpire John Gaffney. Ferguson started the game calling balls and strikes with Gaffney on the bases. They alternated each half inning.[3]

A crowd of 8,445 showed up on October 18 for the opening game of the series.[4] New York was viewed as the favorite.[5] That's because the Giants represented the older league, which was generally seen as superior to the American Association, although the St. Louis AA club had won the 1886 World's Series, and at least broke even in the 1885 one. New York had Tim Keefe, winner of four games in the 1888 World's Series, in the box. He was opposed by Will Terry, at 25 years old already in his seventh year with Brooklyn. The Giants' captain, Buck Ewing elected to hit first, but his team was retired in order in the first.[6] It was a different story in the bottom of the inning, though. Brooklyn captain Darby O'Brien led off with a single up the middle, and before they were retired, the Bridegrooms had pounded out six hits good for five runs. There was some suspicion that Brooklyn was on to Keefe's signs. Rather than being fooled by his changeup, they jumped all over it.[7]

Oyster Burns: His early fielding miscue set a tone for the wild afternoon.

The Giants came back with two runs in the top of the second as right fielder "Oyster" Tommy Burns let a hit go by him for three bases. They could have had more, but Johnny Ward was thrown out stealing third for the first out. Brooklyn got one back in the bottom of the inning on Hub Collins's home run, for a 6–2 lead. It was Collins's second of four runs scored in the game, part of his still-standing record of 13 for the series. But the Giants fought back. After both Ewing and Ward were thrown out trying to steal third in the fourth, Danny Richardson hit a long line drive to center that Pop Corkhill got his hands on but then dropped as he tumbled head over heels. Richardson circled the bases for a two-run homer before Brooklyn could retrieve the ball. Corkhill had to come out of the game with an injured neck; Joe Visner, usually a catcher, replaced him.

Ward's single to center drove in his brother-in-law Keefe in the top of the fifth to make it Brooklyn 6, New York 5.[8] An error by Darby O'Brien and five hits capped by Jim O'Rourke's triple resulted in five runs for New York in the seventh and a four-run lead. But after being shut down for four innings, the Bridegrooms came back with two runs in the bottom of the inning, Dave Foutz's double being the big hit. Terry held the Giants scoreless in the eighth as darkness started to settle over the Polo Grounds. The Bridegrooms came to bat knowing it would be their last chance. After Terry grounded out, Joe Visner doubled. Germany Smith made the second out, Darby O'Brien hit one that Danny Richardson couldn't handle, and doubles by Collins and Burns gave Brooklyn the lead. The Giants appeared to be having a hard time seeing the ball. Dave Foutz drove in another run with a hit, then quickly let himself be put out between second and third to end the inning with Brooklyn ahead 12–10. The umpires called the game for darkness at one minute before sunset, and the Bridegrooms took a one-game lead in the series.[9]

New York	AB	R	H	RBI	Brooklyn	AB	R	H	RBI
Gore, cf	5	1	1	0	O'Brien, lf	5	2	2	1
Tiernan, rf	5	1	2	0	Collins, 2b	5	4	3	2
Ewing, c	4	0	1	0	Burns, rf	5	3	4	3
Ward, ss	2	1	2	3	Foutz, 1b	5	0	2	2
Connor, 1b	3	3	0	0	Pinckney, 3b	4	0	1	1
Richardson, 2b	4	3	3	4	Clark, c	4	1	1	1
O'Rourke, lf	4	0	2	2	Terry, p	4	1	0	0
Whitney, 3b	4	0	0	0	Corkhill, cf	2	0	1	2
Keefe, p	3	1	1	0	Visner, cf	2	1	1	0
					Smith, ss	4	0	0	0
	34	10	12	9		40	12	16	12

New York   020 210 50 -- 10
Brooklyn   510 000 24 -- 12

New York	IP	H	R	ER	BB	SO
Keefe T (L)	8.0	16	12	10	0	2
Brooklyn	IP	H	R	ER	BB	SO
Terry A (W)	8.0	12	10	5	5	3

E -- Collins H, Burns O, Visner J, O'Brien D, Ward M
DP -- Brooklyn 1
LOB -- New York 5, Brooklyn 4
2B -- Collins H 2, Corkhill P, Ewing B, Foutz D 2, Visner J, Burns O
3B -- O'Rourke J
HR -- Collins H, Richardson D
SB -- Connor R
CS -- Ward M 2, Ewing B
PB -- Clark B
T -- 2:07
A -- 8,445

Notes:

1. The Polo Grounds got dark at least a half-hour earlier than Washington Park in Brooklyn, according to the *Brooklyn Eagle*, September 11, 1889.

2. National League Team Versus Team Historical Win Loss Records Baseball Almanac (http://www.baseball-almanac.com/teams/teamvsteam-nl.shtml).

3. Harris, W.I. *New York Press*, October 19, 1889.

4. *New York Times*, October 19, 1889.

5. *New York Times*, October 17, 1889.

6. *New York Evening Sun*, October 18, 1889.

7. Harris, W. I., *New York Press*, October 19, 1889; *Boston Herald*, October 19, 1889.

8. Lewis, Ethan M. "A Structure to Last Forever: The Players League and the Brotherhood War of 1890," http://www.ethan-lewis.org/pl/ch2.html.

9. Henry Chadwick, *Brooklyn Eagle*, October 19, 1889.

Box score compiled by the author from accounts in above cited newspapers as well as the *New York World* and the *New York Tribune*.

Giants Win Back-to-Back World's Series

New York Giants vs. Brooklyn Bridegrooms

Polo Grounds, New York, N.Y.
October 29, 1889

By Peter Mancuso

They might have called it the first "Subway Series" if there had been a subway at the time. That wouldn't arrive in New York for 15 years after the New York Giants of the National League triumphed over the Brooklyn Bridegrooms of the American Association to make the victors the first major-league team to win consecutive World Series.

The 1889 regular season was one of the most exciting in baseball history. Two teams in the National League, New York and Boston, and two in the American Association, Brooklyn and St. Louis, came down to pennant-deciding games on the last day.[1] New York's victory, following the Giants 1888 World Series triumph over the American Association champion St. Louis Browns, gave the Giants a chance to be the first team to win consecutive World Series titles since the two league champions began meeting after the 1884 season.

Adding to the intrigue was the impending rebellion of nearly all key players from both leagues, and the prospect that a third major league, the Players League, would be formed.

Owners of the two teams agreed on a best-of-11 series, the games to alternate between the home parks of the two teams.[2] The first was to be played at the "New" Polo Grounds (opened during the 1889 season) at 155th Street and the Harlem River in Manhattan, and the second at Washington Park between Third and Fifth Streets and Fourth and Fifth Avenues in Brooklyn.[3]

Play commenced on Friday, October 18, with a 12–10 Brooklyn victory at the New Polo Grounds. New York cranks, players, and management were frustrated by what they felt was biased umpiring by Brooklyn native Bob Ferguson.[4]

Game Two in Washington Park drew a huge throng of 16,100 with all seating claimed two hours before the start. Thousands more stood in a great roped-off, horseshoe-shaped portion of the deep outfield and foul territory, and additional hundreds sat atop the outfield fence. The Giants were victorious, 6–2. The series was now tied at one game apiece.[5]

Without Sunday baseball allowed in either city, there was no game on October 20. On Monday 3,000 fans made their way to the upper reaches of Manhattan only to find that the game was canceled because of heavy rain that morning. This left many of the Giants' followers chagrined as the club had failed to alert downtown stations that the game was called off.[6]

Although the weather for Tuesday, October 22, was perfect and the Series was tied, the New Polo

Brooklyn ace Bob Caruthers could not stop a rout in Game 5.

Grounds saw fewer than half the 8,000 who had watched Game One. Many had been frustrated by the previous day's trip made in vain. Perhaps it was better that more New York cranks didn't see the game, which Brooklyn won 8–7. Once they got a slight lead, the Bridegrooms resorted to blatant stalling tactics. At 5:07 P.M. (six minutes before official sundown), with the game in the ninth inning and two New York runners on base, umpire John Gaffney called the game because of darkness. Giants management was furious. Manager James Mutrie referred to his opponents as "schoolboys." Brooklyn led the series 2–1.[7]

Game Four was played back in Washington Park on Wednesday, October 23, in weather that turned very chilly. To make matters less comfortable for the Giants, the Bridegrooms continued their stalling tactics. Coupled with an on-field wrangle that followed a close play, the game was called for darkness after only six innings with Brooklyn ahead, 10–7. The Bridegrooms now led three games to one.[8]

On Thursday, October 24, before the fifth game, scheduled at Washington Park, Giants owner John B. Day met with Brooklyn owner Charles Byrne and umpires Gaffney and Tom Lynch. Day threatened to withdraw from the Series unless the umpires acted impartially and Brooklyn stopped its stalling tactics. The result was a New York landslide, 11–3, against Brooklyn ace Bob Caruthers. The Series now stood at three wins for Brooklyn and two for New York.[9]

For Game Six the teams returned to the New Polo Grounds, where the Giants tied the series at

New York's John Ward was the hero of Game 6.

New York's Hank O'Day was the winning pitcher in Game 9.

three games apiece, prevailing 2–1 in 11 innings on the heroics of shortstop John Montgomery Ward.[10]

On Saturday, October 26, New York beat the Bridegrooms 11–7 and took the Series lead, four games to three. On Monday, October 28, the Giants secured their fifth Series victory in a 16–7 blowout in Washington Park.

The ninth and final game was played Tuesday in Manhattan and was won by the Giants, 3–2. New York pitcher Hank O'Day allowed the Bridegrooms only four hits, two of which came in the first inning. In the bottom of the ninth, Brooklyn raised a last-ditch threat when Germany Smith reached first on an error, but he was erased when Doc Bushong lined out and Smith was caught off first for a double play. The last batter, Darby O'Brien, managed a base on balls, but O'Brien was caught stealing to end the Series.[11] The Giants were again the world champions.

When the Giants had won their second consecutive National League pennant less than a month earlier, there was much celebration, particularly upon their triumphant return to New York from Cleveland. Now, there was nothing beyond a brief post-game high exhibited by the team as various VIPs entered the clubhouse to congratulate them.

Throughout the 1889 World's Series daily newspaper reports of the game frequently appeared side-by-side with the latest reports about the formation of the Players League, which would soon spirit away nearly all National League and American Association regular players, including the biggest stars. Once the clubhouse door at the New Polo Grounds had been secured that evening, the celebration ended and war began.[12]

October 29, 1889

Brooklyn	AB	R	1b	SH	SB	PO	A	E
O'Brien, lf	1	1	0	0	1	3	0	0
Collins, 2b	4	1	2	1	1	2	4	0
Burns, rf	4	0	1	1	0	1	0	0
Foutz, 1b	3	0	0	0	2	10	1	0
Pinkney, 3b	3	0	0	0	1	1	0	0
Terry, p	4	0	0	0	0	1	2	0
Visner, cf	4	0	0	0	0	4	0	0
Smith, ss	4	0	1	0	1	1	3	0
Bushong, c	3	0	0	0	0	1	0	2
	30	2	4	2	6	24	10	2
New York	**AB**	**R**	**1b**	**SH**	**SB**	**PO**	**A**	**E**
Slattery, cf	4	1	1	0	1	3	0	0
Tiernan, rf	3	1	1	0	0	1	0	0
Ewing, c	3	0	0	1	0	4	3	1
Ward, ss	3	1	2	0	1	3	6	1
Connor, 1b	4	0	1	1	2	7	2	0
Richardson, 2b	4	0	0	1	0	5	0	1
O'Rourke, lf	4	0	2	1	2	1	0	0
Whitney, 3b	4	0	0	1	0	3	2	0
O'Day, p	2	0	1	0	0	0	0	1
	31	3	8	5	6	27	13	4

```
Brooklyn  200 000 000 - 2
New York  100 001 10x - 3
```

Earned runs – Brooklyn 1, New York 2. First base on errors – Brooklyn 2, New York 1. Left on bases – Brooklyn 8, New York 8. Base on Balls – Off O'Day 7, off Terry 3. Struck out – By O'Day 5, by Terry 1. Three-base hit – Ward. Two-base hits – Burns, Tiernan. Stolen bases – Connor (2), O'Rourke (2), O'Brien, Collins, Foutz (2), Pinkney, Smith, Slattery, Ward. Sacrifice hits – Ewing, Connor, Richardson, O'Rourke, Whitney, Collins, Burns. Double plays – Whitney and Connor; Smith and Collins. Passed ball – Bushong. Wild pitch – O'Day. Umpires – Messrs Lynch and Gaffney.

Notes:

1. Caillault, Jean-Pierre. *A Tale of Four Cities: Nineteenth Century Baseball's Most Exciting Season, 1889, in Contemporary Accounts* (Jefferson, North Carolina, and London: McFarland & Company, 2003), p. 3.

2. *New York Times*, October 17, 1889, p.3.

3. Benson, Michael. *Ballparks of North America: A Comprehensive Historical Reference to Baseball Grounds, Yards and Stadiums, 1845 to Present* (Jefferson, North Carolina, and London: McFarland & Co.), p. 57, 256-257.

4. *New York Times*, October 19, 1889, p. 2.

5. *New York Times*, October 20, 1889, p. 12.

6. *New York Times*, October 22, 1889, p. 3.

7. *New York Times*, October 23, 1889, p. 3.

8. *New York Times*, October 24, 1889, p. 3.

9. *New York Times*, October 25, 1889, p. 2.

10. *New York Times*, October 26, 1889, p. 2. (See independent story of this game in this volume.)

11. *New York Herald*, October 30, 1889, p. 8; *New York Times*, October 30, 1889, p. 9.

12. *New York Times*, October 30, 1889, p. 9.

Debut of the Players League

Philadelphia Quakers vs. New York Giants
Brotherhood Park, New York, N.Y.;
Chicago Pirates vs. Pittsburgh Burghers
Exposition Park, Pittsburgh, Pa.;
Brooklyn Wonders vs. Boston Reds
Congress Street Grounds, Boston, Mass.;
Cleveland Infants vs. Buffalo Bisons
Olympic Park, Buffalo, N.Y.
April 19, 1890

By John W. Bauer

The Players League opened the 1890 season with seven of eight clubs playing in the same city as National League clubs; Buffalo was the lone exception. Under the sponsorship and direction of the players' Brotherhood, the Players League also commenced play on the same day as the National League, with four games on Saturday, April 19, 1890. The American Association had commenced its campaign two days earlier. New York, Boston, Pittsburgh, and Buffalo hosted games, with all but Buffalo in direct competition with a National League game.

Organized the previous offseason by players disenchanted by labor relations in the existing Organized Baseball structure, the Players League offered teams in which the players themselves retained partial ownership. The concept attracted most of the game's stars, and the popularity of those stars cut deeply into the existing leagues. Of the 72 players appearing in Players League box scores on April 19, all but two had played in either the National League or American Association in 1889. That star power showed itself at the turnstiles of the four Opening Day sites.

Philadelphia at New York. More than 12,000 arrived at the Brotherhood Park on a cold afternoon for the inaugural Players League match in New York. The crowd greeted the Players League Giants with "such cheering and yelling, throwing up of hats and general enthusiasm as, perhaps, had never before been witnessed at a ball game."[1] New York featured a lineup remarkably similar to the regular lineup for the 1889 National League Giants; the entire lineup had played for the '89 National League outfit and seven had been regulars. Tim Keefe, who won 28 games for the National League Giants the previous year and whose sporting goods company supplied the Players League game ball, pitched for New York. Charlie Buffinton, who equaled Keefe's 28 wins with the '89 Phillies, took the mound for the Players League Quakers.

Harry Stovey, who hit a first inning home run for Boston

New York opened the scoring with three runs in the top of the second inning, but Philadelphia answered with seven in the bottom half. The Giants chipped away at Philadelphia's lead with one run in the fourth and two more in the sixth.

After Philadelphia added one run in the bottom of the sixth to take an 8–6 lead, New York regained the lead with a five-run eighth inning and held that 11–8 lead into the ninth. Philadelphia batted last despite playing away from home. A combination of two hit batsmen, two singles, and a double provided the spark for Philadelphia's come-from-behind 12–11 win. As a reward for their season-opening win, the Philadelphia players were promised new suits.[2]

Chicago at Pittsburgh. Pittsburgh hosted Chicago before approximately 8,500 at Exposition Park. The crowd "gave the players a good reception and made them jubilant."[3] Charlie Comiskey, longtime member of the American Association St. Louis Browns, led Chicago into the Players League campaign. His nine comprised of former Browns teammates as well as members of the '89 National League Chicago White Stockings.

Comiskey contributed to his club's cause with one hit in four at-bats and two runs. Those contributions helped Chicago score seven runs in the first three frames. Pittsburgh pitcher Pud Galvin was undone by his defense as well as Chicago's bats. Chicago tagged Galvin for 10 runs and 12 hits over the nine innings, and Pittsburgh's seven errors hurt the home team's cause. Chicago pitcher Silver King scattered six hits and surrendered two unearned runs in a 10–2 Chicago victory.

Brooklyn at Boston. After an exhibition schedule in which it won all 12 matches,[4] Boston hosted Brooklyn at the Congress Street Grounds. Boston's 3–2 win in front of more than 8,000 fans included elements of a modern-day pitchers' duel. Boston's Matt Kilroy and Brooklyn's George Van Haltren allowed only 10 hits between them. Boston third baseman Billy Nash and Brooklyn center fielder Ed Andrews were the only batsmen with multi-hit games.

The New York Players League club of 1890: (from top) George Gore, Mike Slattery, Danny Richardson, Jim O'Rourke, Art Whitney, Gil Hatfield, Tim Keefe, Roger Connor, Buck Ewing, William Brown

Boston opened the scoring with right fielder Harry Stovey's first-inning home run, one of two four-baggers in the four Opening Day games. Boston doubled its lead in the third inning when an error by Brooklyn shortstop John Montgomery Ward allowed Stovey to get on base. He stole second, then scored on a double by catcher and captain Mike "King" Kelly. In the top of the ninth inning, Boston added what proved to be the difference in the game when Nash scored.

After failing to score in the first eight innings, Brooklyn rallied in the bottom of the ninth. Left fielder Emmett Seery's two-out, two-run double allowed Brooklyn to pull within a run. The game ended when the next batter, second baseman Lou Bierbauer, grounded out.

Cleveland at Buffalo. Buffalo hosted Cleveland before 3,125 at Olympic Park, and romped to a 23–2 win over the visiting Infants. The Bisons scored in each of the first six innings and every batter but one crossed home plate at least twice. Pitcher George Haddock scored more runs (four) than he surrendered (two).

The Bisons offense proved effective in garnering 17 hits, with second basemen Sam Wise contributing four and right fielder John Rainey hitting a home run. Cleveland assisted in its own demise with seven errors and pitcher Henry Gruber's 16 walks.

Over the course of the first four games of season, Buffalo would score 79 runs in completing a four-game season-opening sweep of Cleveland. The promise of this fast start was undone with 11 losses in the next 12 games en route to a 36–96 season that left the Bisons 20 games behind seventh-place Cleveland.

After the first day of games, Brotherhood leader Ward pronounced himself satisfied with the start to the season. He asserted that the Brotherhood movement was "in accord with the spirit of the times" and "the Brotherhood grounds … [were] far better than those of the League."[5] Ward had reason to feel satisfied. In the three cities where the Players League and National League went head-to-head, the Players League teams won the attendance battle by approximately 3 to 1.

That pattern continued through the remainder of the season. But with the baseball market glutted by an extra league, all teams in all three leagues lost money. At season's end, the established leagues, relying on their deeper financial reserves, managed to coerce backers of the Players League into going out of business.

Cleveland pitcher Henry Gruber walked 16 batters.

	AB	R	H	PO	A	E
BOSTON						
Richardson, lf	4	0	1	1	0	0
Stovey, rf	4	2	1	0	0	0
Kelly, c	4	0	1	5	0	0
Nash, 3b	4	1	2	1	3	0
Brouthers, 1b	3	0	1	14	1	1
Quinn, 2b	4	0	0	4	1	1
Johnston, cf	4	0	0	1	0	0
Irwin, ss	3	0	0	0	5	1
Kilroy, p	3	0	0	1	2	1
TOTALS	33	3	6	27	12	4
BROOKLYN						
Seery, lf	4	0	1	1	1	0
Bierbauer, 2b	4	0	0	2	2	1
Andrews, cf	4	0	2	0	0	0
Ward, ss	3	0	0	1	4	1
Orr, 1b	4	0	0	12	2	0
McGeachy, rf	4	0	0	3	0	0
Joyce, 3b	1	0	0	2	2	3
Daily, c	4	1	1	1	0	1
VanHaltren, p	2	1	0	5	2	0
TOTALS	30	2	4	27	13	6

Boston	1	0	1	0	0	0	0	1	-	3
Brooklyn	0	0	0	0	0	0	0	2	-	2

Earned runs – Boston 2, Brooklyn 1. Home run – Stovey. Two-base hits – Seery, Andrews. Three-base hit – Kelly. Sacrifice hits – Seery, Nash, Quinn, Stovey, Ward, Van Haltren. Stolen bases – Stovey, Joyce. Double plays – Irwin, Brouthers, Kelly, Seery, Daily; Van Haltren, Ward, Bierbauer. Passed ball – Daily. Wild pitch – Kilroy. Hit by pitcher – Van Haltren. Umpires – Gaffney, Barnes. Tome – 1:37.

Notes:

1. *Sporting Life*, April 26, 1890, p. 3.

2. Op cit, p. 1-2.

3. Op cit, p. 3.

4. Ibid.

5. Ibid.

Other references used in preparation of this article included:

Koszarek, Ed. *The Players League* (Jefferson, North Carolina: McFarland & Company, Inc., 2006).

Nemec, Nemec. *The Great Encyclopedia of Nineteenth Century Major League Baseball* (2d ed.) (Tuscaloosa, Alabama: University of Alabama Press, 2006).

Baseball-reference.com, Retrosheet.org

The Kid, the Bolt, and Silent Mike

Boston Beaneaters vs. New York Giants

*Polo Grounds, New York, N.Y.
May 12, 1890*

By Peter Mancuso

In 1890 the Players League sat on top of the baseball world, such as it was. Perhaps nowhere else was this more apparent than in New York City, where the Giants of the National League played second fiddle to another team composed almost exclusively of their former players, who complicated the situation further by also calling themselves the Giants. The Players League Giants scheduled games in direct conflict with the original Giants and built Brotherhood Park next to their former club's home field, the New Polo Grounds.

The National League Giants, who became the first team to win consecutive undisputed "World's Championships" in 1888–89, were decimated for 1890 when practically all of their star players jumped to the Players League. The only first-string players to remain were pitcher Mickey Welch, a future Hall of Famer, and Silent Mike Tiernan, a hard-hitting outfielder.

The Players League Giants consistently outdrew their National League counterparts. This was the situation on Monday, May 12, 1890, when only 687 cranks[1] showed up for the National League Giants-Boston game, while 1,707[2] patrons attended the Players League Giants-Boston game next door.

National League teams went to great lengths to obtain star players. The Giants managed to convince

*The 1890 Boston Beaneaters.
Back: Chippy McGarr, Pretzels Getzien, Patsy Donovan, Charlie Ganzel, John Taber, Marty Sullivan, Tommy Tucker. Middle: Kid Nichols, Herman Long, Charlie Bennett, Frank Selee, John Clarkson, Pop Smith, Steve Brodie. Front: Bobby Lowe, unknown, Lew Hardie.*

the Indianapolis team's owner, John Brush, that the 18-year-old pitching phenomenon Amos "The Hoosier Thunderbolt" Rusie was more valuable to the National League's success playing his home games in New York City than in Indiana. Thus, Rusie came to the National League Giants, where he would go on to a Hall of Fame career with more than 20 victories in each of the next eight seasons.

To say that Rusie, now only in his second major-league season, was the backbone of the Giants pitching staff in 1890 is an understatement. He pitched in a career-high 67 games. He managed 29 wins against 34 losses for an anemic-hitting team and completed 56 of the 62 games he started, including four shutouts.[3] That day's starting pitcher for the National League Boston Beaneaters, 20-year-old rookie Kid Nichols, would go on to have a 27–19 season, appearing in 48 games and completing all of his 47 starts while pitching a league-leading seven shutouts.[4] Nichols would be one of only three pitchers of the 1890s (Rusie and Cy Young were the others) inducted into the Hall of Fame, leading that decade with seven seasons of 30 wins or better.

"Silent" Mike Tiernan arrived with the National League Giants as a rookie in 1887 and played an integral part as the starting right fielder for the club's back-to-back world's championships. Tiernan hit home runs in double digits five times, leading the league in 1890 and 1891 with 13 and 16 respectively. His .311 lifetime batting average for his 13-year career,[5] all with the Giants, made him a New York fan favorite. His nickname was attributed to his disinclination to argue with umpires in an era when the reverse was the norm.

The home-team National League Giants elected to bat first, hoping to get first crack at the still lively ball. In the bottom of the first inning, Boston stranded its lead runner at third base, the only Beaneater to reach third in the game. The pitching duel continued for 12 innings with remarkable defensive play by both teams, particularly by Herman Long, Boston's great shortstop. Nichols struck out 11 (*New*

The 1890 New York Giants: 1-Jack Sharrott, 2-Artie Clark, 3-Jack Glasscock, 4-Dick Buckley, 5-Charley Bassett, 6-Henry Boyle, 7-Tom O'Rourke, 8-Joe Hornung, 9-Pete Sommers, 10-Mike Tiernan, 11-Mickey Welch, 12-Jesse Burkett, 13-Amos Rusie, 14-Sam Crane, 15-Jim Mutrie, 16-Mort Scanlan, 17-Jerry Denny, 18- Listed as Dooley, identification cannot be verified, 19-Pat Murphy.

York Herald*) or 10 (*New York Times*), while Rusie fanned 12 (*Herald*) or 11 (*Times*).[6]

As the game passed beyond the ninth inning, each putout by the Giants was met with lusty cheers by the small but enthusiastic crowd. This brought many of the spectators in the adjacent Brotherhood Park to the top row of the grandstand that overlooked right field and center field of the New Polo Grounds.[7] Soon, every putout was met with cheering from both parks. Nichols struck out Rusie to start the top of the 13th, and with the game in Brotherhood Park a 12-2 Boston rout, the attention of almost all at that game turned to the National League contest.

The next batter after Rusie was Tiernan, who had one of the three hits that Nichols had allowed. (Rusie had also allowed only three.) Tiernan fouled off the first pitch into the grandstand. Before the foul ball could be retrieved, the Giants quickly provided a brand-new ball to the umpire, who tossed it to Nichols. Nearly simultaneously, the ball that Tiernan fouled off was thrown back to Nichols' feet. Remembering that Tiernan's only other hit in the game, back in the eighth inning, had been off a new ball, Nichols picked up the old ball and asked the umpire, "This ball is all right, isn't it?" "No, the new ball was on the field first," said umpire Phil Powers, "and you will have to use it."[8]

The significance of the new ball was not missed by the cranks, who chanted, "Now, Mike." Nichols' very next pitch was shoulder high and the sound of Tiernan's bat communicated that every pound of his power was behind it. The ball headed for the deepest part of the outfield, more of a line drive than a towering shot. Center field in the New Polo Grounds had been set at 360 feet when the ballpark was hastily built during the start of the 1889 season,[9] but the distance had been increased by 50 feet before play began in 1890.[10] Additionally, a canvas-covered wooden fence sat atop a tall, steep embankment. Tiernan's blow cleared the center-field fence near the flagpole, landed in the narrow alley between the two stadiums and bounded against the wall of Brotherhood Park. The onlookers in both parks erupted in wild cheering as Tiernan circled the bases. Rusie then made quick work of Boston in the bottom of the 13th.[11]

One sportswriter predicted that the flagpole would long mark the spot of Tiernan's great hit. But when the Players League disbanded, the National League Giants took over Brotherhood Park, renaming it the Polo Grounds. The site of the great game of May 12, 1890, passed into obscurity.

New York	R	H	PO	A	E	Boston	R	H	PO	A	E
Tiernan cf	1	2	2	0	0	Tucker 1b	0	0	21	0	1
Glasscock ss	0	0	5	2	0	McGarr 3b	0	0	0	2	2
Easterb'k 1b	0	0	14	0	1	Sul'an lf	0	1	0	0	0
Bassett 2b	0	0	3	4	0	Long ss	0	0	1	9	0
Clarke rf	0	0	0	0	0	Brodie cf	0	1	2	0	0
Denny 3b	0	1	8	1	1	Hardie c	0	0	10	3	0
Hornung lf	0	0	2	0	0	Smith 2b	0	0	5	4	1
Buckley c	0	0	10	5	0	S'hase rf	0	0	0	0	0
Rusie p	0	1	0	2	0	Nichols p	0	1	0	2	1
TOTAL	1	4	39	14	2	**TOTAL**	0	3	39	19	5

New York   000 000 000 000 1 – 1
Boston   000 000 000 000 0 – 0

Earned runs – New York 1. First base on errors – New York 4, Boston 2. Left on base – New York 6, Boston 5. First base on balls – Off Rusie 2, Off Nichols 1. Struck out – By Rusie 11, by Nichols 10. Home run – Tiernan. Sacrifice hits – Glasscock, Tucker, Bassett. Stolen bases – Tiernan, Glasscock. Passed ball – Hardie. Umpires – Messrs. Powers and McDermott. Time of game – Two hours.

Notes:

1. "Over The Fence In Centre Field," *New York Herald*, May 13, 1890, p.8.

2. Ibid.

3. John Thorn, Phil Birnbaum, and Bill Deane, eds. *Total Baseball: The Ultimate Baseball Encyclopedia, 8th Ed.* (Toronto: Sport Media Publishing, Inc.)

4. Thorn et. al., op. cit.

5. Ibid.

6. "Tiernan's Home Run Won It," *New York Times*, May 13, 1890, p.3.

7. *New York Herald*, op. cit., loc. cit.

8. Ibid.

9. Lowry, Philip J. *Green Cathedrals* (Reading, Massachusetts: Addison-Wesley Publishing Co., 1992), p.190.

10. *New York Herald*, op. cit., loc. cit.

11. Ibid.

No Hits—But No Win

Ward's Wonders of Brooklyn vs. Chicago Pirates

South Side Park, Chicago, Ill.
June 21, 1890

By John Zinn

A hit that wasn't a hit turned an exciting, but hardly unique, pitchers' duel into baseball history. The scene was Chicago's South Side Park; the opponents were two Players League teams, the Chicago Pirates and Ward's Wonders of Brooklyn.

Played before a crowd estimated at between 4,000 and 4,500, the game was the first of four scheduled between two struggling teams. Although preseason predictions had Charles Comiskey's Pirates winning "first place in a walk-over," Chicago had played no better than .500 ball. On the other hand, little had been expected of Brooklyn, which got off to a quick start before stumbling in June.

Chicago had major problems on the left side of its infield because of poor performance, injuries, and personal issues. Brooklyn's lineup was also depleted because of injuries, most notably the loss a few days earlier of Dave Orr, one of the league's best hitters.[1]

Although the teams' regular lineups weren't up to par, the same couldn't be said of the starting pitchers. In the pitcher's box for Brooklyn was its best hurler, Gus Weyhing. Opposing him was the even more intimidating Silver King. An ace pitcher with the American Association St. Louis Browns, King had jumped to the Players League with teammate Charles Comiskey, the Chicago player-manager.

Although born Charles Frederick Koenig, the Chicago pitcher was known almost exclusively by his nickname. It derived both from his blond hair, which was said to resemble "burnished silver" and also from the fact that the German word Koenig is King in English.

Whatever he was called, the right-hander used speed and control to dominate hitters. After his last start, the *Chicago Herald* had compared the opposition's offensive efforts to a pig trying to climb a greased pole.[2]

Because of the problems at shortstop and third base, Comiskey was forced to use Jack Boyle and Dell Darling, both primarily catchers, at those positions. Orr's absence from the Brooklyn lineup gave King one break, but there were still three .300 hitters in the Ward's Wonders' batting order.[3]

Home team manager Comiskey chose to bat first, and Weyhing retired the Pirates without incident. With one out for Brooklyn in the bottom half of the inning, John Montgomery Ward, Brooklyn team manager and founder of the Brotherhood of Professional Base Ball Players, which had started the Players League, drew one of the three walks King would issue. The Brooklyn shortstop stole second and third before catcher Charles Farrell picked him off that base. Chicago's infield weakness was demonstrated during Ward's next at-bat as fill-in third baseman Boyle threw his bunt over Comiskey's head at first, one of his three throwing errors in the game. Then one of the two true infielders in the Chicago lineup, second baseman Fred Pfeffer, threw out Ward trying to reach second.[4]

If King was being let down by Chicago's fielding, the hitting was even more futile. The Pirates mustered only four singles and two walks, never advancing a man past second. One potential Chicago threat was short-circuited by Ward, who made a leaping catch of Comiskey's line drive in the sixth and turned it into a double play.

In spite of being the beneficiary of three walks and eight Chicago errors, the Ward's Wonders were hitless and scoreless as they batted in the seventh. With one out George VanHaltren hit a grounder to Darling, who had already made two errors. The catcher-turned-shortstop got to the ball "quickly enough [almost] to hand it to Comiskey" at first, a newspaper reporter at the game told readers the next morning. Instead, he threw "like a crazy man" past Comiskey, and Van Haltren went to second.

*The 1890 Chicago Players League club
(clockwise from the top): Charlie Comiskey, Hugh Duffy, Arlie Latham, Duke Farrell, Charlie Bastian, Silver King, Ned Williamson, Dell Darling, Charlie Bartson, Tip O'Neill, Jack Boyle, Mark Baldwin; (center, left to right): Jimmy Ryan, Fred Pfeffer, Frank Dwyer.*

Brooklyn's Paul Cook then bunted to King, who threw him out at first while Van Haltren advanced to third. At least one writer speculated that King had a play at third, but the Chicago pitcher probably, and understandably, no longer had confidence in the left side of his infield.[5]

The next batter was second baseman Louis Bierbauer, who hit what on most days would have been a single to right field. However, Chicago right fielder Hugh Duffy followed a difficult stop with a strong throw to retire Bierbauer at first, although Van Haltren was able to score the game's first run.

One dramatic moment remained. Chicago's Jim Ryan led off the ninth with a drive out of the park but foul. He struck out on the next pitch, and the last two batters went down. Silver King had not only lost a classic pitcher's duel, but earned the dubious distinction of being the first major-league pitcher to no-hit the opposition and lose. To further add to the bizarre events, Comiskey's decision to bat first meant King had pitched only eight innings.[6]

The biggest challenge to the media was finding enough adjectives to describe the Pirates defense or lack thereof. Recognizing that King had pitched the "best game" of the season, they lamented the "miserably poor infield work" of Boyle and Darling. Stating the obvious, one writer noted that Darling, who had five errors in two consecutive games at short, was "badly out of position." In a final touch of irony, Chicago's regular shortstop, Ned Williamson, who had been away with his dying sister, returned for the remaining three games—all Pirates victories.

Comiskey, Ward, and Duffy would go on to the Hall of Fame, but it is doubtful that they, or anyone else who was there, ever forgot the game. As one eyewitness put it, "It will be a long time before as queer a game will be seen again."[7]

BROOKLYN PLAYERS' LEAGUE TEAM.

Ward's Wonders, the 1890 Brooklyn Players League team: 1-John Ward, 2-Dave Orr, 3- Lou Bierbauer, 4-Bill Joyce, 5-Paul Cook, 6-Tom Kinslow, 7-Jackie Hayes, 8-Con Daily, 9-Gus Wehying, 10-Pete Conway, 11-John Sowders, 12-Con Murphy, 13-Jack McGeachey, 14-Art Sunday, 15-Emmett Seery, 16-Ed Andrews, 17-George Van Haltren.

	AB	R	BH	PO	A	E
Chicago						
Duffy, rf	3	0	0	3	1	0
O'Neill, lf	4	0	1	1	0	0
Ryan, cf	3	0	0	1	0	0
Comiskey, 1b	4	0	0	13	1	0
Pfeffer, 2b	4	0	0	0	3	1
Darling, ss	3	0	1	1	0	3
Farrell, c	2	0	1	2	2	1
Boyle, 3b	3	0	0	1	3	3
King, p	3	0	1	2	4	0
Total	29	0	4	24	14	8
Brooklyn						
Joyce, 3b	4	0	0	0	1	0
Ward, ss	3	0	0	4	2	0
Van Haltran, rf	3	1	0	1	0	0
Cook, 1b	4	0	0	12	0	0
Bauer, 2b	3	0	0	1	2	1
McGeachey, cf	3	0	0	4	0	0
Seery, lf	2	0	0	0	0	0
Kinslow, c	3	0	0	4	2	0
Weyhing, p	3	0	0	1	1	0
Total	28	1	0	27	8	1

Sacrifice Hits—Doyle, Cook. Stolen Bases—Ward (3). Left on Bases—Chicago, 5; Brooklyn, 6. Double Plays—Ward, Cook. Struck Out—By King, 2 by Weyhing, 5. Base on Balls—Off King, 3; off Weyhing, 3. Time—1 hour and 40 minutes. Umpires—Gaffney and Barnes

Notes:

1. Koszarek, Ed. *The Players League: History, Clubs, Ballplayers and Statistics*. (Jefferson, North Carolina: McFarland & Co, 2006), p. 51; *Sporting Life*, October 11, 1890; *The Sporting News*, June 21, 1890, August 2, 1890; *New York World*, June 22, 1890; *Brooklyn Daily Eagle*, June 18, 1890.

2. Koszarek, op. cit., p. 288; *The Sporting News*, May 26, 1938; *Chicago Herald*, June 18, 1890.

3. *Chicago Herald*, June 21 and June 22, 1890; *Chicago Tribune*, June 22, 1890; *Chicago Sunday Inter Ocean*, June 22, 1890; *New York World*, June 22, 1890; *Brooklyn Daily Eagle*, June 15, 1890.

4. Boren, Steven. "Silver King Loses a No-hitter," *Baseball Research Journal*, 1990; *Chicago Sunday Inter Ocean*, June 22, 1890; *Chicago Daily Tribune*, June 22, 1890.

5. *Chicago Herald*, June 22, 1890; *Chicago Tribune*, June 22, 1890; *Chicago Sunday Inter Ocean*, June 22, 1890.

6. *Chicago Tribune*, June 22, 1890; *Chicago Herald*, June 22, 1890; *Brooklyn Citizen*, June 22, 1890.

7. *Chicago Herald*, June 22, 1890; *Chicago Tribune*, June 22, 1890; *Chicago Sunday Inter Ocean*, June 20, 1890, June 22, 1890; *The Sporting News*, June 21, 1890.

The First Worst To First

Louisville vs. Columbus

October 6, 1890

By Jimmy Keenan

In 1889, the Louisville Colonels of the American Association finished in last place, compiling an unenviable record of 27 wins and 111 losses. The following season, Louisville pulled off one of the most amazing turnarounds in the history of our national pastime, clinching the American Association pennant on October 6, 1890 with a 2–0 victory over Columbus.

That turnaround was assisted by a seismic shift in the baseball landscape during the winter of 1889–90 that included the formation of a third major league. Unlike the existing National League and American Association, Players League teams were partly owned by the players themselves. Most of the best players in baseball at the time jumped to the new league. Those jumpers included 27 from Association teams, among them Louisville star Pete Browning, who signed with the Players League Cleveland Infants.

The Association's instability ran even deeper. Two entire teams—including the champions from Brooklyn—switched over to the National League. Their players were among 27 Association regulars from 1889 who played in the National League during 1890. A third club folded and a fourth dropped down to the minors. Four new franchises were added to the American Association to take their place.

The AA champion Louisville Colonels—who came from last place in 1889 to the pennant—as pictured in Sporting Life. Back: Mike Jones, Charlie Hamburg, Jack Chapman, Herb Goodall, Ned Bligh. Middle: Jack Ryan, Phil Tomney, Dan O'Connor, Tim Shinnick, Red Ehret, Farmer Weaver. Front: Scott Stratton, Chicken Wolf, George Meakim, Harry Raymond, Harry Taylor.

To make matters worse, on March 27, 1890 a cyclone tore through Louisville, killing over 100 people. On the night of the disaster, Louisville's baseball team was enjoying a show at a local theatre, just a short distance from where the cyclone touched down. The next day, members of the ballclub assisted the town's citizens in pulling the living as well as the dead from the rubble of the collapsed buildings.

In the aftermath of the disaster, pitcher Red Ehret remarked to a reporter, "We want to strike the other fellows [in the league] as hard as the cyclone struck the town."

Shortly after the tragedy, the press started referring to the ballclub as the Cyclones and the name stuck. The team, under the ownership of Barney Dreyfuss, played outstanding baseball all year. As fall approached, the only formality remaining was when would Louisville officially wrap up the American Association championship?

The Cyclones took the field at Eclipse Park in Louisville on Monday October 6 against the third place Columbus Solons. If the Louisville nine could defeat Columbus and if Toledo knocked off second place St. Louis, the Cyclones would become the first major-league baseball team to go from last place to first in just one year.

Louisville's manager Jack Chapman gave the starting assignment to his best pitcher, Scott Stratton. The 21-year-old hurler had a great year in 1890, posting a 34–14 record with a league-leading 2.36 earned run average.

From the start, things went Louisville's way. Second baseman Tim Shinnick robbed speedy

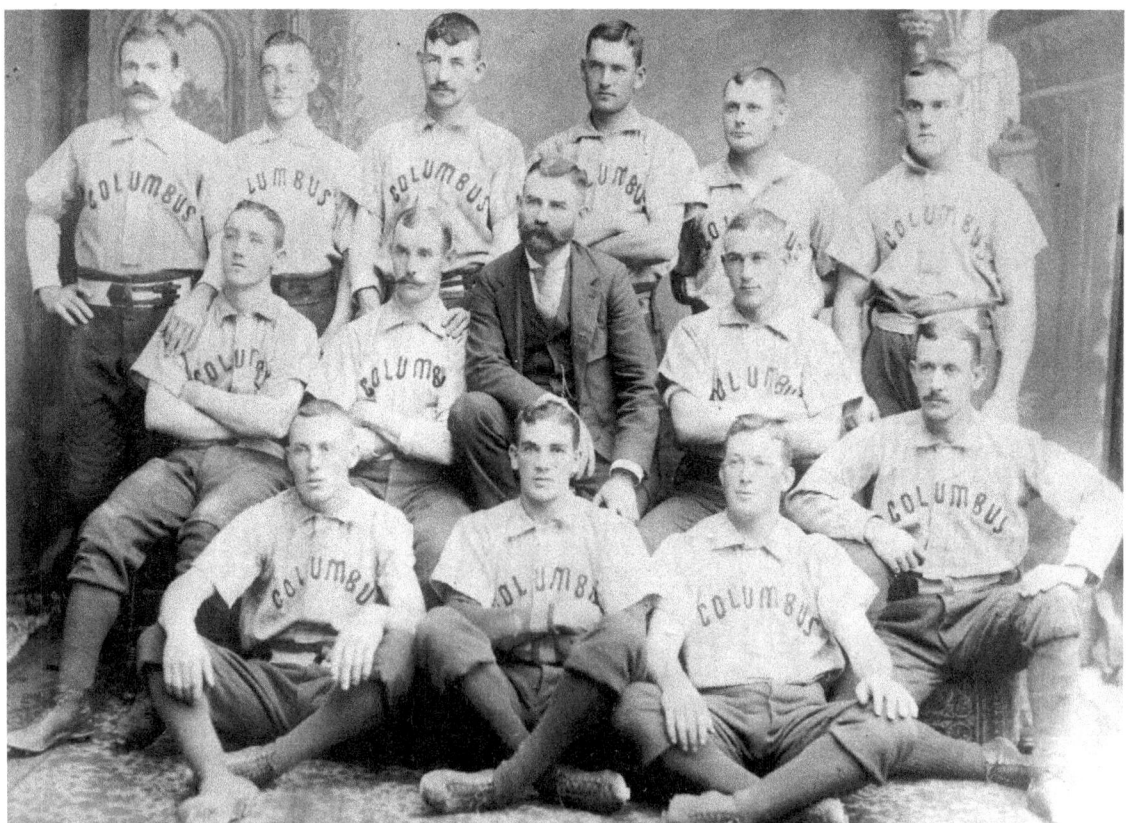

The 1890 Columbus Solons of the American Association. Back: Jim McTamany, Frank Knauss, Mike Lehane, Hank Gastright, Spud Johnson, Jack Crooks. Middle: Jack Doyle, Bill Widner, Gus Schmelz, Icebox Chamberlain, John Sneed. Front: Jack O'Connor, John Easton, Charlie Reilly.

Columbus lead-off hitter Jim McTamany of a sure base hit on a great stop and throw. In the Louisville half of the first, Columbus pitcher Hank Gastright who went 30–14 that season, walked Harry Taylor. A rookie who batted .306 with 45 stolen bases that season, Taylor advanced on a well-placed sacrifice bunt by Harry Raymond, then scored on Farmer Weaver's line single to center. "Taylor started like a quarter horse for home," the *Louisville Courier-Journal* wrote.

Weaver advanced to second on the play, and one batter later took third on a fly to right by Jimmy Wolf, on his way to leading the league with a .363 batting average. Charlie Hamburg drilled a ball that got by leftfielder Spud Johnson, allowing Weaver to score the second and final run of the game.

Stratton retired the Solons on three pitches in the top of the second, inducing a foul fly, pop up, and ground out. Columbus started a two-out rally in the third inning with consecutive hits by Gastright and McTamany, but Stratton retired King Crooks on a ground out to the first baseman to end the threat.

Stratton wound up with a six hitter and didn't allow a Columbus runner to reach third base, although the Solons might have broken the ice in the sixth but for a baserunning gaffe. Crooks, who had been jawing back and forth with the Louisville crowd for most of the day, reached base on a bunt. He advanced to second on a fielder's choice, but in his eagerness to argue a close "out" call at first on the play the runner strayed from the bag and was tagged out by Shinnick. "The King, who moments ago was in his glory, walked back to the bench as meek as a lamb to his seat on the bench, the crowd yelling wildly at his discomfiture," the *Courier-Journal* reported.

The pennant was finally clinched when Louisville left fielder Charlie Hamburg tracked down a long fly ball off the bat of Jack Doyle for the final out. Gastright pitched a good game in the tough 2–0 loss, allowing five hits and tossing shut-out ball for the last eight innings.

Louisville second baseman Shinnick had a phenomenal day, accepting 12 chances flawlessly, some quite difficult, while the rest of the infield played errorless ball. In the outfield, Weaver, Wolf and Hamburg each made outstanding plays to help preserve the win.

Louisville finished with an 88–44 record in 1890, an astonishing 64-game improvement in the standings. The Cyclones went on to play the National League champion Brooklyn Bridegrooms in an early version of the World Series. Each team notched three victories in addition to playing to a 7–7 tie in the third game, but rain, cold weather, and dwindling attendance led to the cancellation of the series. The anticlimactic end to the 1890 campaign did nothing to diminish the Cyclones' remarkable accomplishment of being the first major-league ballclub to go from worst to first in just one season.

	AB	R	BH	PO	A	E	SB	SO	BB
Louisville									
Taylor, 1b	3	1	1	14	0	0	0	0	1
Raymond, 3b	4	0	0	0	0	0	0	1	0
Weaver, c.f.	4	1	1	2	0	0	0	0	0
Wolf, r.f.	3	0	1	2	0	0	0	0	1
Hamburg, l.f.	4	0	1	3	0	0	0	0	0
Shinnick, 2b	3	0	0	3	9	0	0	0	0
Tomney, s.s.	3	0	0	0	2	0	0	1	0
Ryan, c	3	0	0	2	0	0	0	0	0
Stratton, p	2	0	1	1	1	0	0	0	1
Totals	**29**	**2**	**5**	**27**	**12**	**0**	**0**	**2**	**3**
Columbus									
McTamany, c.f.	4	0	1	2	0	0	0	0	0
Crooks, 2b	4	0	1	4	4	0	0	0	0
O'Connor, c	4	0	0	3	0	0	0	0	0
Johnson, l.f.	4	0	0	0	0	1	0	1	0
Doyle, s.s.	4	0	1	1	4	0	0	0	0
Sneed, r.f.	3	0	0	2	0	0	0	1	0
Reilly, 3b	3	0	1	0	2	0	0	0	0
Lehane, 1b	3	0	1	12	1	0	0	0	0
Gastright, p	3	0	1	0	1	1	0	0	0
Totals	**32**	**0**	**6**	**24**	**12**	**2**	**0**	**2**	**0**

```
Innings     1 2 3  4 5 6  7 8 9
Louisville  2 0 0  0 0 0  0 0 x
Base Hits   2 1 0  0 1 0  0 1 x
Columbus    0 0 0  0 0 0  0 0 0
Base Hits   0 0 2  1 1 1  1 0 0
```

Exact Attendance – 1,082.
Earned Runs --- Louisville, 1.
Sacrifice hits --- Raymond 2, Wolf 1
Double Play – Crooks and Lehane
Umpire – Doscher
Time of Game – One hour and thirty-two minutes

The Clouded Finish

New York Giants vs. Boston Beaneaters

South End Grounds, Boston, Mass.
September 28-30, 1891

By Lyle Spatz

When first-place Chicago hosted second-place Boston on September 4, 1891, the Colts' lead over the Beaneaters was six games. Colts manager Cap Anson was so confident of winning the pennant that he entertained the crowd by wearing a white flowing beard throughout the game. The Colts' 5–3 victory increased the lead to seven games.

Ten days later it was down to 4½ games as the Colts prepared to face the Beaneaters in a final three-game series between the contenders. Chicago won the first two games, raising the lead back to 6½ games. A reporter at the *Chicago Daily Tribune* told his readers, "The good captain's men are champions and no mistake."[1]

Moreover, the scheduled pitchers in the third game indicated another likely win for Chicago. For Frank Selee's Beaneaters it was Charles "Kid" Nichols, 0–9 lifetime against Chicago; and for Anson's Colts it was Bill Hutchison, already with eight wins against Boston this season.

But strong pitching by Nichols, together with seven Colts errors led to a Beaneaters victory. Following a tie, the challengers embarked on a 17-game winning streak that would not end until the final day of the season. Boston's 16th consecutive victory, on October 1 against Philadelphia, clinched the pennant.

Fifteen of Boston's 18 wins were against Philadelphia, Brooklyn, and New York, the league's other Eastern teams. Boston's spectacular late-season success against its regional neighbors led to a serious post-season accusation by Chicago president James Hart. Hart charged that the Eastern teams had conspired to ensure that Boston, not Chicago, won the pennant. He alleged that players in the National League as a whole did not want the Colts, a team with the league's lowest payroll, to be its champion.

Additionally, Hart believed that resentment against Anson still existed for his opposition to the Brotherhood-inspired Players League, many of whose former members were back playing in the National League. Adding to the mix was the animosity Giants manager Jim Mutrie harbored toward Anson over his refusal to play a postponed contest on an open date of the Giants' choice.

Hart pointed to several instances during the streak where suspect fielding plays contributed to Boston victories. He focused mainly on the Beaneaters' five games against the Giants on September 28–30. The series took place at Boston's South End Grounds and included back-to-back doubleheaders. The Beaneaters, of course, won all five games, the first four by huge margins: 11-3, 13-8, 11-3, 16-5, and 5-3.

Hart pointed out the Giants had arrived in Boston for this very crucial series without their two best pitchers, Amos Rusie and John Ewing. Also absent were first baseman Roger Connor and second baseman Danny Richardson. And, Hart added, those Giants who played did so in such a casual manner that *Sporting Life*'s comment that "the New York's beat all records for indifferent and rocky playing," was typical of the reaction by the press.

James Hart: Chicago club's president alleged a conspiracy on the part of the Eastern teams to ease Boston's way to the 1891 pennant.

The New York papers were normally fully supportive of the Giants, yet they too wrote of their suspicions. For one, they wondered why Rusie and Ewing were used against Chicago, but not against Boston. Under a headline in the September 30 *New York Evening Telegram* that read, "Are The Giants Trying to Defeat Anson?" the *Telegram* writer claimed that "Anson's opponents are doing all in their power to prevent him from winning, but it is doubtful if New York is trying to win. This is unfortunate for it will probably leave a stigma on the National game."[2]

The Giants' lackadaisical play was so obvious that even the Boston fans booed their performance, and led Anson himself to accuse the Giants of deliberately losing the games. Rumors flew that Boston gamblers had even refused to set odds on the Beaneaters-Giants contests.

The whole controversy might have been rendered moot if Chicago had played better down the stretch. Keep in mind that the Colts had left Boston still in possession of a 5½-game lead over the Beaneaters. But they promptly lost three games in New York before finishing up just 6–5–1 in 12 games against Cincinnati, Cleveland, and Pittsburgh. Until that point, the Colts had been a combined 36–11 against the three teams.

On November 11 the league held a hearing at the Fifth Avenue Hotel in New York to consider Hart's charges. Hart offered two more alleged items of testimony in addition to the previous evidence presented. He claimed that 10 days before the Boston-New York series, umpire Jack McQuaid had told the Chicago players that the Beaneaters would sweep the series. And, Hart added, several Cincinnati players had told certain Colts players that the Giants openly stated they would do whatever was necessary to see that Boston won the pennant.[3]

Despite the seemingly overwhelming evidence to the contrary, owners Arthur Soden of Boston and John Day of New York denied any wrongdoing, and the league dismissed all charges.[4] However, to this day both Boston's 17-game winning streak and its 1891 championship remain clouded with suspicion.[5]

Amos Rusie: The Giants' mound ace.

John Ewing (above) and Amos Rusie won a combined 54 games in 1891, but neither pitched against the Beaneaters.

The 1891 stretch run

Date	Boston	Chicago	Difference
Sept. 16	Chicago 7-2	@ Boston 2-7	Chicago 5½
Sept. 17	Pittsburgh 7-7	@ New York 1-3	Chicago 5
Sept. 18	Pittsburgh 9-3	@ New York 3-9	Chicago 4
Sept. 19	Pittsburgh 11-3	@ New York 0-8	
		Pittsburgh 11-2	Chicago 2½
Sept. 21	Brooklyn 6-1	@ Cincinnati 5-4	Chicago 2½
Sept. 22	Brooklyn 3-0	@ Cincinnati 4-1	Chicago 2½
Sept. 23	Brooklyn 5-1	@ Cincinnati 9-0	
		Brooklyn 9-2	Chicago 2
Sept. 24	Philadelphia 5-2	Pittsburgh 7-4	Chicago 2
Sept. 25	Philadelphia 6-3	Pittsburgh 4-4 (forfeit to Chi)	Chicago 2
Sept. 26	Philadelphia 8-6	Pittsburgh 6-6	Chicago 1½
Sept. 28	New York 11-3	@ Cleveland 2-4	Chicago ½
Sept. 29	New York 13-8	@ Cleveland 14-13	
		New York 11-3	Tied
Sept. 30	New York 16-5	@ Cleveland 5-12	
		New York 5-3	Boston 1½
Oct. 1	@ Philadelphia 6-1	Cincinnati 1-6	Boston 2½ *
Oct. 2	@ Philadelphia 5-3	Cincinnati 16-17	Boston 3½
Oct. 3	@ Philadelphia 3-5	Cincinnati 9-15	Boston 3½

*Clinched pennant

Sept. 30, 1891 (Game 1)

Boston	AB	R	H	PO	A	E	New York	AB	R	H	PO	A	E
Long, ss	4	0	2	2	1	0	Gore, cf	5	0	1	1	0	0
Lowe, cf	4	2	1	4	0	0	Bassett, 3b	4	1	2	1	0	0
Stovey, lf	4	2	1	3	0	2	Connor, 1b	4	2	2	10	1	1
Brodie, rf	4	3	3	0	0	0	Tiernan, rf	5	1	3	0	0	0
Nash, 2b	4	1	1	1	1	0	O'R'ke, lf	4	1	4	3	0	2
Tucker, 1b	4	2	2	4	0	0	Wh'tler, 2b	4	0	1	5	0	1
Quinn, 3b	3	3	2	4	3	1	Gla'ck, ss	5	0	0	3	4	0
Bennett, c	3	2	1	7	3	0	Clarke, c	4	0	0	3	2	0
Nichols, p	3	1	3	1	5	0	Coughlin, p	5	0	0	1	3	0
	–	–	–	–	–	–	Welch, p	4	0	0	0	1	0
TOTALS	33	16	16	27	13	3	**TOTALS**	44	5	13	27	11	4

```
Boston     200 271 040 – 16
New York   200 000 012 –  5
```

Earned runs – Boston 8, New York 2. Home runs – Lowe, Tiernan. Two-base hits – Nichols, Brodie, Bassett, O'Rourke. Three-base hits – Quinn, Long, Connor. Sacrifice hits – Nash, Connor, Coughlin. Passed ball – Clarke. Umpire – Lynch. Time – 1:53. Stolen bases – Stovey 2, Brodie, O'Rourke. First on balls – Nichols 4, Coughlin 3, Welch 4. Struck out – Nichols 1, Coughlin 1, Welch 2.

Notes:

1. *Chicago Daily Tribune*, September 16, 1891.

2. *New York Evening Telegram*, September 30, 1891.

3. *Chicago Daily Tribune*, November 12, 1891.

4. Day was allowed to be present at the entire meeting, while Hart was allowed in only to testify.

5. For a full discussion of Boston's winning streak and the controversy it engendered, see Robert L. Tiemann's "The Forgotten Winning Streak of 1891" in the 1989 *Baseball Research Journal*, pp. 2-5.

Seven Hits in Seven Tries

St. Louis Browns vs. Baltimore Orioles

Union Park, Baltimore, Md.
June 10, 1892

By Jimmy Keenan

Until Rennie Stennett matched the feat in September of 1975, only one man in major-league history had recorded seven hits in seven at-bats during a regulation nine-inning game. This rarest of batting achievements was accomplished on June 10, 1892, by Wilbert Robinson, later to become a Hall of Fame manager but at the time a portly catcher for the cellar-dwelling Baltimore Orioles.

The Orioles hosted the St. Louis Browns that Friday at their two-tiered wooden home ground, Union Park. Those who attended the scheduled doubleheader couldn't have expected anything approaching the history that would unfold before their eyes. The Orioles had won just 10 of their 42 games to that point. The Browns, like the Orioles a remnant of the recently disbanded American Association, stood at 16–27. Those clubs and their fellow Association adoptees to the National League, Louisville and Washington, had formed a cluster at the bottom of the standings where they would remain all season.

It was a cool, overcast summer day with a light breeze blowing in from the northwest when the Browns took the field in the first inning of the opening contest. St. Louis sent veteran pitcher Charlie "Pretzels" Getzien into the box to oppose the Orioles ace right-hander Sadie McMahon. McMahon, 24, was coming off 36- and 35-win seasons. But those victories had been posted in the disbanded American Association, and so far in 1892 McMahon had found the National League to be tougher. His record stood at just 3–10 as the game began.

Wilbert Robinson

Pretzels Getzien was at the end of a career that yielded 145 victories, 29 of them with the pennant-winning Detroit Wolverines in 1887. As recently as 1890, Getzien had won 23 games for Boston's National League team. But that had been his last strong season. Although just 27 years old, he started only 10 games in 1891, winning four and losing six. Nonetheless, in their desire for an experienced arm, the Browns had signed Getzien just a few days before, and he was 2–0 for them as he took to the pitcher's box in Baltimore.

Orioles batters, who exercised their right under the rules of the time to bat first, were all over Getzien's offerings from the outset. Billy Shindle led off with a blistering triple to left field, and by the time the first inning ended, the Orioles had sent 10 men to the plate and scored five runs. Robinson, the eighth hitter in the lineup, contributed a single.

Baltimore hitters continued to tee off on Getzien in the second inning, scoring five more runs, with Robinson adding a second single. The veteran hurler was removed at the end of the inning, his team trailing 10–1. He had given up seven hits and 10 runs in two innings of work. Getzien never recovered from the humiliation, losing eight of his final 11 starts before being released in late July.

Joe Young, making his major-league debut and, as it turned out, his only big-league appearance, replaced Getzien in the third inning. Young had been the star hurler for the Mount Carmel team in the Central Pennsylvania League before signing with the Browns, but he could do nothing to stop the Orioles' onslaught. The Baltimore club pounded him for nine hits and 13 runs during his two innings in the pitcher's box. Amazingly, the leader of the Orioles assault was Robinson, a career .226 batter entering the season, whose third, fourth, and fifth hits were a single in the third inning, a double in the fourth, and a single in the fifth.

Besides being unable to stop Robinson or the Orioles, the visiting Browns had great difficulty catching up to McMahon's offerings. They managed only seven hits and four runs. Browns center fielder Steve Brodie, who later gained fame as an Oriole, was the only St. Louis player to make two hits off McMahon.

Left-hander Ted "Theo" Breitenstein came in to start the sixth inning, allowing the Orioles' 24th and 25th runs but avoiding Robinson, who did not come to the plate. Robinson batted in the seventh, collecting his sixth hit (a single), although the Orioles failed to add to their 25–2 lead. He batted again with two out in the ninth and produced a seventh base hit, his sixth single of the game. That seventh hit was harmless, but Robinson had already done enough damage, driving across 11 runs. The runs batted in were a single-game record that stood until 1924, and represented nearly 20 percent of the runs Robinson sent across the plate for the entire 1892 season.

Robinson was hardly alone in his offensive exploits that June day. The Baltimore lineup, despite the team's poor record, had its share of talented ballplayers. Future Hall of Famer John McGraw, playing second base in his sophomore season in the majors, connected for three singles in the opener, scored three runs, and stole a base. His double-play partner,

Robbie in a Baltimore uniform, 1898.

shortstop George Shoch, connected for five hits, including a two-bagger, and he scored four runs. Baltimore's left-handed right fielder, George Van Haltren, swatted two base hits while crossing the plate five times. Third baseman Billy Shindle stroked a double and a triple. Jocko Halligan, Joe Gunson, and Curt Welch each came through with a pair of safeties for the Orioles in the lopsided victory. (Remarkably, despite 32 hits and seven bases on balls for both teams, the game took only an hour and 50 minutes to complete.)

Following his record performance, which included a stolen base, the durable Robinson caught the second game of the doubleheader, garnering two more singles. The result was a 9–3 Orioles victory that looked like a nail-biter in comparison with the opener. Robinson later told the press that his "lamps got tired during the second game" or he would have done better.

McMahon, who was coming off back-to-back 30-win seasons, fell off a bit in 1892, winning just 19 games. The Orioles played inconsistent ball for the rest of the 1892 season and finished with the worst record in the league. But on that one June day in Baltimore, Wilbert Robinson made baseball history.

Baltimore	R	H	O	A	E	St. Louis	R	H	O	A	E
Shindle, 3b	2	2	1	2	1	Crooks, 2b	1	0	3	3	3
VanHaltren, rf	5	2	2	0	0	Carroll, lf	0	1	1	0	2
Halligan, 1b	3	2	13	0	0	Werden, 1b	1	1	10	0	1
Shoch, ss	4	5	0	4	2	Glasscock, ss	1	1	2	1	0
Welch, cf	3	2	3	0	0	Brodie, cf	0	2	2	2	2
Gunson, lf	4	2	0	0	2	Carruthers, rf	0	0	0	1	1
McGraw, 2b	3	3	4	7	1	Pinkney, 3b	0	1	3	0	1
Robinson, c	1	7	3	0	0	Buckley, c	0	0	2	1	0
McMahon, p	0	0	0	3	0	Getzien, p	0	0	0	1	0
–	–	–	–	–	–	Young, p	0	0	0	0	0
–	–	–	–	–	–	Bird, c	0	0	2	2	0
–	–	–	–	–	–	Breitenstein, p	1	0	0	2	0
–	–	–	–	–	–	Stricker, 2b	0	1	2	1	0
	25	25	27	16	6		4	7	27	14	10

Baltimore 554 632 000 – 25
St. Louis 100 002 101 – 4
Earned runs – Baltimore 9. Two-base hits – Robinson, Glasscock, Shindle, Shoch. Three-base hits – Shindle. First base on errors – Baltimore 8, St. Louis 2. Bases on balls – Baltimore 6, St. Louis 1. Left on bases – Baltimore 11, St. Louis 1. Sacrifice hits – Werden, Glasscock, Halligan, Bird, Carruthers, McMahon. Struck out – By McMahon 3, Young 1, Breitenstein 2. Bases from being hit – Welch, Gunson (2). Double play – Shindle, McGraw, and Halligan. Passed balls – Robinson 1. Stolen bases – McGraw, Robinson. Time of game – One hour and fifty minutes. Umpire – Hurst.

Bumpus Jones: No-hit Phenom

Pittsburgh Pirates vs. Cincinnati Reds

League Park, Cincinnati, Ohio
October 15, 1892

By Jerry Grillo

Bumpus Jones was the talk of the baseball world at 22, a pitcher whose major-league debut foretold more potential than any other twirler who'd come before him. He was a big-league bust before he turned 24.

But for one day on the cusp of two eras, Jones was the best there was in the game.

He began—and for all practical purposes, ended—his major-league career by pitching a no-hitter for the Cincinnati Reds against the Pittsburgh Pirates on October 15, 1892.

It was the final day of the season, making it the last time (other than that year's Boston-Cleveland post-season series) that pitchers would throw with their back foot positioned 55 feet 6 inches from the plate. The distance was pushed back to 60 feet 6 inches the next season.

Cincinnati had signed Jones off the local sandlots a few days before. "This makes his feat against the hard-hitting Pittsburghs at this season of the year the more remarkable," *Sporting Life* said in its October 22, 1892, edition.

Jones had grown up in Cedarville, about 65 miles from Cincinnati in southwest Ohio. A local semipro pitching phenom who went off to play pro ball in the Illinois-Iowa (Two Eyed) League, he became a sort of known commodity in the region. He spent most of the 1892 season pitching spectacularly for the Joliet Convicts, posting a 24-3 record before the team folded in early August. He signed with the Atlanta Crackers of the Southern League, making his debut on September 1, but the arrangement lasted less than a month because the Atlanta team folded on September 20.

So Jones was idling back home in Ohio when a local semipro club, the Wilmington Clintons, tapped him to play for them in an exhibition game against the visiting Reds on October 12. Jones started in the outfield, but with the Reds winning easily, he came in to pitch the final three innings and shut them out.

Reds manager/first baseman Charlie Comiskey was so impressed that he hired Jones to pitch his team's National League season finale against Pittsburgh, and Jones made history.

It was the second game of a two-game set for the two evenly matched teams. Cincinnati would finish the year at 82–68–5, and the Pirates would finish 80–73–2, although they won the season series with the Reds, nine games to five. The Reds took the first game, 8–6, on Thursday, October 13.

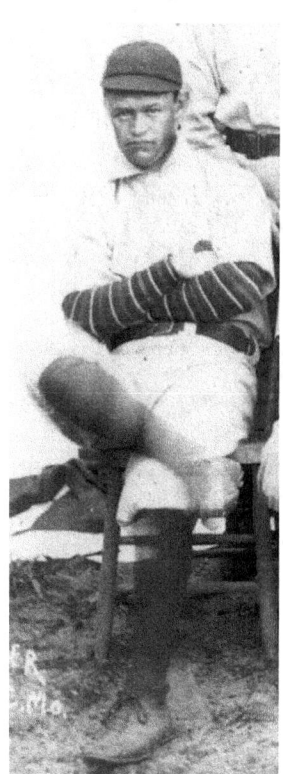
Bumpus Jones

On Saturday, instead of seeing one of their veteran pitching stars, occasionally ambidextrous wonders Elton Chamberlain and Tony Mullane, take the box, Cincinnati fans watched the jittery Jones face a veteran Pittsburgh club that featured players like Jake Beckley, Patsy Donovan, and Connie Mack.

Fortunately for Jones, he had a good defensive club backing him up. He walked the first two batters he faced, Donovan and Duke Farrell, but escaped trouble on an unusual double play. Arlie Latham fielded

George Van Haltren's bunt and threw to first for one out, then Comiskey fired home to catcher Farmer Vaughn, who tagged out the ambitious Donovan trying to score from second.

Jones got another swashbuckling defensive boost in the second after walking Elmer Smith. Second baseman Bid McPhee made a fine running catch in shallow right field near foul territory, then threw to Comiskey to double up Smith, who was running on the play.

The Reds took a 1–0 lead in the bottom of the second when Comiskey doubled, driving in Vaughn, who had reached on a throwing error by Pittsburgh pitcher Mark Baldwin. Pittsburgh tied it in the third when Donovan walked (Jones's final free pass of the afternoon), stole second, and hustled home when Jones slipped trying to field Farrell's soft tap, then made a bad throw to Comiskey.

Farrell was the last batter who would reach base for the Pirates that day. Jones retired the last 19 batters he faced, deceiving Pittsburgh's batters with a motion that had him doubling his body into a knot before each offering. Meanwhile, the Reds pulled away with two runs in the fifth on Germany Smith's home run, and added four more in the eighth against the beleaguered Baldwin.

According to the *Pittsburgh Dispatch*, "Farrell and Van Haltren tried hard for safe bunts in the ninth, but failed and when Smith shot the last ball over to Comiskey which led Pittsburgh down without a hit, the crowd spread into the field with cheers for a newborn favorite."

Sporting Life reported that Jones's performance, while "certainly wonderful … may have the effect … of making the Cincinnatians next season expect too much of him. The Pittsburgh players claim his wildness made him effective, they being afraid of being injured or maimed."

The *Stark County Democrat* (Canton, Ohio) added to that sobering tone in its November 17 edition, "Two or three days next spring may be enough to send Jones into the pit of oblivion. It takes more than one swallow to make a spring and more than one game to make a great pitcher. Cincinnati should bide a bit with Jones."

Sure enough, Jones was never that good again at the major-league level. Maybe the change in the pitching distance threw him off. He posted a 1–4 record with an ERA of 10.19 for the Reds and Giants in 1893, and didn't pitch in the majors again.

Two other pitchers have thrown no-hitters recognized by Major League Baseball in their first major-league start: Ted Breitenstein (who actually preceded Jones by a year) and Bobo Holloman (1953).[1] But both had pulled relief duty earlier, which means Bumpus Jones is the only player in the long history of baseball to throw a no-hitter in his first major-league game—so far.

	AB	R	B	P	A	E
Pittsburgh						
Donovan, rf	2	1	0	1	0	0
Farrell, 3b	3	0	0	0	1	0
Van Haltren, cf	4	0	0	1	0	1
Miller, ss	3	0	0	3	5	0
Beckley, 1b	3	0	0	9	1	0
E. Smith, lf	2	0	0	0	0	0
Mack, c	3	0	0	5	2	0
Bierbauer, 2b	3	0	0	3	5	0
Baldwin, p	3	0	0	2	0	1
Cincinnati						
Holiday, cf	4	1	2	3	0	0
Latham, 3b	3	1	1	1	3	0
McPhee, 2b	4	0	0	3	2	0
Browning, rf	4	1	1	1	0	0
Vaughn, c	4	1	1	4	0	0
Hoover, lf	4	1	0	1	0	0
Comiskey, 1b	4	1	3	1	–	–
Jones, p	2	0	0	0	0	1

Earned runs – Cincinnati 5. Two-base hit – Comiskey. Home run – Smith. Stolen base – Donavan. Double plays – Miller, Bierbauer, Beckley 2; Latham, Comiskey, Vaughn; McPhee, Comiskey. First on balls – By Jones 4, by Baldwin 2. Hit by pitcher – By Baldwin. Struck out – By Jones 3, by Baldwin 5. Passed ball – Vaughn. Umpire – McQuaid. Time—1.18.
Source: *Sporting Life* (Oct. 22, 1892 edition)

Note:
1. George Nicol allowed no hits in his first game with St. Louis in 1890 and Red Ames did the same in 1903, but those games are not recognized as no-hitters by MLB because neither went the required nine innings.

The Split-Season Playoff

Cleveland Spiders vs. Boston Beaneaters

League Park, Cleveland, Ohio;
South End Grounds, Boston, Mass.
October 1892

By Terry Gottschall

Major-league baseball faced a serious crisis in the early 1890s. Players rebelling against the reserve clause had created the independent Players League to challenge the existing National League and the American Association in 1890. The ensuing season, in which three major leagues competed for fans and revenues, weakened baseball overall. The Players League folded after a single season, the American Association neared insolvency in late 1891, and even the venerable National League languished.

National League and American Association representatives found a solution when they met in Indianapolis in December 1891 and agreed to consolidate the two leagues. The new organization combined the eight National League teams with four American Association franchises to create what *Sporting Life* editor Francis Richter called the "big league." In order to accommodate more teams, league directors decided to expand the standard 140-game season to 154 games, and they also established a split-season format. Hoping that a different team would win each season, the directors tentatively planned a postseason "world championship series."

The Indianapolis agreement also needed to reconcile significant differences between the two organizations. The new league established a standard 50-cent admission, but allowed the former American Association teams to charge their traditional "two bits"—25 cents. Likewise, former AA ballparks could sell alcohol—the Association had acquired the nickname Beer and Whiskey League—forbidden at teetotaling National League grounds, and could schedule games on Sunday, violating the long tradition of blue laws in National League cities.[1]

The 1892 season began on April 12 with more than 40,000 fans turning out. The Boston Beaneaters quickly moved into first place, with the Brooklyn Bridegrooms and the Cleveland Spiders competing for second. When the first half ended on July 13, Boston (52–22) led second-place Brooklyn (51–26) by 2½ games. *Sporting Life* attributed Boston's success to pitching, baserunning, and teamwork. The report described Cleveland (40–33), which finished fifth, as "one of the best-balanced teams in the League, being equally strong in batting, fielding and base-running, well-handled and aggressive."[2]

Cy Young: Cleveland's ace won once, but lost twice in the 1892 playoff.

When the second half of the season began, on July 15, Boston started slowly while Cleveland, Brooklyn, Philadelphia, and Cincinnati dominated. Cleveland broke away from the pack at the end of the month, remaining solidly in first for the remainder of the season. Although Boston (50–26) made a late-season run, the Spiders (53–23) finished the second half on October 15 with a three-game lead.[3] The dual champions enabled a best-of-nine "world's championship series" to begin, with the teams playing three games each in Cleveland, Boston, and, if necessary, New York.[4]

Both teams engaged in a bit of trash-talking. When Boston manager Frank Selee complained that late-October weather would lead to postponed games and reduce attendance, Cleveland's player-manager, Patsy Tebeau, suggested that "the Beaneaters fear the humiliation of possible defeat." Tebeau termed the cold weather a "dodge … simply an excuse to avoid playing Cleveland."[5] Selee responded that "the Boston players are willing to go for broke on their ability to beat the club that has been 'easy' for [us] all year."[6]

Bettors made the Spiders the early favorite based on their pitching staff. Cy Young had gone 36–12 with a 1.93 earned-run average, while rookie George "Nig" Cuppy had a 28–13 record with a 2.51 ERA. Meanwhile, fans attributed Boston's second-half decline to the poor performance of aging superstar Mike "King" Kelly. Described as "one of the biggest failures of the base ball season," Kelly batted only .189, well below his career .308 average.[7]

The series began in Cleveland on Monday, October 17, as more than 6,000 fans watched the two teams play to a 0–0 tie. *Sporting Life* described the game succinctly: "It was altogether a pitchers' battle and not a run had been scored, when, after the eleventh inning, the game was called owing to darkness."[8]

Cleveland: 0 4 1 Young
Boston: 0 6 0 Stivetts

Boston, choosing to bat first, edged Cleveland, 4–3, in the second game, on October 18. The Beaneaters' center fielder, Hugh Duffy, led Boston to victory with a double and two triples, while the Spiders sent "the ball time and again into some fielder's waiting hands."[9]

Boston: 4 10 2 Staley
Cleveland: 3 10 2 Clarkson

Boston won Game Three, 3–2, in an excellent contest whose "agony was not over until the last man was out."[10]

Cleveland: 2 8 0 Young
Boston: 3 9 2 Stivetts

The series moved to Boston's South End Grounds, where the Beaneaters won Game Four, 4–0, on Friday, October 21.

Cleveland: 0 7 2 Cuppy
Boston: 4 6 0 Nichols

Frank Selee: Boston's manager feared the cold weather in Cleveland.

The Spiders started strong in Game Five on Saturday, October 22, scoring six runs in the top of the second inning. But Boston came back to win, 12–7.[11]

Cleveland: 7 9 4 Clarkson
Boston: 12 14 3 Stivetts

Both league rules and state laws required the two teams to take Sunday off before playing Game Six on Monday, October 24. A Cleveland victory would have moved the series to New York for the next game but Boston won, 8–3.

Cleveland: 3 10 4 Young
Boston: 8 11 5 Nichols

Sporting Life provided an apt description for the series: "The Clevelands put up a stiff game and fought every inch, but they [played] against a team that has proved their superiors in all the points of the national game." Cranks also ignored manager Selee's fear of bad weather as more than 32,000 attended the series' six games.

League directors nonetheless decided to abolish the split-season format and cut the season back to 132 games for 1893. The "big league" itself continued through the 1899 season, when the league dropped four teams. A true World Series would not return until 1903 with the advent of the American League.[12]

McAleer, McCarthy 2, Nash. Struck out – Tebeau, Young 2, Burkett, O'Connor, Lowe, Zimmer, Nichols, Bennett, Virtue. Passed ball – Bennett. Wild pitches – Young 3. Umpires – McQuaid and Gaffney. Time of game – 1:55.

Notes:

1. "The Revolution," *Sporting Life*, December 19, 1891, 1.

2. "The Record," *Sporting Life*, July 16, 1892, 3.

3. "The Season's End," *Sporting Life*, October 22, 1892, 4.

4. "The Big League," *Sporting Life*, September 24, 1892, 2.

5. "Tebeau Talks," *Sporting Life*, October 8, 1892, 11.

6. "20/3," *Sporting Life*, October 15, 1892, 3: "Editorial Notes and Comments"

7. "Editorial Views, News, Comment," *Sporting Life*, October 22, 1892, 2.

8. "The World's Championship Series," *Sporting Life*, October 22, 1892, 4.

9. "Boston Wins the Second Game," *Sporting Life*, October, 1892.

10. "Boston Wins Again," *Sporting Life*, October, 1892.

11. "The Final Game." *Sporting Life*, October, 1892.

12. "The Big League," *Sporting Life*, October 8, 1892, 2.

October 24, 1892

BOSTON	AB	R	H	PO	A	E	Cleveland	AB	R	H	PO	A	E
Long, ss	5	1	1	3	4	1	Childs, 2b	5	1	2	3	3	0
McCarthy, rf	3	2	1	0	0	1	Burkett, lf	4	1	2	1	0	0
Duffy, cf	5	0	2	1	0	0	Virtue, 1b	5	0	1	13	1	1
Nash, 3b	4	1	1	1	0	0	McKean, ss	5	0	2	0	1	2
Lowe, lf	4	0	0	4	0	1	McAleer, cf	3	0	0	0	0	0
Tucker, 1b	4	1	1	7	0	0	O'Connor, rf	3	0	1	2	0	0
Quinn, 2b	4	0	1	3	0	0	Zimmer, c	4	0	1	4	1	0
Bennett, c	4	2	2	8	2	2	Tebeau, 3b	4	0	0	1	4	1
Nichols, p	4	1	2	0	2	0	Young, p	4	1	1	0	3	0
Totals	37	8	11	27	8	5	Totals	37	3	10	24	13	4

| Cleveland | 003 000 000 – 3 |
| Boston | 002 211 11x – 8 |

Earned runs – Boston 6 Cleveland 2. Two-base hits – Duffy, McCarthy. Three-base hits – Quinn. Sacrifice hits – Lowe 2, McAleer, Tucker 2, O'Connor, McCarthy. First on errors – Boston 3, Cleveland 2. Home run – Bennett. Stolen bases – McCarthy, Nichols, Burkett 2, Zimmer, Tucker, Duffy, Long. Double plays – Long, Quinn; Tebeau, Virtue, Zimmer. First on balls – O'Connor,

Bill Hawke's No-Hitter

Baltimore Orioles vs. Washington Senators

Boundary Park, Washington, D.C.
Aug. 16, 1893

By Jimmy Keenan

In the early days of baseball, a multitude of changes occurred over time in relation to how far the pitcher stood from the batter when he released the ball. Originally, the pitcher was positioned behind a line that was 45 feet from the center of home plate. As time went on, rules changed, and the line was modified to a box that was moved back to 50 feet from home plate with the pitcher working from the back line five-and-a-half feet further back.

In 1893, the National League replaced the pitcher's box with a rubber slab 12 inches by four inches that was set in the ground 60 feet, six inches from the back of home plate. Batting averages had been on the decline for years and the extra distance was meant to handicap the pitcher, thus making the game more exciting. The added distance had its desired effect; more than 30 batters hit .300 or better in 1893, after nine reached the mark the previous year.

On Wednesday, August 16, 1893, Bill Hawke of the Baltimore Orioles became the first pitcher to toss a no-hitter from the new distance, defeating the Washington Senators 5–0. Based on his lackluster major-league pitching record up to that point, the 23-year-old right-hander was an unlikely candidate to achieve this milestone. The Delaware native started out his amateur career as a catcher and third baseman. In 1890, Hawke began pitching on a full-time basis for a team from Elkton, Maryland. Bill signed his first professional contract with Reading of the Pennsylvania State League in the spring of 1892 and in late July signed with the St. Louis Browns. Hawke finished out the season with the Browns, going 5–5 with a 3.70 earned-run average. St. Louis released him the next season after he was hit hard in his first start. Hawke signed with Baltimore in June and his work with the club had been creditable but not spectacular during the weeks leading up to his no-hit game.

It was a clear, humid summer day in Washington with temperatures ranging in the high 80s when the Baltimore Orioles took the field against the Washington Senators. Neither team had been setting the league on fire. Baltimore was struggling, 12 games below .500, and the Washington club, which was floundering in last place, had 33 wins and 59 losses. The game was played at Boundary Park, which was on the future site of Griffith Stadium. The umpire was Bob Emslie, who had been an outstanding pitcher, winning 32 games for Baltimore in 1884, and now in his fourth year as an umpire.

The starting pitchers were Hawke for Baltimore and Ben Stephens, who was making his debut with the Senators. Stephens had been a rising star in the Midwestern leagues before signing a major-league contract with Baltimore in July 1892. He had won 18 and lost seven for the Western League champion Columbus team before joining the Orioles. Washington's left fielder, Charles Abbey, also made his major-league debut in this game.

Washington batted first and lead-off hitter William "Dummy" Hoy drew a base on balls off Hawke. Hoy attempted to steal second base, but Orioles catcher Wilbert Robinson threw him out. Washington's only other baserunner was catcher Duke Farrell, who walked in the fourth inning but was left stranded at second.

Hawke was backed by a number of fine defensive plays. Orioles third baseman Billy Shindle and shortstop John McGraw made a number of outstanding stops and throws that cut down batters. Hawke himself hustled over and covered first base on a sharply hit ball to first baseman Harry Taylor. Baltimore outfielders Joe Kelley and George Treadway also made clutch grabs that helped preserve

Hawke's no-hit bid.

The Orioles scored two runs in the second inning. George Treadway singled and advanced to second on a passed ball by Farrell. Jim Long sacrificed Treadway to third and he scored on a single by second baseman Heinie Reitz. The next hitter, Wilbert Robinson, drilled a groundball that caromed off Washington shortstop Joe Sullivan and ended up in center field. Reitz advanced to third. Hawke hit a sacrifice fly to center that sent Reitz home.

Bill Hawke

Stephens settled down after that and the Orioles didn't score again until the eighth inning. Shindle reached on an error by Washington second baseman Cub Stricker and Taylor walked. Both runners scored when Jim Long smashed a double to left field, and Reitz followed with a double to right that plated Long.

Stephens deserved a kinder fate, working all nine innings, allowing seven hits and just two earned runs. The 25-year-old struck out two (the first two batters he faced), walked two, and uncorked a wild pitch. Stephens also went winless in his next five starts, and was released after appearing in three games for the Senators in 1894. He returned to the minors and pitched for the Milwaukee Brewers of the Western League for two seasons before dying of tuberculosis at the age of 28 on August 5, 1896.

Hawke's sinkerball kept the Senators off-balance for the entire game. He struck out six and walked two. Hawke finished the 1893 campaign with an 11–17 record (including one loss with St. Louis). He hit his stride the next season, going 16–9 for the National League champion Orioles. *Sporting Life* said of him on October 6,1894, "He is what is called a 'phenom' and pitches a very swift, puzzling ball, difficult to fathom." Unfortunately for Hawke, he suffered a broken wrist before the start of the 1895 season and never won another major-league game. He made a short-lived comeback in the minors in 1899 but was never the same pitcher. Like his pitching opponent on August 16, 1893, Hawke died young, a victim of cancer at the age of 32 on December 11, 1902.

Washington	R	H	O	A	E	Baltimore	R	H	O	A	E
Hoy, cf	0	0	1	0	0	McGraw, ss	0	0	4	2	0
Farrell, c	0	0	2	2	0	Kelley, cf	0	0	2	0	0
Wise, 1b	0	0	1	3	0	Shindle, 3b	1	2	0	3	0
O'Rourke, 1b	0	0	10	0	1	Taylor, 1b	1	0	8	1	0
Abbey, lf	0	0	4	0	1	Treadway, rf	1	1	3	0	0
Sullivan, ss	0	0	2	4	1	Long, lf	1	1	1	0	0
Radford, rf	0	0	1	0	0	Reitz, 2b	1	2	0	0	0
Stricker, 2b	0	0	2	2	1	Robinson, c	0	0	8	2	0
Stephens, p	0	0	0	2	1	Hawke, p	0	1	1	0	0
	0	0	24	13	5		5	7	27	8	0
Washington	000		000		000 - - 0						
Baltimore	020		000		030 - - 5						

Washington 000 000 000 – 0
Baltimore   020 000 030 – 5

Earned runs – Baltimore 2. First base on errors - Baltimore 3. Left on base - Washington 1 Baltimore 6. First base on balls – Off Stephens, 2, off Hawke 2. Struck out – By Stephens, 2, by Hawke, 6. Three base hit – Shindle. Two base hit – Long. Sacrifice hits – Long, Hawke. Stolen bases – Robinson, Taylor, Farrell. Wild Pitch – Stephens. Umpire Emslie. Time of game- 1:46.

"It Was a Hot Game, Sure Enough!"

Baltimore Orioles vs. Boston Beaneaters

South End Grounds, Boston, Mass.
May 15, 1894

By Terry Gottschall

Nineteenth-century baseball often suffered game delays, suspensions, and even cancellations due to weather or dusk. But a game between the Baltimore Orioles and Boston Beaneaters on May 15, 1894, at Boston's South End Grounds concluded prematurely for a more life-threatening reason: fire. "It was a hot game, sure enough," the *Boston Globe* reported.[1] *Spalding's Guide* for 1895 described the game in equally brief terms: "Baltimore vs. Boston stopped by fire (3rd inning), 3–3."[2]

The South End Grounds, constructed in the city's Roxbury section in 1888, was considered one of the most beautiful ballparks of the time, with striking twin spires rising from each corner of the Grand Pavilion. A *Boston Globe* reporter audaciously asserted that the Boston Tea Party, the battle of Bunker Hill, and Paul Revere's ride would "fade into nothingness" when compared to the park's beautiful "cathedral-like grand stand."[3] The double-decked area seated approximately 2,000 in the lower deck and 800 in the upper deck, while bleachers along each foul line provided seats for another 2,600 cranks.[4] But like all ballparks of the era, it was built largely of wood, making fire a constant threat. Indeed, similar fires would damage the ballpark in Chicago and destroy the one in Philadelphia on consecutive August days that same season.

Unexpected fireworks first broke out on the field. As the Beaneaters' Tommy "Foghorn" Tucker slid into third, the Orioles' John McGraw kicked him in the face. Although the umpire broke up the ensuing brawl, Tucker nursed his sore jaw while awaiting an opportunity to avenge his injury.

That opportunity didn't come because with the Orioles at bat in the next inning, Boston right fielder James "Foxy" Bannon spotted a fire under the right-field bleachers. He rushed over to the stands and tried "to stamp out the flames with his feet." At first, most fans ignored the fire, preferring to watch the fiery Tucker in anticipation that he would "get even with the young Baltimore sport." The Beaneaters expected the game to resume momentarily "as the visitors were acting very fresh, especially catcher [Wilbert] Robinson, who kept shooting off his big mouth at a lively rate."

But a sudden, powerful gust of wind spread the fire, causing the "blackened and exhausted" Bannon to give up his "gallant efforts." Panicking fans "in the 25-cent bleachers rushed out on to the field, breaking the fence and tumbling over one another to get away from the heat."

The conflagration swept swiftly around the outfield fence to the left-field bleachers, then up the line to the grandstand, setting "the whole pavilion ablaze [with] the fire running wizard-like up to its highest tower." Witnesses later estimated that the fire destroyed the South End Grounds in less than 45 minutes, leaving the "jagged cornice of the east end of the grandstand, and that charred and broken, as the only relic remaining of the big pavilion."

The fire's rapid spread caused consternation among the players. They quickly returned to their locker rooms to grab their clothes but then had to change outside "in the open field." John Haggarty, the Beaneaters equipment manager, saved the team's bats and uniforms but lost four dozen balls when he could not find the key to the storage closet. He also reported that the fire had destroyed the team's championship pennant from 1893, but promised fans that "the Bostons would win another pennant just as good." Catcher Charlie Ganzel bravely saved the team's large photograph from the pavilion's foyer but lost three suits of clothes when his boarding house across the street burned down. Another player cut his hand severely while trying to help fans out of the burning ballpark.

Boston firefighters sent requests for assistance to fire stations 20 miles from the blaze. The nine-alarm fire caused no fatalities, but burned more than 12 acres, destroying about 200 buildings valued at more than $300,000. A total of 1,900 people were left homeless.[5]

The *Globe* initially blamed the fire on two young fans who it was said had set fire to an empty peanut bag and then dropped it underneath the bleachers. But Fire Marshal Edward J. Flynn, citing the eyewitness account of 14-year-old Jimmy Lasky, who had sneaked into the bleachers to avoid paying the 25-cent admission, said an adult fan had carelessly tossed away a cigarette that had set fire to trash underneath the bleachers.

Municipal officials cited the team's miserly ways for the destruction of the South End Grounds and the ensuing Roxbury fire. The city had installed a hydrant on the grounds, but team owners had failed to pay the fee necessary to have the water turned on. "If this is true, it would appear for the sake of saving $15, the grand stand, worth $80,000, was imperiled," the *Globe* remarked.[6]

Team directors moved the next day's game to the Congress Street Grounds, where other Boston teams had played in previous seasons. Fear of fire failed to deter a crowd of 2,000 who watched Boston defeat Baltimore, 10–8.[7]

The team built a new ballpark at the South End site. But because inadequate insurance coverage meant the owners had less money to invest, it had a smaller, one-story grandstand. Contractors also used more steel and brick to provide both "comfort [and] safety for the patrons of the game." When the new grounds opened on July 20, more than 5,200 fans watched Boston defeat the Giants.[8]

The Bostons did not, however, get their replacement pennant at season's end. It went to the other fire-stricken team that day, the Orioles, who outlasted the Giants by three games. The burned-out Beaneaters faded to third.

Notes:

1. "Editorial Points," *Boston Globe*, May 16, 1894, p. 6.

2. *Spalding's Base Ball Guide and Official League Book for 1895*, edited by Henry Chadwick (New York: American Sports Publishing, 1895), p. 32.

3. "Editorial Points," *Boston Globe*, May 26, 1888, p. 1.

4. Foulds, Alan E. *Boston's Ballparks & Arenas* (Boston: Northeastern University Press, 2005), p. 13.

5. "1900 Persons Homeless," *Boston Globe*, May 16, 1894, p. 1.

6. "Dread Doubt," *Boston Globe*, May 17, 1894, p. 5.

7. "Lively Batting," *Boston Globe*, May 17, 1894, p. 5.

8. "Bat Like Fiends," *Boston Globe*, July 21, 1894, p. 2.

The beautiful South End Grounds grandstand before the fire.

Four For Bobby Lowe

Cincinnati Reds vs. Boston Beaneaters

Congress Street Grounds, Boston
May 30, 1894

By Charles F. Faber

Fans arriving for the second portion of the Boston Beaneaters' morning-afternoon Memorial Day twin bill with Cincinnati on May 30, 1894, had reason to anticipate a pleasant afternoon. It was warm and sunny, with a breeze blowing from the south and southwest.[1] Beyond the pleasant conditions, their three-time defending National League champions had won four straight (including the morning game) and six of their last seven.

The crowd of 8,500 did indeed cheer their heroes on to a fifth straight victory. But beyond that, they witnesssed an unprecedented achievement. Bobby Lowe, the team's popular second baseman, that afternoon became the first player to hit four home runs in a game.

The crowd for the afternoon portion of the split-admission holiday twin bill was much larger than the 3,000 who had showed up for the morning game, won by Boston in a 13–10 slugfest. Kid Nichols, on his way to his fourth straight 30-victory season, started for the home team in the second game. But the Reds treated Nichols roughly, with Bug Holliday's first-inning home run over the left-field fence giving the visitors a 2–0 lead. Cincinnati hurler Elton "Icebox" Chamberlain, winless since the season's second game, disposed of Lowe leading off the home half of the first, but a walk followed by hits by Tommy McCarthy and Billy Nash knotted the score at 2–2.

Boston took the lead in the bottom of the third on Lowe's first home run, a line drive that cleared the left-field fence. The rest of the Beaneaters took it from there. Herman Long was hit by a pitch, Hugh Duffy sacrificed, McCarthy singled, and Nash walked, loading the bases. Tommy Tucker hit a fly to right field for the second out, but Jimmy Bannon, Jack Ryan, and Nichols followed with consecutive singles. Lowe, who had started the rally with his first home run, climaxed it with his second, again clearing the left field fence. The champions produced nine runs off Chamberlain that inning, taking an 11–2 lead.

The Reds attempted to get back into the game in the fifth when Dummy Hoy and Jack McCarthy singled, Arlie Latham connected for a double, and Holliday drove them in with his second home run. That made the score 11–6. But in the home half of the inning, Lowe clouted his third round-tripper, this one easily clearing the left-field fence. That tied the major-league record for home runs in a game, held by six players.

Bobby Lowe

Already leading 12–6, Boston added five more runs in the sixth. Nash walked, Tucker was hit by a pitch, and Bannon singled. That brought up Lowe again, and he etched his name in the record books by hitting his fourth home run, the ball again sailing over the left-field fence. The crowd, aware that it was witnessing an exceptional exhibition, cheered Lowe wildly, some throwing coins at him. Teammates helped the player gather the loot, which was later found to total $160. Long followed that blast with one of his own.

Neither Lowe nor his teammates were through yet. In the seventh inning, bases on balls to Tucker and Bannon and hits by Nash, Ryan, and Lowe scored two more runs. Lowe's fifth hit, a single, gave him 17 total bases for the game, another National League record and one that stood for more than 60 years until it was broken by Joe Adcock on July 31, 1954. In the eighth inning Boston scored its 20th and final run on a single by Long and a double by McCarthy.

Trailing 20–6, the Reds mounted a ninth-inning comeback against Nichols that produced five runs, including two more home runs, by Farmer Vaughn and Jimmy Canavan. The latter's carried into the top of the center-field bleachers. Amazingly, for a game that saw 31 runs scored, 33 hits, nine bases on balls, and two hit batsmen, both Chamberlain and Nichols pitched a complete game.

In recent years, some have questioned whether Lowe's accomplishment was aided by the fact that the game was played at the Congress Street Grounds—a facility abandoned by the Boston Reds when the American Association ceased play in 1891—rather than the Beaneaters' usual home, the South End Grounds. That park had burned in the Great Roxbury Fire just two weeks earlier. The fences at Congress Street Grounds were generally much closer than at South End Grounds.[2] Those on the scene, however, saw it differently. "His home runs were on line drives far over the fence, and would be good for four bases on an open prairie," wrote the *Boston Globe*'s Tim Murnane in his account of the game the following day.[3]

Two years after Lowe accomplished his batting

Lou Gehrig and Lowe.

feat, Philadelphia slugger Ed Delahanty duplicated it in Chicago. But not until Lou Gehrig in 1932 did any of the great 20th-century sluggers hit four home runs in one game. Just a few weeks after Gehrig did so, photographers in Detroit, where the Yankees were playing, arranged for the famed slugger to pose with a plain-looking, 66-year-old, 20-year Detroit city employee with whom the Yankee powerhouse had something in common. The city employee was Bobby Lowe. As reported in the newspapers of the time, Gehrig's first question upon meeting the small, quiet man was, "Did you really hit four home runs in a single game?"[4]

Yes, he did.

	AB	R	H	TB	PO	A	E
Boston							
Lowe, 2b	6	4	5	17	2	2	1
Long, ss	3	5	2	6	2	4	2
Duffy, cf	5	0	1	1	1	0	0
T. McCarthy, lf	6	2	3	4	3	0	0
Nash, 3b	4	3	3	3	0	1	0
Tucker, 1b	2	1	0	0	10	2	0
Bannon, rf	4	2	2	2	1	0	0
Ryan, c	5	2	2	3	5	0	0
Nichols, p	5	1	1	1	3	2	0
Totals	40	20	19	37	27	11	3
Cincinnati							
Hoy, cf	5	1	1	1	3	0	1
J. McCarthy, 1b	5	2	2	2	9	0	1
Latham, 3b	4	3	2	4	0	3	2
Holliday, lf	4	3	2	8	1	1	0
McPhee, 2b	5	0	2	2	4	5	0
Vaughn, c	5	1	2	5	3	3	1
Canavan, rf	5	1	1	4	2	0	0
Smith, ss	5	0	1	2	1	5	1
Chamberlain, p	5	0	1	2	1	0	0
Totals	43	11	14	30	24	17	6

Cincinnati	2	0	0	0	4	0	0	0	5	-	11
Boston	2	0	9	0	1	5	2	1	x	-	20

Earned runs, Boston 7, Cincinnati 8. Two-base hits, T. McCarthy, Ryan, Latham 2, Chamberlain, Lowe, Smith. Home runs, Holliday 2, Lowe 4, Long, Vaughn, Canavan. Stolen bases, Long, Duffy, Nash 2, Hoy, Latham. Sacrifice hit, Duffy. First base on balls, Long 2, Tucker 3, Nash 2, Latham. Struck out, Bannon, Ryan, T. NcCarthy, Vaughn, McPhee, Chamberlain. Hit by pitched ball, Long, Tucker, Vaughn. Umpire, Swartwood. Time, 2:10. Attendance, 8,500.

Notes:

1. *North Adams Daily Transcript*, May 31, 1894.

2. The dimensions at Congress Street Grounds were 250 feet to left field and 400 feet to center field. The South End Grounds dimensions were 250 feet to left field, 445 to left center, 500 feet to center field, 440 feet to right center and 255 feet to right field. Source: Philip J. Lowry, *Green Cathedrals*. New York: Walker & Company, 2006, p. 25. Lowry does not give the dimensions to right field at Congress Street Grounds.

3. *Boston Globe*, May 31, 1894.

4. Bobby Lowe File, A Bartlett Giamatti Research Library, National Baseball Hall of Fame and Museum.

Ed Delahanty's Four-Home Run Game

Philadelphia Phillies vs. Chicago Colts

West Side Park, Chicago, Ill.
July 13, 1896

By Jerrold Casway

The Philadelphia Phillies had high hopes for the 1896 season. It was hoped that Billy Nash, acquired in a trade from Boston to be the new third baseman and manager-captain, could bring teamwork and playing fundamentals to the talent-laden team. The ballclub also signed Big Dan Brouthers to play first base. But after a good start, their pitching soured and the team lost eight straight games. From May 11 to the end of June the club went 16–24. One writer suggested that the team looked like they were "dosed on morphine."[1]

A closer look revealed a troubled team. Nash was beaned and could not play. Brouthers played poorly and was dropped after a salary dispute. Injuries and illnesses laid up Bill Clements, Al Orth, Lave Cross, and Con Lucid. The most troubling injury was to Ed Delahanty, who had reinjured his old separated shoulder. At one point he was hospitalized and missed eight games. Yet when the Phillies departed for Cincinnati after a July 4 doubleheader, Ed was in the midst of a 19-game hitting streak. He ultimately batted safely in 27 out of 28 games.

Despite Delahanty's effort, the ball club did not improve its standing, arriving in Chicago 0-for-6 on the road trip including three losses to last-place Louisville. The city, which had just hosted the Democratic Party convention that nominated William Jennings Bryan for president, gave little thought to the Monday afternoon midsummer ballgame. A heat wave that recorded 133 deaths the day of the game also hurt interest, and only about 1,000 hardy fans turned out at West Side Park. The thermometer in the grandstand read in the triple digits.

The Phillies started a lanky rookie hurler, Virgil Garvin. He was opposed by the veteran William "Adonis" Terry. This handsome right-handed curveball specialist had already won more than 180 major-league games. Delahanty had had previous success against the clever offspeed Terry, with 16 hits in 48 at-bats for a .333 average. But he had never hit a home run off Terry.

The ballpark that hosted this memorable game was oddly fashioned. The foul lines were 340 feet to the perimeter fence, and the on-field clubhouses in center field were more than 450 feet from home plate. The right-field wall was 40 feet high with a scoreboard and a canvas screen fastened to telephone poles in order to block the view of rooftop spectators. It was an unlikely setting for the greatest hitting performance of the 19th century.

The Phillies began the game with Dick Cooley getting a walk and being sacrificed to second base. With two outs, Delahanty, batting fourth in Dan Brouthers' former spot, swung at an outside pitch and hit it over the inner, lower bleacher fence in front of the right-field wall. Jimmy Ryan chased the ball into the narrow bleachers between the two fences as Cooley and Delahanty scored. In the third inning, Ed hit a vicious line drive toward shortstop that knocked over the leaping Bill Dahlen and went into left field for a single. Del's third at bat came with two runners on base. This time he struck a towering blow that soared over the scoreboard and canvas-topped right-field wall. It landed across the road in a flock of chickens. A young boy picked up the ball and was chased by a panting policeman. This home run was said to be the longest ever hit at West Side Park.

With the Phillies losing, 9–6, Delahanty came to the plate in the seventh inning. He swatted a fastball that went over the head of the fleet-footed Chicago center fielder, Billy Lange. The ball rolled to the distant clubhouses, giving Delahanty his third home run. When Delahanty came to bat in the ninth inning, fans had forgotten the score and were cheering for another home run. Chicago manager Cap Anson threatened to fine his whole team "the price of three meals at World Fair rates" if any Philadelphia player was put on base before Delahanty got his last at bat.[2] To make sure everything was in order, center fielder Lange called time and retreated to the farthest part of the grounds—the uncut grass before the center-field clubhouses. Delahanty, in his soaking-wet woolen uniform, laughed at the spectacle of the retreating center fielder.

With Chicago fans behind him, many standing on their seats, Delahanty fooled everyone and bunted the first pitch foul. His action brought shouts from the grandstands: "Line it out, Del!" Ed enjoyed this stunt and waited on Terry's next pitch, a slow, outside curve. The bat, it was reported, impacted with the sound of a "rifle shot." The hit carried over 450 feet, beyond Lange, and bounded onto the roofs of the center-field clubhouses. Delahanty easily scored his fourth home run without a throw. As he crossed the plate, Terry was waiting to shake his hand. Outfielder Lange hid the ball under the clubhouse for a souvenir, and the fans remained standing on their seats cheering wildly for about 10 minutes. After the game, spectators followed Del to the omnibus and offered him congratulatory claps on his back. A local gum factory recognized Ed's achievement by giving him a box of gum for each home run. One Chicago paper wrote that if it were not for Delahanty's hitting the overheated fans would have "cursed the day baseball was invented."[3]

The Phillies lost the game, 9–8, their seventh setback in a row. Ed had five of the team's nine hits. He knocked in seven runs and had 17 total bases. That evening, back at the hotel, many commiserated with Delahanty. They told him it was a tough loss after the way he batted. Ed replied, "I did the best I could. I couldn't hit any more."[4] Queried about "Adonis" Terry, Delahanty confessed that he never hit hard

Ed Delahanty

against him, but "Today they came just right. Tomorrow I probably would not get a hit. Those things can't be explained."[5]

Before Delahanty, only Boston's Bobby Lowe, in 1894, had hit four homers in a game. Nothing again rivaled Delahanty's power display until Lou Gehrig hit four cork-centered baseballs out of Philadelphia's Shibe Park in 1932.

Delahanty finished the year with 13 home runs and 126 RBIs. In a *Sporting Life* feature, he was praised: "Amid the wreck of the year the performance of Delahanty shines out luminously and marks him as indeed the star of the team."[6]

Chicago	AB	R	H	PO	A	E	Philadelphia	AB	R	H	PO	A	E
Everitt, 3b	3	1	2	1	3	0	Cooley, lf	3	1	1	1	0	0
Dahlen, ss	2	2	0	0	0	0	Hulen, ss	4	1	1	1	4	0
Lange, cf	4	2	2	4	0	0	Mertes, cf	5	1	0	1	0	0
Anson, 1b	3	0	1	12	2	0	Delahanty, 1b	5	4	5	9	0	0
Ryan, rf	4	1	1	2	0	1	Thompson, rf	5	0	1	2	0	0
Decker, lf	4	1	1	0	0	1	Hallman, 2b	4	1	1	5	3	0
Pfeffer, 2b	4	0	2	1	4	0	Clements, c	2	0	0	5	3	0
Terry, p	4	1	2	2	3	0	Nash, 3b	4	0	0	0	3	1
Donohue, c	3	1	0	5	0	0	Garvin, p	4	0	0	0	1	0
TOTALS	31	9	11	27	12	2	**TOTALS**	36	8	9	24	14	1

Philadelphia 210 030 101 – 8
Chicago   104 040 00x – 9

Earned runs – Chicago 7, Philadelphia 5. Two-base hits – Lange, Terry, Thompson, Decker. Three-base hits – Lange, Pfeffer. Home runs – Delahanty 4. Sacrifice bunt hits – Hulen, Everitt. Stolen bases – Everitt 2, Dahlen 2, Lange, Anson, Mertes, Thompson. Struck out – By Terry 5, By Garvin 4. Hit by pitcher – By Terry 1. First on balls – By Terry 3, by Garvin 5. Wild pitch – Garvin. Double play – Hulen, Hallman, Delahanty. Umpire – Emslie. Time – 2:15.

Notes:

1. *Philadelphia Inquirer*, June 3, 1896, June 10, 1896.

2. Randall Papers (Letters and Papers of Norine Delahanty, Mobile, Alabama), packet one.

3. Ibid., packet two.

4. *Sporting Life*, August 1, 1896, August 8, 1896; *Philadelphia Inquirer*, August 2, 1896.

5. *Sporting Life*, July 14, 1896.

6. *Sporting Life*, August, 22, 1896, October 17, 1896.

Arrested on a Day of Rest

Washington Senators vs. Cleveland Spiders

League Park, Cleveland, Ohio
May 16, 1897

By Bill Felber

All Frank and Stanley Robison wanted was for their Cleveland Spiders to make as much money as possible. That meant scheduling home games when fans could watch them.

But scheduling at convenient times was a tough proposition before the turn of the century, an age of six-day, 50-hour work weeks. Even given the usual 3 P.M. starting time for games, that left only Sunday as a day when most potential fans could easily come to the park. And Sunday baseball was illegal in Ohio.

In 1897 the Robisons challenged the law, which they felt was not only wrongheaded but inequitably enforced. They noted that Sunday baseball was being played openly in Cincinnati, where city and state officials looked the other way. Less than a year earlier, the Reds had drawn a record crowd of 24,000 to a Sunday game with the defending champion Baltimore Orioles. The Robisons wanted that revenue. They also needed it because attendance in Cleveland badly lagged behind the team's performance, which had included a Temple Cup victory in 1895 and a runner-up finish in 1896.

If Sunday baseball was not permitted, the Robisons announced, they would consider relocating the team to a more tolerant city. Speculation fed the threat. "Cleveland is the poorest patronage of the League cities, but has one of the strongest teams to represent it," observed *The Sporting News*, which added that "the Cleveland team in St. Louis would be a gold mine to its owners."[1]

But Robert McKisson was mayor of Cleveland, and McKisson was an archfoe of Sunday ball. In that he had the support of unlikely allies: several of the city's churches as well as the local saloon league. The churches' motivation was obvious and—once you thought about it—so was the saloon keepers'. Unlike ballparks, the law did not force the closing of saloons on Sunday, making that day their best for revenue. Neither the churches nor the saloon owners craved the competition the Robisons' Spiders would provide. "Men and boys will … go to the games and spend the 75 cents they would otherwise leave with us," a tavern keeper told *Sporting Life*.[2]

The first of the Sunday games on Cleveland's 1897 schedule was to be played on May 16, and McKisson made it known in advance that he was prepared to make a scene. Privately, he and the Robisons worked out a more civil arrangement. The game would be allowed to begin, but it would be halted after a single inning, the players arrested and one prosecuted in what amounted to a test case of the state law. The Robisons cooperated by disbursing "rain checks" to each paying fan—and there were an estimated 10,000 of them. Spiders

Stanley Robison, owner of the Spiders, pushed the issue of Sunday baseball. When Robison lost in court, he sabotaged the team.

The 1898 Cleveland Spiders, many of whom were also members of the 1897 team: (Back row) Sport McAllister, Emmet Heidrick, Cy Young, George Bristow, Jesse Burkett, Chief Zimmer. (Middle) Jake Stenzel, Ed McKean, Ossee Schreckengost, Jack O'Connor, Patsy Tebeau, Cupid Childs, Zeke Wilson, Harry Blake, Bobby Wallace. (Front) Jack Powell, Lou Criger, unidentified person, unidentified person, Frank Bates.

captain Patsy Tebeau juggled his lineup, inserting rookie pitcher Jack Powell at first base and designating him as the player to be formally charged. The game was in fact halted after a scoreless first inning, and the players on both teams (along with umpire Tim Hurst) were led away to be booked at the police station, where they signed autographs for the arresting officers. All were released on $100 bail posted by Frank Robison.

Immediate reaction in the press favored the players. "About seventy-five games of ball were played in the city yesterday, the police not interfering," alleged Elmer Bates, Cleveland's correspondent to *Sporting Life*.

But that had little impact in the courts. Powell was quickly tried and convicted, prompting Robison to cancel a game scheduled for Sunday, May 23. Powell, funded by Robison, appealed, contending that the prohibition essentially forced him to observe a religious holiday against his will. When Judge Walter Ong rendered his ruling in August, he sided with Powell and threw out the law. Although the state appealed that decision to the Ohio Supreme Court, the Robisons were for what remained of 1897 free to play Sunday ball. "It means," wrote Bates, "that 20,000 workingmen, heretofore deprived of an opportunity of seeing a National League game, can with perfect assurance of two hours of rare enjoyment go out to League Park on Sunday afternoon without fear of police interfering in their effort to enjoy personal liberty."[3] They staged six such games, drawing a crowd in excess of 14,000 to the July 25 game with Baltimore. It was the largest baseball crowd in the city until 1902.

But the Robisons' victory was short-lived. In April of 1898, the Ohio Supreme Court reversed Ong and upheld the ban on Sunday ball. The ruling effectively killed the Spiders. Opening Day attendance that season barely topped 1,000, driven downward both by the ruling and by the owners' renewed threats to move the team. When the Robisons' ongoing efforts to play Sunday games in a small town outside Cleveland were again thwart-

The 1899 St. Louis NL club: All players except Jones and Cuppy also appear in the previous Cleveland photo. 1-Cy Young 2-Cupid Childs 3-Jake Stenzel 4-Harry Blake 5-Bert Cowboy Jones 6-Emmet Heidrick 7-Ossee Schreckengost 8-Patsy Tebeau 9-Jesse Burkett 10-Bobby Wallace 11-Ed McKean 12-Jack Powell 13-George Cuppy 14-Frank Bates 15-Jack O'Connor 16-Lou Criger 17-Zeke Wilson 18-Chief Zimmer

ed by local sentiment, they reacted by taking the team on the road ... permanently. From late June until season's end, the Spiders played just three more games at their home park, scheduling everything else either at neutral sites or at their opponents' fields.

In 1899 the Robisons went further, transferring Cleveland's best players—Cy Young, Lou Criger, Jesse Burkett, Bobby Wallace, Powell, Tebeau—to the St. Louis team, which they simultaneously owned. The moves effectively ransacked the 1899 Spiders ... but that's a separate story.

Did the Sunday baseball decision destroy National League baseball in Cleveland? Not necessarily, for it may have been doomed anyway. There is a line of argument that the NL, which had operated with a dozen teams since 1892, was inevitably bound to contract, that one of the Robisons' two teams would have been liquidated, and that Cleveland was always the logical choice for that distinction ahead of St. Louis.

But if the events of May 16, 1897, and subsequent legal rulings did not kill the Spiders directly, they certainly ensured the franchise's demise.

Notes:

1. *The Sporting News*, March 27, 1897.

2. *Sporting Life*, February 13, 1897.

3. *Sporting Life*, June 19, 1897.

Hit 'Em Where They Ain't

Pittsburgh Pirates vs. Baltimore Orioles

*Union Grounds, Baltimore, Md.
June 19, 1897*

By Bill Felber

Presumably due to his size, William Henry "Wee Willie" Keeler had a hard time convincing managers he could play the rough-and-tumble game in vogue in the 1890s. The New York Giants gave the 5-foot-4, 145-pound Brooklyn-born 21-year-old just 77 at-bats in 1892 and 1893. They were not persuaded by his .325 batting average and cut him loose. Keeler caught on with Brooklyn for 20 games, batting .313, good enough to make him a throw-in on a deal designed to unload aging veteran Dan Brouthers to Baltimore in return for journeyman Billy Shindle and coveted young outfielder George Treadway.

In Baltimore Keeler fell in with the one gang that could see beyond his physical limitations. Beyond the 6-foot-2, 200-pound Brouthers, the undersized Oriole team being assembled by Ned Hanlon cared far more about brains and hustle than bulk. John McGraw and Heinie Reitz stood just 5-foot-7; Hughie Jennings and portly Wilbert Robinson barely reached 5-foot-8 and even slugging outfielders Joe Kelley and Steve Brodie failed to top six feet.

That absence of size failed to slow the Orioles, who more than made up for it with a slashing, inventive style of ball designed to take advantage of every available physical, mental, and emotional edge. From 1894 through 1896, the Orioles slashed their way to three consecutive National League championships. They did it with their bats; the Orioles averaged about .332 over the three-year span. They did it with their feet, averaging more than 350 steals per season over their championship run. When necessary, they did it with their bodies. Orioles batters were hit by pitched balls 324 times between 1894 and 1896, 133 times more than the team that ranked second over that time span.

The Orioles also did it with their brains. They spent more time than any other team devising strategies to take advantage of, and sometimes circumvent, the rules. Finally, they did it with their mouths. They were unapologetic in their desire to intimidate. "Baseball as she is played," Hanlon explained of the approach, whose elements included distracting batters, blocking runners, upending fielders, and baiting umpires.

Keeler was never much for the umpire-baiting, but in all other respects he was the focus of the Oriole offense. A superb contact hitter before the phrase was invented, he specialized in slapping the ball to precise areas of the outfield. This precision, which Keeler explained as an effort to "hit 'em where they ain't," made him virtually impossible to retire easily. Between his first full season in 1894 and 1904 Wee Willie made fair contact in 98.6 percent of his official at-bats. Through 1906, he never batted below .313 and won two batting titles. Keeler topped .360 annually between 1894 and 1900.

It was in 1897 that Keeler attained his greatest batting glory. He singled and doubled in the season opener against Boston, had at least two hits in eight of the Orioles' first nine games, and by the end of the first week of June had collected 70 hits. His average stood at .446.

To that point the closest any pitcher had come to stopping Keeler was St. Louis left-hander Duke Esper, who held him to a bunt single on June 5. The

Frank Killen held Baltimore to five singles.

bunt extended Keeler's consecutive-game hitting streak for the season to 35.[1] He ran it to 40 against Louisville a week later, and on June 16 hit safely in his 43rd consecutive game, breaking the record set by Bill Dahlen of the Chicago Colts three seasons earlier.[2] On June 18 he thrashed Pink Hawley of Pittsburgh for a single, double, and triple.

Left-hander Frank Killen pitched for Pittsburgh on June 19, hoping both to stop Keeler and to atone for his own poor performance of three days earlier, when he left after less than one inning of work. He did more than that, holding the Orioles to just five hits, all of them singles. Meanwhile, two late and costly errors by Orioles shortstop Jennings permitted four unearned runs to score in the eighth and ninth innings. The final score was 7–1.

Keeler faced Killen four times, and never got a good piece of him. His closest brush with a hit occurred in the third when he ticked a weak ground ball toward third and lit out for first base. He wasn't fast enough; Harry Davis raced in, grabbed the roller, and threw to first just in time to record the out. When Keeler was retired twice more on routine plays, the longest batting streak in the game's history had been ended. The streak remained in the record book for more than four decades, until Joe DiMaggio erased it on the way to his 56-game streak of 1941.

Keeler and Killen met once more in 1897, that coming in the first game of a doubleheader on September 6 in Baltimore. Willie went 3-for-5. His season-ending .424 average won the league's batting title by 34 points.

Pittsburgh	AB	R	H	PO	A	E	Baltimore	AB	R	H	PO	A	E
Smith lf	2	2	1	7	0	1	McGraw 3b	4	0	0	0	1	0
Padden 2b	5	1	0	3	1	0	Keeler rf	4	0	0	2	0	0
Davis 3b	5	0	1	0	2	0	Jennings ss	3	0	1	1	6	2
Brodie cf	5	0	1	2	0	0	Doyle 1b	3	1	0	15	0	0
Donovan rf	4	2	1	1	0	0	Reitz 2b	4	0	2	0	3	0
Ely ss	4	0	0	3	7	0	O'Brien lf	4	0	1	3	0	0
Merritt 1b	4	0	1	10	1	1	Quinn cf	3	0	0	3	0	0
Sugden c	3	1	1	1	1	1	Bowerman c	3	0	0	3	0	0
Killen p	4	1	1	0	4	0	Hoffer p	3	0	1	0	4	0
TOTAL	36	7	7	27	16	3	TOTAL	31	1	5	27	14	2

Pittsburgh 010 000 015 – 7
Baltimore 010 000 000 – 1

Earned runs—Pittsburgh 3. Two-base hit – Smith. Three-base hit – Davis. Sacrifice bunt hits – Padden, Ely. Stolen bases – Doyle 2, Quinn, Donovan 2. Struck out – By Hoffer 2, by Killen 1. First base on balls—By Hoffer 4, By Killen 2. Passed balls – Bowerman 2. Umpire – Hurst. Time – 2:00.

Notes:

1. That total did not include the final game of the 1896 season, in which he also had hit safely.

2. Some historians credit Denny Lyons, playing for the Athletics of the American Association, with a 52-game hitting streak in 1887. That streak is not officially recognized, however, because it included games in which Lyons reached base only via walks—which were counted as hits in 1887.

Willie Keeler, no hits in four at bats vs. Killen.

The Colts' Record Romp

Louisville Colonels vs. Chicago Colts

*West Side Grounds, Chicago, Ill.
June 29, 1897*

By Bill Felber

Nothing in the buildup suggested it would be remembered more than 100 years later. The Colonels arrived at West Side Park that afternoon for the second of a scheduled three-game series in 10th place in the 12-team National League. The Colts stood 11th. Chicago had lost eight of its last 10 games, while the Colonels had lost 14 of 18.

As might be surmised, Chicago fans didn't expect much; only 1,150 of them paid to see the game. Even after it was over, *The Sporting News* managed to dismiss the afternoon's events in a single-sentence writeup lost amid a sea of page 2 box scores. This was the writeup from start to finish: "The greatest picnic of the season in the line of base ball occurred at the West Side Park today when the Colts broke the record by scoring 36 runs on 32 hits for a total of 51 bases."[1]

The laconic nature of that summation says more about sports journalism in the 1890s than it does about the game, which more than a century later remains the most prolific one-team offensive explosion in the history of major-league baseball.

Chick Fraser, a 23-year-old right-hander in his second big-league season, made the start for the Colonels. Fraser would win 175 games—15 of them that season—in a big-league career that lasted into 1909. The club's 1897 Opening Day starter, Fraser was arguably Louisville's most reliable arm, although with the Colonels that wasn't saying much. This was decidedly not Fraser's day. He allowed three runs in the first inning, five in the second, and six more just one out into the third before being removed in favor of Sheriff Jim Jones, a 20-year-old prospect making his big-league debut.

That was all right with the Colts, who added a seventh run before Jones retired the side in the third, and proceeded to score in every subsequent inning. Barry McCormick, a lightly recalled infielder playing shortstop that afternoon, batted eight times and produced six hits, among them a triple and a home run. Just to rub salt in the numerous Louisville wounds, McCormick also stole two bases. The Colts stole six bases in all. Why? Because, obviously, they could. Right fielder Jimmy Ryan also homered.

The chief beneficiary of this explosion was Colts pitcher Nixey Callahan, who led by 15 runs after 2½ innings—the Colts having exercised their option as the home team of batting first. "Callahan made but little effort to pitch after the third," the next morning's papers reported.[2] Callahan's pitch-

Nixey Callahan: The Colts hurler was so far ahead that he hardly bothered to pitch after the third inning.

ing labors may have been half-hearted, but he certainly worked at the plate. He contributed five hits, two of them doubles.

About the only Colt frustrated by what passed for the Colonels' pitching that day was the best known one, first baseman and manager Cap Anson. The Chicago legend, 45 years old and in the last of his 22 big-league seasons, managed only one hit, although he did walk three times.

Fraser and Jones may have been ineffective, but they didn't get much help, either. Louisville fielders committed nine errors that afternoon, permitting a staggering 16 unearned runs to cross the plate. Center fielder Ollie Pickering made three of them. That was a sorry fielding performance even by the relatively low standards of 1897.

Perhaps the most amazing offensive statistic of the entire afternoon was this: Chicago led 21–7 at the completion of seven innings, *then* produced 15 more runs in the eighth and ninth innings alone. Because they had chosen to bat first, the White Stockings hit in the ninth inning despite already leading by 22 runs. The gratuitous insult that followed produced eight additional runs, Chicago's biggest inning of the afternoon.

It would improve the story to report that the offensive explosion got the Colts rolling, but that is only partly true. Recovering from his record defeat, Fraser returned to the mound the next day and defeated Chicago 8–7. And although Anson's Colts did win seven of their next nine games, that brief run lifted them only into 10th place. They finished ninth. The Colonels stumbled home 11th in the 12-team National League.

The 1897 Louisville Colonels, victims of the worst drubbing in baseball history. Back: Joe Dolan, Abbie Johnson, Bill Hill, Perry Werden, Bill Wilson, Dick Butler, General Stafford. Middle: Dad Clarke, Billy Clingman, Fred Clarke, Honus Wagner, Bill Magee. Front: Roy Evans, Bert Cunningham, Chick Fraser, Charlie Dexter.

But nobody had it worse than Jones, the young Louisville reliever who absorbed most of the Chicago onslaught. After playing one more game, he was released and kicked around in the minors before being signed by the desperate Giants at the tail end of New York's forgettable 1901 season. They threw him out on the mound against the St. Louis Cardinals, and Jones lasted five innings, surrendering six more runs. He never pitched again in the majors, having allowed 28 runs in fewer than a dozen career innings.

Chicago	AB	R	H	Louisville	AB	R	H
Everitt, 3b	7	3	2	Clarke, lf	4	0	3
McCormick, ss	8	5	6	McCreery, rf	4	1	0
Lange, cf	7	4	4	Pickering, cf	5	1	2
Anson, 1b	4	4	1	Stafford, ss	5	1	0
Ryan, rf	6	5	2	Werden, 1b	5	1	3
Decker, lf	4	2	3	Dexter, 3b	5	0	4
Connor, 2b	6	4	4	Butler, c	5	0	0
Callahan, p	7	4	5	Johnson, 2b	0	0	0
Donahue, c	6	3	3	Fraser, p	0	0	0
Thornton, lf	2	2	2	Jones, p	3	2	1
				Delahanty, 2b	3	1	1
Totals	57	36	32	**Totals**	39	7	14

Chicago	3	5	7	1	2	1	2	7	8	-	36
Louisville	0	0	1	0	5	0	1	0	0	-	7

Earned runs – Chicago 19, Louisville 6. Left on bases – Chicago 6, Louisville 7. Two-base hits – Everitt, Ryan, Decker, Callahan (2), Donahue, Werden (2), Dexter (2), Jones, Delahanty. Three-base hits – McCormick, Lange, Connor. Home runs – McCormick, Ryan. Sacrifice hits – Everitt, McCreery. Stolen bases – McCormick (2), Lange (2), Connor, Callahan. Struck out – By Callahan, 4. Passed ball – Butler. Bases on balls – Off Callahan, 2; off Fraser, 5; off Jones, 5. Hit by pitch – Ryan, Decker. Time––– 2:15. Umpire – Sheridan.

Notes:

1. *The Sporting News,* July 3, 1897, p. 3.

2. *Baltimore Sun,* June 30, 1897, p. 4.

Cap Anson's 3,000th hit?

Louisville Colonels vs. Chicago Colts

*West Side Grounds, Chicago, Ill.
September 19, 1897*

By Bill Felber

Among more than two dozen men credited with at least 3,000 career base hits, the first to do it is also easily the most controversial. Cap Anson broke through the 3,000-hit barrier in 1897. Or did he?

More than any other achievement in the statistically obsessed game that is baseball, Anson's hit totals are subject to debate. The most respected statistical references in the game disagree on how many hits the 19th-century Chicago star actually had … or whether he even reached 3,000. The Hall of Fame credits Anson with 3,081 hits. But *The ESPN Baseball Encyclopedia* gives him 3,012. Baseball Reference says Anson had 3,435 hits. Project Retrosheet accepts both the 3,012 and 3,435 figures, while the *Macmillan Encyclopedia* gives him an even 3,000. *Total Baseball* credits Anson with 2,995. Anson biographer David Fleitz puts the figure at 2,995 or 3,418.[1]

There are as many reasons for the differing totals as there are totals themselves. One relates to the 423 hits Anson achieved while playing for National Association teams in Rockford and Philadelphia between 1871 and 1875. The National Association was a precursor to the National League, and whether its statistics are counted hinges on who's doing the counting.

But the legitimacy of the Association as a major league is hardly the only question. The keeping of statistics was an imprecise science in the 19th century, occasionally flavored by favoritism depending on who was keeping the stats. In no case was this truer than with Anson, whose presence engendered strong sentiments, both favorable and unfavorable. There is evidence that scorekeepers and league officials tampered with the record books to inflate his hit totals. Although Anson was the game's first great star, the major reference works today agree on his hit totals for a mere nine of his 22 seasons. For example, in 1894 *Total Baseball*, *Macmillan*, and Fleitz credit Anson with having made 132 hits. But ESPN, Baseball Reference, and Retrosheet say he made 133, and the Hall of Fame puts the total at 137.[2]

Changes in rules contribute another source of controversy. In 1887 the National League adopted a rule counting bases on balls as hits. Anson had 60 walks that year, and the Hall of Fame counts those walks as hits because that's how they were recorded in 1887. None of the other major references do.[3]

Those difficulties in verifying Anson's achievement are magnified by the fact that at the time he did it, nobody paid the slightest attention to his career hit total, or to the notion that he might be approaching a milestone.

In short, it is today impossible to reconstruct exactly how many hits Anson made, or say with certainty whether and when he reached 3,000. We can, however, fashion some sort of consensus or estimate out of the cumulative judgments of the major reference works. When you delete Anson's performance in the National Association as well as the 60 walks he got in 1887, then examine the various versions of his remaining hit record side by side, the expert consensus arrives at 3,012 hits. Although it's coincidental because the year-by-year figures don't track, that sum happens to be precisely the number put forward by *The ESPN Baseball Encyclopedia*, Baseball Reference, and Retrosheet (in the case of the latter two, minus the NA games).

If we accept the 3,012 hit total as a best estimate, then Anson reached 3,000 during the last game he ever played in Chicago. The date was September 19, and the Colts—preparing for a season-ending road trip to Cleveland, Pittsburgh, and St. Louis—were hosting Louisville's Colonels in what gave every appearance of being an insignificant game between the ninth- and eleventh-place teams.[4]

A good crowd of 6,000 showed up on a Sunday afternoon at West Side Park for what was presumed to be, if not officially designated as, Anson's final home game. What they witnessed could hardly be termed an artistic success, given that the eight errors—six by Louisville—led to all of the runs in the 5–2 Colts victory being unearned.

Nor was there anything remarkable about the "3,000th" hit. It was a second-inning lead-off single, and although the Chicago fans cheered their hero lustily for it, that amounted to more of a "lifetime achievement" recognition than any response to a batting milestone. He got an equally enthusiastic ovation following an uneventful double later in the game.

The precise date—and even the legitimacy—of Anson's achievement is still debated today. But Anson was the most consistent and durable hitter of the 19th century. Whatever his final hit total, it remained a record for 17 years. Not until 1914 did Honus Wagner and Napoleon Lajoie join him in what would eventually become recognized as the 3,000-hit club. (Wagner, by the way, played in center field for the Colonels in the September 19 game and had one hit, a single.)

Cap Anson

	AB	R	H	O	A	E
Chicago						
Ryan rf	3	1	1	1	0	0
Callahan ss	0	0	2	5	1	1
Lange cf	3	1	1	2	0	0
Anson 1b	4	0	2	12	0	0
O'Connor 2b	3	1	1	3	3	0
Decker lf	4	1	1	1	0	0
McCormick 3b	3	1	0	1	3	1
Kittredge c	3	0	1	5	1	0
Griffith p	3	0	0	0	2	0
Totals	**29**	**5**	**7**	**27**	**14**	**2**
Louisville						
F Clarke lf	5	1	0	1	1	0
Stafford ss	4	0	1	1	3	2
Wagner cf	4	0	1	1	0	1
Nance rf	3	0	0	3	0	0
Werden 1b	3	0	0	12	0	0
Dexter c	3	0	0	2	0	1
Clingman 3b	4	1	1	0	8	1
Smith 2b	4	0	1	4	3	1
D Clarke, p	3	0	1	0	2	0
Wilson*	1	0	0	0	0	0
Totals	**34**	**2**	**6**	**24**	**17**	**6**

*Batted for D Clarke in ninth.

Louisville 000 010 100 – 2
Chicago   000 022 10x – 5

Earned runs – None. Left on bases – Chicago 6, Louisville 8. Two base hits – Anson, Decker. Sacrifice hits – Connor, McCormick, Kittridge. Stolen bases – Ryan, Lange (2), Wagner, Clingman. Double plays – Kittredge and Callahan, Smith, Stafford and Werden. Struck out – By Griffith 3, by Clarke 3. Passed balls – Decker. Bases on balls – Off Griffith 3, off Clarke 3. Wild pitch – Clarke. Hit with ball – Callahan. Time – 1:50. Umpire – O'Day.

Notes:

1. Hall of Fame data from www.baseballhall.org/hof/anson-cap; Total Baseball data from *Total Baseball. Revised and Updated. 2004*. ESPN Baseball Encyclopedia data from *2006 ESPN Baseball Encyclopedia* by Gary Gillette and Pete Palmer; Baseball Reference data from www.baseballreference.com/players/a/ansonca01.shtml; Fleitz data from David Fleitz, *Cap Anson, The Grand Old Man of Baseball*, (Jefferson, N.C. McFarland 2005). Macmillan data from *The Macmillan Baseball Encyclopedia, 1996*. The Fleitz hit total discrepancy is attributable to the author's ambivalence on the question of whether to count the 423 hits Anson is credited with during his years playing in the National Association.

2. Ibid.

3. The Hall of Fame's inclusion of the 1887 walk totals as hits (see the citation above), is not decisive to Anson's 3,000-hit total, since even if those 60 walks were subtracted from his career hits the Hall would still credit him with 3,021 hits.

4. The game account is based primarily on reporting from the *Chicago Tribune*, September 20, 1897, supplemented by the *Baltimore Sun*, September 20, 1897.

Good vs. Evil

Boston Beaneaters vs. Baltimore Orioles

*Union Grounds, Baltimore, Md.
Sept. 27, 1897*

By Bill Felber

More than a battle for the 1897 National League pennant, the contest played out at Baltimore's Union Grounds was a living, breathing metaphor. To the 30,000 fans who literally broke down the park's gates and walls to see it, and to the thousands nationally who followed telegraphed accounts in locations as distant as Los Angeles, it was the real world playing out of the eternal struggle of good vs. evil.

Few confused the assigned roles. Virtually across the nation outside Baltimore itself, the Orioles were the embodiment of all that was wrong with baseball. Led by third baseman John McGraw, shortstop Hughie Jennings, first baseman "Dirty Jack" Doyle and right fielder Wee Willie Keeler, the team managed by Ned Hanlon had since 1894 terrorized the rest of the league, sweeping to three successive pennants by both skill and intimidation. "The dirtiest ball ever seen in this country,"[1] Boston sports writer Tim Murnane lamented of the Orioles' style. A reporter in New Orleans, commenting on a spring training exhibition, had characterized McGraw as having adopted "every low and contemptible method that his erratic brain can conceive to win a play by a dirty trick."[2]

Though hardly saints themselves, the Beaneaters—three-time champions from 1891–93 before being dethroned by the Orioles—assumed the mantle of fan favorites once it became clear in 1897 that either they or the Orioles would win the pennant. Between August 27 and September 26, they combined to win 39 of 49 decisions (three games ending in ties), neither team ever leading the other by more than one game in the standings. A fated schedule ordered the clubs together for three games the final week in Baltimore. As the series opened, the Orioles held a one percentage point lead over Boston, although thanks to having played three more games the Beaneaters were actually a half game ahead in the standings.[3]

The frantic first two games did nothing to resolve the tension. Boston won 6–4 on Friday behind ace pitcher Charles "Kid" Nichols with a throng of 13,000 overflowing onto the field. Another 14,000 turned out Saturday, again spilling onto the field and climbing atop the outfield fence, to watch the Orioles win 5–3 and draw the race back into a virtual deadlock. The illegality of Sunday baseball merely ensured that the drama would build one more day.

Despite the fact that Monday was a work day, fans overwhelmed the tiny baseball grounds to witness the decisive game. The attendance is commonly estimated at 30,000—easily surpassing the previous record for any game—but the truth is that nobody knows how many people watched. Fans

Baltimore pitcher Joe Corbett was forced from the game by a hand injury.

broke through the outfield gate and knocked down part of the fence to get access. Others stormed the turnstiles, erected seats on the roofs of houses across the street, or perched themselves on telegraph poles. A delegation of more than 100 fans from Boston—the genesis of the famed "Royal Rooters"—showed up complete with a brass band to challenge the home team's noise advantage. Thousands more crowded the streets of Boston's "Newspaper Row" to "watch" on large play-by-play boards in a scene repeated on smaller scales in cities across the country. Nichols, already a 30-game winner, returned to the rubber on two days' rest as did the Orioles' Joe Corbett, who was seeking his 25th victory.

But chance had it in for Corbett. The game's fourth batter, Chick Stahl, lined a drive off his hand that jammed several fingers. Hanlon was forced to remove his ace. The Beaneaters got a run out of that first inning, but Keeler's base hit led to two Oriole runs in the bottom half of the inning. The lead changed hands three more times by the end of the third inning, which ended with the score tied at 5–5. In the Boston fourth, Billy Hamilton, the era's premier baserunner, singled and stole second, Fred Tenney walked, and Bobby Lowe singled to drive Hamilton across. Chick Stahl followed with a single that produced Tenney, and an error by Wilbert Robinson allowed Lowe to score an eighth run.

Bill Hoffer, whose 22nd victory had been Saturday's complete game triumph, pitched scoreless ball from that point through the sixth. But by the beginning of the seventh inning Hoffer had worked 13 innings in less than two days against the league's best offense, and he was exhausted. What ensued turned the top of the seventh into one of the most productive (or, depending on your perspective, disastrous) half innings ever played. Hugh Duffy opened for Boston with a solid base hit. Jimmy Collins drilled a fastball into the crowd in right field for a ground rule double, and Dutch Long's double into the crowd in center scored both runners. When three more hits produced three additional runs, Hoffer did what in 1897 was the unthinkable: He motioned to team captain Robinson and manager Hanlon to

"Evil" John McGraw

relieve him. Both men ignored the gesture, imploring Hoffer to continue. He did, but by the time the slaughter had ended with Long's second double of the inning, nine Boston runs crossed the plate. The champion Orioles were, for the first time since 1893, effectively unseated.

When Nichols retired the last Baltimore batter and the final score 19–10 score was posted, a remarkable scene ensued. Although the Baltimore and Boston fans had exchanged epithets all season long, they now joined on the field in a series of mutual salutes. Their bands serenaded each other with renditions of "Yankee Doodle," "Dixie," "There'll Be a Hot Time in the Old Town Tonight," and "Maryland, My Maryland."[4]

The nation treated the outcome as something of a purgative for what were widely perceived as the game's ills. "Never was interest keener in America's great national game than it is today," said the *Boston Globe*.[5] The outcome put Boston a game and a half in front with just three to play; two victories in Brooklyn the following weekend formalized the pennant that ended the pennant run of the 19th century's most feared and despised team at three.

BOSTON	AB	R	H	BALTIMORE	AB	R	H
Hamilton, cf	6	3	4	McGraw, 3b	5	0	0
Tenney, 1b	2	1	0	Keeler, rf	4	4	4
Lowe, 2b	5	1	1	Jennings, ss	4	3	3
Stahl, rf	5	1	2	Kelley, lf	4	1	2
Duffy, lf	5	4	2	Stenzel, cf	3	0	0
Collins, 3b	6	3	5	Doyle, 1b	5	0	2
Long, ss	6	2	4	Reitz, 2b	5	0	0
Bergen, c	6	2	2	Robinson, c	5	1	2
Nichols, p	4	2	3	Corbett, p	0	0	0
–	–	–	–	Nops, p	0	0	0
–	–	–	–	Hoffer, p	3	1	1
–	–	–	–	Amole, p	2	0	0
TOTALS	**45**	**19**	**23**	**TOTALS**	**40**	**10**	**14**

Boston   131 300 911 – 19
Baltimore 230 000 320 – 10

Earned runs – Baltimore 8, Boston 10. Two base hits – Keeler (2), Kelley (2), Jennings (2), Doyle, Robinson, Hoffer, Collins (4), Long (2), Duffy. Sacrifice hits – Jennings, Lowe, Tenney. Bases stolen by – Kelley, Doyle, Hamilton (2), Long. Double plays – McGraw and Doyle, Long and Tenney. Bases on balls By -- Nops (1), Hoffer (2), Nichols (3). Bases on balls to – Keeler, Kelley, Stenzel, Tenney, Stahl, Duffy. Batters hit – By Corbett 1 (Tenney), by Nops 1 (Tenney), by Amole 1 (Nichols), by Nichols 1 (Stenzel). Struck out – By Hoffer 2 (Long, Nichols), by Nichols 2 (Hoffer, Amole). Passed ball – Bergen. Wild pitch – Hoffer. Left on bases – Baltimore 8, Boston 7. Innings pitched by – Corbett 2/3, Nops 1 1/3, Hoffer 5, Amole 2. Base hits off – Corbett 1, Nops 2, Hoffer 17, Amole 3. Errors—Baltimore 1, Boston 4. Time of game: 2:30. Umpires: Emslie and Hurst.

Notes:

1. Murnane, Tim. *The Sporting News,* June 30, 1894

2. Alexander, Charles. *John McGraw,* (Lincoln: University of Nebraska Press, 1988)

3. The Orioles had four games remaining on their schedule compared to Boston's three. Due to travel problems, rained-out Orioles games in Cleveland and Louisville had not been made up.

4. *Baltimore Sun,* Sept. 28, 1897

5. Editorial, *Boston Globe,* Sept. 28, 1897

"Good" Kid Nichols got his 31st win.

The Ducky Holmes Game

Baltimore Orioles vs. New York Giants

Polo Grounds, New York, N.Y.
July 25, 1898

By Bill Lamb

In the fourth inning of an otherwise unremarkable game at the Polo Grounds, Orioles left fielder Ducky Holmes struck out. On his way back to the bench, Holmes responded to the heckling of New York fans by referring to the Giants team owner as a *Sheeney*. The utterance of this now obscure anti-Semitic epithet would have immediate consequences, setting in motion events that prompted the Giants to forfeit the game. But the incident would produce far more than just another entry in the New York loss column. The Holmes remark helped fuel a bruising 17-month battle among National League magnates that culminated in nothing less than the restructure of major league baseball.

Nothing so momentous was in the offing that July 25, 1898 afternoon as a crowd of some 3,000 gathered for a Monday contest between two teams struggling to maintain contact with league leader Cincinnati. Manager Ned Hanlon's Orioles boasted a Hall of Fame-studded lineup (John McGraw, 3b; Hugh Jennings, ss; Joe Kelley, cf; Willie Keeler, rf; and Wilbert Robinson, c) but inconsistent pitching had hampered the team, then mired in fourth place with a 48–32 record. The sixth-place Giants (44–38) were struggling as well, in imminent danger of falling out of the first division in the 12-team circuit. Although New York featured Cooperstown-bound George Davis at short and fireballer Amos Rusie on its pitching staff, the team had more than its share of non-entities on the roster. Worse yet, the dominant actor in team fortunes did not even wear a uniform. He was, rather, Giants majority owner and team president Andrew Freedman.

An astute businessman and powerful Tammany Hall insider, Freedman was a train wreck as a baseball magnate. His acquisition of the financially troubled New York franchise in January 1895 had been hailed, but the combination of Freedman's autocratic manner and his abrasive personality quickly proved toxic. Frequently out of step on league affairs and isolated, Freedman fought—at times, literally, for he was short-tempered and pugnacious—with most anyone who opposed him. In the process, the Giants boss managed to alienate NL officials, fellow team owners, players, umpires, the sporting press and baseball fans, all in about equal measure. By July 1898, Andrew Freedman was easily the most detested figure in the game.

During that summer, Freedman, preoccupied with business and political concerns, had made only infrequent appearances at the Polo Grounds, the last being at a July 4 game marred by an unseemly public row between Freedman and umpire (later NL President) John Heydler. Freedman had not been to the Polo Grounds since. But as the opposing pitchers for the July 25 contest, Jerry Nops, a young southpaw on his way to a 16-win season for Baltimore, and Giants veteran righthander Jouett Meekin, began warming up, Andrew Freedman assumed his seat in the owner's box. Both Nops and Meekins were in good form and at the end of three crisply played innings, the score was knotted 1–1. With one out and one on in the top of the fourth, Orioles left fielder Holmes, a former Giant, came to the plate. He promptly struck out, much to the delight of jeering New York fans. As Holmes trudged back to the bench, the following exchange, as recorded in likely sanitized press accounts, ensued:

Unidentified Fan: Oh Ducky, you're a lobster. That's why you're not here anymore.
Holmes: Well, at least I don't have to play for a Sheeney no more.

Whether Freedman heard the slur personally is unclear. But if not, it was swiftly relayed to him. As the teams switched sides, a deeply offended Freedman dispatched factotum Fred Hoey toward the Baltimore bench with the demand that Manager Hanlon remove Holmes from the game. Hanlon refused, referring Hoey to home plate umpire Tom Lynch. At this, Freedman, escorted by his NYPD bodyguards, strode onto the field to confront Lynch directly. But Lynch refused to take action, informing Freedman that he had not heard the offending remark. With Holmes resolutely stationed in left field and the Giants due to bat, a near apoplectic Freedman had had enough. He immediately ordered Giants player-manager Bill Joyce to keep New York batsmen on the bench. Seeing no way beyond the impasse, umpire Lynch thereupon forfeited the game to Baltimore. The final score was listed as 9-0.

The incident left league officials in a quandary. Freedman, branding Holmes' remark not only personally offensive but "an insult to the Jewish people and the Hebrew patrons of the game," demanded disciplinary action against Holmes. Simultaneously, Hanlon demanded punitive sanctions against Freedman for causing the game forfeiture and for withholding Baltimore's share of the July 25 gate. Trying to placate both sides, the NL Board of Discipline only made the situation worse. The $1,000 game forfeiture fine imposed on the Giants aggravated Freedman while the season-long suspension imposed on Holmes infuriated Baltimore, as well as players throughout the league.

The truly pivotal event, however, was the stance publicly adopted by Freedman's fellow team owners. Deeming Holmes' suspension illegal (because it had been imposed without first affording the player a hearing), the NL magnates sided with Holmes and urged the lifting of the sanction on him. This development stunned Freedman, who viewed the controversy as a matter of personal honor. In Freedman's mind, the magnates' position and the subsequent reinstatement of Holmes represented nothing less than league countenance of a gross insult. And Andrew Freedman would not abide it.

Freedman's revenge took the form of a punishing financial lesson for the other NL owners. Using his personal fortune—Freedman's wealth probably exceeded that of the other NL magnates combined—to ruthless advantage, Freedman decided to effect the ruination of the league's most important financial asset: Freedman's own New York Giants franchise. Over time, the lost revenues occasioned by fan disinterest in the dismal 1898–99 Giants teams forced the other owners to capitulate to the game-related demands that fig-leafed the deeply personal nature of Freedman's ire. Syndicate club ownership was abolished and the NL contracted to eight teams for the 1900 season, the structure that it would maintain for the next 60 years. And all because of a journeyman ballplayer's insult to Andrew Freedman on July 25, 1898.

Ducky Holmes

The Misfits

Cleveland Spiders vs. Washington Senators

Boundary Field, Washington, D.C.
September 16, 1899

By Bill Felber

It was a "Ladies Day," but there were few ladies—or gentlemen, for that matter—present on September 16, 1899, when the Washington Senators beat the visiting Cleveland Spiders in a sloppy 15–10 game. Only 400 fans came to Washington's Boundary Field to see Cleveland put up an eight-run inning and hold a seven-run lead yet still lose for the 24th time in a row. That's the National League record, and the 1899 Spiders are still the uncontested worst team to ever play in one of the existing major leagues.

The Spiders were a victim of syndicate ownership, a system prevalent in the late 1890s through which the same people owned two teams. Miffed by the failure of city leaders to permit them to play Sunday baseball in Cleveland, brothers Stanley and Frank Robison bought the St. Louis team in March 1899, and moved their best players there. Cy Young, Jesse Burkett, and others vanished in exchange for a collection of second-stringers. The result was a 20–134 record that would have placed the Spiders 12 games behind the 1962 New York Mets, one of the worst teams of the 20th century. In addition to the record 24-game losing streak, the Spiders remain the only team with six different losing streaks of 10 games or more; and the only team to lose 40 out of 41 consecutive games. Scrappy Bill Joyce was slated to manage Cleveland but, in the prime of his career, walked away from baseball instead.

The "Misfits," as they were called, lost 10–1 on Opening Day, April 15, and grabbed last place for good on May 3 with a 3–10 record. Fans stopped coming to games, and players stopped trying to win. Stanley Robison moved the last two players of merit, Lave Cross and Willie Sudhoff, to St. Louis and begged the National League to permit his team to finish its schedule on the road. Only New York and Boston refused, thinking their teams could draw fans anywhere. They were wrong. Two hundred fans watched Cleveland beat New York on August 25, during a home series that ended Cleveland's record 50-game road trip. Then the losing streak began.

The Spiders were outscored 209–65 during the streak, and there were few heartbreaking losses among the 24 games. The game-losing run in 10 losses came in the first inning. Loss number 14 was the only one with late-inning drama. Cleveland's big right-hander Charlie Knepper had a 6–4 lead with three outs to go in Chicago. He hit opposing pitcher Jack Taylor with a pitch, got two quick outs, and gave up singles to Bill Everitt and Sam Mertes. With the Spiders still leading by a run, Chicago's Bill Bradley seemed to end the game with a chopper that shortstop Harry Lochhead scooped up. But first baseman Tommy Tucker dropped the ball and failed to find it until Everitt and Mertes had scored. The frustrated Tucker, once an American Association batting champion, was released a few days later.

The next season was the one in which the modern "visiting-team-bats-first" convention gained favor, so the Septem-

Cy Young

Jack Fifield

ber 16, 1899, game was one of the last in which the home team chose to bat first. Washington scored a run that first half-inning when center fielder Jimmy Slagle singled, Win Mercer - a pitcher trying to become a third baseman - walked, and outfielder Buck Freeman singled home Slagle.

Cleveland's eight-run bottom of the second began with the major-league debut at bat of Otto Krueger: a ground-ball single to shortstop off aging utilityman Jimmy Stafford's glove. The floodgates opened. Jim Duncan singled. Harry Lochhead bunted poorly back to the mound, but pitcher Jack Fifield thought he heard someone yell "Third base!" and threw there although Krueger was already safe. Bases loaded.

Lew McAllister seemed to hit into a double play, but Stafford dropped the toss at second base for an error. Pitcher Charlie Knepper walked with the bases loaded for another run, and Harry Colliflower, a pitcher filling in for center fielder Tommy Dowd, who had a fever, ripped a two-run single up the middle. Cleveland 4, Washington 1. Dick Harley beat out a bunt. After one out, Charlie Hemphill singled for two runs when center fielder Slagle threw in wild for an error. Another out later, Jim Duncan singled and two runs scored when Buck Freeman threw in wild for an error. The Misfits had put together the eight runs on six hits and three errors.

Washington countered right away with four in the third inning aided by three straight bunts against the inept Cleveland infield. Washington's Jack Fifield went on to pitch four perfect innings while the Senators continued to chip away. Three two-out singles in the fifth put Washington down by two. In the eighth Slagle led off with another bunt single, advanced on a groundout, and scored to make it 8-7 on Jack O'Brien's single. Knepper was getting tired, but relief pitching was not a popular idea in the 19th century. Dan McGann singled and Buck Freeman doubled both runners home to put Washington in front. By inning's end, the Spiders trailed 11-8.

Although the Spiders appeared doomed to another loss, they rallied. Hemphill tripled in a run in the bottom of the seventh, and Colliflower singled in a run in the bottom of the eighth. That made it Washington 11, Cleveland 10. The Misfits seemed on their way to tying the game in the eighth when Lew McAllister broke an 0-for-19 slump with a single, but Freeman gunned out Duncan at the plate with a beautiful throw. Freeman added a run-scoring triple in the top of the ninth, and Shad Barry applied the finishing touches to the score with a rattling inside-the-park home run that gave him six RBIs for the day.

Cleveland manager-second baseman Joe Quinn, Hemphill, and Krueger went out in order in the bottom of the inning to make the 24th consecutive loss complete. The winning pitcher Jack Fifield, never got another major-league victory.

Sunday was an off-day. On Monday Cleveland took the third game of the series to snap its string of losses. Jack Harper, in his major-league debut, beat journeyman Bill Magee, 5-4, in ten innings. Tommy Dowd, back in the lineup, doubled in the last frame and scored on a Charlie Hemphill single. That raised Cleveland's win total to 20 for the season.

The loss gave Magee, who had already lost to the Misfits while pitching for the Louisvilles and Phillies, an unlikely distinction. For three different clubs he had been defeated by the worst team ever.

Washington	AB	H	PO	A	E	Cleveland	AB	H	PO	A	E
Slagle, cf	6	3	3	0	1	Col'wer, rf	5	2	2	0	0
Mercer, 3b	5	2	2	0	0	Harley, lf	5	3	0	0	0
O'Brien, lf	5	1	4	0	0	Quinn, 2b	5	0	1	7	0
McGann, 1b	5	4	9	1	0	Hemphill, rf	5	2	1	0	0
Freeman, rf	5	3	1	1	1	Krueger, 3b	5	1	2	0	0
Barry, ss-2b	5	3	2	2	0	Duncan, 1b	4	3	17	0	0
Stafford, ss-2b	3	3	2	3	1	Lochhead, ss	3	0	2	0	0
McManus, c	4	2	3	0	0	McAllister, c	4	1	2	2	1
Fifield, p	5	0	1	1	0	Knepper, p	3	0	0	1	0
TOTALS	43	21	27	8	3	TOTALS	39	12	27	10	1

Washington	1	0	4	0	1	0	5	0	4	–	15
Cleveland	0	8	0	0	0	0	1	1	0	–	10

Two-base hit – Freeman. Three-base hits – Harley, Stafford, Freeman, Hemphill. Home run – Barry. Stolen bases – O'Brien, Freeman. Double plays – Quinn, Lochhead, Duncan, Freeman and McManus. Bases on balls – Off Fifield 1, off Knepper 2. Hit by pitcher – Lochhead. Struck out – By Knepper 2. Passed ball – McAllister. Left on base – Washington 8, Cleveland 7. Umpire – Betts.

Frank Vaccaro served as researcher and fact-checker on this essay.

A "Basket of Fresh Goose Eggs"

Buffalo Bisons vs. Detroit Tigers

Bennett Park, Detroit
April 19, 1900

By Jeff Samoray

On April 19, 1900, hundreds of baseball fans gathered outside the Russell House in Detroit to cheer their Tigers and begin Opening Day festivities. A marching band led a parade of carriages carrying city and county officials, reporters, and the Tigers, wearing their new white uniforms with black trim. The Buffalo Bisons rode in their own carriage at the rear, dressed in their road grays. About 400 members of the Elks joined the parade en route to Bennett Park, while streetside fans blew tin horns and cheered lustily.

Detroiters had reason to feel optimistic about the coming baseball season. Just a month earlier, local businessman James Burns and team manager George Stallings had purchased the Tigers, ending speculation that the newly christened American League—fashioned from the former Western League—might drop the team because of ongoing legal disputes. The acquisition ended six tumultuous years under quarrelsome owner George Vanderbeck.

It was also the first game for the re-christened league (Chicago had been scheduled to host the inaugural game, but it was rained out.) Western League owners had renamed the circuit during the offseason, signaling league President Ban Johnson's ambitions of achieving major-league status. Although the caliber of play among American League teams during the 1900 season is debatable,[1] fans still felt enthusiastic about the league's major-league aspirations, which it achieved in 1901.

Aside from being the first game in the history of the American League, the afternoon was made memorable by Morris "Doc" Amole's pitching performance. The Buffalo starter silenced the hometown favorites without a hit, winning 8–0.

About 5,000 fans packed the grandstand and bleachers—hundreds more ringed the field. It was the largest Opening Day crowd in Detroit since its National League days in the late 1880s. Before that afternoon, Amole, a 21-year-old left-hander, was probably best known for a prank he pulled when he was 17 years old during his first season of professional ball with Wilmington (Delaware) of the Atlantic League. During a poorly planned exhibition night game on July 4, 1896, Amole replaced the ball with a "torpedo" firecracker that ignited on impact. Batter Honus Wagner couldn't see the explosive device in the dim light. He smacked the torpedo, resulting in a flash of light and a loud pop. The game ended abruptly as Wagner stood stunned at the plate. The Wilmington players fled the field while fans left the stands and angrily demanded refunds.[2]

Amole compiled a 4–10 record in 18 major-league games with Baltimore and Washington in 1897. He joined Buffalo in 1898, going 11–11 with one shutout. During the 1899 season, Amole ran into trouble—the team fined him and a teammate $25 apiece for "keeping late hours."[3] Buffalo released Amole that July, then re-signed him.

Detroit right-hander Jack Cronin retired the side in the first before Amole took the mound. He initially looked shaky, as Tigers left fielder and leadoff hitter Harry Bay reached base on an error and advanced to second on a wild pitch. Center fielder Dick Harley walked and the runners advanced on a sacrifice. Amole escaped damage by striking out second baseman Suter Sullivan and getting right fielder Lew "Sport" McAllister out on a foul fly.

The Tigers' only other scoring opportunity came in the fourth. Amole walked shortstop Norman "Kid" Elberfeld, who advanced to third after a wild pitch and a sacrifice bunt. With one out, Elberfeld attempted to score on an infield grounder, but Bi-

Detroit's 1900 American League team. Back: Emil Frisk, Pop Dillon, Bill Hill, Ed Siever, Roscoe Miller, Jack Cronin, Jack Ryan. Front: Ducky Holmes, George Nicol, Frank Owen, Dick Harley, unidentified man in suit, Sport McAllister, Doc Casey, Joe Yeager, Al Shaw.

sons shortstop Bill Hallman threw him out at the plate. Third baseman Ed Wheeler ended the inning with a grounder to second. Detroit didn't get another baserunner until there was one out in the ninth, when Amole hit Elberfeld. But the Tigers went quietly as Sullivan flied to center fielder Jake Gettman and McAllister popped foul to first baseman George "Scoops" Carey.

Amole didn't have perfect control, but he struck out four and used his curveball effectively to keep Tigers hitters mystified. Cronin pitched credibly for Detroit but was backed by sloppy play. The Tigers committed eight errors, including three by Elberfeld.

The next day's *Detroit Free Press* headline said it all: "BASKET OF FRESH GOOSE EGGS." The anonymous sportswriter praised Amole's performance, albeit in backhanded fashion:

> *Doc Amole ... was in grand form, had all sorts of curves and speed and kept the Tigers guessing so effectually that only once in the game was there anything that approached a base hit. ... Perhaps the wound will heal sufficiently to allow forgiveness to be granted and due credit allowed the twirler for his wonderful feat; but forgotten, never!*[4]

Amole's performance raised Buffalo's expectations for the left-hander, but his past digressions also raised concerns. "[Amole] is in grand form and promises to be the star twirler in the American League this season," wrote the Buffalo correspondent for *Sporting Life*. "But he must take care of himself in order to sustain this reputation. Manager [Dan] Shannon declares that Doc is good and has promised to keep in the straight and narrow path. Every fan in Buffalo hopes that this is true."[5]

Amole's success was short-lived. Indianapolis pounded him for a 7–1 loss four days later, and he finished the season 22–22 with two shutouts in 47 games (41 starts). He continued to pitch for Buffalo through 1903, splitting that season with Providence. Amole remained with Providence through the 1904 season and finished his professional career in 1905, bouncing between Syracuse, Utica, and Scranton of the New York State League. He never reached the level of dominance he displayed in the 1900 season opener.

Major-league records don't consider Amole's performance to have been an Opening Day no-hitter because the American League was not considered a major league at the time. In all of baseball history there has been only one, that pitched by Bob Feller of the Cleveland Indians against the Chicago White Sox on April 16, 1940.

Little is known about Amole's life after baseball. He was found dead at the age of 33 in his Wilmington boardinghouse in March of 1912.[6] He had arrived in town three weeks earlier to work as a carpenter for a local contractor. Amole had been complaining about his health but was not known to be seriously ill.

A no-hitter for Doc Amole.

	AB	R	H	O	A	E
BUFFALO						
Knoll, LF	4	2	0	1	0	0
Flood, 2B	5	2	1	2	6	1
Shearon, RF	4	1	1	2	0	0
Gettman, CF	5	2	2	1	0	0
Carey, 1B	5	0	2	16	0	0
Hallman, SS	4	0	1	0	2	0
Andrews, 3B	4	0	0	0	1	0
Speer, C	4	0	0	5	0	0
Amole, P	3	1	0	0	4	0
	38	8	7	27	13	1
DETROIT						
Bay, LF	4	0	0	0	1	0
Harley, CF	3	0	0	0	3	0
Elberfeld, SS	1	0	0	6	3	3
Sullivan 2B	3	0	0	0	3	1
McAllister, RF	3	0	0	0	0	1
Ryan, 1B	3	0	0	15	0	1
Wheeler, 3B	3	0	0	1	4	1
Shaw, C	3	0	0	2	2	1
Cronin, P	3	0	0	0	5	0
	26	0	0	27	18	8

Buffalo   001 001 303 – 8
Detroit   000 000 000 – 0

Two-base hits: Flood, Shearon, Gettman. Sacrifice hits: Elberfeld, McAllister, Shearon. Stolen base: Gettman. First base on balls: Off Cronin 2, Off Amole. Hit by pitcher: Sullivan, Elberfeld, Knoll, Amole. First base on errors: Detroit 1, Buffalo 8. Left on bases: Detroit 5, Buffalo 7. Struck out: Sullivan, Wheeler, Cronin, Harley. Wild pitch: Amole. Time: 1:40. Umpire: Dwyer. Attendance: 5,000.

Notes:

1. Wayman, Joseph M. "Major League Status for the AL: If 1901, Why Not 1900?" *Baseball Research Journal* 27 (1999), p. 74-76. Shiner, David "Another Look at the AL of 1900," *National Pastime* 21 (2001), p. 28-31.

2. Hittner, Arthur D. *Honus Wagner: The Life of Baseball's "Flying Dutchman."* (Jefferson, North Carolina: McFarland & Company, 1996).

3. "News And Gossip," *Sporting Life*, July 22, 1899.

4. "Basket of Fresh Goose Eggs," *Detroit Free Press*, April 20, 1900.

5. "Buffalo Briefs," *Sporting Life*, April 28, 1900.

6. "Latest News by Telegraph Briefly Told," *Sporting Life*, March 16, 1912.

Photo Credits

Special thanks goes to archivist Pat Kelly at the Hall of Fame for helping us find so many of the images that appear in this book, and to senior curator Tom Shieber for helping with some of the identifications. Several auction houses graciously provided photos for this project. Thanks go to Doug Allen of Legendary Auctions (www.legendaryauctions.com), Eric Caren of The Caren Archive, Rob Lifson of REA Auctions (www.robertedwardauctions.com), Lou Lipset of Old Judge Auctions (www.oldjudge.com), and David Kohler of SCP auctions (www.scpauctions.com). Thanks also to John Rogers of The Rogers Archive/The Conlon Collection. A number of private collectors provided images. They include Brian Campf, Jerry Casway, Frank Ceresi, Paul Conan, Clint Cox, David Dyte, Phil Garry, Dennis Goldstein, Doug Goodman, John Husman, Mark Macrae, Jay Miller, David Nemec, Chris Rainey, John Thorn, and Erich Wolters. William Wheaton descendant Bruce Marshall allowed us to use an excellent photo of his ancestor. Thanks also to Ronald Shafer for his magical digital restoration of a torn Library of Congress image of Charlie Byrne.

Photos not included in this list are considered to be in the public domain. Please context SABR directly for more information.

Chapter	Description	Credit
In the Beginning	Olympics of Philadelphia Constitution	Courtesy of John Thorn
The Legendary Doubleday Game	Abner Doubleday	Library of Congress Prints and Photographs Division
The First Recorded Games	William Wheaton	Courtesy of Bruce Marshall
Caught On The Fly	New York Knickerbockers 1859	National Baseball Hall of Fame and Library, Cooperstown, N.Y.
Baseball Goes To College	Amherst Express Front Page	Library of Congress Rare Book and Special Collections Division
The Massachusetts Champions	Exselsior Bannes	Upton Historical Society
The Grand Excursion	Asa Brainard	National Baseball Hall of Fame and Library, Cooperstown, N.Y.
No Gentlemen's Game	Brooklyn Excelsior 1860	National Baseball Hall of Fame and Library, Cooperstown, N.Y.
	Excelsior vs. Atlantic Woodcut	Courtesy of The Caren Archive
The Grand Excursion, Part II	Edwin Russell	National Baseball Hall of Fame and Library, Cooperstown, N.Y.
	Jim Creighton	National Baseball Hall of Fame and Library, Cooperstown, N.Y.
The POW Game	Johnson's Island Lithograph	Library of Congress Prints and Photographs Division
	Union Prisoner Game Lithograph	Library of Congress Prints and Photographs Division
The "Silver Ball" Game	Al Reach	National Baseball Hall of Fame and Library, Cooperstown, N.Y.
	Charlie Smith	National Baseball Hall of Fame and Library, Cooperstown, N.Y.
	Joe Start	National Baseball Hall of Fame and Library, Cooperstown, N.Y.
The Martyrdom of Jim Creighton	Henry Chadwick	National Baseball Hall of Fame and Library, Cooperstown, N.Y.
	Jim Creighton	National Baseball Hall of Fame and Library, Cooperstown, N.Y.
The First Fixed Game	Ed Duffy	Courtesy of REA Auctions/Rob Lifson
	New York Mutuals 1864	National Baseball Hall of Fame and Library, Cooperstown, N.Y.
Money Ball	Athletics and Atlantics Teams Woodcut	Courtesy of The Caren Archive

Photo Credits

	Athletics and Atlantics Game Action	Courtesy of The Caren Archive
The Most Important Game in Baseball History?	Al Barker	Courtesy of Phil Garry
	George Wright	National Baseball Hall of Fame and Library, Cooperstown, N.Y.
	Al Spalding	Courtesy of Phil Garry
	Frank Norton	National Baseball Hall of Fame and Library, Cooperstown, N.Y.
A Cunning Play Saves the Streak	John Hatfield	Courtesy of REA Auctions/Rob Lifson
Unbeaten, But Tied	Cincinnati Reds 1869	Library of Congress Prints and Photographs Division
Inter-racial Baseball	Octavius Catto	Courtesy of Jerry Casway
	Catto Shooting Woodcut	Courtesy of Jerry Casway
The Atlantic Storm	Atlantic vs. Red Stockings	Courtesy of David Dyte
	George Zettlein	Courtesy of REA Auctions/Rob Lifson
The First "Chicago" Game	Levi Mayerle	Courtesy of Lou Lipset
	NY Mutuals 1870	Courtesy of REA Auctions/Rob Lifson
The Birth of the NA	Tom Foley	Courtesy of REA Auctions/Rob Lifson
Association Ball	Bobby Mathews	Courtesy of Lou Lipset
	Deacon White	Courtesy of Legendary Auctions/Doug Allen
The First Pennant Race	Chicago NA 1871	Courtesy of REA Auctions/Rob Lifson
	Philadelphia A's 1871	National Baseball Hall of Fame and Library, Cooperstown, N.Y.
	Nate Berkenstock	Brace Photo
New Game in The Old Country	UK Game ACtion	Library of Congress Prints and Photographs Division
The Unbeatable Red Caps	Al Spalding	Courtesy of Legendary Auctions/Doug Allen
	St. Louis Brown Stockings 1875	Courtesy of the Rogers Archive/John Rogers
	Cal McVey	Courtesy of REA Auctions/Rob Lifson
The "Model" Game	Hartford Club 1875	Courtesy of Legendary Auctions/Doug Allen
	Paul Hines	Courtesy of Lou Lipset
The First Professional No-Hitter	Joe Borden	National Baseball Hall of Fame and Library, Cooperstown, N.Y.
A New Age Begins	Jim O'Rourke	Courtesy of Paul Conan
	Tim McGinley	National Baseball Hall of Fame and Library, Cooperstown, N.Y.
Wearin' of the "Grin"	St. Louis Browns 1876	National Baseball Hall of Fame and Library, Cooperstown, N.Y.
The Double Shutout	Syracuse Stars 1877	National Baseball Hall of Fame and Library, Cooperstown, N.Y.
Gray Outcomes	George Hall	National Baseball Hall of Fame and Library, Cooperstown, N.Y.
	Jimmy Delvin	National Baseball Hall of Fame and Library, Cooperstown, N.Y.
Three In One?	Charlie Sweasy	Courtesy of Legendary Auctions/Doug Allen
	Paul Hines	National Baseball Hall of Fame and Library, Cooperstown, N.Y.
Farewell To Old-style Ball	Harry McCormick	National Baseball Hall of Fame and Library, Cooperstown, N.Y.
Lee Richmond's No-Hit Debut	Lee Richmond	Courtesy of John Husman
The Cameo of Bill White	Brown University 1879	Courtesy of John Husman
Baseball Perfection	Lee Richmond	Courtesy of Lou Lipset
	Perfect Game Scorecard	Courtesy of John Husman
Perfection Revisited	John Ward	National Baseball Hall of Fame and Library, Cooperstown, N.Y.

Photo Credits

Night Baseball	Weston Arc Lamp	United States Patent and Trademark Office
Mullane vs. Reccius For Eighteen Innings	John Reccius	University of Louisville, Special Collections
	Tony Mullane	Courtesy of Lou Lipset
Roger Connor's Grand Slam	Roger Connor	National Baseball Hall of Fame and Library, Cooperstown, N.Y.
The Beer and Whiskey League	Cincinnati 1882	National Baseball Hall of Fame and Library, Cooperstown, N.Y.
Mullane Goes Both Ways	Louisville Eclipse 1882	University of Louisville, Special Collections
Radbourn The Slugger	Detroit 1882	Courtesy of Legendary Auctions/Doug Allen
	Providence 1882	National Baseball Hall of Fame and Library, Cooperstown, N.Y.
The First Meeting of Champions	Jimmy Macullar	National Baseball Hall of Fame and Library, Cooperstown, N.Y.
	Will White	National Baseball Hall of Fame and Library, Cooperstown, N.Y.
A Grasshopper Ruins The 'Eaters	Boston NL 1883	National Baseball Hall of Fame and Library, Cooperstown, N.Y.
Nipped At The Wire	St. Louis AA 1883	National Baseball Hall of Fame and Library, Cooperstown, N.Y.
Fleet Walker's Major League Debut	Guy Hecker	National Baseball Hall of Fame and Library, Cooperstown, N.Y.
Sweeney Strikes Out Nineteen	Charlie Sweeney	Courtesy of Mark Macrae
	Hoss Radbourn	Courtesy of REA Auctions/Rob Lifson
One-Arm Baily Strikes Out 19 (or 20)	Cannonball Crane	Library of Congress Prints and Photographs Division
	Tim Murnane	Courtesy of Lou Lipset
Hoss Radbourn: 59 or 60?	Cyclone Miller	Courtesy of Jay Miller
	Hoss Radbourn	National Baseball Hall of Fame and Library, Cooperstown, N.Y.
The First "World Series"	Tim Keefe	Courtesy of Legendary Auctions/Doug Allen
	Providence Grays 1884	Courtesy of REA Auctions/Rob Lifson
Capping A Pennant Chase	Chicago NL 1885	Courtesy of SCP Auctions/David Kohler, www.scpauctions.com
"A Glorious Victory"	Cuban Giants 1886	Courtesy of FC Associates, www.fcassociates.com
Guy Hecker, Hitting Pitcher	Guy Hecker	Courtesy of Legendary Auctions/Doug Allen
Matt Kilroy, Strikeout King	Icebox Chamberlain	PhotOhio, www.photohio.org
	Matt Kilroy	Courtesy of Legendary Auctions/Doug Allen
Curt Welch's Winning Slide	Abner Dalrymple	Library of Congress Prints and Photographs Division
	Chris Von Der Ahe	Library of Congress Prints and Photographs Division
Sam's Triple Trouble	Detroit 1887	Courtesy of Erich Wolters
	Yank Robinson	Library of Congress Prints and Photographs Division
Tim Keefe Finally Loses	DeWolf Hopper	Library of Congress Prints and Photographs Division
	New York Giants 1888	National Baseball Hall of Fame and Library, Cooperstown, N.Y.
The Little Steam Engine That Could	Indianapolis Hoosiers 1888	Library of Congress Prints and Photographs Division
A Wondrous Ballpark	All-Americas 1889	Courtesy of Brian Campf
	Pyramid Game Action	National Baseball Hall of Fame and Library, Cooperstown, N.Y.
	The Sphinx	National Baseball Hall of Fame and Library, Cooperstown, N.Y.
Sad-sack Colonels	Louisville 1889	National Baseball Hall of Fame and Library, Cooperstown, N.Y.
	St. Louis 1889	Courtesy of David Nemec
	Nat Hudson	Library of Congress Prints and Photographs Division

Photo Credits

The Candlelight Game	Brooklyn Bridegrooms 1889	Library of Congress Prints and Photographs Division
	Tip O'Niel	Courtesy of Legendary Auctions/Doug Allen
	Charlie Duffee	Library of Congress Prints and Photographs Division
A King's Downfall	John Clarkson	National Baseball Hall of Fame and Library, Cooperstown, N.Y.
	King Kelly	National Baseball Hall of Fame and Library, Cooperstown, N.Y.
The Giants Win the Pennant on the Last Day	Boston Beaneaters 1889	National Baseball Hall of Fame and Library, Cooperstown, N.Y.
	NY Giants 1889	Courtesy of Legendary Auctions/Doug Allen
Genesis of a Rivalry	Oyster Burns	Library of Congress Prints and Photographs Division
Giants Win Back-To-Back World Series	Bob Caruthers	Library of Congress Prints and Photographs Division
	John Ward	Library of Congress Prints and Photographs Division
Debut of the Players League	New York Players League Team 1890	Courtesy of Paul Conan
The Kid, The Bolt and Silent Mike	New York NL 1890	Courtesy of Phil Garry
The First Worst to First	Columbus Solons 1890	PhotOhio, www.photohio.org
The Clouded Finish	John Ewing	National Baseball Hall of Fame and Library, Cooperstown, N.Y.
	James Hart	National Baseball Hall of Fame and Library, Cooperstown, N.Y.
Seven Hits in Seven Tries	Wilbert Robinson	Library of Congress Prints and Photographs Division
Bumpus Jones: No-Hit Phenom	Bumpus Jones	Courtesy of Chris Rainey
The Split-Season Playoff	Frank Selee	National Baseball Hall of Fame and Library, Cooperstown, N.Y.
Bill Hawke's No-Hitter	Bill Hawke	Courtesy of REA Auctions/Rob Lifson
"It Was a Hot Game, Sure Enough	South End Grounds	National Baseball Hall of Fame and Library, Cooperstown, N.Y.
Four For Bobby Lowe	Lou Gehrig and Bobby Lowe	Courtesy of Legendary Auctions/Doug Allen
Ed Delhanty's Four Home-Run Game	Ed Delhanty	Courtesy of Jerry Casway
Arrested on a Day Of Rest	Cleveland 1898	National Baseball Hall of Fame and Library, Cooperstown, N.Y.
	St. Louis 1899	Library of Congress Prints and Photographs Division
	Stanley Robinson	Library of Congress Prints and Photographs Division
Hit 'Em Where They Ain't	Franke Killen	Library of Congress Prints and Photographs Division
The Colts' Record Romp	Louisville 1897	National Baseball Hall of Fame and Library, Cooperstown, N.Y.
The Misfits	Jack Fifield	Courtesy of Legendary Auctions/Doug Allen
	Cy Young	National Baseball Hall of Fame and Library, Cooperstown, N.Y.
A "Basket Of Fresh Goose Eggs"	Detroit AL 1900	Courtesy of Legendary Auctions/Doug Allen

Contributor Biographies

Edward Achorn, an editor with the *Providence Journal*, is a Pulitzer finalist and author of *Fifty-nine in '84: Old Hoss Radbourn, Barehanded Baseball and the Greatest Season A Pitcher Ever Had* (HarperCollins).

David Arcidiacono is the author of three books on 19th-century baseball in Connecticut, including his latest, *Major League Baseball In Gilded Age Connecticut: The Rise and Fall of the Middletown, New Haven and Hartford Clubs*. He has also been a featured speaker at the National Baseball Hall of Fame in Cooperstown, New York.

Bob Bailey is the author of History of the Junior World Series and Baseball Burial Sites. He has written extensively on the Louisville franchise in the nineteenth century. He currently edits *Nineteenth Century Notes*, the newsletter of the Nineteenth Century Committee of the Society for American Baseball Research.

Jon Barnes is vice president of the Dix & Eaton public relations firm in Cleveland, Ohio, and a former business journalist. He has ghost-written many articles, books and speeches for clients, but is only beginning to pursue writing projects for SABR. He has been a SABR member since 1998.

John Bauer resides with his wife and two children in Parkville, Missouri, just outside of Kansas City. By day, he is an attorney specializing in insurance regulatory law and corporate law. By night, he spends spring and summer evenings cheering for the San Francisco Giants after the kids go to bed, and he spends many fall and winter evenings reading history: baseball, American and European.

Parker Bena is a lobbyist by trade. He lives in Jefferson City, MO with his wife of 23 years, Karen, his three sons Jordan, Jeremy, and Brendan, three cats, and a Chocolate Lab named Shimmy. He is a devoted fan of the St. Louis Cardinals, following their doings on Fox Sports Midwest, and is especially fascinated with 19th Century Base Ball. He contributed a biography on Daryl Patterson to the SABR-published book, *"Sock It To 'Em Tigers!"*

Clifford Blau, a retired CPA living in White Plains, NY, is a frequent contributor to SABR publications.

Rich Bogovich is the author of a book published in 2003 about the rock and roll band The Who and, at this writing, is finishing his manuscript of a biography of Kid Nichols to be published by McFarland & Co. He joined SABR in 2010. A Chicago native, he recently moved to Rochester, Minnesota, after living 25 years in Madison, Wisconsin.

Paul Browne has been a member of SABR since the mid-1990s and has several player biographies posted at the *SABR BioProject* site. He has also contributed articles to SABR's Nineteenth and Minor League's Committees, as well as local newspapers.

JP Caillault is a long standing member of SABR who has published articles in *Baseball Digest* and the *Baseball Research Journal* and two books about the early history of baseball: *A Tale of Four Cities: 19th-Century Baseball's Most Exciting Season, 1889* and *The Complete New York Clipper Baseball Biographies*. He is a Professor of Astronomy at the University of Georgia, where he has also has taught freshman seminars on the physics of baseball, baseball statistics, and the history of major-league baseball.

Jerrold Casway, Ph.D. is the Chairman of the Social Sciences and Teacher Education Division at Howard Community College in Columbia, Maryland. A Professor of History, his latest book, Ed Delahanty in the Emerald Age of Baseball, is complemented by numerous articles on nineteenth-century baseball, specializing on Philadelphia and the game's early ethnicity. Presently he is completing a book on the culture and ethnicity of nineteenth-century baseball and is working on the history of the national pastime in Philadelphia from 1832 to 1909. He is a frequent presenter at Hall of Fame symposiums.

Philip Dixon is an environmental and land use attorney in Albany, New York. He has been a SABR member since the 1980s.

Charles F. Faber is the author of six books on baseball. His latest is *Major League Careers Cut Short: Leading Players Gone by 30*, published by McFarland in 2011. He has been a member of SABR since 1995. Faber is a retired educator, having served in both public schools and universities as a teacher and administrator.

Jim Farmer has worked for the Cincinnati Reds Hall of Fame and Museum since its grand opening in 2004. He is the president and founder of the Society for Cincinnati Sports Research (SCSR) which produced the documentary *Cincinnati Kelly's Killers: The Story Of Cincinnati's Forgotten Baseball Team*. He has also done extensive research on the 19th century era of Cincinnati baseball for both SCSR and the Reds Museum. Farmer is the co-founder of the Ludlow Base Ball Club, a vintage baseball team that plays in Ludlow Kentucky. He joined SABR in 2008.

Bill Felber is the author of five books on baseball, including *A Game of Brawl*, the story of the 1897 pennant race. He is editor of *Inventing Baseball: the 100 Greatest Games of the Nineteenth Century*. Felber has been a SABR member since 1983. He has been executive editor of The Manhattan, Ks., *Mercury*, since 1986.

Mark Fimoff is an electronic engineer residing in Illinois. He is cochair of SABR's Pictorial History Committee and has produced the committee's Mystery Photo Supplement (now known as Reflecting the Past) since 2008.

Contributor Biographies

Irving Goldfarb has been a member of SABR since 1999 and a New York Mets fan for much longer. He has written columns and book reviews for *The Deadball* and *Black Sox Scandal Committee* newsletters and has contributed to *Deadball Stars of the NL and AL* along with writing the Jerry Koosman bio for *The Miracle Has Landed*. Irv works at ABC Television and lives in New Jersey with his fiancee, Mercedes.

Terry Gottschall teaches European and German history at Walla Walla University. He has published *Here by the Order of the Kaiser: Otto von Diederichs and the Development of the Imperial Germany Navy, 1865-1902* (Naval Institute Press, 2003). He has recently developed professional schizophrenia as he alternates research between 19th-century German overseas naval operations and the development of 19th-century town teams in the interior Pacific Northwest.

Jerry Grillo is a lifelong baseball fan, occasional playwright and an award-winning journalist who writes about business, music, the environment, energy, sports and just pretty much anything else under (and sometimes beyond) the sun. His work for SABR includes the profile of Johnny Mize for *The Baseball Biography Project* and a profile of Joe Reliford, the youngest person to play professional baseball, for *The National Pastime: Baseball in the Peach State*.

Mike Harrington is a member of the SABR 19th Century Committee. He is a retired school psychologist. He has been a baseball card collector since the 1950s and a card dealer since the 1970s. He is an avid Detroit Baseball fan and historian from the Detroit Wolverines in the 19th century until the present 21st century Detroit Tigers.

Richard Hershberger is a paralegal in Maryland. He has written numerous articles on early baseball, concentrating on its origins and its organizational history. He is a member of the SABR 19th Century and Origins committees

Joanne Hulbert is co-chair of the Boston Chapter, co-chair of SABR's Baseball Arts Committee, and is a collector of baseball poetry. She lives in Holliston, MA and if she had attended the 1859 game at Worcester she would have enthusiastically rooted for the Medway Unions.

John Richmond Husman has been a member of SABR since 1982 and is a former chair of the 19th Century Committee. He is a great grandson of 19th century pitcher J. Lee Richmond and is historian for the Toledo Mud Hens.

Don Jensen, a long-time SABR member, is the author of "The Timeline History of Baseball" and a contributing author to *Deadball Stars of the National League* and *Deadball Stars of the American League*. He is a Senior Fellow at the Center for Transatlantic Relations, Nitze School of Advanced International Studies, Johns Hopkins University.

W. Lloyd Johnson edited the *Encyclopedia of Minor League Baseball, Third Edition* (Baseball America) with Miles Wolff and the *Complete Book of the Negro Leagues*. Among nearly a dozen published works are the *Total Baseball Catalog*, *Baseball's Book of Firsts*, five editions, and the *Encyclopedia of Minor League Baseball*, which won the SABR-Macmillan Award for the year's best baseball research book. Formerly the executive director (1985–1989) and president (1991–1992) of the Society for American Baseball Research (SABR), Johnson chaired the SABR National Convention in 1996, and the Jerry Malloy Negro Leagues Conference, in Kansas City, June 22–24, 2001, and July 7–9, 2006. Between stints with SABR, Johnson, along with John "Buck" O'Neil and Larry Lester, founded the Negro Leagues Baseball Museum in 1989, and he served as the NLBM's first director and Executive Director (1989–1992).

Jimmy Keenan has been a SABR member since 2001. His grandfather Jimmy Lyston, along with his great- grandfather John M. Lyston and John's two brothers Marty and Bill were all professional baseball players. He is the author of the book, *The Lystons: A Story of One Baltimore Family and Our National Pastime*. His biography of Cupid Childs was published in SABR's *The National Pastime* in 2009. In addition, he was the writer and historian for the *Forgotten Birds Documentary* that chronicles the fifty- year history of the minor league Baltimore Orioles. He has also written biographies for SABR's Bio-Project and has contributed biographies for Bio-Project books on the 1947 Brooklyn Dodgers and the 1947 New York Yankees. Jimmy is a 2010 inductee into the Oldtimers Baseball Association of Maryland's Hall of Fame and was elected Chairman of the organization's Board of Governors in 2011.

Bill Lamb is a retired state/county prosecutor. A member of SABR since 1993, he has contributed essays to *The National Pastime, Base Ball, A Journal of the Early Game, SABRgraphs*, and various SABR committee newsletters.

Len Levin, a longtime newspaper editor, is now the grammarian and copy editor for the Rhode Island Court. When he's not busy editing the justices' decisions, he works on a variety of SABR projects and cheers for the Red Sox.

Peter Mancuso has been a member of SABR since 1998 and has chaired its' 19th Century Committee since 2007. He retired from the NYPD in 1987 as the Department's Assistant Director of Training and has co-owned an events production company since then.

Dick McBane, a retired newspaperman, has been a member of SABR since 1986. He is the author of two books: *Glory Days: The Akron Yankees of the Middle Atlantic League 1935-1941*, and *A Fine-Looking Lot of Ball Tossers: The Remarkable Akrons of 1881*. He also contributed five brief items to the 2010 edition of *The National Pastime: Baseball in the Peach State*.

Eric Miklich has been the Vintage Base Ball Association Historian (VBBA) since 2009. He began playing 19th-century base ball in 1998 and is approaching 700 matches. Miklich has recently written for *Base Ball* and was a contributing author to

Contributor Biographies

Major League Baseball Profiles 1871–1900 and *The Rank and File of 19th Century Major League Baseball: Biographies of 1,081 Players, Owners, Managers and Umpires*. He is the founder and owner of 19c Base Ball Inc., which includes a 500+ page web site; www.19cbaseball.com.

Patricia Millen has been a museum professional for more than 30 years in museums in New Jersey and in New York State. Patricia holds a BS degree in American Studies and teaching certificates in US and world history. She is the author of two published books and dozens of articles on 19th-century American history including several articles on baseball during the Civil War. Her second book, *From Pastime to Passion: Baseball and the Civil War*, was the first book published on the subject in 2001. Patricia is currently the Executive Director of the new Roebling Museum in Roebling, New Jersey and lives in Titusville.

Bill Nowlin is national Vice President of SABR and the author of close to 30 Red Sox-related books, including *Red Sox Threads: Odds and Ends from Red Sox History*. Bill is also co-founder of Rounder Records of Massachusetts, and a finalist for a Grammy Award for Best Liner Notes on an album of Woody Guthrie recordings. He never saw any 19th-century games, but very much enjoys visits to Boston's Fenway Park.

Jim Overmyer is the author of *Queen of the Negro Leagues: Effa Manley and the Newark Eagles* and a contributing author for *Shades of Glory*, a history of the black baseball in America. He has also authored several articles on baseball history in general. He was a member of the special Baseball Hall of Fame committee that in 2006 elected 17 black baseball figures to the Hall. He has been a member of the Society for American Baseball Research since 1985.

Mark Pestana has been a SABR member since 1990. He has written for *Moonstone Magazine* and *The Pearl*, both of Lowell, MA, and published and edited a news and literary journal, *The Scrawl*, from 1981 to 1985. His essays here are his first published works on baseball.

Greg Rhodes, who holds a doctorate in education from Indiana University, was the founding director of the Cincinnati Reds Hall of Fame and Museum. He now serves as the Team Historian of the Reds. He has written seven books on the Reds, including two that won the *The Sporting News*-SABR Baseball Research Award (*Reds in Black and White*, with Mark Stang, and *Redleg Journal*, with John Snyder). He is a past-chairman of the Cincinnati SABR chapter.

James Rygelski is a retired newspaper reporter and editor who lives in St. Louis and has had articles on 19th-century baseball published in several publications over the past twenty-five years. He and fellow SABR member Robert L. Tiemann are co-authors of the recently published *10 Rings: Stories of the St. Louis Cardinals' World Championships* (2011, Reedy Press).

Jeff Samoray is a freelance health care copywriter and lifelong Tigers fan based in metro Detroit. He has authored numerous articles about baseball, including "A New 'Field of Dreams' for Detroit" (*DBusiness*, May-June 2011). Jeff is working on a biography of Detroit Tigers founder George A. Vanderbeck.

Lyle Spatz has been a SABR member since 1973 and chairman of the Baseball Records Committee since 1991. He is the author of six books on baseball history and the editor of two baseball record books. His book, *1921*, written with co-author Steve Steinberg, was awarded the 2010 Seymour Medal. Lyle's latest book is *Dixie Walker: A Life In Baseball*.

John Thorn is the Official Historian of Major League Baseball. Apart from his creation, with Pete Palmer, of *Total Baseball*, his many baseball books over the past three decades also include *Treasures of the Baseball Hall of Fame*, *The Game for All America*, and *Our Game*, a history of the game which also supplies the title for his blog at mlb.com. In 2011 Simon & Schuster published his major work, *Baseball in the Garden of Eden: A Secret History of the Early Game*.

Casey Tibbits is an information technology manager living in San Diego, California. He is the author of the historical novel *Place of Honor* and a lifelong student of Major League Baseball's history and traditions.

Robert L. Tiemann is a Bob Davids Award winner and a former chairman of SABR's 19th Century Research Committee.

Kathy Torres has been a member of SABR for about four years and a baseball fan since childhood. She is a great-granddaughter of 19th-century Boston second baseman John Joseph "Jack" Burdock and is in the process of completing a biography of him for the SABR Biography Project. Kathy is retired and lives in Indiana.

Frank Vaccaro is a longtime SABR member and Teamsters Local 812 shop steward for Pepsi-Cola (KBI) in Northern Queens, NY. He lives in Long Island City with his wife Maria and their cat Furgood.

Craig B. Waff, who joined SABR in 1992, was, prior to his June, 2012 death, the creator and compiler of the Protoball Web site's "Games Tabulation," a detailed directory of all recorded games of "base ball" played from 1845 to 1860. He wrote on the early history of the Atlantic and Star clubs of Brooklyn for the Pioneer Project. The holder of a doctorate in the history of science, he was a historian at the Air Force Research Laboratory at Wright-Patterson AFB near Dayton, Ohio. When not working on the history of early baseball, he researched the popular-astronomy lecture tours (1842–1861) of Ormsby MacKnight Mitchell, the founder and first director of the Cincinnati Observatory.

John Zinn is the author/co-author of three books including *The Major League Pennant Races of 1916* and an upcoming book on Ebbets Field (both with Paul Zinn). A longtime SABR member he is also a contributor to the Pioneer Project and the Deadball Era's World Series Project. Retired since 2007, he is an independent historian.

INDEX

NAME INDEX

Abbey, Charles 244
Adams, Doc 17
Allen, Dick 111
Allison, Art 80
Allison, Doug 65, 93
Amole, Morris "Doc" 272-274
Andrews, Ed 223, 230
Angell, Walter F. 113-114, 119
Anson, Adrian "Cap" 92n1, 113, 127-128, 144-145, 147-148, 149-150, 152, 154, 175-176, 181, 185, 189-190, 196, 201-203, 234-235, 252, 260, 262-264
Atwater, E.P. 81
Ayers (Brooklyn player, 1845) 7

Baldwin, Lady 193
Baldwin, Mark 189-190, 201, 229, 240
Bancroft, Frank 113, 133, 141, 170, 172-173
Bannon, James "Foxy" 246, 248-249
Barker, Al 55-56
Barlow, Tom 56
Barnes, Ross 90-92
Barnie, Billy 88, 205
Barry, Shad 271
Bartson, Charlie 229
Bassett, Charlie 199, 226
Bastian, Charlie 229
Bates, Elmer 255
Battin, Joe 91, 100-101, 103
Bay, Harry 272
Beach, Waddy 40
Beam (Excelsior of Baltimore player, 1860) 34
Beatin, Ed 211-212
Becannon, Buck 174
Bechtel, George 82-83
Beckley, Jake 199, 239
Beecher, Robert Edes 20
Bennett, Charlie 114, 120, 133, 141, 143, 193, 214, 225
Benson (New York player, 1858) 10
Berkenstock, Nate 82-83
Berthrong, Harry 56
Bierbauer, Lou 224, 229-230
Bingham, Thomas 3
Birchall, Jud 159-160
Bligh, Ned 231

Blondin, Charles 24, 26
Blong, Joe 91, 100-101
Boerum, Folkert Rapelje 11, 28
Boetticher, Otto 36-37
Bond, Tommy 93-94, 100
Booth, Amos 101
Borden, Joseph Emley 95-96, 97
Boyd, Benjamin "Ben" 179
Boyd, Bill 88
Boyle, Henry 199, 226
Boyle, Jack 206, 228-230
Bradley, Bill 270
Bradley, George Washington "Grin" "Foghorn" 91, 100-102, 103, 143, 159
Brady, Steve 114
Brainard, Asa 24, 29, 34, 60, 63-64, 65-66, 72
Brannock, Mike 82
Breitenstein, Ted "Theo" 238, 240
Brewer, Nelson 3
Briggs, Charlie 168
Briody, Fatty 193
Brockway, John 66
Brodie, Steve 225, 238, 257
Brouthers, Dan 192-193, 214, 251, 257
Brown, Tom 138, 202, 214
Brown, William 195, 215, 223
Browning, Louis Rogers "Pete" 130-131, 137, 138-139, 180-181, 183, 205-206, 231
Brush, John 226
Buckley, Dick 199, 226
Buffinton, Charlie 152-153, 222
Burdick, Bill 199
Burdock, Jack "Blackie" 93-94, 100-101, 108-109, 152
Burkalow, Ike Van 131
Burke, James 168
Burkett, Jesse 226, 255, 270
Burns, James 272
Burns, Mark 74-75, 76n2
Burns, Tommy 128, 144-145, 175-177, 185, 190, 201
Burns, Tommy "Oyster" 209, 217-218
Bush, Archibald McClure 60-61
Bushong, Doc 185, 209, 220
Butler, Dick 260
Butler, Frank 168
Byrne, Charles 208, 210, 220

Calihan, Thomas 188
Callahan, Nixey 259
Cammeyer, William 32
Campbell, George 110
Canavan, Jimmy 249
Cannon, John 70
Cantz, Bart 189
Carey, George "Scoops" 273
Carey, Tom 80, 93-94, 108
Carpenter, Hick 103-104, 110-111, 134, 135-137, 147-148, 178
Carroll, Cliff 173
Carroll, Fred 202
Caruthers, Bob 181, 185, 192-193, 209, 219-220
Casey, Doc 273
Cassidy, John 133
Catto, Octavius 68-70
Cauldwell, William 16
Caylor, O.P. 96, 147
Chadwick, Henry 3, 17, 18n6, 25, 29-30, 44, 71, 76, 78, 82, 93, 103, 144, 201, 203
Chaffee, Joseph 3
Chamberlain, Elton "Icebox" 139, 183, 206, 232, 239, 248-249
Champion, Aaron 64, 65, 67, 73
Chapman, John "Jack" 44, 52, 91, 231-232, 236
Claflin, James 19-20
Clapp, John 100-101
Clark, Artie 226
Clark, Bob 209
Clarke, Dad 260
Clarke, Fred 260
Clarkson, John 175-177, 185, 190, 195, 200, 211-212, 214-216, 225, 242-243
Clarkson, Josephus 37-38
Clements, Bill 251
Cleveland, Elmer 195
Cline, Monk 162
Clingman, Billy 260
Clinton, Jim 103-104
Collier, James W. 79
Colliflower, Harry 271
Collins, Hub 183, 209, 218
Collins, Jimmy 266
Comiskey, Charlie 136, 158-160, 185, 192-193, 205-206, 208-209, 223, 228-230, 239-240

Index

Conley, Ed 173
Connor, Roger 133-134, 176, 195, 215, 223, 234
Conway, Dick 180
Conway, Pete 230
Cook, Paul 205, 229
Cooley, Dick 251
Coon, Bill 97
Corbett, Joe 265-266
Corcoran, Larry 128, 139, 148, 152-153, 175-176
Corkhill, Pop 178, 209, 218
Cottrelly, Mathilde 196
Crane, Ed "Cannonball" 167, 168, 195, 202, 215
Crane, Fred 40, 51-52
Crane, Sam 226
Craver, Bill 66, 74-75, 106-107
Creighton, James P. 24-25, 28-30, 34-35, 43-44, 187
Criger, Lou 255-256
Cronin, Jack 272-273
Crooks, Jack "King" 232-233
Cross, Amos 183
Cross, Lave 251, 270
Crossley, William 36
Crowley, Bill 107, 111, 123, 156, 165
Cummings, William Arthur "Candy" 60-61, 93-94, 104, 110-111
Cunningham, Bert 260
Cuppy, George "Nig" 242
Cuthbert, Ned 74-75, 82-83, 91, 101

Dabney, Milton 179
Dahlen, Bill 251, 258
Daily, Con 230
Daily, Hugh "One Arm" 155-156, 165, 167-168, 182-183
Daley, Bill 214
Dalrymple, Abner 113-114, 127-128, 148, 153, 175-177, 185
Daly, Tom 190, 201-202
Darling, Dell 189-190, 228-230
Davidson, Mordecai 204-207
Davis, George 268
Davis, Harry 258
Davis, James Whyte 17
Davis, Jumbo 183
Day, G. 179
Day, John B. 112, 172, 174, 214, 216, 220, 235, 236n4
Deasley, Pat 158, 176
DeBost, Charles 10, 17
Decker, Reuben S. 51

Dehlman, Herman "Dutch" 91, 100-101
Delahanty, Ed 249, 251-252
Denny (Princeton catcher, 1875) 87
Denny, Jerry 142, 145, 165, 173, 199, 226
Derby, George 141
Devlin, Jim 93-94, 106-107
Devyr, Thomas 40, 46-47
Dexter, Charlie 260
Dillon, Pop 273
Dolan, Joe 260
Dolan, Tom 111, 158, 160
Donovan, Patsy 225, 239-240
Dooley (New York Giants PL player, 1890) 226
Dorgan, Mike 104, 112, 176
Doubleday, Abner 3-4
Doubleday, Abner Demas 3-4
Doubleday, John 4
Dowd, Tommy 271
Doyle, Jack 232-233, 265
Dreyfuss, Barney 232
Duffee, Charlie 205-206, 208
Duffy, Edward 46-47, 78, 81
Duffy, Hugh 229-230, 242, 248, 266
Duncan, Jim 271
Dunlap, Fred 120, 193
Dunning, Frank 87
Dutton, Pat 168
Dwyer, Frank 229

Earle, Billy 202
Easton, John 232
Eggler, David 74-75, 98, 111
Ehret, Red 204-205, 231-232
Elberfeld, Norman "Kid" 272-273
Ellick, Joe 91
Emslie, Bob 244
Epps, S. 179
Esper, Duke 257
Esterbrook, Dude 176
Evans, Jake 133
Evans, Roy 260
Everitt, Bill 270
Ewing, Buck 133-134, 176, 195, 214-215, 217-218, 223
Ewing, John 206, 234-235

Faatz, Jay 215
Farrell, Charles "Duke" 228-229, 239-240, 244-245
Farrell, Jack 103-104, 111, 128, 142, 145, 173
Farrell, Joe 141

Fennelly, Frank 178
Ferguson, Bob 72-73, 88, 94, 106, 217, 219
Fifield, Jack 270-271
Fisher, Charlie 168
Fisher, Cherokee 95
Fisler, Wes 52, 82-83, 97-98
Fitzgerald, Thomas 69
Flanley, George 28, 29, 44
Fleitz, David 262
Flint, Silver 91, 128, 145, 175-176, 190
Flynn, Clipper 74-75, 77
Flynn, Edward J. 247
Flynn, Jocko 190
Fogarty, James 202-203
Foley, Tom 77-78, 81
Folk, John S. 52
Force, David 98, 103, 105, 111
Forman, Theodore 7
Foster, Tom 143
Foster, Elmer 195, 215
Fouser, Bill 97-98
Foutz, Dave 192-193, 209, 218
Fowler, John "Bud" 178, 190
Fox, George 56
Fraser, Chick 259-260
Freedman, Andrew 268-269
Freeman, Buck 271
Frisk, Emil 273
Fry(e), Jack 178-179
Fuller, Shorty 205, 209
Fulmer, Chick 88, 111, 136-137, 148

Gaffney, John 192, 217, 220
Galligan, Jim 204
Galvin, James "Pud" 95, 110-111, 122-123, 155, 198-200, 223
Galvin, John 52
Ganzel, Charlie 192-193, 214, 225, 245-246
Garvin, Virgil 251
Gastright, Hank 232-233
Geer, Billy 103-104
Gehrig, Lou 249, 252
George, Bill 195, 215
Gerhardt, Joe 106, 176
Gettman, Jake 273
Getzien, Charlie "Pretzels" 193, 225, 237
Gilks, Bob 216
Gillespie, Pete 176
Gilligan, Barney 142, 170, 173
Gilmore, William 7
Glasscock, Jack 199, 226

- 283 -

Index

Glazier, Willard W. 36
Gleason, Bill 137, 158-159, 193
Gleason, Jack 136-137
Glenn, John 94
Goldsmith, Fred 104, 111, 128, 145, 148, 152-153, 208-209
Goodall, Herb 231
Gore, George "Piano Legs" 113-114, 127-128, 145, 148, 153-154, 175-176, 195, 215-216, 223
Gould, Charles 63, 65, 72
Gould, Edward 36
Govern, Stanislaus Kostka "Cos" 178
Grant, Frank 178
Graves, Abner 3-5
Graves, John 4
Gray, Charles 36
Green, Jimmy 131
Gridley, Henry 20
Gross, Emil 127
Gruber, Henry 216, 224
Gunson, Joe 238

Hackett, Charles 189
Hackett, Mert 152
Hackett, Walter 167-168
Haddock, George 224
Haggarty, John 246
Hague, Bill 91, 106
Haldeman, John A. 106
Haldeman, Walter 106
Hall, George 73, 97-98, 106-107
Halligan, Jocko 238
Hallman, Bill 273
Hamburg, Charlie 231-233
Hamilton, Billy 127, 266
Hankinson, Frank 114, 133
Hanlon, Ned 120, 141-142, 193, 201-202, 257, 265-266, 268-269
Hannegan, Bernie 43, 45n4
Harbridge, Bill 100, 114
Hardie, Lew 190, 225
Hardy, John 7
Harley, Dick 271, 272-273
Harper, Jack 271
Harrison, Abraham "Abe" 178-179
Harrison, William Henry 5n4
Hart, James A. "Jim" 183, 212, 214-215, 234-235
Hastings, Scott 93-94
Hatfield, Gil 195, 215
Hatfield, John 63-64, 75
Hawes, William 145
Hawke, Bill 244-245
Hawley, Pink 258

Hayes, Jackie 230
Hayhurst, E. Hicks 68
Healy, John "Egyptian" 202-203
Hecker, Guy 137, 138-139, 162, 180-181, 183, 205
Hemphill, Charlie 278
Henry, John 188
Heubel, George 82-83
Heydler, John 267
Higham, Dick 101, 103-105
Hill, Bill 259, 273
Hines, John 7
Hines, Mike 152-154
Hines, Paul 93-94, 108-109, 123, 142-143, 173, 199
Hodes, Charlie 75, 81
Hodnett, Charlie 158
Hoey, Fred 269
Hoffer, Bill 258, 265
Holder, John 16, 29
Holdsworth, Jim 107
Holliday, Bug 248
Holmes, Ben 178-179
Holmes, Ducky 268-269, 273
Hopper, DeWolf 196-197
Hornung, Joe 111, 152-153, 226
Hotaling, Pete 103-105, 111, 120
Householder, Charlie 136, 138-139
Hoy, William "Dummy" 244, 248
Hoyt (New York player, 1858) 10
Hudson, Nat 206
Hughes, Mickey 187-188, 189, 209
Hulbert, William 97, 100
Hurst, Tim 255
Hutchison, Bill 234
Hyde, Henry 20

Irwin, Arthur 108, 113-115, 120, 164, 167, 173
Irwin, John 167-168
Ivor-Campbell, Frederick 171

Jennings, Hughie 257-258, 265
Johnson, Abbie 260
Johnson, Ban 272
Johnson, Harry 179
Johnson, Spud 232-233
Johnston, Dick 214
Jones, Bumpus 239-240
Jones, Charley "Baby" 101, 178
Jones, Frank 57
Jones, Jack 159
Jones, Joseph B. 44
Jones, Mike 231
Jones, Sheriff Jim 259-261

Josephs, Joseph E. see Borden, Joseph Emley
Joyce, Bill 230, 269, 270

Keefe, Tim 133-134, 172-174, 176-177, 195-197, 200, 214-216, 217-218, 222, 223
Keeler, William Henry "Wee Willie" 257-258, 265-266
Keenan, Jim 135-136, 178
Kelley, Joe 244, 257, 268
Kelly (reporter, 1867) 58
Kelly, Michael "King" 127-128, 144-145, 147, 150, 152-154, 175-177, 185-186, 201, 211-212, 214, 223, 242
Kerns, James N. 83
Killen, Frank 257-258
Kilroy, Matt "Matches" 168, 182-183, 223
King, Marshal "Mart" 81-82
King, Silver 205, 223, 228-230
Kinslow, Tom 230
Kissam, Samuel 16
Knauss, Frank 232
Knepper, Charlie 270-271
Knight, Lon 98, 114, 120, 133, 141, 160
Krieg, Bill 169
Krock, August "Gus" 196
Krueger, Otto 271

Landis, Doc 138
Lange, Billy 251-252
Larkin, Terry 107
Lasky, Jimmy 247
Latham, Arlie 158, 185, 193, 205-206, 208-209, 229, 239, 248
Latham, Juice 107
Leary, Jack 136
Leggett, Joseph B. 10, 29-30, 34-35
Lehane, Mike 232
Lennon, Billy 80
Leonard, Andy 65-66, 91, 97
Lewis, Fred 160
Libby, Steve 111
Lochhead, Harry 270-271
Loftus, Tom 215
Long, Herman "Dutch" 225-226, 248-249, 266
Long, Jim 245
Lovett, Len 70
Lovett, Tom 209
Lowe, Bobby 181, 225, 248-250, 252, 266
Lucid, Con 251
Lynch, Jack 172-173

- 284 -

Index

Lynch, Tom 217, 220, 269
Lyons, Denny 258 (n2)

Mack, Connie 239
Mack, Denny 101, 111, 139
Mack, Reddy 183
Macullar, Jimmy 110, 135, 137, 147-148, 183
Madden, Kid 214
Magee, Bill 260, 271
Magnum, Adolphus 37
Mahn, L.H. 105
Maitland, James 76
Malinowski, W. Zachary 117
Malloy, Jerry 178
Malone, Fergy 82
Mann, George Williamson 87
Mann, Joseph McElroy 87-89
Manning, Jack 90, 98, 108-109, 164-165, 181, 183
Manning, Jimmy 202
Manola, Marion 196
Manolt, Harry 40
Mansell, Mike 103-104, 111-112
Mansell, Tom 104
Martin, Phonney 75
Maskrey, Leech 139
Massey, F.S. "Mace" 40
Masten (Brooklyn player, 1858) 11
Mathews, Bobby 79-80, 127, 158
McAllister, Lew "Sport" 255, 271-274
McAtee, Bub 75, 78, 81
McBride, Dick 51-52, 81-83, 84
McCarthy, Jack 248
McCarthy, Tommy 205-206, 209, 248-249
McCormick, Barry 259
McCormick, Jim 119-120, 155-156, 175-177
McCormick, Patrick Henry "Harry" 103-104, 110-112, 137
McDermott, Joe 80
McGann, Dan 271
McGarr, Chippy 225
McGeachey, Jack 199, 200, 230
McGeary, Mike 95, 100-101, 141
McGinley, Tim 98, 101
McGinnis, George "Jumbo" 136, 158-159
McGraw, John 238, 244, 246, 257, 265-266, 268
McGunnigle, Bill 111, 209
McKenna, Brian 189-190
McKeon (Haymakers of Troy president, 1869) 66
McKinnon, Alex 103-104, 111
McKisson, Robert 254
McLean, William 92 (n1)
McMahon (Mutuals of New York right fielder & catcher, 1865) 46
McMahon, Archie 29
McMahon, Sadie 237-238
McPhee, Bid 130, 135-137, 147-148, 178, 240
McQuaid, John "Jack" 212, 235
McSorley, Trick 111
McTamany, Jim 232-233
McVey, Cal 63, 65-66, 72-73, 90-92
Mayer, George J.E. 79-80
Meakim, George 231
Meekin, Jouett 268
Melville, Tom 7
Mercer, Win 271
Mertes, Sam 270
Meyerle, Levi S. 74-75, 82-83, 97
Meyers (Brooklyn player, 1845) 7
Millar, Henry 66
Miller, Cyclone 170-171
Miller, Joe 162
Miller, Roscoe 273
Milligan, Jocko 205-206
Mills, Abraham G. 170
Mills, Andy 40
Mills, Charlie 47, 75, 78
Mills, Everett 75, 93, 94, 100
Mincher, Ed 80
Mitchell, Bobby 114
Moreland, George 109
Morrill, John 95, 152, 153, 165
Morris, Peter 116-117
Morrisey, John 66
Morton, Charlie 135-136, 150
Mullane, Tony "Count" 130-131, 138-140, 158-159, 162, 178, 200, 239
Murnane, Tim 97-98, 109, 167-168, 249, 265
Murphy, Con 230
Murphy, Pat 195, 215, 226
Mutrie, James "Jim" 172-173, 176, 187, 195, 215, 220, 226, 234
Myers, Henry 138

Nash, Billy 212, 214, 223, 248-249, 251
Nava, Sandy 142, 143 (n2), 145, 173
Nedrob, Joseph *see* Borden, Joseph Emley
Nelson, Candy 75
Nichols, Al 106-107
Nichols, C.W. 110
Nichols, Charles "Kid" 225-227, 231, 242-243, 248-249, 265-267
Nichols, Fred 103-104
Nichols, Tricky 114
Nicol, George 240 (n2), 273
Nicol, Hugh 128, 144-145, 148, 158-159
Nops, Jerry 268
Norcross, Tip 22
Norton, Frank 56

O'Brien, Darby 208-209, 217-218, 220
O'Brien, John Joseph "Jack" 271
O'Brien, John K. "Jack" 136, 159
O'Brien, Matty 10, 28-29, 40
O'Brien, Peter 29, 40
O'Connor, Dan 231
O'Connor, Jack 232
O'Day, Hank 220
Oliver, John 29
O'Neill, Tip 185, 205-206, 209, 229
Ong, Walter 255
Orem, Preston 51, 125-126
O'Rourke, Jim "Orator" 90-91, 97-98, 108, 116, 176, 195, 215, 218, 223
O'Rourke, Tom 226
Orr, Dave 180-181, 228, 230
Orth, Al 251
Owen, Frank 273

Palmer, Harry Clay 202
Parago, George 178-179
Parker, George Alanson 20
Parks, Bill 98
Patchen, S. 34-35
Patterson (umpire, 1867) 58
Patterson, Tom 46, 75
Pearce, Dickey 10, 29, 52, 91, 100-101
Pearsall, Aleck T. 17, 29, 35
Peters, John 93, 123
Pettit, Robert 202
Pfeffer, Fred 130-131, 153-154, 175-176, 185, 190, 201, 228-229
Phillips, Bill 120
Phinney, Elihu 4
Pickering, Ollie 260
Pierce, Edward 19-20
Piercy, Andy 128
Pike, Lipman 49-50, 52, 91, 100-101
Pinckney (New York player, 1858) 10
Pinkham, Ed 77-78, 81-82
Pinkney, George 209
Polhemus, Harry Ditmas 16-17, 29

Index

Powell, Jack 255-256
Powell, Martin 141-142
Powers, Pat 191
Powers, Phil 137, 147-148, 227
Pratt, Tom 52, 82
Price, John 29
Purcell, Blondie 156
Pyle, Shadow 190

Quest, Joe 128, 144-145, 158
Quinn, Joe 214, 271

Radbourn, Charles "Old Hoss" 128, 141-143, 145, 155, 164-165, 170-171, 172-174, 196, 200, 214
Radcliffe, John 82, 88
Radford, Paul 152-153, 173, 215
Rainey, John 224
Ramsey, Tom "Toad" 168, 180, 182, 206
Randolph, Andrew 179
Raymond, Harry 205-206, 231, 235
Reach, Al 39-40, 51-52, 82
Reccius, John 130-131, 139
Reilley, Charlie 142
Reilly, Charlie 232
Reitz, Heinie 245, 256
Remsen, Jack 93-94, 100, 104
Renfro, William 190
Reynolds, Thomas 16-17, 29, 34
Richardson, Danny 176, 195, 215, 218, 223, 234
Richardson, Hardy 192-193, 212, 214
Richmond, Lee 113-115, 117, 119-121, 122-124, 133-134
Richter, Francis 202, 241
Robinson, Wilbert 237-238, 244-245, 246, 257, 266, 268
Robinson, Yank 185, 192-193, 205-206, 209
Robison, Frank 254-256, 270
Robison, Stanley 254-256, 270
Rowe, Jack 123, 192-193
Rusie, Amos 226-227, 234-235, 268
Russell, Edwin 16-17, 29, 34-35
Ryan, Jack 231, 248-249, 273
Ryan, Jimmy 185, 190, 202, 229, 251, 259

Saltzman, Edward G. 13
Scanlan, Mort 226
Scanlon, Pat 168
Schafer, Harry 98
Schmelz, Gus 232
Schoeneck, Jumbo 168

Sears (Excelsior of Baltimore player, 1860) 34-35
Seery, Emmett 199, 223, 230
Selee, Frank 225, 234, 242-243
Sensenderfer, Count 82
Shadney, G. 179
Shafer, Orator 114, 120
Shannon, Dan 204-205, 273
Sharp, William H. 7
Sharrott, Jack 226
Shaw, Al 273
Shetzline, John 136
Shieber, Tom 44
Shindle, Billy 193, 237-238, 244-245, 257
Shinnick, Tim 231-233
Shoch, George 238
Shreve, Lev 199
Shriver (Excelsior of Baltimore player, 1860) 34
Sidney, Capt. 14
Sidway, Franklin 25
Siever, Ed 273
Simmons, Joe 81
Slagle, Jimmy 271
Slattery, Mike 168, 195, 215, 223
Smith, Charles 29, 40, 51-52
Smith, Edgar 152
Smith, Elmer 240
Smith, Germany 209, 218, 220, 240
Smith, J. 40
Smith, Pop 214, 225
Sneed, John 232
Snyder, John 46
Snyder, Pop 135-137, 147
Soden, Arthur 235
Sommer, Joe 135-137, 147, 180, 183
Sommers, Pete 226
Sowders, John 230
Spalding, Albert G. 3, 56-57, 76, 84-85, 90-92, 95-96, 127, 184, 201, 203
Spence, Harry 199
Spence, Peter 40
Sprague, Joe 40
Stafford, Jimmy "General" 260, 271
Stahl, Chick 266
Staley, Harry 242
Stallings, George 272
Starkweather, John 3
Start, Joe 40, 51-52, 72, 106, 110, 142, 173
Stearns, Dan "Ecky" 135-137, 148
Stephens, Ben 244-245
Stivetts, Jack 205, 242-243
Storrs, Sam 19

Stovey, George 150, 187-188, 189-191
Stovey, Harry 134, 159-160, 222, 223
Stratton, Scott 204, 231, 233
Stricker, Cub 136, 159-160, 245
Strief, George 135, 159
Sudhoff, Willie 270
Sullivan, Daniel "Link" 131, 137, 139
Sullivan, Joe 245
Sullivan, Martin "Marty" 190, 202, 225
Sullivan, Sleeper 136
Sullivan, Suter 272-273
Sunday, Art 230
Sunday, Billy 150, 175, 190
Sutcliffe, Sy 175, 215-216
Sutton, Ezra 97-98, 108-109, 152-153
Swandell, Marty 74-75
Swartwood, Ed 131, 136
Sweasy, Charlie 65, 72-73, 91, 108-109
Sweeney, Charlie 164-165, 167, 170, 172-173

Taber, John 225
Taylor, Billy 135-136
Taylor, Harry 231, 233, 245
Taylor, Jack 270
Tebeau, Patsy 242, 255-256
Tener, John 201, 203
Tenney, Fred 266
Terry, Will "Adonis" 209, 217-218, 251-252
Thomas, Arthur 179
Thompson, Frank P. 178
Thompson, Sam 192-193
Thorn, Dick 11
Thorn, R.H. 29-31
Tiernan, Mike 195, 215, 225-227
Tierney, Bill 135-136
Titcomb, Cannonball 195, 215
Tomney, Phil 204, 231
Tower, Frank 19
Treacey, Fred 74-75, 81, 83
Treadway, George 244-245, 257
Trott, Sam 141-143
Troy, Dasher 141
Trusty, Shepard "Shep" 178-179
Tucker, Tommy "Foghorn" 225, 246, 248-249, 270
Tucker, William H. 6-7
Twitchell, Larry 193

Van Cott, Theodore 10-11
Vanderbeck, George 272
Van Haltren, George 223, 228-230, 238, 240
Vaughn, Farmer 204, 206, 240, 249

Index

Visner, Joe 209, 218
Von der Ahe, Chris 184, 186, 208-210

Wadsworth (New York player, 1858) 10
Wagner, Honus 260, 263, 272
Waitt, Charlie 91, 138
Walker, Moses Fleetwood "Fleet" 140, 149-150, 161-162, 178, 187-188, 189-191
Walker, Oscar 136
Wallace, Bobby 255, 256
Walsh, Michael 188
Wansley, William 46-48
Ward, John Montgomery 116, 122-124, 141-142, 145, 175-176, 195, 201-203, 214-215, 218, 220, 223-224, 228-230
Waterman, Fred 63-64, 65, 72
Watkins, Bill 193
Weaver, Farmer 206, 231-233
Weed, Hamilton A. 51
Welch, Curt 184-186, 193, 238
Welch, Mickey 133-134, 175-176, 188, 195, 200, 215, 225-226
Werden, Perry 260
Werrick, Joe 183
West, Buck 190
Weyhing, Gus 228
Wheaton, William Rufus 6-8
Wheeler, Ed 273
Wheeler, George 139
Wheeler, Harry 137, 147-148
White, Bill 183
White, C.D. 189
White, Jim "Deacon" 79, 90-92, 193
White, Sol 178
White, Will 135-137, 147-148
White, William Edward "Bill" 116-117, 161
Whiting, Ed 136
Whiting, John C. 17, 29, 34-35
Whitney, Art 120, 133, 215, 223
Whitney, James Evans "Grasshopper" 152-154, 164-165, 181
Whyte, Billy 179
Widner, Bill 232
Wiedman, George "Stump" 141-142, 193, 195
Wildey, John 47
Williams, Clarence 178-179
Williams, James A. 110
Williamson, Ned 113, 128, 146, 148, 154, 175-176, 181, 185, 190, 202, 229, 230
Wilson, Bill 259

Wilson, Zeke 255
Winslow, W.H. 113-114
Wise, Sam 152, 224
Wolf, Jimmy "Chicken" 139, 162, 183, 206, 231-233
Wolters, Rynie 64, 74-76, 77-78
Wood, George A. 133, 141, 143, 202
Wood, Jimmy 75, 81-82
Wright, George 55-57, 63-64, 65, 72-73, 84, 86, 90-91, 97-98, 116, 142-143, 144-145, 201
Wright, Harry 10, 17, 63-64, 65, 71, 84-86, 90, 96, 97, 141-143, 144-145
Wright, Sam 84

Yeager, Joe 273
York, Tommy 94, 100, 128, 142, 145, 156, 182
Young, Denton True "Cy" 200, 226, 241-243, 255, 256, 270
Young, Joe 237

Zettlein, George "The Charmer" 72-73, 81, 83, 93, 95

CLUB/TEAM INDEX

The pages for clubs and teams named in chapter titles are given in boldface.
Abbreviations:
AL = American League
IA = International Association
IL = International League
NA = National Association of Professional Base Ball Players
NL = National League
PL = Players' League
UA = Union Association

Akrons **130-132**
Albany (NY), Champions of 24
Alerts of Danville (PA) 49-50
All Americas **201-203**
Amherst College **19-21**
Athletics of Philadelphia (1866-1870) **49-50**, **51-54**, 68-69, 74, 77
Athletics of Philadelphia (NA) 79, **81-83**, **84-86**, 95, 97-99
Atlantics of Brooklyn 10, 26, **28-31**, **39-42**, 49-50, **51-54**, 64, **71-73**, 77, 79
Atlantics of Chicago 56

Baltimore, Excelsiors of 34-35
Baltimore, Marylands of 79-80

Baltimores, Lord **136**, **138-140**
Baltimore Orioles (AA) **180-181**, **182-183**, 204-205
Baltimore Orioles (NL) **237-238**, **244-245**, **246-247**, **257-258**, **265-267**, **268-269**
Binghamton Bingos (IL) 190
Boston, Lowells of 60
Boston, Tri-Mountains of **13-14**
Boston Beaneaters (NL) **152-154**, **164-166**, **211-213**, **214-216**, **225-227**, **234-236**, **241-243**, **246-247**, **248-250**, **265-267**
Boston Red Caps (NL) **90-92**, **96**, **97-99**, **108-109**
Boston Red Stockings (NA) 79, 81-82, **84-86**, **90-92**, 97
Boston Reds (AA) 249
Boston Reds (PL) **222**, 223
Boston Reds (UA) 165, **167-169**
Brooklyn, Atlantics of 10, 26, **28-31**, **39-42**, 49-50, **51-54**, 64, **71-73**, 77, 79
Brooklyn, Constellations of 32
Brooklyn, Continentals of 39, 41n4
Brooklyn, Eckfords of 28, 32, **39-42**, 46-48, 64, 74, 77, 79
Brooklyn, Enterprise Club of 28
Brooklyn, Excelsiors of 10, **16-18**, **24-27**, **28-31**, **34-35**, **43-45**, **60-62**
Brooklyn, Monitors of 59
Brooklyn, Niagaras of 43
Brooklyn, Putnams of 30n3, 32
Brooldyn, Stars of 43
Brooklyn all-stars **10-12**, 51
Brooklyn Base Ball Club 7, 8
Brooklyn Bridegrooms (AA) **208-210**, **217-218**, **219-221**
Brooklyn Bridegrooms (NL) 233, 241, 257
Brooklyn Wonders (PL) **222**, **228-230**
Buffalo, Niagaras of **24-25**
Buffalo Bisons (AL) **272-274**
Buffalo Bisons (IA) **110-112**
Buffalo Bisons (IL) **187-188**
Buffalo Bisons (NL) **122-124**
Buffalo Bisons (PL) **222**, 224

Camdens of Camden (NJ) 1
Champions of Albany (NY) 24
Chicago, Atlantics of 56
Chicago, Excelsiors of 56
Chicago, White Stockings of (1870) 74-76, 77-78, 79
Chicago Browns (UA) **167-169**

Index

Chicago Colts (NL) 231-232, **251-253, 258-260, 261-263** *see also* Chicago White Stockings (NL)
Chicago Pirates (PL) **222-223, 228-230**
Chicago White Stockings (NA) **81-83, 93-94, 95-96**
Chicago White Stockings (NL) **113-115, 127-129,** 130, **144-146, 147-148, 149-151, 152-152-154, 175-177, 184-186, 189-191, 195-197, 201-203** *see also* Chicago Colts
Cincinnati Red Stockings (1869-1870) 56, **63-64, 65-67,** 70, **71-73,** 76, 77, 79-80
Cincinnati Red Stockings (AA) **135-136,** 139, **147-148, 178-179**
Cincinnati Red Stockings (NL) 96, 106-107, 135
Cincinnati Reds (NL) **239-240, 248-250,** 254
City Item (Philadelphia) team 70
Cleveland, Forest Citys of **79-80**
Cleveland Blues (NL) **116-118, 119-121,** 123, 130, **155-157**
Cleveland Infants (PL) **224**
Cleveland Spiders (NL) **211-213, 214-216, 241-243, 254-255, 270-271**
Columbus Colts (AA) **234-236**
Constellations of Brooklyn 32
Continentals of Brooklyn 39, 41n4
Cuban Giants **178-179**

Danville (PA), Alerts of **49-50**
Detroit Tigers (AL) **272-274**
Detroit Wolverines (NL) **141-143, 192-194**

Eagles of New York 10, 12
Eckfords of Brooklyn 28, 32, **39-42, 46-48,** 64, 74, 77, 79
Eclipse of Louisville **130-132,** 136
Empires of New York 28
Enterprise Club of Brooklyn 28
Excelsiors of Baltimore **34-35**
Excelsiors of Brooklyn 10, **16-18, 24-27, 28-31, 34-35, 43-45, 60-62**
Excelsiors of Chicago 56
Excelsiors of Philadelphia **58-59**
Excelsiors of Upton (MA) **22-23**

Flour Citys of Rochester (NY) 25
Forest Citys of Cleveland **79-80**
Forest Citys of Rockford (IL) **55-56,** 79
Fort Wayne (IN), Kekiongas of **79-80**

Gothams of New York 6, **8-9,** 10, 12-13, 28

Hartford Dark Blues (NA) **93-94**
Hartford Dark Blues (NL) **100-102, 106-107**
Harvard College **60-62**
Harvard University 105
Haymakers of Troy (NY) **65-67,** 74, 79, 81
Hudson Rivers of Newburgh (NY) 25

Indianapolis Hoosiers (NL) **198-200**

Jersey City Skeeters (IL) 187, 189, 190
Jordan Marsh and Company (Boston) team 125-126

Kekiongas of Fort Wayne (IN) **79-80**
Keystones of Philadelphia 60
Knickerbocker Base Ball Club of New York 6-7, **8-9,** 10, 12, **16-18**

Lansingburgh (NY), Unions of 65
Live Oaks of Rochester (NY) 25
Lord Baltimores 136, **138-140**
Louisville, Eclipse of **130-132,** 136
Louisville Colonels (AA) **180-181, 182-183, 204-207, 234-236**
Louisville Colonels (NL) **259-261, 262-263**
Louisville Cyclones (AA) *see* Louisville Colonels (AA) **232-233**
Louisville Eclipse (AA) **136-137, 138-140, 161-163**
Louisville Grays (NL) **106-107**
Lowells of Boston 60

Magnolia Ball Club of New York 7
Manchester (NH) Manchesters (IA) 105
Marylands of Baltimore 79-80
Marylebone Cricket Club 84
Medway (MA), Unions of **22-23**
Monitors of Brooklyn 59
Morrisania (NY), Unions of **43-45,** 55, 76, 77
Mutuals of New York 28, **46-48, 63-64,** 71, **74-76, 77-78, 79-80,** 86, 90, 93

Nationals of Washington (DC) 32, **55-57,** 79
New York, Eagles of 10, 12
New York, Empires of 28

New York, Gothams of 6, **8-9,** 10, 12-13, 28
New York, Mutuals of 28, **46-48, 63-64,** 71, **74-76, 77-78, 79-80,** 86, 90, 93
New York, Washingtons of 6, **8-9**
New York all-stars 10-12, 51
New York Base Ball Club 6-7, 8
New York Giants (NL) 101, 128, **175-177,** 187-188, **195-197,** 211-212, **214-216, 217-218, 219-221, 234-235, 268-269**
New York Giants (PL) **222, 225-227**
New York Metropolitans (AA) **172-174,** 178
Newark (NJ) Little Giants (IL) **187-188, 189-191**
Newburgh (NY), Hudson Rivers of 25
Niagaras of Brooklyn 43
Niagaras of Buffalo 24-25

Olympics of Philadelphia 1-2, **32-33, 68-70**
Olympics of Washington (DC) 79

Philadelphia, Athletics of (1866-1870) **49-50, 51-54, 68-69,** 74, 77
Philadelphia, Athletics of (NA) 79, **81-83, 84-86,** 95, **97-99**
Philadelphia, Excelsiors of **58-59**
Philadelphia, Keystones of 60
Philadelphia, Olympics of **1, 32-33, 68-70**
Philadelphia, Pythians of **68-70**
Philadelphia Athletics (AA) 136, **158-160**
Philadelphia Athletics (NL) 96, **97-99**
Philadelphia Phillies (NL) **155-157, 170-171, 251-253**
Philadelphia picked nine (1860) 35
Philadelphia Quakers (PL) **222**
Philadelphia White Stockings (NA) **95-96**
Pittsburgh Alleghenies (AA) 135-136
Pittsburgh Alleghenies (NL) **198-200,** 215-216
Pittsburgh Burghers (PL) **222-223**
Pittsburgh Pirates (NL) **239-240, 257-258**
Portland (ME) Base Ball Club 13-14
Princeton College **87-89**
Providence Grays (NL) **116-118, 122-124, 127-129, 141-143, 144-146,** 152, **164-166, 170-171, 172-174**
Providence Rhode Islanders (NL) **108-109**

Putnams of Brooklyn 30n3, 32
Pythians of Philadelphia **68-70**

Red Stockings of Boston *see* Boston Red Stockings
Red Stockings of Cincinnati *see* Cincinnati Red Stockings
Red Stockings of St. Louis *see* St. Louis Reds
R.H. White and Company (Boston) team 125-126
Rochester (NY), Flour Cities of **25**
Rochester (NY), Live Oaks of **25**
Rockford (IL), Forest Cities of **56-57**, 79

St. Louis Brown Stockings (AA) **136-137**
St. Louis Brown Stockings (NA) 90, 95
St. Louis Brown Stockings (NL) **100-102, 103-105**
St. Louis Browns (AA) **158-160, 184-186, 192-194, 204-207, 208-210**
St. Louis Browns (NL) **237-238**
St. Louis Perfectos (NL) 270
St. Louis Red Sox *see* St. Louis Reds
St. Louis Red Stockings *see* St. Louis Reds
St. Louis Reds (NA) **90-92**, 93
Stars of Brooklyn 43
Syracuse Stars (IA, 1878) **110-112**
Syracuse Stars (Keystone Association, 1877) **103-105**

Toledo Blue Stockings (NA) **161-163**
Toledo Blue Stockings (Northwestern League, 1883) **149-151**, 161
Tri-Mountains of Boston **13-14**
Troy (NY), Haymakers of **65-67**, 74, 79, 81
Troy (NY), Victorys of **24**
Troy Trojans (NL) **133-134**

Unions of Lansingburgh (NY) 65
Unions of Medway (MA) **22-23**
Unions of Morrisania (NY) **43-45**, 76, 77
Uniques of Williamsburg (NY) **58-59**
Upton (MA), Excelsiors of **22-23**

Victorys of Troy (NY) **24**

Washington (DC), Nationals of 32, **55-57**, 79
Washington (DC), Olympics of 79
Washington (DC) Nationals (NA) 90
Washington (DC) Senators (NL) **244-245, 254-255, 270-272**
Washington (DC) Statesmen (NL) 199
Washingtons of New York 6, **8-9**
White Stockings, Chicago *see* Chicago White Stockings
White Stockings of Chicago (1870) **74-76, 77-78**, 79
Williams College **19-21**
Williamsburg (NY), Uniques of **58-59**
Worcester (MA) Brown Stockings (NL) **119-121**, 123, **133-134**
Worcester (MA) Worcesters (NA) **113-115**

Yale College **87-89**

SUBJECT INDEX

admission charges 10, 22, 32-33, 39, 51-52, 72, 135, 241, 247
African Americans 58-59, 68-70, 116-117, 140, 149-150, 161-162, 178-179, 187-188, 189-190
alcohol 135, 170, 172, 211-212, 241
all-star games 10-12
ambidextrous pitcher 138-139
American Association (AA) 135-137, 147, 158, 161, 172-174, 208-210, 217, 219, 237, 241
American League (AL) 272, 274
anti-Semitic epithet 268-269

ballparks, enclosed 32-33, 39, 51, 53, 58, 63
baseball (the ball) 20, 49, 87, 105, 227
baseball, origin of 1-3, 6
baserunning 144-145, 233
battery 187-191
Beer and Whiskey League *see* American Association
bound rule 14, 16-18
Brotherhood of Professional Base Ball Players 203, 214-216, 222-224, 228
Brown University 113, 116-117, 119, 123
bunts 56

Camac Woods, Philadelphia 32-33, 35
candles, lighted 208-210
Capitoline Grounds, Brooklyn 32, 51-53, 71-72

"Casey at the Bat" 196-197
catchers 187-188
champions, determination of 78, 81, 147-148
chess 19-20
Chicago (verb and noun) 74-76, 148
Chicago Fire, Great 81
Civil War 20, 36-38, 39-40, 55
color line 149-150, 189-190
competition, beginning of 9
contract jumping 172, 187, 190
cricket 6-7, 32-33, 44, 84-86
curveball 60-61, 87, 93, 104, 110, 114, 164-165, 168, 182, 251

discrimination, racial 68, 149-150, 161
double plays 64, 72, 97-98, 144

Egypt 201-203
ejections 212
Elysian Fields, Hoboken (NJ) 6-8, 16-18, 46-48
England 84-86
errors *see* fielding, poor

Fashion Race Course, Flushing (NY) 10-12, 32
fielding, good 25, 34, 40, 46, 64, 80, 84, 97-98, 104, 108-109, 114, 119, 123, 141-142, 159, 161, 200, 208, 226, 229, 244
fielding, poor 19, 40, 46-47, 91, 98, 100, 106, 120, 125, 127, 131, 134-137, 153, 158, 162, 176, 180, 196, 199, 206, 217, 223, 228-230, 234, 260, 273
fines 205, 207, 209-210, 269, 272
fires 81, 246-247
fixing of games 23, 46-48, 53, 65-66, 106-107, 231-233
fly rule 14, 16-18
forfeits 29-30, 66-67, 184, 208-210, 268-269
Fourth of July games 1

gambling 10, 22-23, 29-30, 47, 51, 63, 65-66, 74, 97, 106-107, 110, 186, 235
gate receipts 53, 67, 69, 150, 173, 184-186, 269
grand slams 133-134

home runs 14, 49-50, 56, 84, 117, 133-134, 141, 180-181, 224, 248-250, 251-253

Index

injuries 11, 43-45, 91, 97-98, 111, 136, 147, 155-156, 167, 183, 199, 211, 218, 228, 251, 265-266
inside baseball 257, 265
intercollegiate game, first 19-21
International Association 105, 110-112
International League 111, 189-191
Ireland 85-86

Jews 49, 268-269
Johnstown (PA) Flood 96, 204
July 4th games 1

Knickerbocker rules 6-8, 13

Massachusetts Association of Base Ball Players 13-14, 50
Massachusetts game / rules 13-14, 19, 22
match games / play, concept of 1, 8
McCaull's Light Opera Company, New York City 196

National Agreement 172
National Association (1879) 113
National Association of Base Ball Players (NABBP) 17, 47, 63, 67
National Association of Professional Base Ball Players (NA) 78, 79-80, 81-83, 86, 90, 90-92, 97, 199, 262
National League (NL) 97-98, 100, 105, 106, 112, 147, 172-174, 175, 201, 210, 217, 219, 241, 268
New York game / rules 1-2, 4, 13-14, 38
night baseball 125-126
no-hitters 87-89, 95, 96, 100-102, 113-115, 119-121, 122-124, 139, 156, 228-230, 239-240, 244-245, 272-274
Northwestern League 149, 161, 172

Pennsylvania Association of Amateur Base Ball Players 68
perfect games 119-121, 122-124
pitching distance 239, 244
platooning 120
Players' League 216, 219, 221, 222-224, 225, 227, 228-230, 231, 234, 241

Polo Grounds, New York City 172-174, 195-197, 214, 217-218, 219-221, 225, 227, 267-268
professionalism 49-50, 55, 63, 79-80
Putnam Club Grounds, Brooklyn 28-31
Pyramid Game 201-203

racism 70, 149-150, 161
records, batting 180-181, 237-238, 248-250, 251-253, 259-260, 262-263
records, pitching 167-169, 170-171, 182-183, 195-197, 198-200
reserve clause 103, 111, 139, 144, 241
round ball 1, 19, 22
rounders 3
Royal Rooters 266

salaries 49, 76-77, 96, 155
Salisbury (NC) Prison 36-38
scientific baseball 16, 93, 187, 257, 265
scorecards 51
segregation, racial 149-150
shutouts 74-76, 87-89, 93-94, 95, 96, 100-102, 103-105, 113-115, 119-121, 122-124, 130-131, 141-143, 148, 156, 167-169, 226-227, 228-230, 231-233, 242, 244-245, 272-274
sign stealing 217
silver ball 39, 41n4
sliding 22, 31n10, 185
South End Grounds, Boston 152-153, 164, 234, 241-243, 246-247, 249, 250n2
Spalding Commission 3
spectators, crowd control of 50, 51-52, 70, 92n1
spectators, interference by 72-73
spectators, rowdy behavior of 29-30, 65-66
Sphinx 203
split season 241-243
spotting 22
stolen bases 127-128
streaks, hitting 251, 258
streaks, losing 204-207, 270-272
streaks, winning 63-67, 71, 195-196, 234-236

strike, player 205
strikeouts 164-166, 167-169, 182-183
Sunday baseball 208, 241, 243, 254-256, 265, 270
suspensions 128, 140, 170, 172, 269
switch-hitting 120
syndicate baseball 255, 269-270

temperance 63
Temple Cup 254
3,000 hits 262-264
thrown games *see* fixing of games
tours 24-27, 34-35, 55, 63-67, 71-73, 74, 84-86, 201-203
town ball 1-2, 4, 13-14, 38, 69, 84-86
Tripartite Agreement 172
triple plays 34-35, 108-109, 164-165, 192-193
trophy ball 20, 39, 41n4

umpires / umpiring 29-30, 58, 66, 69, 72, 77-78, 87, 92n1, 110, 112, 143, 145, 153, 168, 182, 185, 208-210, 212, 217, 219-220, 227, 235, 244, 246, 255, 257, 268-269
uniforms 65, 72, 82
Union Association (UA) 156, 167, 172
Union Grounds, Brooklyn 32, 39-40, 63, 81-83, 106

walks as hits (1887) 262
Wallack's Theatre, New York City 79, 196
whip pennant 83
women spectators 19, 22, 32-34, 58, 140, 142, 165, 270
World's Championship Series (1884) 172-174
World's Championship Series (1886) 184-186
World's Championship Series (1887) 192-194
World's Championship Series (1889) 217-218, 219-221
World's Championship Series (1890) 231

SABR BioProject Books

In 2002, the Society for American Baseball Research launched an effort to write and publish biographies of every player, manager, and individual who has made a contribution to baseball. Over the past decade, the BioProject Committee has produced over 2,200 biographical articles. Many have been part of efforts to create theme- or team-oriented books, spearheaded by chapters or other committees of SABR.

DETROIT TIGERS 1984: What a Start! What a Finish!
The 1984 Detroit tigers roared out of the gate, winning their first nine games of the season and compiling an eye-popping 35–5 record after the campaign's first 40 games—still the best start ever for any team in major league history. This book brings together biographical profiles of every Tiger from that magical season, plus those of field management, top executives, the broadcasters—even venerable Tiger Stadium and the city itself.

Mark Pattison and David Raglin, editors
$19.95 paperback (ISBN 978-1-933599-44-1)
$9.99 ebook (ISBN 978-1-933599-45-8)
8.5" x 11" / 250 pages (Over 230,000 words!)

SWEET '60: The 1960 Pittsburgh Pirates
A portrait of the 1960 team which pulled off one of the biggest upsets of the last 60 years. When Bill Mazeroski's home run left the park to win in Game Seven of the World Series, beating the New York Yankees, David had toppled Goliath. It was a blow that awakened a generation, one that millions of people saw on television, one of TV's first iconic World Series moments.

Edited by Clifton Blue Parker and Bill Nowlin
$19.95 paperback (ISBN 978-1-933599-48-9)
$9.99 ebook (ISBN 978-1-933599-49-6)
8.5" x 11" / 340 pages, 75 photos

RED SOX BASEBALL IN THE DAYS OF IKE AND ELVIS:
The Red Sox of the 1950s
Although the Red Sox spent most of the 1950s far out of contention, the team was filled fascinating players that captured the heart of their fanbase. In *Red Sox Baseball*, members of SABR present 46 biographies on players such as Ted Williams and Pumpsie Green as well as season-by-season recaps.

Edited by Mark Armour and Bill Nowlin
$19.95 paperback (ISBN 978-1-933599-24-3)
$9.99 ebook (ISBN 978-1-933599-34-2)
8.5" x 11" / 372 PAGES, over 100 photos

OPENING FENWAY PARK IN STYLE:
The 1912 World Champion Boston Red Sox
Opening Fenway Park in Style details a season played 100 years ago, the first season played at Fenway Park by the World Series winning Boston Red Sox. Included are player and owner biographies and a variety of essays considering the role of the press and facets of baseball during that era.

Edited by Bill Nowlin
$19.95 paperback (ISBN 978-1-933599-35-9)
$9.99 ebook (ISBN 978-1-933599-36-6)
8.5" x 11" / 304 PAGES, over 200 photos

The SABR Digital Library

The Society for American Baseball Research, the top baseball research organization in the world, disseminates some of the best in baseball history, analysis, and biography through our publishing programs. The SABR Digital Library contains a mix of books old and new, and focuses on a tandem program of paperback and ebook publication, making these materials widely available both on digital devices and as traditional printed books.

MEMORIES OF A BALLPLAYER
by Bill Werber and C. Paul Rogers III
Bill Werber's claim to fame is unique: he was the last living person to have a direct connection to the 1927 Yankees, "Murderers' Row," a team hailed by many as the best of all time. Rich in anecdotes and humor, *Memories of a Ballplayer* is a clear-eyed memoir of the world of big-league baseball in the 1930s. Werber played with or against some of the most productive hitters of all time, including Babe Ruth, Ted Williams, Lou Gehrig, and Joe DiMaggio.

$14.95 paperback (ISNB 978-0-910137-84-3)
$6.99 ebook (ISBN 978-1-933599-47-2)
6" x 9" / 250 pages

BATTING
by F. C. Lane
First published in 1925, *Batting* collects the wisdom and insights of over 250 hitters and baseball figures. Lane interviewed extensively and compiled tips and advice on everything from batting stances to beanballs. Legendary baseball figures such as Ty Cobb, Casey Stengel, Cy Young, Walter Johnson, Rogers Hornsby, and Babe Ruth reveal the secrets of such integral and interesting parts of the game as how to choose a bat, the ways to beat a slump, and how to outguess the pitcher.

$14.95 paperback (ISBN 978-0-910137-86-7)
$7.99 ebook (ISBN 978-1-933599-46-5)
5" x 7" / 240 pages

NINETEENTH CENTURY STARS: 2012 EDITION
First published in 1989, *Nineteenth Century Stars* was SABR's initial attempt to capture the stories of baseball players from before 1900. With a collection of 136 fascinating biographies, SABR has re-released *Nineteenth Century Stars* for 2012 with revised statistics and new form. The 2012 version also includes a preface by John Thorn.

Edited by Robert L. Tiemann and Mark Rucker
$19.95 paperback (ISBN 978-1-933599-28-1)
$9.99 ebook (ISBN 978-1-933599-29-8)
6" x 9" / 300 pages

GREAT HITTING PITCHERS
Published in 1979, *Great Hitting Pitchers* was one of SABR's early publications. Edited by SABR founder Bob Davids, the book compiles stories and records about pitchers excelling in the batter's box. Now updated for 2012 by Mike Cook, *Great Hitting Pitchers* contain tables including data from 1979–2011 and corrections to reflect recent records.

Edited by L. Robert Davids
$9.95 paperback (ISBN 978-1-933599-30-4)
$5.99 ebook (ISBN 978-1-933599-31-1)
8.5" x 11" / 102 pages

SABR Members can purchase each book at a significant discount (often 50% off) and receive the ebook edtions free as a member benefit.

Each book is available in a trade paperback edition as well as ebooks suitable for reading on a home computer or Nook, Kindle, or iPad/tablet.

Join SABR today!

If you're interested in baseball—writing about it, reading about it, talking about it—there's a place for you in the Society for American Baseball Research.

SABR was formed in 1971 in Cooperstown, New York, with the mission of fostering the research and dissemination of the history and record of the game. Our members include everyone from academics to professional sportswriters to amateur historians and statisticians to students and casual fans who merely enjoy reading about baseball history and occasionally gathering with other members to talk baseball.

SABR members have a variety of interests, and this is reflected in the diversity of its research committees. There are more than two dozen groups devoted to the study of a specific area related to the game—from Baseball and the Arts to Statistical Analysis to the Deadball Era to Women in Baseball. In addition, many SABR members meet formally and informally in regional chapters throughout the year and hundreds come together for the annual national convention, the organization's premier event. These meetings often include panel discussions with former major league players and research presentations by members. Most of all, SABR members love talking baseball with like-minded friends. What unites them all is an interest in the game and joy in learning more about it.

Why join SABR? Here are some benefits of membership:

- Two issues annually of the *Baseball Research Journal*, which includes articles on history, biography, statistics, personalities, book reviews, and other aspects of the game.
- One issue annually of *The National Pastime*, which focuses on baseball in the region where that year's national convention is held (in 2013, it's Philadelphia)
- Regional chapter meetings, which can include guest speakers, presentations and trips to ballgames
- "This Week in SABR" e-newsletters every Friday, with the latest news in SABR and highlighting SABR research
- Online access to back issues of *The Sporting News* and other periodicals through *Paper of Record*
- Access to SABR's lending library and other research resources
- Online member directory to connect you with an international network of passionate baseball experts and fans
- Discount on registration for our annual conferences
- Access to SABR-L, an e-mail discussion list of baseball questions and answers that many feel is worth the cost of membership itself
- The opportunity to be part of a passionate international community of baseball fans

SABR membership is on a "rolling" calendar system; that means your membership lasts 365 days no matter when you sign up! Enjoy all the benefits of SABR membership by signing up today at SABR.org/join or by clipping out the form below and mailing it to: **SABR, 4455 E. Camelback Rd., Ste. D-140, Phoenix, AZ 85018**.

SABR 2013 MEMBERSHIP FORM

2013 dues payable by check, money order, Visa, MasterCard or Discover Card;
online at: http://store.sabr.org; or by phone at (602) 343-6455

	Annual	3-year	Senior	3-yr Sr.	Under 30
US	❏ $65	❏ $175	❏ $45	❏ $129	❏ $45
Canada/Mexico	❏ $75	❏ $205	❏ $55	❏ $159	❏ $55
Overseas	❏ $84	❏ $232	❏ $64	❏ $186	❏ $55

Add a Family Member: $15 each family member at same address (list on back)
Senior: 65 or older before 12/31/2013
All dues amounts in US dollars or equivalent

Participate in Our Donor Program!
I'd like to designate my gift to be used toward:
❏ General Fund ❏ Endowment Fund ❏ Research Resources ❏ _____
❏ I want to maximize the impact of my gift; do not send any donor premiums
❏ I would like this gift to remain anonymous.

Note: Any donation not designated will be placed in the General Fund.
SABR is a 501(c)(3) not-for-profit organization & donations are tax-deductible to the extent allowed by law.

NAME _____
ADDRESS _____
CITY _____ STATE ____ ZIP _____
HOME PHONE _____ BIRTHDAY _____
E-MAIL: _____
(Your e-mail address on file ensures you will receive the most recent SABR news.)

Dues $ _____
Donation $ _____
Amount Enclosed $ _____

Do you work for a matching grant corporation? Call (602) 343-6455 for details.
❏ check/money order enclosed   ❏ VISA, Master Card, Discover Card
CARD # _____
EXP DATE _____ SIGNATURE _____

Mail to: SABR, 4455 E. Camelback Rd., Ste. D-140, Phoenix, AZ 85018

www.ingramcontent.com/pod-product-compliance
Lightning Source LLC
Chambersburg PA
CBHW051400070526
44584CB00023B/3238